*Library and
Information Center
Management*

Library and Information Science Text Series

Library and Information Center Management

Fifth Edition

Robert D. Stueart
Asian Institute of Technology
Professor and Executive Director, CLAIR
Bangkok

Barbara B. Moran
University of North Carolina
Dean and Professor
Chapel Hill

1998
LIBRARIES UNLIMITED, INC.
Englewood, Colorado

For
Marlies and Joe
&

LIBRARIES UNLIMITED, INC.
P.O. Box 6633
Englewood, CO 80155-6633
1-800-237-6124
www.lu.com

Production Editor: Carmel A. Huestis
Copyeditor: Alison Auch
Proofreader: Pamela J. Getchell
Indexer: Susan Olason
Interior Design and Typesetting: Judy Gay Matthews

Library of Congress Cataloging-in-Publication Data

Stueart, Robert D.
    Library and information center management / Robert D. Stueart,
Barbara B. Moran. -- 5th ed.
    xxv, 509 p. 17x25 cm. -- (Library and information science text series)
    Includes bibliographical references and index.
    ISBN 1-56308-593-3. -- ISBN 1-56308-594-1 (pbk.)
    1. Library administration--United States. 2. Information
services--United States--Management. I. Moran, Barbara B.
II. Title. III. Series.
Z678.S799 1998
025.1--dc21   98-23574
                                                CIP

Contents

List of Illustrations

Figures *(continued)*

Tables

Foreword

Libraries are among the oldest social and cultural institutions in existence. Many great libraries flourished in ancient times, and these institutions continue their importance in the modern information age. Although libraries have been developed by various nations and cultures, they all share one overriding feature: They provided and still provide access to information recorded on some type of medium. Over the years the form of the medium has changed from stone to clay tablets, from papyrus and palm leaf to vellum, from scrolls to hand-copied books, and most recently from print-on-paper to magnetic, optical, and interactive multimedia.

It is likely that there was as much concern and consternation among information professionals working in libraries when scrolls were replaced by books as there is today when print-on-paper technology is being supplemented by online interactive access mechanisms. It must always be remembered, however, that the form in which the information is recorded is not the primary concern. What is far more important is the retrievability and accessibility of information in an efficient and effective manner. To make that retrieval and accessibility possible, managers need to employ successful management processes and to create appropriate work environments.

Over the centuries, the science—some would call it an art—of management has changed as dramatically as have libraries and information services. From the days of slaves managed by a few privileged classes to the age of the free craftsman or traders; to the age of cottage industries, in which a whole family worked to produce a living; to the age of the Industrial Revolution, which caused a violent social upheaval; and now to the information age, where information is the single most important resource in the political, economic, social, and technological development of society, and where information professionals play a key role as information advocates and intermediaries, standards of and approaches to viewing management have changed dramatically. It has never before been so important for organizations of all types to be responsive to changes in what their customers want and need and to be creative and innovative in delivering a product or service to meet those needs.

Libraries and other information-intense enterprises have, over the years, adopted and adapted many management principles from business, industry, and government. In some cases, as part of a government structure or other larger organization, libraries and information centers have been required to do so. But in all cases, library managers have attempted to adopt proven principles from the nonlibrary world that they think will contribute to the successful operation of their organizations.

There is, of course, a major difference between most libraries and businesses: Almost all libraries are nonprofit organizations. Whatever the nature of the enterprise, whether profit-making or not-for-profit, it must operate to please the customer or client, to give the employees and employers a sense of well-being and self-esteem, to maintain an attractive and healthy environment, and to provide consistent and efficient services.

A well-managed library or information center not only presents a better image to its constituency but also provides better service. A cluttered, unattractive workplace leads to disregard of its importance by customers. A laissez-faire attitude toward organizational structure and service objectives can be both demoralizing and destructive to employees and patrons. A high turnover of staff is a likely indicator of personnel problems that will affect service. A budget deficit at the end of a reporting period reflects lack of proper attention to control. Management techniques are vital to libraries of all types.

Because of their long history, libraries have tended to perpetuate practices that have worked effectively in the past. There is a natural tendency in mature organizations to become stagnant and disinclined to innovate. Mature organizations often are marked by inflexibility and an inability to compete and to respond to the needs of customers. Although libraries have changed tremendously over the past few decades, the changes must continue. If libraries and information centers are to remain viable entities into the next century, they must be able to compete with the burgeoning and often aggressive information industry. To remain competitive, they cannot simply keep doing what they have always done, instead they must remain open to new methods and techniques. And there is an abundance of new techniques to be considered. As a recent article in *Business Week* stated:

> Mobility. Empowerment. Teams. Cross-training. Virtual offices. Telecommuting. Re-engineering. Restructuring. Delayering. Outsourcing. Contingency. If these buzzwords don't sound familiar, they should: They are changing your life. The last decade, perhaps more than any other time since the advent of mass production, has witnessed a profound redefinition in the way we work.[1]

Effective organizations cannot rest on past success. Instead they must focus on quality and customer satisfaction, must respond quickly to changes in the external environment, must be creative and innovative, and must be committed to continuous learning. Although libraries and information centers have changed tremendously over the course of their existence, they will need to continue to change to succeed in the future as libraries along with all other organizations face the redefined world of information provision.

Notes

1. "The New World of Work," *Business Week* (October 17, 1994): 76.

Preface

The title of this edition, and of the previous one published five years ago, reflects a coming of age and continual development of principles and processes of management in libraries and information center organizations. More than twenty years ago, when the first edition of this book was published, little had been written about the management of libraries and information centers. Those seeking advice on, examples of, and information about how organizations function were forced to seek answers in the literature of public administration or business management. Since then there has been a spate of articles and monographs on various aspects of management as applied to library and information center operation.

The first edition of *Library Management*, published in 1977, was conceived as a basic text for library and information science management courses primarily in North America, because the authors were both faculty in schools on that continent. Many students in programs for which the textbook was intended had work experience in libraries or other types of information centers before entering graduate school, but they had little understanding of the theories or philosophies that directed and controlled the environments in which they worked or would be working in the future. They simply accepted patterns of library and information center organization, personnel procedures, budgetary controls, and planning processes, with their mission and goals—if they were even stated—as a given, without understanding why processes and procedures were followed. They were subjected to the *what* and *how* without understanding the *why*. Even when examples and forms, such as budgetary and personnel evaluation forms, were available, they were mostly regional or type-of-center specific. These materials did not reflect a broad cross section of libraries and information centers in the United States, not to mention the rest of the world. The second edition, written as the first by colleagues Robert D. Stueart and John T. Eastlick, was much broader in scope. While maintaining its usefulness as a basic text, it also served as a primary source of information and reference for lower- and middle-management personnel. Its geographic scope was broadened to be more representative of practices throughout North America. The third edition, published in 1987, addressed new and more complex issues and reflected contemporary developments in addition to the basic core of information. A new coauthor with Stueart for this edition, Barbara B. Moran, brought additional insight, expertise, and depth to the discussions. With the fourth edition, published in 1993, the two authors expanded the coverage to include themes for an international audience. In the meantime, previous editions had been translated into several languages—some of these without prior knowledge of the authors and publisher. The fourth edition also changed its title to *Library and Information Center Management* to more accurately reflect the focus and to incorporate a deeper discussion on each topic, and it included new materials, features, topics, examples, and insights. Quotes by experts were used to emphasize particular points.

The present edition updates and expands the materials contained in the previous four editions. It discusses new thoughts and techniques and reemphasizes those which have stood the test of time. This edition uses contemporary examples to illustrate such topics as strategic planning and total quality management.

Since publication of the first edition of *Library Management*, libraries and information services have changed drastically. These changes have been precipitated by both the internal and the external environment, and the continuous change process requires a more systematic approach to reviewing functions and developing strategies in the organization's setting. Technology and the political, economic, and social environments are powerful forces that influence the planning for information services today. New knowledge, skills, and techniques are required by staff at every level of an enterprise's operations. Different organizational structures, communications techniques, and budgeting strategies are required now. In the information age the focus is upon strategic initiatives for services necessary to connect the customer with the information being sought—whether for cultural, educational, economic, or entertainment purposes.

Even while established theories and practices of management have been modified and expanded, new theories, concepts, and practices have been developed. For example, an understanding of the concept of contingency management is essential for the planned growth and viability of an institution in the current social and technological climate. Changing demographic patterns, ethical issues, social responsibilities, and other economic, social, and technological forces, require reexamination of how effectively and efficiently resources of a human, material, and technological nature are utilized.

Teaching colleagues, practicing librarians and other information managers, and students require a text addressing established theories and reflecting contemporary practices. Although the chapter titles have remained the same, the volume has been rethought, reworked, and reedited to reflect recent changes and new issues in the information services environment. A great deal of thought was given to completely restructuring the volume. However, in final analysis the authors came to the conclusion that the chapter themes together represent the best approach to describing a contemporary organization. Although Planning, Organizing, Staffing, Directing, Coordinating, and Budgeting (POSDCORB) is not a new concept, it remains a viable one. Citations and examples have been updated, and additional readings are suggested at the end of each chapter. Examples of library and information service practice are included, and although they are from U.S. institutions, their purpose has international appeal. Some provide direct application for those seeking to establish new processes and procedures, and others provide useful guidelines for establishing standards throughout the world.

The basic theme of the book remains unchanged. The book focuses on the complex and interrelated functions common to all organizations and their current and future managers: planning, organizing, staffing, directing, and controlling. Although these functions are presented and discussed separately, it is important to remember that they are carried out simultaneously and concurrently. The actual operation of a library or information center follows no precise linear pattern. Most managerial functions progress simultaneously; they do not exist in a hierarchical relationship. For instance, budgeting is not likely to be reflective of the enterprise's success without some measure of planning where goals and objectives are established. Therefore, management cannot be viewed as a rigid system, and the concepts discussed in this text must be viewed as a whole. In this volume, each concept discussed is related to or builds upon others, and each relates to all levels of management and supervision in information services organizations. The purpose of separating and individually discussing the functions that comprise the management process is to permit an examination of the various threads in the fabric of what managers actually do.

This book was not written in a vacuum, nor is it intended for use in one. In-basket exercises, case studies, action mazes, and other simulation techniques should be used to supplement and magnify the principles discussed. Volumes on case studies may be helpful. Anderson's volume[1] was specifically developed as a companion piece for earlier editions of this text. In writing this book, the authors drew freely from writings and research in cognate fields, including business management, public administration, and the social sciences. The readings and notes at the end of each chapter represent a classified bibliography on the chapter topic.

Finally, it is important to point out that anyone who is supervising another person is involved in the management process. With the growth of participative management processes, more individuals are contributors to the management of organizations. Further, anyone involved in an organizational setting that requires interaction among individuals should understand the dynamics that relate to managing situations and organizations. In all organizations, everyone is either managing or being managed, and the principles of management are essential to individuals in both groups. Therefore, the principles discussed in this volume have relevance for each person whose job involves interacting with others to achieve the common goals and objectives of their organization.

Notes

1. A. J. Anderson, *Problems in Library Management* (Littleton, CO: Libraries Unlimited, 981).

Acknowledgments

As with previous editions, many people have contributed to the final product of this, our fifth edition. Readers of previous editions, both students and practitioners from America to Zimbabwe, have made encouraging comments and useful suggestions. Many have been incorporated into this latest edition. Colleagues throughout the world have indicated the value and use of such a general text, providing the principles with the practices. To them we are grateful for such encouragement.

The authors would especially like to thank those, too numerous to name here, who read and made comments on the content of various chapters. We are also grateful to colleagues who helped in the preparation of this manuscript, especially Krongtong Smitobol, Jessica Mathewson, Charlotte Sears, Kristin Chaffin, and Susan Thomas. Many libraries and information center managers permitted us to reproduce documents that are used as examples in the book, and we thank them. Their management practices and procedures make our discussions and illustrations of the issues and challenges more relevant and effective.

Finally, and once again, Bohdan Wynar of Libraries Unlimited is recognized for his continuing encouragement to do yet another edition.

Introduction

Readers of previous editions will note extensive revisions to this current edition. The authors have incorporated new issues and concepts of management thought and theory with an emphasis on a systems view of management. Technology, change, and human development dictate a holistic view of organizations and how they employ techniques, skills, and knowledge to accomplish identified goals. Today, employees of libraries and information centers are more sophisticated, better educated, and more responsive than at any point in the past. They are at the same time facing greater challenges than ever before resulting from increased competition, growing globalization, ever-changing technology, and the pace of change. The only constant in today's organizations is change. And as Charles Handy has stated, it is not change as we have known it in the past, but discontinuous change, which is particularly disturbing and confusing.

> It is not just because the pace of change has speeded up, which it has done, of course. . . . Faster change by itself sits quite comfortably with the "more only better" school. It is only when the graph goes off the chart that we need to start to worry, because then things get less predictable and less manageable. Incremental change suddenly becomes discontinuous change. In mathematics, they call it catastrophe theory.[1]

Handy feels that discontinuous change does not have to be catastrophic but can provide great opportunities. Discontinuous change will allow us to make great leaps forward because we cannot continue to do things as we have in the past. He advocates that we must, individually and organizationally, adopt "upside-down thinking" to confront this change. "It is time for new imagining, of windows opening even if some doors close. We need not stumble backward into the future, casting longing glances at what used to be; we can turn around and face a changed reality."[2]

One is reminded of Giuseppe Di Lampedusa's writing in *The Leopard,* when he warned that if things are to stay as they are, they will have to change. With that fact in mind, individuals working in dynamic organizations called libraries or information centers must use organizational knowledge in the mission of dispensing new knowledge to customers. This means understanding the organization and its potential for change to meet new goals that are now made more immediate by the acceleration of technology and the globalization of society. Tolerating ambiguity and risk taking are factors in organizational change and are reflected in each element of a structured work environment.

The practice of managing in such an environment requires awareness of the political, economic, social, and technological (PEST) factors that influence goals, the structures necessary to achieve these goals, the value systems embedded in that structure, and the human and monetary resources committed to that effort.

> ॐ We can say that organizations consist of (1) goal-oriented arrangements, people with a purpose; (2) psychosocial systems, people interacting in groups; (3) technological systems, people using knowledge and techniques; and (4) an integration of structured activities, people working together in patterned relationships.[3]
>
> —Fremont E. Kast and James E. Rosenzweig,
> *Organization and Management*

As management is a key concept in an organization, linking all of the various interrelated units and purposes together into a whole, it involves skills, techniques, and knowledge about organizations and how they behave. The authors have chosen to examine the elements of management under traditional headings of planning, organizing, staffing, directing, coordinating and budgeting. Others might cover similar concepts by considering each of those as a subsystem of the larger whole. For instance, instead of "staffing" one might look at a "structural subsystem," which views people working together on integrated activities.

All organizations change over their lifetime, and over a span of years theories that have been developed and applied may need to change also. What is right at one point in an organization's development may not be appropriate at a different stage when the organization has developed into a more sophisticated organism. Some theories used in the past may no longer have relevance for organizations preparing for the twenty-first century. Most of the traditional principles, however, are still useful in modern organizations, and managers should be familiar with them so they can choose the most appropriate methods for their own particular situation. There simply is not one best way of doing things, and techniques such as Total Quality Management, Management by Objectives, and others that have achieved widespread application are not appropriate in all organizations. The various concepts discussed in this volume will provide managers (and future managers) with information about the techniques and processes available. The book describes the various tools available in the managerial tool kit, but only an individual who is knowledgeable about the particular circumstances in a specific organization will be able to choose which tool to use to build a competitive and strong organization.

Notes

1. Charles Handy, *The Age of Unreason* (Boston: Harvard Business School Press, 1989), 8.

2. Ibid., 28.

3. Fremont E. Kast and James E. Rosenzweig, *Organization and Management: A Systems and Contingency Approach* (New York: McGraw-Hill, 1985), 5.

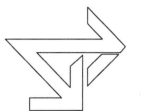

1

Management Development

A Historical Overview

Introduction

Each body of theory purports to rest on a scientific foundation. . . .
Each theory offers its own version of what organizations are like
and its own version of what they should be like. . . .
A modern manager who wants to improve an organization thus
encounters a cacophony of different voices and visions. . . .
As managers . . . turn to the theory base for help,
they will find a conceptual pluralism:
a jangling discord of multiple voices.[1]

—Lee G. Bolman and Terrence E. Deal,
Reframing Organizations

Anyone studying the history of management thought, with a glimmer of hope that past practices might shed some guiding light on future operations, may be both enlightened and disappointed. Experiences and experiments in any profession do add to the body of knowledge, and for the field of management this relates to how organizations were created in the past and how people working in them interacted in pursuing the mission of various types of organizations. But those experiences and experiments are relative, and when placed into a modern context of constant change, often present only interesting reading. Further, unlike principles in other disciplines upon which there seems to be specific agreement, there is none for management, where the focus varies from time to time, from situation to situation, and from person to person. Segments of the management process have developed unique principles and ethics such as for personnel management, marketing, and planning; nevertheless, some general theories do present a solid foundation upon which to view the present management milieu.

A hundred years ago, most organizations were relatively small and focus was upon techniques, with little recognition of underlying principles that guided development. Since then organizations have grown in size and multiplied in number. Some have disappeared completely, while others have been able to build upon their initial strengths to become stronger and more focused over time. Most dynamic organizations have changed; some have dissolved and reappeared in different configurations. New ones have emerged with strength and vitality. There also have been mergers, splits, and strategic partnerships, which form the nucleus of today's organizational life. Networking and adaptation to change, both technological and personal, now play primary roles in all organizational life. Both profit-making and not-for-profit organizations continue to struggle with changes brought on by political, economic, social, and technological (PEST) factors.

Libraries and information centers have not been immune to such dynamic development. Today, most are market driven, with service performance the primary criterion for resource allocation and measurement against set standards becoming the norm. Entrepreneurship and risk taking have become a way of life in the modern organization, including libraries and information centers.

Myriad concepts and theories have been put forward, particularly over the decades of the twentieth century, as historians and management theorists have struggled with identifying the experiments and defining the influences and functions that allow organizations to develop the way they do. They have tried to envision those that are likely to survive into future generations of organizations, and on the threshold of the twenty-first century, several thoughts, theories, and trends have merged in current management practice. All of these have been driven by consideration of the work, the people who perform it, and the environment that influences both.

> A person who knows only the skills and techniques, without understanding the fundamentals of management, is not a manager, he (she) is, at best, a technician.[2]

—Peter F. Drucker,
Management: Tasks, Responsibilities, Practices

Today's management has evolved from earliest practice, principles, and research that provide a body of scientific knowledge about organizations and the way they function. Throughout the development of the art of management, philosophers have tried to capture the concepts of what is happening and why, condensing those notions into theories that can be tested and expounded upon. Several attempts have been made to identify and delineate the "schools of thought" and "approaches" to management theories, both developed during the twentieth century. Adding to those experiments and theories, one also can learn from many management experiences recorded before modern times. For a variety of reasons, the categorization of the ideas and findings into various schools of thought continues to be met with as much confusion as clarity. Some researchers and instructors would place an idea, a theory, and an observation into one school, while others might place it in a different, though aligned, school.

The topic of management and observations about how it works have been of concern to organized society throughout civilized history, although its systematic study as a separate branch of human knowledge has received most attention during the second half of the twentieth century, primarily after World War II. Although formal management inquiry and research is a relatively recent phenomenon, historical records make it obvious that the forces that affect organizations today are much the same as those of the past: Political, Economic, Social, and Technological, PEST being an appropriate acronym for those forces.

The twentieth century has produced an enormous number of large, profit-driven organizations, as well as a variety of smaller institutions, limited in size and scope, some of them social or other kinds of not-for-profit agencies or units. Both organization profiles provide great opportunities for observation and speculation. Through analysis, researchers working in different schools of thought have attempted to scientifically formulate underlying principles of management and to postulate various theories based upon the practice of the occasion, as is evidenced in those various types of organizations.

A retrospective glance at the development of management reveals that, in most situations, management actions can be observed to have been guided by underlying theory or theories observable in practice. Thus management is both a science, grounded in theory, and an art, practiced by those who have the inspiration and drive to encourage others in their assigned organizational responsibilities. Theory provides the cornerstone, the *why*, while practice provides the laboratory for observation, the *what* and *how*.

Management in Ancient History

As early as 3000 B.C., the Sumerians kept records on clay tablets; many of those records applied to the management practices of the priests of Ur. Early Babylonia implemented very strict control of business enterprises with its Codes of Akkadian and Hammurabi. Nebuchadnezzar, for instance, used color codes to control production of the Hanging Gardens of Babylon, considered to be one of the great wonders of the ancient world. Checks were performed every week and cumulated yearly, with rewards being given for piecework, thereby establishing some of the earliest norms for performance. The Hebrews' understanding of hierarchy and the importance of delegation is reflected in the Old Testament, particularly in Exodus, chapter 18:25–26, in which Moses "chose able men out of all Israel and made them heads over the people, rulers of thousands, rulers of hundreds, rulers of fifties, and rulers of tens. And they judged the people at all seasons; the hard cases they brought unto Moses, but every small matter they judged themselves."

Construction of one pyramid in Egypt around 5000 B.C. was accomplished by about 100,000 people working for 20 years. It is obvious that such a magnificent feat could not have been accomplished without extensive planning, organizing, and controlling.

Around 2000 B.C., the principle of decentralized control was introduced, as is illustrated by the vesting of control in the individual states of Egypt; it was only later that the pharaoh established central control over all.[3] There is also evidence that Egyptians employed long-range planning techniques and staff advisers. Interpretations of early Egyptian papyri, extending as far back as 1300 B.C., indicate that the bureaucratic states of antiquity recognized the importance of organization and administration. Similar records exist for activities in ancient China. Claude George points out that one could find, in the China of 3000 years ago, "concepts that have a contemporary managerial ring: organization, functions, cooperation, procedures to bring efficiency, and various control techniques."[4] The staff principle, later perfected by military organizations, was used very effectively by Chinese dynasties as far back as 2250 B.C.

Although the records of early Greece offer little insight to the principles of management, the very existence of the Athenian commonwealth, with its councils, popular courts, administrative officials, and board of generals, indicates an appreciation of various managerial functions. Socrates's definition of management as a skill separate from technical knowledge and experience is remarkably close to current understanding. The Greek influence on scientific management is revealed in their writings, for example, Plato wrote about specialization and Socrates described management issues.[5]

In ancient Rome the complexity of the administrative job evoked considerable development of management techniques. It is thought that the secret of the Roman Empire's success lay in the ability of the Romans to organize work and people for the cause. Confucius, the great Chinese sage, a civil servant and teacher of management around 500 B.C., wrote parables that offered practical suggestions for public administration. Some of them are still quoted in and applied to modern organizations.

Many ancient leaders were not only charismatic individuals but skillful organizers as well. Hannibal's crossing of the Alps in 218 B.C., with his Carthaginian troops and equipment, was a remarkable organizational feat.

About the same time, Qin Shi Huang Di, the First Emperor of China, was able to organize hundreds of thousands of slaves and convicts to create his burial complex at Xian and to connect portions of the Great Wall. He also unified warring factions and standardized weights and measures as part of his centralization initiative. He is referred to as the "First" Emperor of China.

The earliest documentation of motion studies appeared in the time of Cyrus, the Persian king, about 600 B.C. Records of those studies indicate that musical instruments—the flute and the pipe—governed workers' tempo and motions, while songs designated each of the various tasks. The Persians further added to the developing body of management practice by introducing rhythm, standard motion, and other motion-related work aspects.[6] Thus, many of the techniques that are employed today in modern organizations can be traced to ancient times and civilizations.

Modern History of Management Thought

Bringing the management process into modern times, the most efficient formal organization in the history of Western civilization has been the Catholic Church. This is due not only to the sustained appeal of its objectives but also to the effectiveness of its organization and management techniques. Early in the organization of the church, the scalar chain of command, along with the concept of specialization, was introduced to establish a path of communication from the highest level in the organization, the pope, down to the bottom rung of a ladder-like hierarchy.

The Arsenal of Venice in Italy, probably the sixteenth century's largest industrial plant, is an outstanding example of organizational efficiency. It was established during the time of Machiavelli, whose writings emphasized the principle that authority develops from the consent of the masses. His ideas, particularly as set forth in his classic work, *The Prince*, apply to current study of leadership and communications.

Some of the most important principles and practices of modern business management can be traced to military organizations. The principles of unity of command, staff advisers, and division of work all evolved from early military order, probably as early as Cyrus and certainly refined by Alexander the Great, who effectively used staff organization to coordinate activities.

The military has been a strong organization throughout history and in many countries. Among the most important management practice developed by the military is the staff principle. For example, the general staff, organized under a chief of staff, furnishes specialized advice and information and supplies auxiliary services. The general staff and its services have come to be essential features not only of the military but also in business enterprises. In addition, the line-of-command concept originated in the armies of antiquity and medieval times, and the scalar principle, to be discussed later, is still a very important part of military organizations today.

The development of technology during the Industrial Revolution, at the end of the nineteenth and beginning of the twentieth centuries, produced a factory system that brought workers into a central location and into contact with other workers. It was during the development of effective and efficient management control of these newly founded organizations that many management concepts began to emerge. Adam Smith in his writing, particularly in *The Wealth of Nations*, described division of work and time-and-motion studies, as they should be employed in organizations. Other writers of the period, including Robert Owen, Charles Babbage, and Charles Dupin, wrote about the problems of management in factories.[7] Many of the principles that were later reemphasized and further refined in the scientific management approach and the human relations approach were first developed by those writers during the eighteenth and nineteenth centuries. For instance, Charles Babbage, a mathematician, stressed the importance of distinguishing mental activity from physical work, and wanted to improve efficiency by encouraging managers to use time-study techniques, to centralize production, to inaugurate research and development, and so forth.[8] He contributed much to the scientific management approach and was a pioneer in developing the principles that are used in computing. Both Owen and Babbage identified human resources as a major contributing force to the success of organizations. Owen was committed to human comforts, including working conditions and wages, while Babbage emphasized staff benefits, including profit sharing.

> ॐ Those who look for library administrative theory search for it outside of librarianship. Because library administration is so pragmatically oriented, it seems impossible that a theoretical framework for viewing administrative practice already exists within libraries. Yet this is indeed the case. It remains only to ferret it out.[9]
>
> —Charles McClure,
> *Strategies for Library Administration*

Various methods have been used in the study of management in this century. The first systematic approach was legalistic, being devoted to a study of the organization, powers, and activities and limitations of public authorities. Later, a more scientific approach was considered, concerned chiefly with the administrative organization as an instrument of management. An attempt was made to determine, on the basis of empirical evidence, rules for administrative organization and operation. More recently, behavioral scientists have used the methods of psychology, sociology, and anthropology in efforts to secure a better understanding of group behavior, leadership, and decision making. These pioneering contributions to schools, movements, or approaches are referred to by various names, but the major focus or core of each can be recognized, although their factors sometimes overlap.

No student of management thought can afford to be unfamiliar with the contributions of the major pioneer thinkers in the field. This is not to say that their ideas must be accepted without question. However, their ideas are the basis for the development of management techniques currently in practice, and their contributions provide insight into the background theories that are the essence of management today.

> There are the behaviorists . . . who see management as a complex of interpersonal relationships and the basis of management theory, the tentative tenets of the new and undeveloped science of psychology. There are also those who see management theory as simply a manifestation of the institutional and cultural aspects of sociology. Still others, observing that the central core of management is decision-making, branch in all directions from this core to encompass everything in organization life. Then, there are mathematicians, who think of management primarily as an exercise in logical relationships expressed in symbols and the omnipresent and ever revered model. But the entanglement of growth reaches its ultimate when the study of management is regarded as one of a number of systems and sub-systems, with an understandable tendency for the researcher to be dissatisfied until he [or she] has encompassed the entire physical and cultural universe as a management system.[10]
>
> —Harold Koontz, "The Management Theory Jungle"

It is apparent, when one studies the schools of management thought that developed in this century, that each reflects the problems of the changing times. There is a progression of concerns detailed in those studies. In management practice, the theory that is most relevant and applicable at one point in its evolution seems not to be the most appropriate one at the next level of the organization's development. Also, the theory that is prominent at one point in time may no longer be in vogue during the next decade. A few theories have survived and continue to influence management thought and practice today. For purposes of discussion, these are grouped into three approaches: scientific, human relations, and systems.

Scientific Approach

Scientific Management Movement

The term *scientific management* is said to have been coined in 1910 by Louis Brandeis in his appearance before the Interstate Commerce Commission in the United States. The basic assumption of this school of thought is that workers, at the operational level, are primarily economically motivated and that they will put forth their best efforts if they are rewarded financially. Further, the emphasis is on maximum output with minimum strain, eliminating waste and inefficiency. Planning and standardization of efforts and techniques are viewed as important factors. In the United States, the pioneering work of Frederick Winslow Taylor dominates the thinking of this school. Although one cannot say that he developed the theory, his concepts, based upon experiments on the shop floor, have contributed to general management theory of the scientific management movement.

> ⚘Scientific management requires the establishment of many rules, laws and formulae which replace the judgment of the individual [worker] and which can be effectively used only after having been recorded, indexed, etc.[11]
>
> —Frederick W. Taylor,
> *Principles of Scientific Management*

During his day, Taylor's views coincided closely with those of proponents of the Protestant work ethic, who had no difficulty with the fusion of religion and worldly success. Taylor's attitude toward work was that the human and machine are similar. "It is no single element, but rather the whole combination, that constitutes scientific management, which may be summarized as: Science, not rule of thumb; Harmony, not discord; Cooperation, not individualism; Maximum output, in place of restricted output; The Development of [all workers to their] greatest efficiency and prosperity."[12] Taylor expounded several principles:

1. To gather all traditional knowledge and classify, tabulate, and reduce it to rules, laws, and formulas to help workers in their daily work.

2. To develop a science for each element of man's work to replace the rule-of-thumb method.

3. To scientifically select and then train, teach, and develop the worker.

4. To cooperate with workers to ensure that work is done according to developed scientific principles.

5. To effect an almost equal division of work and responsibility between workers and managers; that is, managers are to be given work for which they are best fitted, as are employees.[13]

Efficiency was Taylor's central theme. As a steel works manager in Philadelphia, Pennsylvania, in the United States, he was interested in knowing how to get more work out of workers who were "naturally lazy and engage[d] in systematic soldiering." Poor management, he speculated, fostered this attitude. He observed "when a naturally energetic man works for a few days beside a lazy one, the logic of the situation is unanswerable. 'Why should I work hard when the lazy fellow gets the same pay that I do and does only half as much work?' "[14] Taylor proposed using scientific research methods to discover the one best way to perform a job. He felt that faster work could be assured only through enforced standardization of methods, enforced adaptation of the best instruments to be used for the work, adoption of good and hygienic working conditions, and enforced cooperation. This attitude moved away from a more experiential approach to a more scientific one. Among the several experiments he performed were:

1. Work study. One particular experiment detailed movements of workers in a shop and suggested shortcuts as well as more efficient ways of performing certain operations. Within three years of implementing the new ways, the output of the shop had doubled.

2. Standardized tools for shops. In another area he found that the coal shovels being used weighed between 16 and 38 pounds. After experimenting, it was found that 21–22 pounds was the best weight. Shovels weighing that amount were employed. Again, after three years, efficiency increased as 140 men were doing what had previously been done by between 400 and 600 men.

3. Selecting and training workers. Taylor insisted that each worker be assigned to do what he or she was best suited for and that those who exceeded the defined work be paid bonuses. With this motivation, production, as might be expected, rose to an all-time high.

As a result of these experiments, Taylor also advocated assigning supervisors by function, that is, one for training, one for discipline, and so on. As can be imagined, this required the principles of planning, organizing, and controlling as input measures to increase output. A related functional approach is still successful as is evident today in many organiza- tions, including some libraries and other types of information centers throughout the world.

However, in the industry of that time, Taylor's efforts were resented by unions and managers alike: managers, because their intuition and discretion were challenged, unions because their role was questioned. Taylor was fired from his original job in Philadelphia, Pennsylvania. He then went to Bethlehem Steel, still in Pennsylvania, where, again he was fired after only three years. The unions, indignant by this time, were instrumental in having his methods investigated by a special U.S. congressional committee; they succeeded in forbidding the use of stopwatches and bonuses in U.S. army arsenals until World War II. His concepts, however, spread to Europe and Great Britain and later to the Soviet Union after the Russian Revolution. Many researchers and scholars maintain that this movement represented techniques only and thwarted the development of a true philosophy of management.

An often-repeated criticism of the scientific management approach is that it overemphasizes productivity and underemphasizes human nature. Amitai Etzioni wrote that "although Taylor originally set out to study the interaction between human characteristics and the characteristics of the machine, the relationship between these two elements which make up the industrial work process, he ended up by focusing on a far more limited subject: the physical characteristics of the human body in routine jobs— e.g., shoveling coal or picking up loads. Eventually Taylor came to view human and machine resources not so much as mutually adaptable, but rather man functioning as an appendage to the industrial machine."[15] Similar criticism could be leveled at other movements within the scientific management approach.

While Taylor was the most important advocate of the scientific management movement, others worked in the same arena, including Frank and Lillian Gilbreth. Frank, an engineer, and Lillian, who held a doctorate in psychology, were concerned with the human aspects of managing, and they expanded the concepts of motion study and fatigue. Their merit systems eventually evolved into performance analysis and appraisals. They tried to identify the one best way to perform a task in the most comfortable manner. In the process they identified 17 basic elements in on-the-job motions, such as grasp, hold, position, and search. These motions came to be called THERBLIGS, *Gilbreths* spelled backward, with one transposition.[16] Taylor's experiments and the Gilbreths' work were complementary, Taylor stressing time study and the Gilbreths emphasizing motion study. From these two merged systems emerged the industrial engineering discipline.

Henry L. Gantt, experimenting at about the same time, developed the task-and-bonus system, which was similar to Taylor's awards incentive. Gantt's system set rates of output; if those rates were exceeded, bonuses were paid. In some cases, production more than doubled; therefore, he developed what might be considered the first set of output measures. The Gantt Chart is still widely used in production schedules and is used in many libraries and information systems to chart and calculate work schedules. Along the horizontal axis of the chart, Gantt placed the time, work schedule, and work-completed aspects; along the vertical axis he placed the individuals and machines assigned to those schedules. In this way, the path to completion could be easily calculated.

In its early development, scientific management had little concern for the external environment of the organization, but was almost exclusively concerned with internal operations. Taylor took many of his concepts from the bureaucratic model developed by Max Weber in Germany, particularly in regard to rules and procedures for the conduct of work in organizations. Weber, the first to articulate a theory of authority structure in organizations, distinguished between power and authority, between compelling action and voluntary response. He identified three characteristics that aided authority: charisma (personality), tradition (custom), and bureaucracy (through rules and regulations). This concept of bureau-cracy developed on one side of the Atlantic at about the same time as scientific management was developing on the other. Further, thoughts on specialization of work, levels of authority, and control all emerged from Weber's writings.

Weber was more concerned with the structure of the organization than with the individual. Most of his writings and research related to the importance of specialization in labor, regulations and procedures, and the advantages of a hierarchical system in making informed decisions. Weber, a German behavioral scientist, characterized a bureaucratic organization as an organization of functions bound by rules in which:

1. area of competence or division of labor provides specialization and contributes to standardization;

2. the principle of hierarchy exists;

3. promotion into management ranks is only by demonstrated technical competence; and

4. rules are to be recorded in writing.[17]

Weber further stated that "experience tends universally to show that the purely bureaucratic type of administrative organization . . . is, from a pure theoretical point of view, capable of attaining the highest degree of efficiency and is in this sense formally the most rational known means of carrying out imperative control over human beings."[18] But Weber later recognized the dangers of too rigid a bureaucratic control.

> It is horrible to think that the world could one day be filled with nothing but little cogs, little men clinging to little jobs and striving towards bigger ones. This passion for bureaucracy is enough to drive one to despair.[19]
>
> —Max Weber, in J. P. Mayer,
> *Max Weber and German Politics*

Classical Movement

Another movement began to develop in France about the same time as Taylor's experiments in the United States. Using some of the same scientific management methods, it sought to establish a conceptual framework for management, identify principles, and build a theory. However, unlike the scientific management movement, which focused on shop operations, this approach, referred to as the classical or traditional or universalist school, took a holistic view of the organization in order to define an ideal structure. Some refer to the body of knowledge that came out of this process as the administrative management theory.[20]

The father of the classical or generalist theory of movement was a Frenchman, Henri Fayol. Fayol took a scientific approach, but he looked at administration from the top down. As an industrialist, he concentrated on the roles that managers should perform as planners, organizers, and controllers. He believed that managers needed guidelines, basic principles upon which to operate, and he emphasized the need to teach administration at all levels. He identified elements in the administration of organizations as including planning, organization, command, coordination, and control. Briefly, his stated principles are:

1. Division of work. As the enterprise grows, there should be an early division of duties. The activities concerning management should be separate and distinct. Specialization naturally develops with division of work.

2. Authority. The authority that individuals possess in an organization should be equal to their responsibility. A person who is responsible for the results of a task should be given the authority to take actions necessary to ensure its success.

3. Discipline. There should be complete obedience to, total energy devoted to, and behavior in the best interest of the organization.

4. Unity of command. An employee should receive orders from only one superior. (This unity of command is in direct opposition to Taylor's idea of having workers take instructions from several superiors.)

5. Unity of direction. A body with two heads is a monster and has difficulty in surviving. There should be one head and one plan to ensure a coordinated effort.

6. Subordination of individual interest to general interest. Primary concern should be the growth of the organization.

7. Remuneration of personnel. Wages should be fair.

8. Centralization. Everything that goes to increase the importance of the subordinate's role is decentralization, everything that goes to reduce it is centralization. Centralization is the desirable arrangement within an organization.

9. Scalar chain. Gangplanks should be used to prevent the scalar chain from bogging down. The gangplank (illustrated in fig. 1.1) can be used without weakening the chain of command, as long as the gangplank relationship is advisory and not policy making.

Fig. 1.1. A gangplank can be used to communicate across scalar boundaries.

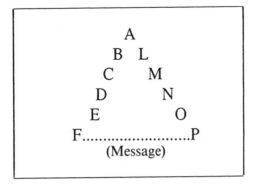

10. Order. There is a right place for everything and everyone in the organization. That place or job must be identified.

11. Equity. Equality of treatment must be taken into account in dealing with employees. Justice should be tempered with kindness.

12. Stability of tenure of personnel. It is important to keep people on the job.

13. Initiative. Incentive rewards must be provided to stimulate production.

14. Esprit de corps. Communication is the key to a satisfied working group.[21]

Like Taylor, Fayol believed workers are naturally lazy, resist work more effectively when working in groups, must be subject to sharp discipline, can best be motivated by the incentive of higher wages, can do much better when properly instructed, and differ markedly in native ability and capacity. Unlike Taylor in other views of the organization, Fayol was more concerned with human relations and defining the activities of managers. He and Luther Gulick, among others, advised managers to break down complicated jobs into specialized activities. This was achieved through a "pyramid of control." Gulick and Lyndall Urwick followed Fayol's lead by popularizing several principles:

1. Fit people to the administrative structure.

2. Recognize one top executive as the source of authority.

3. Adhere to unity of command.

4. Use special and general staff.

5. Departmentalize by purpose, process, person, and place.

6. Delegate and use the exception principle.

7. Make responsibility commensurate with authority.

8. Consider appropriate spans of control.[22]

> When management principles can be developed, proved and used, managerial efficiency will inevitably improve. Then the conscientious manager can become more effective by using established guidelines to help solve . . . problems, without engaging in original laborious research or the risky practice of trial and error.[23]
>
> —Harold Koontz and Cyril O'Donnell,
> *Principles of Management*

Taylor and Fayol, then, may be considered the founders of the theory of management. There is little doubt that many organizations, libraries, information centers, and other information agencies still depend heavily on these classic theories for the base of their formal organization. The greatest criticisms of those schools is that they place undue emphasis on the formal aspects of organization and neglect entirely the effects of individual personality, informal groups, intraorganizational conflicts, and the decision-making process on the formal structure.

Organization and System Movement

World War I gave great impetus to the study of efficiency, and by 1930 the idea of applying theory to organization and system was emphasized in the organization and system movement. This theory distinguished between administration, representing the ownership point of view, and scientific management, an approach to work at the operational level, as they related to organization and system. This movement expanded the work of Fayol and at the same time began to explore the behavioral aspects of management. Weber's theory about authority structures in complex organizations is a classic foundation of the system movement.[24] Mooney and Reiley added further substance to the systems movement by focusing on principles of coordination, scalar chaining, functionality, and staffing.[25] They developed organization charts, job descriptions, and policy manuals for procedures in organizations.

Other significant writers about this movement, already mentioned, were Lyndall Urwick, an Englishman, and Luther Gulick, an American, who edited a landmark work on scientific administration. In a paper to U.S. President Franklin Roosevelt in 1937, they summed up an executive's functions in the acronym POSDCORB. The focus was on:

- Planning, that is, working out in broad outline the things that need to be done and the methods for doing them in order to accomplish the enterprise's set purpose.

- Organizing, that is, the establishment of the formal structure of authority through which work subdivisions are arranged, defined, and coordinated for the defined objectives.

- Staffing, that is, the whole personnel function of bringing in and training the staff and maintaining favorable conditions for work.

- Directing, that is, the continuous task of making decisions and embodying them in specific and general orders and instructions, and serving as the leader of the enterprise.

- COordinating, that is, the all-important duty of interrelating the various parts of the work.

- Reporting, that is, keeping those to whom the executive is accountable informed through records, research, and inspection.

- Budgeting, that is, all that goes with budgeting in the form of fiscal planning, accounting, and control.[26]

Readers will quickly realize that the early systems approach, originally developed by Urwick and Gulick, is a simplified yet comprehensive way of viewing management. It is based upon a combination of experiences and philosophy. The reader will also recognize that the concepts detailed in their work, with modifications and additions, have been used as a framework in developing some of the discussion in this textbook. It is a simplified view, recognizing that there are many segments of management, each of which has developed its own principles. For instance, when one talks about organizing, staffing, and directing it is obvious that Urwick and Gulick's principles of personnel management come into play.

Human Relations Approach

During the 1930s management studies began to give more attention to the concerns of individuals working in organizations. The primary belief of this approach was that, because managing involves getting things done through people, management study should naturally center on interpersonal relations. The main emphasis of observation and study became that of the individual and the informal group in the formal organization; the primary concern was with integrating people into the work environment. The phrase *personnel administration* came into prominence and increasing efforts toward democratization and staff participation was evident. It became important to study people as human beings rather than as work units, as individuals rather than as cogs in a wheel. Of paramount concern in this approach is the recognition of basic human needs, with the idea that once those primary needs are satisfied and a willing ear given to suggestions and complaints made by the individual, morale will increase and production will go up. The maxim "a happy workforce is a productive workforce" well describes this approach. Both sociologists and psychologists have contributed to these developments.

Human Behavior Movement

This movement focuses on behavior of the individual and his or her quality of life in the organization, and the individual's needs, aspirations, and motivations, as well as those of the group and the organization. The major assumption is that if management can make employees happy, maximum performance will result. Mary Follett, a political philosopher writing in the early 1900s, was one of the first to be concerned with the human aspect.

She emphasized the psychological and sociological aspects of management, viewing it as a social process and the organization as a social system in which coordination was the most important principle: coordination by direct contact with the people concerned, coordination that was a continuous process, coordination found in the initial steps of every endeavor, and coordination as a reciprocal process. Her main concern was with workers and their involvement in deciding their destiny within the organization.

Elton Mayo and a group of industrial psychologists at the Western Electric Hawthorne Plant in Chicago, Illinois, conducted early efforts in this type of research in the United States. Mayo promoted internal communications by providing decision-makers with insights into the attitudes of workers and by looking at the informal groups and focusing on human factors. Researchers, led by Mayo, began to study physical working conditions and their influence on worker productivity.[27] The studies established that each individual is different; that they act to protect their own position in a group rather than to help management achieve higher production; and that this self-interest has an impact upon the behavior of others within the group. These studies also revealed the importance of social interaction and psychological factors in determining productivity and satisfaction. Several principles have been demonstrated in their studies:

1. Workers are more motivated by social rewards and sanctions than by economic incentives.

2. The group influences workers' actions.

3. Whenever formal organizations exist, both formal and informal norms exist.

The researchers, after hypothesizing that motivation and supervision, as well as basic social relations on the job were responsible for increased productivity, found that indeed, when the work group felt itself to be in opposition to management, productivity stayed close to the minimum accepted level. For the first time it was recognized that those social factors were important to organizational output. In general, the human behavior movement maintains that if the organization makes employees happy, it will gain their full cooperation and effort and reach optimum efficiency.

> ❧A major concern of management must be that of organizing teamwork, that is to say, of developing and sustaining cooperation.[28]
>
> —G. Elton Mayo,
> *The Social Problems of an
> Industrialized Civilization*

Mayo's conclusions were quite opposite from those of Taylor, who stated that a person at work is an entirely economic person. Mayo maintained that workers are primarily motivated by togetherness and crave individual recognition within the group.

Self-Actualizing Movement

This movement is closely related to the human relations movement and is often confused or intertwined with it. It encourages management to let employees develop social groups on the job, to move toward employee participation in management, and to allow democracy in the organization. The spiritual father of this movement is Chester Barnard, who dwells on the contribution-satisfaction equilibrium, as he examined the organization as a social system. He was the first to introduce the issue of social responsibility of management, including fair wages and security and the creation of an atmosphere conducive to work. He identifies four inducements: material inducements, including money and other physical securities; personal, nonmaterial opportunities for distinction, prestige, and personal power; desirable physical conditions of work; and ideal benefactions, such as pride of workmanship, sense of adequacy, loyalty to the organization, and so on.[29] Barnard emphasized communication as the first function of managers.

> Man is a perpetual wanting animal. The average member of society is most often particularly satisfied and particularly unsatisfied in all of his wants.[30]
>
> —Abraham Maslow,
> "A Theory of Human Motivation"

Several later theories and concepts regarding the individual have emerged from the works of other authors in this movement. Abraham Maslow's needs theory builds on the concept that humans have a hierarchy of needs starting with the basic physical necessities of food, shelter, and clothing, and ascending five steps to the intangible needs of self-actualization and fulfillment, with emphasis on self-actualization.[31] The whole concept of organizational behavior has been advanced by Maslow's motivational theory. Management by Objectives, another management concept, was introduced in the 1950s by Peter Drucker and is supported by Douglas McGregor in his Theory X and Theory Y work, which advocates substituting a more participative approach for authoritarianism.[32] Frederick Herzberg's "hygienic" factors are considered deterrents to dissatisfaction in the work environment. Chris Argyris suggests that organizational structure can curtail self-fulfillment.[33] The theories all express the idea that information sharing is desirable and that management and workers should divide planning and analysis of operations. Other disciples of this approach include Rensis Likert, Warren G. Bennis, and Robert Blake and Jane Mouton. Discussion of these and other theorists are incorporated into the discussions in chapter 5.

> ☙ The average person learns, under proper conditioning, not only to accept but also to seek responsibility. The capacity to exercise a relatively high degree of imagination, ingenuity and creativity in the solution of organizational problems is widely, not narrowly, distributed in the population.[34]
>
> —Douglas McGregor,
> *The Human Side of Enterprise*

Systems Approach

Most recently, attention has been paid to the matter of individuals and group behavior in the work situation and the relationship between individuals and groups within a larger social, cultural, and political system. Concepts emerging from the Japanese management approach fall into this category. A topic of current exploration is the behavior of both individuals and groups within organizations and the behavior of organizations as social systems in the environment. Although the term *systems* is used here, it is used in a very different way than the previously mentioned *organization and system movement*.

The systems approach, also known as the decision theory approach, regards the organization as a total system. Terms common in this approach include *management science* and *operations research*. In many ways, the systems approach is similar to the earlier scientific management approach. As Herbert Simon points out, "no meaningful line can be drawn any more to demarcate operations research from scientific management or scientific management from management science."[35] Proponents of this approach gather information by microstudies of units in the system to discern how individual units interrelate and depend on other units to create a whole.[36] Generally, the systems approach draws on the basic science and theory of several disciplines and relates those principles to the structure and management of organizations (see fig. 1.2).

Fig. 1.2. The systems approach to management incorporates a wide array of disciplines. From H. Koontz, "The Management Theory Jungle Revisited," *Academy of Management Review*, vol. 5, no. 2 (April 1980): 179. Reprinted with permission.

Decision Theory Movement

Since the 1950s, disciplines like mathematics, statistics, and economics have contributed to management through the use of mathematical models for decision making and prediction. Control techniques, such as cost-benefit analyses, linear programming, systems analysis, simulation, Monte Carlo techniques, and game theory have been used in creative planning. However, even though this is a recent phenomenon, an operations research team was used as early as the 1940s in England, when the various phases of operations research were developed.[37] The disciplines of psychology and sociology have contributed to theories of leadership and organization, human motivation and behavior, organizational relationships, and the nature of authority. Elements from each of those theories and disciplines have been drawn together in the decision theory movement to focus on the process of making decisions.

The decision theory movement is primarily concerned with the study of rational decision-making procedures and the way managers actually reach decisions. The implication is that mathematical models and quantitative processes can serve as the basis for all management decisions. Many of the researchers have concentrated on describing the decision-making process, drawing on psychology and economics,[38] or on prescribing how decisions should be made.[39] The mathematical branch of the decision theory movement is concerned with both what to measure and why, the goal being to indicate how best to improve a system or solve a problem. Managing information for timely decision-making has become a major focus of some research efforts. Management Information Systems (MIS) has developed as a sophisticated technique for systematically gathering relevant information for decision-makers. The advent of technology has greatly aided researchers in the development of management information systems and has allowed others to more quickly test theories using simulation models. The MIS approach was further facilitated and enhanced by the development of Decision Support Systems (DSS) using computer technology to address complex problems requiring human decisions.[40]

Management scientists share common characteristics, namely the application of scientific analysis to managerial problems; the goal of improving the manager's decision-making ability; high regard for economic effectiveness criteria; reliance on mathematical models; and the use of computers.[41] The decision theory movement, primarily through DSS, uses techniques such as game theory, simulation, and linear programming in presenting alternatives for decision-makers to consider.

General Systems Theory Movement

Undoubtedly the most widely accepted theoretical base for modern management is called the General Systems Theory (GST). This movement integrates knowledge gleaned from the biological, physical, and behavioral sciences. Its disciples, who call themselves revisionists, are working to combine the thoughts of the behavioral scientists with those of systems theorists, mathematicians, statisticians, and computer scientists by merging the theories of the scientific management movement with those of the human relations movement. Some of the previously mentioned researchers are also part of this movement, including Mary Parker Follett, Chester Barnard, Herbert Simon, Chris Argyris, and Rensis Likert. They maintain that external and internal forces influence workers' attitudes. Therefore, it is important to encourage interaction with both environments to benefit the organization. Effective planning systems, organizing systems, and controlling systems, discussed later in this text, are cognizant of this unifying drive. The emphasis is upon communications and developing organizational structures best suited to benefit the organization. Some consider the GST movement not a theory but "a direction in the contemporary philosophy of science."[42]

Ludwig von Bertlanffy is considered the founder of GST because he was the first to talk about the "system theory of the organism."[43] He defines a system as "a set of elements standing in interrelation among themselves and with the environment. The really important aspect is the interaction among the elements to create a whole, dynamic system. This system, if it is an open one, interacts with its environment."[44] The system draws from the environment and feeds back into it. The system is influenced by the environment and in turn influences the environment. If the system is dissected it becomes evident that it comprises a number of subsystems; likewise, the organization is but one subsystem of a larger environment. Fremont Kast and James Rosenzweig summarize nicely by stating that "an organization is not simply a technical or a social system. Rather, it is the structuring and integrating of human activities around various technologies. The technologies affect the types of inputs into the organization, the nature of the transformation processes, and the outputs from the system. However, the social system determines the effectiveness and efficiency of the utilization of the technology."[45]

Psychological Movement

Brief mention should be made of a fledgling psychological movement that, in many ways, fits into several categories already discussed. Based upon personality theory, the psychological movement views the human as a complex being metamorphosing through physiological and psychological stages to maturity. The ego, as it develops, learns to adjust to factors of the environment, the conscience, and basic sexual and aggression drives. Work is the great equalizer in this development; therefore, the organization becomes an important psychological tool, if you will. The major theorists of this movement are Harry Levinson, Abraham Zaleznik, and Elliot Jaques.

Believing that an individual can fashion his or her own existence, researchers have explored how unconscious motives affect decision making and how irrational behavior relates contemporary pressures to childhood conflicts. The researchers are attempting to create a psychology model that identifies the driving force behind the ego, believing that one's self-esteem is a product of the gap between ego ideal and self-image.

Contingency Approach

A current management concept that has gained some attention in recent years is contingency management. This school takes the situational approach. It considers the circumstances of each situation and then decides which response has the greatest chance of success.[46] The contingency or situational approach asserts that: (1) there is no best management technique; (2) there is no best way to manage; (3) no technique or managerial principle is effective all of the time; and (4) should the question be posed as to what works best, the simple response is, "It all depends on the situation."[47] The challenges of the contingency approach are in perceiving organizational situations as they actually exist, choosing the management tactic best suited to those situations, and competently implementing those tactics.[48] The approach requires an analysis and diagnosis of the entire managerial environment, thereby synthesizing all approaches. "It promises to integrate the best of the existing strands of management knowledge."[49]

Summary

The scientific movement's approach to organization is to study the activities that need to be undertaken to achieve objectives; the human relations approach starts with the study of people's motives and behavior; and the decision theory (systems) approach concentrates on the decisions that need to be made to achieve objectives. All of these approaches interrelate to provide a total management picture. For the purposes of this chapter, the major management theories have been placed in categories that are frequently used in the management literature. These categories have been labeled with terms drawn from the literature, although writers disagree about which terms can best be used in a strict classification of management theory. All of the approaches are concerned with the management process, but no one theory can begin to provide a comprehensive view. All have strong points and weak points, and some of the best and some of the worst of each can be observed in library and information center operations today.

This general overview does not permit detailed discussions of concepts or theorists, instead it simply mentions them because the intent is to provide the basic background necessary for a student or other interested professional who can then place into perspective the observed theories as they apply to today's libraries and information centers. Applications of some of these theories mentioned are cited in later chapters of this text. For instance, contemporary theories—such as McGregor's Theory X and Theory Y, Herzberg's motivation-hygiene theory, and Maslow's hierarchy of needs theory—are discussed in appropriate chapters.[50] This discussion of the various approaches to management provides a perspective of the foundation upon which contemporary management rests. The various approaches, each with its own techniques and proponents, contribute to an understanding of the nature of management and how it can be practiced more skillfully.

One way to view management is as a set of common processes or functions that, when properly carried out, lead to organizational efficiency and effectiveness. Another way is to think of management as the roles played by managers. Henry Mintzberg observed what managers did over a period of time and from his observations drew conclusions about what managers actually do. Based on this research, Mintzberg described managers' various roles. These roles can be grouped into three broad categories: interpersonal roles, information roles, and decision roles.[51] Mintzberg's approach offers an interesting and useful alternative to the traditional view of managerial functions. Mintzberg sees managers performing many activities, such as acting as a figurehead and representing the organization to the outside world, that have not been considered strictly managerial functions. This is not surprising, because only top managers perform many of the roles that Mintzberg describes.

> Most managers spend most of their time on things that are not "managing." A sales manager makes a statistical analysis or placates an important customer. A foreman repairs a tool or fills out a production report. A manufacturing manager designs a new plant layout or tests new material. A company president works through the details of a bank loan or negotiates a big contract—or spends hours presiding at a dinner in honor of long-service employees. All of these things pertain to a particular function. All are necessary and have to be done well. But they are apart from the work which every manager does whatever his (or her) function or activity, whatever rank and position, work which is common to all managers and peculiar to them.[52]
>
> —Peter F. Drucker,
> *Management: Tasks, Responsibilities, Practices*

Although management can and should be viewed as a synthesis of functions and roles, the five functions common to all managers, whether first-line supervisors or chief executives, are planning, organizing, staffing, directing, and controlling. These functions are carried out by all levels of library and information center managers in all types of information-providing organizations. If a manager is able to perform all of these functions skillfully, he or she will ensure that the organization is managed well.

Conclusion

Management theory has not changed greatly over the past couple of decades. New ideas have helped "new cohorts of professional managers climb up the bureaucratic ladder; mathematicians, natural scientists, economists, computer programmers, artificial intelligentsia, and even humanistic psychologists came to influence."[53] Perhaps the best way of viewing the maze called management theory is to consider each movement as a subsystem that contributes to the overall system of people working together in organizations that are changing. Each theory brings new means of examining organizations. The proliferation of management theories has resulted in semantic difficulties and a tension among proponents of the various schools, as each has tried to establish its approach as the most logical. Current trends, such as technology, are forcing a reevaluation of some processes and of how some theories have worked in the past or are applied today. Basically, however, the theories have remained the same over the past several years.

Notes

1. Lee G. Bolman and Terrence E. Deal, *Reframing Organizations* (San Francisco: Jossey-Bass, 1991), 10-11.

2. Peter F. Drucker, *Management: Tasks, Responsibilities, Practices* (New York: Harper & Row, 1973), 17.

3. J. H. Breasted, *Ancient Records* (Chicago: University of Chicago Press, 1906), 150-250.

4. Claude S. George Jr., *The History of Management Thought*, 2d ed. (Englewood Cliffs, NJ: Prentice-Hall, 1972), 12.

5. Daniel Wren, *The Evolution of Management Theory*, 3d ed. (New York: John Wiley, 1987).

6. Ibid.

7. Larry N. Killough, "Management and the Industrial Revolution," *Advanced Management Journal* 7 (July 1970): 67-70.

8. Charles Babbage, *On the Economy of Machinery and Manufacturers* (London: Charles Knight, 1831).

9. Charles McClure, *Strategies for Library Administration* (Littleton, CO: Libraries Unlimited, 1982), 11.

10.   Harold Koontz, "The Management Theory Jungle," *Academy of Management Journal* 4, no. 3 (December 1961): 174-75.

11.   Frederick W. Taylor, *Principles of Scientific Management* (New York: Harper & Row, 1941), 47.

12.   Frederick W. Taylor, *Scientific Management* (New York: Harper & Row, 1947), 10.

13.   Taylor, *Principles of Scientific Management*, 36-37.

14.   Taylor, *Scientific Management*, 31.

15.   Amitai Etzioni, *Modern Organizations* (Englewood Cliffs, NJ: Prentice-Hall, 1964), 21.

16.   Edna Yost, *Frank and Lillian Gilbreth* (New Brunswick, NJ: Rutgers University Press, 1949), 262.

17.   Max Weber, *The Theory of Social and Economic Organizations,* trans. and ed. A. M. Henderson and T. Parsons (Oxford: Oxford University Press, 1947).

18.   Weber, *The Theory of Social and Economic Organizations*, quoted in Gerald D. Bell, ed., *Organizations and Human Behavior* (Englewood Cliffs, NJ: Prentice-Hall, 1967), 88.

19.   J. P. Mayer, *Max Weber and German Politics* (London: Farber, 1956), 127.

20.   James G. Marshall and Herbert A. Simon, *Organizations* (New York: John Wiley, 1958), 22.

21.   Henri Fayol, *General and Industrial Management,* trans. Constance Storrs (New York: Pitman, 1949), 22.

22.   Luther Gulick and Lyndall Urwick, eds., *Papers on the Science of Administration* (New York: Institute of Public Administration, Columbia University Press, 1937).

23.   Harold Koontz and Cyril O'Donnell, *Principles of Management*, 5th ed. (New York: McGraw-Hill, 1972), 14-15.

24.   Weber, *Theory of Social and Economic Organizations*.

25.   James D. Mooney and Alan C. Reiley, *Onward Industry* (New York: Harper & Row, 1931).

26.   Gulick and Urwick, *Science of Administration*.

27.   G. Elton Mayo, *The Social Problems of an Industrialized Civilization* (New York: Macmillan, 1933), 30.

28.   G. Elton Mayo, *The Social Problems of an Industrialized Civilization* (London: Routledge, 1949), 76.

29.   Chester I. Barnard, *The Functions of the Executive* (Cambridge: Harvard University Press, 1938).

30.   Abraham Maslow, "A Theory of Human Motivation," *Psychological Review* 50 (July 1943): 394.

31. Abraham Maslow, *Toward a Psychology of Being* (Princeton, NJ: Van Nostrand, 1964).

32. Douglas McGregor, *The Human Side of Enterprise* (New York: McGraw-Hill, 1960).

33. Chris Argyris, *Integrating the Individual and the Organization* (New York: John Wiley, 1964).

34. McGregor, *The Human Side of Enterprise,* 78.

35. Herbert A. Simon, *The Shape of Automation for Men and Management* (New York: Harper & Row, 1965), 69.

36. D. Katz and D. Kahn, *The Social Psychology of Organization* (New York: John Wiley, 1966), 18.

37. C. West Churchman, Russell L. Ackoff, and E. Leonard Arnoff, *Introduction to Operations Research* (New York: John Wiley, 1957), 12-13.

38. James G. March and Herbert A. Simon, *Organizations* (New York: John Wiley, 1958).

39. Sheen Kassouf, *Normative Decision Making* (Englewood Cliffs, NJ: Prentice-Hall, 1970).

40. Paul R. Watkins, "Perceived Information Structure: Implications for Decision Support System Design," *Decision Sciences* (January 1982): 38-59.

41. Richard M. Hodgetts, *Management: Theory, Process and Practice* (Philadelphia: W. B. Saunders, 1975), 113.

42. Anatol Rapoport, "General Systems Theory," in *International Encyclopedia of the Social Sciences*, ed. David Sills, vol. 15 (New York: Macmillan, 1968), 452.

43. Ludwig von Bertlanffy, "The History and Status of General Systems Theory," *Academy of Management Journal* 15 (December 1972): 407.

44. Ibid., 417.

45. Fremont E. Kast and James E. Rosenzweig, *Organization and Management: A Systems and Contingency Approach,* 4th ed. (New York: McGraw-Hill, 1985), 113.

46. Don Helbriegel, J. S. Slocum, and R. W. Woodman, *Organizational Behavior* (St. Paul, MN: West, 1986), 22.

47. Chimezie A. B. Osigweh, *Professional Management: An Evolutionary Perspective* (Dubuque, IA: Kendall/Hunt, 1985), 160.

48. Samuel C. Certo, *Modern Management,* 5th ed. (Boston: Allyn & Bacon, 1992), 48.

49. Fred Luthans, "The Contingency Theory of Management: A Path Out of the Jungle," *Business Horizons* 16, no. 3 (June 1973): 62.

50. McGregor, *The Human Side of Enterprise*. Frederick Herzberg, *Work and the Nature of Man* (Cleveland, OH: World, 1966). Abraham Maslow, *Motivation and Personality,* 2d ed. (New York: Harper & Row, 1970).

51. Henry Mintzberg, *The Nature of Managerial Work* (New York: Harper & Row, 1980).

52. Drucker, *Management*, 399-400.

53. Stephen P. Waring, *Taylorism Transformed: Scientific Management Theory Since 1945* (Chapel Hill: University of North Carolina Press, 1991), 203.

Readings

Alston, Jon P. *The American Samurai: Blending American and Japanese Management Practice.* New York: Walter de Gruyter, 1986.

Anderson, Carl. *Management: Skills, Functions and Organization Performance.* 2d ed. Boston: Allyn & Bacon, 1988.

Argyris, Chris. *Organization and Innovation.* Homewood, IL: R. D. Irwin, 1965.

Barnard, Chester I. *The Functions of the Executive.* Cambridge: Harvard University Press, 1968.

Blake, Robert Rogers, and Jane S. Mouton. *The Managerial Grid.* Houston, TX: Gulf, 1964.

Drucker, Peter F. *The Effective Executive.* New York: Harper & Row, 1967.

———. *Management: Tasks, Responsibilities, Practices.* New York: Harper & Row, 1974.

———. *Managing for the Future: The 1990s and Beyond.* New York: Truman Tally Books/Dalton, 1992.

Duncan, W. Jack. *Great Ideas in Management.* San Francisco: Jossey-Bass, 1989.

Fayol, Henri. *General and Industrial Management.* New York: Pitman, 1949.

Flood, Robert. *Liberating Systems Theory.* New York: Plenum Press, 1990.

George, Claude S., Jr. *The History of Management Thought.* 2d ed. Englewood Cliffs, NJ: Prentice-Hall, 1972.

Graham, Pauline. *Integrative Management.* Cambridge, MA: Basil Blackwell, 1991.

Gulick, Luther, and Lyndall Urwick, eds. *Papers on the Science of Administration.* New York: Institute of Public Administration, Columbia University Press, 1937.

Hersey, Paul, and Kenneth H. Blanchard. *Management of Organizational Behavior.* 5th ed. Englewood Cliffs, NJ: Prentice-Hall, 1988.

Herzberg, Frederick, Bernard Mausner, and Barbara Bloch Snyderman. *The Motivation to Work.* 2d ed. New York: John Wiley, 1959.

Ivancevich, John, and Michael T. Mattson. *Organizational Behavior and Management.* Homewood, IL: BPI/Irwin, 1990.

Jackson, Michael C. *Systems Methodology for the Management Sciences.* New York: Plenum Press, 1991.

Koontz, Harold, and Cyril O'Donnell. *Principles of Management.* 5th ed. New York: McGraw-Hill, 1972.

Likert, Rensis. *The Human Organization.* New York: McGraw-Hill, 1967.

McGregor, Douglas. *The Human Side of Enterprise.* New York: McGraw-Hill, 1960.

Machiavelli, Niccolo. *The Prince.* New York: Norton, 1977.

Maslow, Abraham H. *Motivation and Personality.* 2d ed. New York: Harper & Row, 1970.

Mayo, G. Elton. *The Human Problems of an Industrial Civilization.* 2d ed. Cambridge, MA: Harvard University Press, 1946.

Mintzberg, Henry A. *The Nature of Managerial Work.* New York: Harper & Row, 1980.

Morgan, Gareth. *Creative Organization Theory: A Resourcebook.* Beverly Hills, CA: Sage Publications, 1989.

Odiorne, George S. *Management by Objectives.* New York: Pitman, 1965.

Pollard, Harold R. *Development in Management Thought.* New York: Crane, Russak, 1974.

Quinn, R. E., and K. S. Cameron, eds. *Paradox and Transformation: Toward a Theory of Change in Organization and Management.* Cambridge, MA: Ballinger, 1988.

Ruben, Brent D., and John Y. Kim. *General Systems Theory and Human Communications.* Rochelle Park, NJ: Hayden Book, 1975.

Schoderbek, Peter P. *Management Systems.* Homewood, IL: BPI/Irwin, 1990.

Taylor, Frederick W. *Scientific Management.* New York: Harper & Row, 1947.

Waring, Stephen P. *Taylorism Transformed: Scientific Management Theory Since 1945.* Chapel Hill: University of North Carolina Press, 1991.

Wren, Daniel. *The Evolution of Management Theory.* 3d ed. New York: John Wiley, 1987.

Wright, Robert Granford. *Systems Thinking: A Guide to Managing in a Changing Environment.* Dearborn, MI: Society of Manufacturing Engineers, 1989.

2

The Planning Process

Planning Information Services

Management has no choice but to anticipate the future, to attempt to mold it, and to balance short-range and long-range goals. . . . The future will not just happen if one wishes hard enough. It requires decisions—now. It imposes risk—now. It requires action—now. It demands allocation of resources, and above all, of human resources—now. It requires work—now.[1]

—Peter F. Drucker,
Management: Tasks, Responsibilities, Practices

Management is all of what Drucker says—and more. It encompasses activities directed toward developing a mission, setting goals, motivating individuals, appraising performance of both personnel and systems, evaluating results, adjusting directions to account for the outcome of those activities, and developing a financial base to accomplish all of that. Planning is at the heart of management activities because its effectiveness—or in some cases ineffectiveness—is reflected in every segment of an organization's developmental process.

Despite the need for it, a systematic planning process remains one of the most elusive and easily avoided activities in libraries and other information centers, as in many other organizations, both for-profit and not-for-profit. This phenomenon continues to exist despite the fact that planning is *the* most basic function—all other functions must reflect it, and the growth or decline of an organization depends in no small measure upon the soundness of the planning process.

Many recently imposed factors now have come together to force planning decisions and focus on more formalized processes than were necessary in a more leisurely past. The multidimensional interrelationships between external and internal forces and among levels of staff in the library organization are causes for that consideration. Changing environments and anticipated future environments—including declining or stabilized budgets, inflation, technological developments, the explosion of information in many formats, staffs' growing sophistication coupled with their needs and expectations, patterns of use, user interests and satisfaction, and nonuser resistance and reasons thereof—all make planning for information services in information centers more vital and more alive today than it has ever been. This dynamic environment provides an opportunity to redefine and strengthen information sources and services for growth and survival; that is why planning is imperative. An added benefit, of course, is that it is likely that staff at various levels in the library and information center organization, as they become involved in the process, will buy into the vision of the organization and the goals and objectives that are outcomes of planning and will act as spokespersons and advocates in explaining, enhancing, and supporting the identified needs and directions to other staff members.

Although there are numerous reasons given for why libraries and other information centers neglect planning, the main reason seems to be that it is an extremely difficult, time-consuming, and, sometimes, confusing process. That is further complicated by the macroenvironment, including economic uncertainty, technological innovations that are necessary, shifting demographics, changing societal priorities, and shrinking financial support from primary sources. Further, changes occur in reporting relationships in organizations of which libraries are a part—university presidential tenures are shorter, sometimes another administrative layer is inserted in the chain of command, and boards of trustees change, as do school committees, corporate bosses, and mayors or other chief management officers of the larger organization of which the information services are just one part. Such changes may encourage libraries and information centers to make decisions now that will affect operations of the foreseeable future and, in some cases, to even project needs beyond that known future. Added to these complications and resistance is the fact that many managers simply avoid proper planning, while others naively do not understand how to plan.

Some library and information center professionals in decision-making positions tend to emphasize current operations at the expense of planning. Resistance to systematic and comprehensive planning is often couched in phrases like "Planning is just crystal ball gazing in these days of technological change," or "There's no time to devote to planning because we are too busy with the present operations."

Some managers in libraries and information centers look to past success as a guide for projecting future trends, while others rely on intuition as a decision-making device. Former successful operations that were the result of an overabundance of funds are sometimes attributed to the manager's own imagination and intuition. Lack of success, on the other hand, is blamed on "circumstances beyond the library's or the information center's control" instead of on a lack of planning.

Planning styles and approaches, where they can be identified, seem to be more retrospective in nature, drawing upon past experiences with the thought of projecting any past successes into the future. When the climate, internal and external, was more stable than in current times, such experience was accepted as a basis for decision making. This is no longer a realistic approach. Although experience still is one legitimate factor in the overall analysis of a plan, it is no longer the only and certainly not the most important factor. Experience, intuition, and snap judgment are no longer effective enough with so many variables now determining eventual outcomes. As libraries and other information centers have matured organizationally, and in order to avoid continual crisis, information professionals have taken it upon themselves—or, in some cases, have been mandated by parent institutions—to think more strategically and to develop strategic plans in an attempt to anticipate the processes and programs that will be desirable and sustainable in the future. The outcome of such thinking and planning then becomes the basis for financial considerations leading to operational plans covering staff utilization, materials acquisition, technological development, and physical plant maintenance, each of which is a part of the service matrix. Many libraries and information centers have turned to a self-evaluation planning process in order to identify strengths and weaknesses that support or hinder priorities identified in the process. Some are surprised that those priorities may be completely different from what was previously perceived to be the primary focus of activities.

> 𝔔 Institutions are often the product of a formative idea. The extent to which an institution is successful depends on the degree to which it is guided by this idea and its underlying principles and assumptions. . . . The enormous growth in the quantity and kinds of research materials, escalating publication costs, the introduction of new technologies, changing patterns of research and institutions, and finite resources have undermined the assumptions of the past and prompted the library to seek a new vision and a strategy for creating it.[2]
>
> —Harvard College Library,
> *Commitment to Renewal*

Change is the key factor in this equation. As detailed in the final chapter of this text, change can be viewed from two opposite extremes: It can be random, haphazard, and unpredictable, or it can be anticipated and reasonably controlled by deliberate actions taken to adjust the organizational thinking about the challenges and opportunities of the future. When actions are deliberate and conscious, there is greater likelihood of successfully incorporating change as a dynamic force. Various change dimensions and predictive management approaches are used in the planning process and are extensively discussed in the literature. *Crisis management, contingency planning* and *conditional thinking* are terms sometimes used to describe the art of predicting and planning. These techniques capitalize on opportunities to change. They are techniques for removing some of the risk and uncertainty from an organization's future, replacing that uncertainty with some measure of control over the direction and outcome of the future, and placing the organization on a deliberate course through the planning process.

Because planning is an effort to anticipate future change, it can be accomplished only by choosing from among possible alternatives. Though planning is most often a *line* function performed by managers in a direct supervisory relationship, some libraries and information centers have developed cadres of people whose primary function is planning. Officers in *staff* positions, rather than replacing line responsibilities, augment and support line supervisors' planning efforts, sometimes acting as information sources, sometimes as catalysts, sometimes as devil's advocates. Such officers might, for example, provide factual data and propose new services, but their primary role is to coordinate the entire planning program. Some libraries and information centers have instituted planning committees; others, mainly large public and academic library systems, have created planning offices within the staff structure of the library, while information centers in for-profit organizations often relate a portion of their activities to a planning division. These groups are responsible for developing or guiding the development of certain plans, particularly those that are long range or more strategic in nature. Such groups, with clearly defined responsibilities, are able to perform more intensive investigations and to analyze and coordinate plans more thoroughly.

As an example, one of the earliest such units in libraries was established at Columbia University more than 25 years ago when the library's Planning Office was created and administered by the then newly created position of Assistant University Librarian for Planning. It is a pattern that has been successfully repeated in other information oriented organizations. The specific objectives of that office were to:

1. provide a direction and framework for library and information service operations that will guide decision making and problem solving.

2. improve library service, operations, and fiscal control through the application of computer technology and management science to library procedures.

3. ensure the rational and effective development of information services and resources in the context of university academic planning.

4. permit the anticipation of future resource needs for information service by establishing plans based on present decisions.

5. bring the skills and experience of university and libraries staff members in the planning process.[3]

Over the years, to encourage and facilitate the planning process, several libraries have used self-study guides, such as those developed by the Office of Management Studies of the U.S.-based Association of Research Libraries, including its *Library Management Review and Analysis Program* (MRAP), the *Planning Process for Small Academic Libraries*, and the *Academic Library Development Program* (ALDP), which were particularly popular during the mid-1980s, as well as others for public and academic libraries that were developed by divisions of the American Library Association.[4]

Now, more than ever before, a new, more formalized approach to planning, based upon forecasting and examination of environmental factors, is the key to success in library and information services. However, this simply stated feat is not easily accomplished. Librarians and information specialists new to the planning process should be cautioned that some formal planning methods and models can be quite complicated and may not apply to the current library and information services needs of their own organization. Some of these sophisticated models do not lend themselves to smaller information service operations and, therefore, may not be cost-effective; others are so complex that they may be of no use in a library or information center setting.

Additionally, it is important to recognize that, because of rapid environmental changes, many plans may become dated or obsolete before they can even be implemented. A balance between efforts expended and outcome is desirable. Further, it should be recognized that there is a downside to an extensive planning process. If, in the larger organization, the library or information center is the only unit, or one of the few that performs a planning process, it may be held strictly accountable for the priorities in its plan, or risk being criticized for not meeting stated expectations. This alone should not divert librarians and information specialists from planning strategically, and such cautions should not be viewed as discouragement but as reminders that planning is an evolving process with political overtones.

What Planning Is

A plan is a goal, indicating certain beliefs; a schedule, specifying steps to be taken; a theory, considering relationships; and a precedent, established for existing decisions.[5]

—R. M. Cyert and J. G. March,
A Behavioral Theory of the Firm

A textbook definition of planning is that it is an "analytical process which involves an assessment of the future, the determination of desired objectives in the context of that future, the development of alternative courses of action to achieve such objectives and the selection of a course, or courses, of action from among these alternatives."[6] Planning is both a behavior and a process; it is the process of moving an organization from where it is to where it wants to be in a given period of time by setting it on a predetermined course of action and committing its human and physical resources to that goal. Basic questions of *who, what, when, where,* and *how* are preceded by the most important philosophical question of *why*. All must be addressed in the process. Perhaps the most important reasons for planning are to offset uncertainty and to prepare for change, to focus attention on a clear direction for the future, to gain economical control of the operation, and to facilitate control. It is, of course, impossible and impractical to plan for every single action. Put in perspective, the extent and sophistication of planning depends upon the situation at hand, whether it is charting the future of the library or information center, or negotiating next month's staffing of the reference or information desk. Although both of those examples require some planning effort, some thought being given to needs, the level and required involvement in developing plans is very different.

A successful planning approach must build an understanding of the library's or the information center's current services and capabilities as an essential first step to identifying future directions. To create a planning attitude, the concept must involve all levels of the organization, beginning at the top and filtering down throughout the various levels to be accepted and implemented through policies, procedures, projects, and programs. The outcome, a planning document, becomes today's design for tomorrow's action, a road map, if you will, an outline of the steps to be taken starting now and continuing into the future. The process leading to the development of a written document should involve all segments concerned with and affected by the process, both inside the immediate library or information center and outside through individuals with vested financial and programmatic interests. This planning process, then, forces action on the parts of the whole institution. This is an idealistic approach, one that should be aspired to, because it is not always feasible for everyone to participate in all of the stages of a planning process.

Because planning is a delicate, complicated, time-consuming process, it cannot be forced on an organization that is not prepared for self-analysis and the change that will result from the process. A bifurcation exists, in which scientific evidence and rational thinking must be balanced by a planning attitude and the interpersonal skills that facilitate the process. Discretion must be exercised so that while staff overinvolvement in the planning process does not interfere with fulfillment of the basic mission of the organization, members must still sense that they are an important component in the success of the process. Occasionally, services can suffer if resources are diverted to the planning process and staff become so wrapped up in planning that current basic library and information services tasks are ignored. On the other hand, the success of the effort requires commitment that cannot be forced but must be earned. One cautionary note relates to the fact that when large amounts of energy and resources are committed, expectations are likely to be high, foreseeing miraculous results and significant instant change. Such expectations must be put into a realistic perspective.

The degree of extensive staff involvement in planning depends on cost, time, the importance of the plan, and the perceived knowledge and interest of participants. It is imperative that each person involved knows clearly the purpose of the planning, the expected outcomes, and his or her role as well as that of every other individual throughout the process. Keeping the whole organization informed about the plans taking shape is also an important component. If this type of communication and involvement takes place, the greatest commitment is likely to be achieved. Even prior to the start of the process, the right organizational climate needs to be created to encourage the success of the planning process. If the staff and the funding authorities are in agreement at this initial stage and buy in to the process, then it is realistic to expect that those members of the library or other information services organization will consistently use the written plan as a guide. After the plan is accepted as a document for future directions, planning should be conducted daily, addressing activities and developing procedures to achieve the objectives identified in the plan. The planning process should never be considered as an activity the manager uses only occasionally when he or she thinks there is time for it. Without daily planning as follow-up, decisions revert back to becoming ad hoc choices, activities become random, and confusion and chaos can prevail.

Factors in Planning

The impetus for planning, which is now a required approach for most complex organizations and a desirable approach for others, came primarily after World War II, when postwar planning was necessary in for-profit organizations. This was true because technology was changing, becoming more expensive, and companies had to be sure of the need to expend resources in that arena. Factors in the planning process might be arbitrarily divided into at least five elements: time, collecting and analyzing data, levels of planning, flexibility, and accountability.

Time

There are two categories of plans with respect to time: long-range, or strategic plans, and short-term, or operational plans. These categories refer to the span of time over which the plan is effective, starting with the time when the plan is initiated and ending with the time when the objectives of the plan are actually measured for achievement.

A variety of terms, including *long-range, normative, strategic,* and *master planning* have been used to describe what is now most popularly conceived as the strategic planning process, a type of planning that has become widely used and accepted over the last couple of decades. There are nuances of differences in each of those approaches, but, for purposes of this text, the focus will be on strategic thinking and planning. Strategic planning has become central to the whole management strategy. Exacerbating this development are technological developments and applications combined with circumstances outside and, therefore, beyond the library or information center's environment and control. Those forces dictate an organized, extended view to planning library and information services operations. The strategic planning concept, discussed in greater detail later, has more or less absorbed what was previously viewed as the intermediate long-range view. Long-range, strategic, and master planning each necessitates looking at library and information center operations in a critical and comprehensive way in order to develop a planning network and time frame that combines the subplans of individual units, departments, and divisions of the library or information center into one master plan that charts the course of the whole organization for a foreseeable future. Perhaps the most touted of strategic plans are those produced by various national communities in the form of five- or ten-year plans.

On the other hand, short-term, operational, or tactical plans encompass the day-to-day planning that takes place in any organization; this type of planning is more task-oriented. It involves a shorter time frame and the resolution of specific problems, usually of an internal nature. Such plans often coincide with the accounting or bookkeeping year. An example of short-term plans is the calculation of one year's budget that is expressed in operational terms. Short-term plans provide the guidelines for day-to-day operations and the procedures by which they are accomplished. These plans are much more detail intensive and immediate than strategic plans, and their objectives are much more short-term and specific. They encompass more known factors and, therefore, might be more quantitative. Short-term plans bring the general guidelines developed in long-range plans to the operational stage. One might view the two approaches as complementary; strategic plans provide the overview and operational plans provide the specific budgetary factors for a specified period of time. Because short-term plans are specific and immediate, they do not carry the uncertainty that strategic plans do. However, both types of plans can be considered action oriented and, therefore, measurable and attainable.

Collecting and Analyzing Data

The more pertinent the information on which a plan is based, the better the planning process will be. Therefore, the second element in planning is collecting and analyzing data. This step includes systematic collection of data concerning the library or information center, its activities, operations, staff, use, and users at a given time and over a given period of time. In other words, it is a study of the whole organization and its operation. One must fight the urge to allow data collection to dominate or bog down the planning process, instead viewing this step as a means to an end: the collection of data relating to past activities with the view of making decisions about future activities. Needs assessment and data collection cannot be stressed to the exclusion of translating the needs into goals and objectives, developing programs to address those needs, and evaluating the effectiveness of new and ongoing library operations and programs. Evaluation, as an element of the planning process, and techniques for collecting data are discussed in chapter 6.

Levels of Planning

All supervisors, whether they are at the upper, middle, or lower level in the organizational structure, should engage in planning on two levels: They should be responsible for planning in their individual units, and they should work with others in the organization to develop the overall plan. Involvement of lower echelon personnel in planning has the advantages of incorporating the practical point of view of those closest to the scene of operations while enticing them to recognize the need for planning and to support the direction the plan takes. Traditionally, primarily the upper echelons have carried out long-range planning, while middle- and lower-level supervisors conduct short-term planning. In libraries and information centers that have planning committees or officers, and in smaller organizations, this hierarchical approach is forfeited in favor of input from all levels and segments of the organization.

It should be easy to recognize the consequences of failing to coordinate long-range and short-term plans. The whole concept of planning is to create a network of mutually dependent components ranging from overall mission-oriented plans to detailed technical plans for specific operations.

Flexibility

Flexibility, or adaptability in meeting changing needs, is the essence of good planning. Flexibility applies to both short-term and strategic planning processes. Any planning that is too rigid to accommodate change as it occurs is an exercise in futility. This is why it is important to review strategic plans periodically with the intent of revising priorities that might change over time, as well as identifying objectives that have been accomplished. In this respect, it is important to be sure that the library's or the information center's plans remain compatible with those of the larger organization of which the information unit is a part and that they reflect the changing environment in which the library or information center exists.

Accountability

Accountability is key to future success. Accountability means the obligation and initiative to carry out established plans. For managers, this means delegating authority and making individuals responsible for achieving the plan's objectives once they have been established. Ultimately, however, the manager is accountable for the action—or inaction—toward the established goals. This, again, ties control to the planning process. A plan can be no better than the control mechanisms established to monitor, evaluate, and adjust efficiency and effectiveness.

Environment for Planning

Planning is committing library or information center resources—physical, personnel, and material—based upon the best possible knowledge of the future. It requires systematically organizing the effort needed to use these resources, and it requires measuring the results of planning decisions through systematic feedback so that needed changes can be effected. In libraries and other information services organizations, the planning process may be resisted by individuals and groups who fear that change—in goals and objectives as well as in responsibilities and organizational structure—will threaten their positions in the organization. In its extreme, this planning climate can create a competitive relationship with other departments in the larger organization—whether they are academic units of an educational institution, departments of a governmental entity, or divisions of a business—of which the library is a part. This competition places greater responsibility on the librarian to sell programs and exert pressures for their successful execution.

Strategic Planning

&Organizations engage in formal planning, not to create strategies but to program the strategies they already have, that is, to elaborate and operationalize their consequence formally.[7]

—Henry Mintzberg,
The Rise and Fall of Strategic Planning

Not everyone would agree with that statement by one planning expert. The demands of a changing environment require the use of systems, methods, models, and options that are responsive to rapid and sometimes unpredictable change. Strategic planning is a major tool for effective identification of organizational priorities in that milieu. Although it was introduced in the business world in the 1960s to address market shifts, it now has much wider application. The concept is relatively new to libraries and information centers, whether one considers university planning, affecting academic libraries; city planning, affecting public libraries; school systems planning, affecting media centers; or corporate planning, affecting special libraries. Most large library and information centers and many smaller ones are now involved in some form of strategic planning. Figure 2.1 illustrates the strategic planning process common to libraries and other information centers.

According to Peter Drucker, strategic planning is the continuous process of making entrepreneurial—or risk-taking—decisions systematically and with the greatest knowledge of their future consequences; systematically organizing the efforts needed to carry out these decisions; and measuring the results of these decisions against the expectations through organized, systematic feedback.[8] He maintains business is not determined by the producer, but by the customer. The world is a buyer's market; services must be developed to meet buyers' needs and must be marketed to discerning audiences. Therefore, strategic planning must start with the patron. That focus is prevalent in all types of libraries and information centers today, as librarians have focused their attention and services on the users and potential users of library services.

Fig. 2.1. Strategic planning is a continuous process.

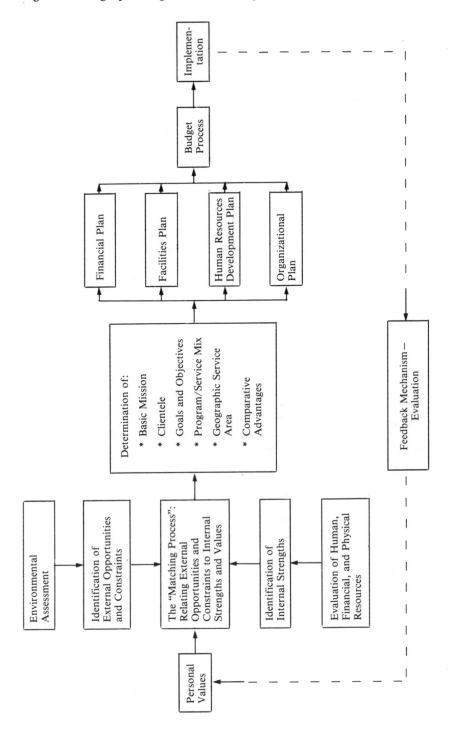

With greater hype and with specific focus on business enterprises, the concept of *reengineering* has developed. Its proponents emphasize that "at the heart of . . . reengineering lies the notion of *discontinuous thinking*—identifying and abandoning the outdated rules and fundamental assumptions that underlie current . . . operations."[9] There is little difference between the reasoning presented in this approach and that of strategic thinking, which is a prelude to any successful strategic planning effort.

Although strategic planning is automatically associated with growth and new resources management, it is equally important for successful retrenchment and maintenance of efforts. Strategic planning, along with other forms of deliberative planning, requires describing a vision for the organization, identifying a mission within that context, setting realistic goals, establishing attainable objectives, and developing activities that are stated as policies and procedures to accomplish those goals and objectives. In its simplest definition, it is a process of translating decisions into policies, and policies into actions. The approach is being utilized more and more by both for-profit and not-for-profit organizations that have recognized the need for change and are determined to make a successful transition, not only from where they are to where they want to be, but also from the current scenario to that of one envisioned in the next century. Systematic, planned change is the only way to effectively implement new services and preserve existing ones. But planned change requires an organizational arrangement that makes orderly change possible and attainable within a realistic time frame.

The very fact that strategic planning involves a cross section of staff members may be threatening to people who have never been involved in such a decision-making process. To establish a climate for strategic planning within the library or information center, at least two things are desirable: The entire organization should know the direction, goals, and expectations of information services, and both the information services unit and institutional administration should know all decisions, commitments, and efforts of the organizational members. Within this climate the library can proceed with a systematic planning process that has a chance of maximum success.

Most experts agree that strategic plans should project at least five years and that they should be part of an ongoing, periodic planning process, not a one-time affair resulting in a document that is never again consulted.[10] The ongoing process addresses one of the most difficult aspects of strategic planning, which is the projections and assumptions that must be made about internal and external forces. Such forces include population trends for higher education or urban settings in addition to those already mentioned. The further ahead one projects, the greater the uncertainty and therefore the greater the challenge. Uncertainty makes it even more imperative that strategic long-range plans receive periodic review and assessment so that certain aspects can be updated, deleted, or rethought as the library's goals are achieved and as priorities shift or change. As Fred Luthans points out, one weakness is that strategic planners seldom, if ever, plan for cutbacks or failures.[11] But strategic planning is designed to address that eventuality as well.

> ☡ To be effective planners librarians and administrators need a great deal more information about their own organizations and their environment than most have tried or been able to gather. Effective goal setting and decision making for the future are dependent upon extensive, up-to-date, and accurate information about the current state of the organization.[12]
>
> —Edward R. Johnson, "Academic Library Planning, Self-Study, and Management Review"

Strategic Planning as Self-Analysis

The process of strategic planning can be thought of as a self-analysis or self-study that identifies the organization's strengths and weaknesses and develops priorities within the framework of the organization's physical and financial capabilities. The library or information center is an open social system with specific goals of service. It interacts with the larger environment through the underlying values that it exists to support—sources and services for social, informational, and educational good upon which the environment depends. To state an overused example, "The right information to the right person at the right time and in the right format at the right cost and for the right reason" is a plan of service. The self-examination begins with identifying the beliefs, values, and ethos of the library or information center. Commitment of individuals working in the organization to organizational strategies is most evident through those common values and shared beliefs or ideologies deemed good and desirable. These can then act as guidelines that influence actions and the implementation of decisions.

Strategic thinking about those factors encompasses who the organization is and what its set of core values or philosophy is. For instance, the concept of "right to know" encompassed in the Library Bill of Rights[13] might be an aspect of the value system. Focus on the organizational values most commonly agreed upon by members of the workforce sets the stage for both daily work and decision making. Those shared values and understandings help build commitment to the organization's mission. From that analysis emerges a concise statement of what the organization is, whom it serves, and how it will achieve its mission. In order to identify priorities of service and to direct decision making, a mission focuses on strategies for action.

This mission statement should be shared with all members of the organization, funding authorities, and supporters so that everyone understands and is committed to its principles. This reduces the possibilities of fragmentation and dissension. In the simplest terms, the mission statement should proclaim the *who, what, why, when, where*, and *how* that guide the operation and future management decisions.[14] As examples, the mission statement of Emory University Libraries is "To support the University's teaching and research programs as well as scholarly research and resource sharing within the broader research community. The libraries fulfill this mission by providing timely access to information in a range of formats from print to multimedia either on site or accessed from remote locations within the networked environment"[15]; and the mission of the Free Library of Philadelphia is to "provide to all segments of the population of Philadelphia a comprehensive collection of recorded knowledge, ideas, artistic expression and information; to assure ease of access to these materials; and to provide programs to stimulate the awareness and use of these resources."[16]

> ≥The mission, vision and values statements are the principal products of the . . . strategic planning process. They, and the process itself which, either directly or indirectly, involve nearly every member of the library staff, are the glue that binds and connects the various parts of the community to the whole.[17]
>
> —Richard DeGennaro, *Shared Understanding*

The self-examination allows the library or information center to coordinate what it would like to be, envisioned in the mission statement, with what it can afford to be, regulated by the organization's physical and financial capabilities. If great disparity exists, a resolution must be sought by reducing expectations, increasing resources, or both. That same Emory Libraries statement, quoted above, identifies six areas that are necessary to make the strategic plan operational: Services; Collections and Bibliographic Control; Human Resources; Physical Facilities and Environment; Collaboration; and Institutional Advancement. Both for-profit and not-for-profit organizations often focus their planning strategies on similar concerns: new directions, marketing, growth, finances, organizational concerns, personnel, and public relations.

&Strategic planning supplies a forum for announcing, selling, negotiating, rationalizing and legitimizing strategic decisions and it also offers means for controlling their implementation.[18]

—Arthur Langley,
"The Role of Formal Strategic Planning"

Strategic planning is similar to other planning activities in that it analyzes capabilities, assesses environmental pressures and opportunities, sets objectives, examines alternate courses of action, and implements a preferred course. However, strategic planning differs from other forms of planning in that it deliberately attempts to concentrate resources in those areas that can make a substantial difference in future performance and capability.

Thus, strategic planning is more a frame of reference and a way of thinking than a set of procedures. It does not concentrate, as long-range planning often does, upon projecting past experiences into future practices. Rather, it concentrates upon understanding the environment into which the library is moving. It encourages creativity, has the potential of improving communications within the organization, and allows libraries and other information organizations and their staffs to identify and adopt options that may be unique to their settings and to this particular time in the organization's life. At the same time, intangible inputs in this strategic thinking process, including the culture, values, vision, and mission—already mentioned—can be converted into the outputs of trust identified through honesty; openness and reliability; satisfaction; team spirit; and commitment of pride, loyalty, and ownership of the process. Strategic planning assists libraries and information centers by developing a thinking mode that facilitates projecting the organization into a desired future.

The plan itself encourages managers to experiment with various alternatives before committing resources by promoting a systems approach in:

- providing a mechanism to avoid overemphasizing organizational parts at the expense of the whole;

- guiding managers to make decisions that are in line with the aims and strategies of the whole organization;

- providing a basis for measuring the performance of the organization as a whole, of an operating unit, and of an individual;

- forwarding to higher levels of management those issues of strategic importance with which they should be concerned;

- serving as a training device by requiring participants to ask and answer the very questions that managers must address; and

- improving managerial motivation and morale through a sense of creative participation in the development of known expectations.[19]

Models for Strategic Planning

Several models have been developed for strategic planning, including some sophisticated ones developed with the aid of appropriate computer software. Each model has its strengths, descriptions of which can be found in the literature of library and information science, as well as in the more extensive literature of business and management. Those who are beginning to seriously approach the subject of strategic planning and those who wish more detail than is possible to present in this brief overview should consult these sources.

Although somewhat mechanical planning models can be helpful in many situations, a more desirable approach emphasizes creativity and innovation. "The key to uniqueness is creativity."[20] Figure 2.2 shows the steps taken in developing the strategic plan for library service in Massachusetts. In addition to the steps in the planning process, the figure indicates which segments the strategic planning committee is expected to complete and which are the responsibility of the organization staff. Strategic thinking is the key component in that creativity.

Getting Started

The initial step in undertaking strategic planning is to identify a planning team that will be responsible for carrying out the major planning phase and will involve other work teams and task forces at appropriate times in the process. Many organizational planning teams work with a strategic planning consultant, who facilitates the process. The primary role of the consultant is to help the team decide what data is to be collected, how it will be collected and by whom, and how it will be analyzed and used. The consultant acts as a catalyst and facilitator in identifying organizational goals and objectives. A realistic time frame—certainly not less than six months but probably not more than a year for the initial plan—should be set for the strategic planning process. During that year the team will need a number of concentrated periods of time to complete its charge.

Before the team or task force begins the strategic planning process, several basic questions need to have been answered: Why plan strategically and, particularly, why at this point in the organization's life? Who should be involved, and how involved should they be? What does strategic thinking and planning entail, and what needs to be known beforehand? When should it be done, and how long will it take? How will the process be accomplished? And, just as importantly, what is happening in the larger context, including the global environment? The latter question can be answered using a formal process variously called environmental scanning or "looking around" in order to develop strategies to deal with the external PEST (political, economic, social, and technological) change that is occurring. See figure 2.3.

Fig. 2.2. Before strategic planning can begin, its strategy must be mapped.

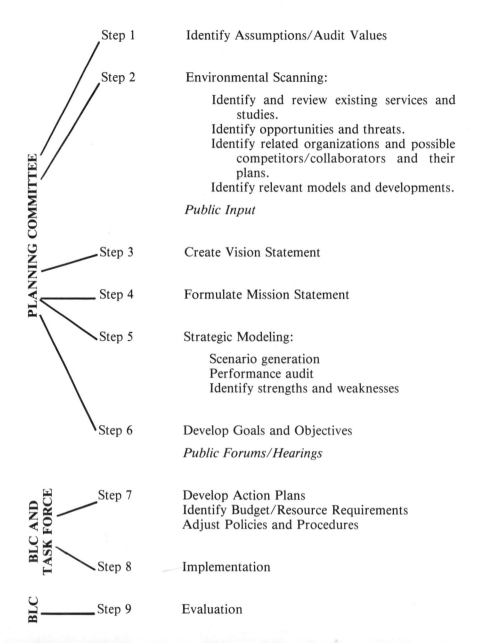

MASSACHUSETTS BOARD OF LIBRARY COMMISSIONERS

Proposed Process for Development of a Strategic Plan
for the
Future of Library Service in Massachusetts

Step 1   Identify Assumptions/Audit Values

Step 2   Environmental Scanning:

    Identify and review existing services and studies.
    Identify opportunities and threats.
    Identify related organizations and possible competitors/collaborators and their plans.
    Identify relevant models and developments.

Public Input

Step 3   Create Vision Statement

Step 4   Formulate Mission Statement

Step 5   Strategic Modeling:

    Scenario generation
    Performance audit
    Identify strengths and weaknesses

Step 6   Develop Goals and Objectives

Public Forums/Hearings

Step 7   Develop Action Plans
    Identify Budget/Resource Requirements
    Adjust Policies and Procedures

Step 8   Implementation

Step 9   Evaluation

PLANNING COMMITTEE

BLC AND TASK FORCE

BLC

Fig. 2.3. Political, economic, social, and technological (PEST) factors impact planning.

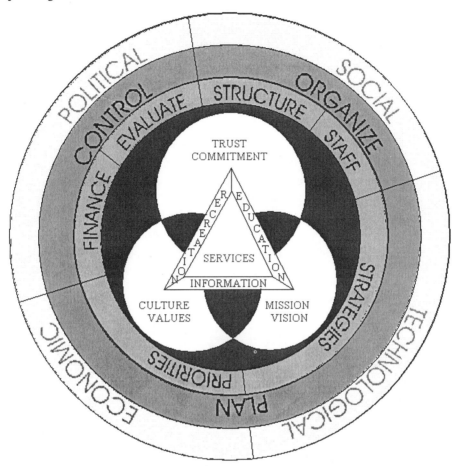

This process views the environment in at least two ways:

1. Looking at the overlapping layers including, but not limited to, the macroenvironment—economic trends, inflation, demographics, and technological factors; the customer environment—who they are and what their needs are; and the internal environment—facilities, personnel resources, and structure of the organization. Positive and negative events inside and outside of the library or information services organization can influence changes in any or all of the these categories.

2. Looking at the environment as a simple dichotomy: the external opportunities and constraints, factors identifiable in the acronym PEST—political, economic, social, and technological forces; and internal analysis—personnel, tasks to be done, finances available, and organizational structure, an exercise identified by the acronym SWOT—strengths, weaknesses, opportunities, and threats. Both views help focus planning on the organization's mission.

By combining the PEST factors with the opportunities and threats, those external components in the SWOT exercise, one is likely to identify factors—technology, demographics, government regulations, multicultural society, etc.—that play a role in promoting or constraining the development of information services. At the same time, internal forces—identifiable in the strengths and weaknesses portion of a SWOT exercise—including facilities, technology, staffing, communications, and financial resources—all tangible input factors—as well as morale, values, and style of management must be factored into the strategic thinking and planning process. See figure 2.4.

Fig. 2.4. Strengths, weaknesses, opportunities, and threats (SWOT) must be identified.

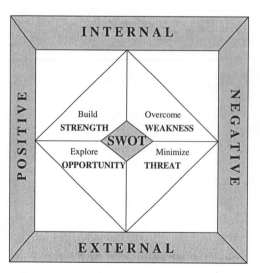

The external environmental scan and the internal self-analysis come together in the process to provide the focus for developing strategies and converting them into plans, policies, processes, and procedures. As the strategic planning document develops, the first component becomes a vision statement, followed by the identification of the aim or mission statement, then come priorities and strategies, goals and objectives, activities and specific tasks, each of which builds upon the previous one in order to achieve the outcomes identified in the various steps of the plan. Figure 2.5 lists some of the factors to be considered in the initial steps of strategic planning.

Once in place, strategic plans can provide guidelines for daily decision-making operations as well as guidelines for overarching decisions today which affect the future of the library or information center. Implementing the strategic plan requires setting up processes and procedures at the functional level. It requires developing strategies to achieve, at various levels, the overall vision of the organization. If this process is followed, the strategic plan can automatically be used at the functional level for decision making. This, of course, entails designating responsibilities for implementing the various steps in the planning process.

Fig. 2.5. Several factors must be considered in initial strategic planning steps.

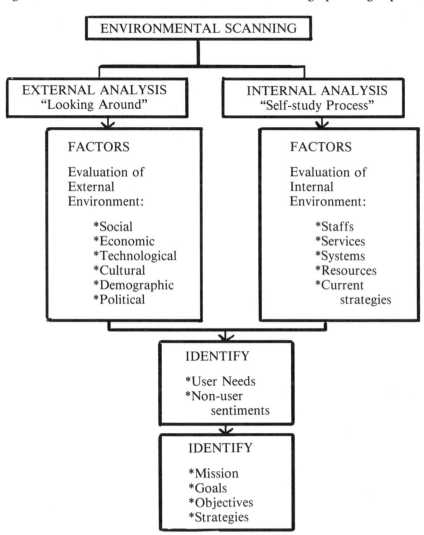

The steps in the strategic planning process, after the planning team has been identified are:

1. Identify the organizational culture and the values or assumptions that are the organization's guiding principles.

2. Conduct the environmental scan: identify the opportunities and challenges, the related competitors/cooperators and their plans, and the relevant existing models and developments.

3. Create a vision statement that focuses on a better future by communicating enthusiasm and excitement.

4. Formulate a mission statement that identifies distinctiveness.

5. Develop the goals and objectives.

6. Develop strategies and action plans. This requires identifying resource funds and developing policies and procedures to accomplish the objectives.

7. Implement the strategic plan.

8. Monitor, evaluate, and adjust the plan as objectives are accomplished and as priorities shift.

A final comment on strategic planning, which relates to planning of any magnitude, is that the planning process should be viewed as only the initial step. No plan, no matter how well formulated, can or will implement itself. It requires direction and commitment to succeed. Therefore, the final step—monitoring, evaluating, and adjusting—is essential to the process. Following through with clearly developed implementation steps, measuring progress toward the goals, and incorporating feedback, is a continuation of the process of planning. The greatest cause for failures of the process lies in poor execution of the plan: a lack of follow-through accompanied by a lack of commitment to see that it is accomplished.

Concise, yet complete strategic plans have been developed by Harvard University Libraries and the Baltimore County Public Library System. They are included in appendix A.

Planning Techniques

Many techniques must be considered for use in the planning process. However, they should not be mistaken for the process itself. Some of the most important techniques are developing standards or guidelines and forecasting.

Developing Standards or Guidelines

One concise definition of *standards* is "being able to designate any measure by which one judges a thing as authentic, good or adequate." Standards are measurable, enforceable, and can be directly related to goals. They should provide guidance for actions in the present climate while being flexible enough to allow for future development. General, industry-wide or professionwide standards or guidelines established by various professional groups provide a basis for planning. For example, standards developed by the American Library Association exist for most types of libraries and library service.[21] They are based on actual, or known, demands for library services. But these standards are not plans; they are a means of defining acceptable service. Each library must develop individual plans based on the demands of its clientele, using industry standards as guidelines. Both human and technical factors must be considered in developing sound standards.

Forecasting

> Planning is an effort to anticipate the future and the inevitable change that comes with it. It must be accomplished by choosing from among possible alternatives, and with full knowledge and use of techniques and tools available for such action.[22]
>
> —Robert D. Stueart, "Long-Range Planning in U.S. Public Libraries"

The term *forecasting* elicits visions of crystal ball gazing, but more appropriately designates a process of projection or prediction. Predictions are, basically, opinions about facts. Projections, on the other hand, are based on some type of systematic review, whether that review employs quantitative data analysis or qualitative judgment using techniques like the Delphi method. Forecasts are predictions based on assumptions about the future. Forecasting helps reduce uncertainty because it anticipates the results of a decision about a course of action described in the forecast.

Forecasting is the most valuable planning technique. It attempts to find the most probable course of events or range of possibilities. H. G. Wells, more than a century ago, argued that if the long-term course of events is principally determined by society's collective response to economic and technological circumstances, we can, in fact, make meaningful projections of what the future is likely to bring through the continued use of analytical tools, including forecasting.[23] A problem very basic to planning in any library is estimating future trends, influences, developments, and events that will affect the library but are beyond the control of the library manager. Forecasts account for this uncertainty; they are the foundation on which managers plan. Forecasting requires good information on trends and developments in society and the economy as well as in the profession and its system of user interaction. Many techniques, some of which are subjective and qualitative, can be used to prepare forecasts, but effective forecasting involves both qualitative and quantitative approaches. Three strategies for forecasting are:

1. Deterministic. This strategy assumes that there is a close causal relationship between the present and the future. This strategy places great reliance upon information about the future.

2. Symptomatic. This strategy searches for signs that might be indicators of the future, for example, the Leading Economic Indicators. This approach is based on the concept that the sequence of events in a cycle is a consistent pattern.

3. Systematic. This strategy looks for underlying regularities over a period of time. Econometrics is an example of this type of forecasting.[24]

Various new techniques are currently employed to predict the future. From opinion polling to informal gathering of information, qualitative approaches are used. Futurology has become particularly popular among managers of business enterprises. Some forecasting techniques used in industry have been adapted for library and information services. These include the survey approach, which is used in technological forecasting. Probably the most important type of technological force testing, one that is popular among librarians and information specialists, is the Delphi technique. Delphi is most useful when judgment is required, when several responses to an issue might be viable, or when it is politically expedient to have strong support for the alternative that eventually will be chosen. The steps for this technique are:

1. A panel of experts on a subject, for example, library funding, is identified.

2. Working independently, selected members of the panel predict developments over a specified period of time. There is no group interaction.

3. The list of predictions is used to create a survey that is sent to each panelist for further reaction. This process is repeated and ideas are refined until the investigator is convinced that no further refinement is necessary.

This technique, based on the opinions of experts, is sure to gain popularity as more libraries and information centers become involved in strategic planning.

Another forecasting technique that has been used quite effectively in libraries and other information centers is trend projection. In its more formal approach, this technique graphically plots future trends based on past experience and current hard data. For instance, the number of volumes put on reserve and the number of times they have circulated during a semester, if plotted on a graph, can reveal significant trends for future planning.

These are only two of the forecasting techniques that can be used in libraries and information centers. Other mathematical and statistical models are used by for-profit organizations to provide quantitative data, and econometric models of the economy are also used. Some of these models are appropriate for not-for-profit organizations. With the availability of computers for modeling and the development of software for that purpose, it is certain that forecasting techniques will become even more attractive to library and information services planners. However, it would be virtually impossible to mold all the various factors into any one explicit, well-defined model that can be used to quantify and solve problems via computational techniques. Therefore, the emphasis is likely to remain, at least for the immediate future, on collecting and analyzing the most relevant information and introducing that information into a flexible framework to serve as a guide for library and information service development. One recent modeling attempt is the Library Costing Model (LCM), which is a computer program that provides means for estimating staff, materials, and costs needed to handle library operations and services. LCM is comprehensive in coverage of cost elements for library operations and services. LCM incorporates them into a standard structure or model, ensuring that analyses and comparisons are consistent and providing default values for its elements.[25]

Vision, Mission, Goals, and Strategies for Information Services

In order for planning to work at the operational level, there must be a common understanding of the meanings of terms used in the strategic planning process. The *vision* (an act of foresight) and *values* (principles intrinsically desirable) of the organization set it within a context of the future, envisioning the changes that will affect systems and services. As an example, Emory University places its *vision* within the context of: Impact of Technology; An Integrated Service Model for Effective Information Support; Links Between Print and Electronic Information Sources; An Opportunity for Quality

Library Support of Graduate and Research Programs; More Active Role for Librarians: Laboratory for Projects; Collaboration Among Libraries; Planning a Virtual Library; and Library as Place.[26] The *values* espoused by the Denver Public Library are expressed in a contextual statement: "In the daily life of the Library, we are guided by values whose application extends throughout our dealings with each other, with our customers, and with the community at large" and encompasses categories of: Services; Communication; Innovation, Creativity, Initiative; Problem Solving; Balance of Life and Work; Accuracy; Diversity; Free and Equal Access to Information; Privacy; Dignity; Negotiation; Safety; Staff Development and Recognition; and Teamwork.[27]

Following from the identified *values* and a *vision* for the future, components can be more accurately stated. One of the difficulties in stating components of the strategic thinking and planning process is the confusion that exists in the terminology used. In the literature, *objective* is often used as a generic term variously referring to philosophy, vision, mission, purposes, goals, guiding principles, strategies, targets, quotas, policies, activities, and even deadlines. This lack of consistency creates confusion.

To help clarify the terminology—at least for the purposes of this discussion—the following list presents the terms in an order that indicates their relative positions or functions in the planning process. Definitions are paraphrased in figure 2.6.

Fig. 2.6. Planning terminology.

Activity	a predetermined act toward achieving an objective
Aim	a determinant to a course of action
Deadline	a time before which something must be done
Ethos	a guiding belief
Goal	a purpose toward which effort is directed
Mission	a self-imposed duty
Objective	a measurable action to be achieved
Philosophy	a viewpoint, a system of values
Plan	a method of achieving an end, implying mental formulation
Policy	a written guideline for action
Principle	an assumption
Procedure	a particular way of accomplishing something
Purpose	an intention
Quota	a production assignment
Strategy	a guide for making decisions
Target	a desired goal to be achieved
Values	a set of intrinsically desirable principles
Vision	an object of imagination

Just as planning may be thought of as a hierarchical process from strategic plans to long-range to short-range and finally to operational plans, so the objectives for library and information services can be indicated in a hierarchy (see fig. 2.7). The peak of the pyramid consists of the most general, all-encompassing objectives, and the lower objectives develop from the higher. In the formulation of plans, if there is to be an integral relationship among them, mission precedes goals, which precede objectives or strategies, which precede activities. Each goal interacts with and is influenced by every other goal, just as every objective or strategy interacts with every other objective related to the goal for which they are designated, just as every activity does with every other activity related to the designated objective.

Fig. 2.7. Strategic planning identifies hierarchy of interactive missions, goals, objectives, and activities.

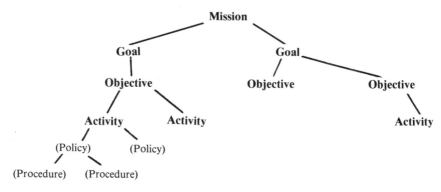

With those understandings, activities and policies can be developed and directed toward the achievement of the goals and objectives through strategic thinking and strategy formulation. Clear objectives encourage consistent planning and decision making over the long term and at various levels of the information organization. Unfortunately, sometimes objectives exist in the thinking of management but are not made explicit by verbalizing and publishing them. Such a casual approach can lead to confusion and discouragement, and a great deal of energy can be expended on faulty assumptions. It is difficult, if not impossible, to be accountable for achieving objectives if they are not clearly communicated. Objectives can and should set the pattern for the structure of the organization and, therefore, must be action oriented. The objectives cannot be viewed as passive but should provide direction as well as incentive toward achievement. Four levels of objectives—here used in the generic sense of the word—can be identified in libraries and information centers: the general mission, organization-wide goals, specific objectives, and activities.

General Mission

The mission is the overarching concept or principle that guides the organization in establishing goals and developing strategies to achieve those goals. Defining its mission is the most important strategic step an organization can take. Identification of this broad service aspiration is the first step in the planning process. Only by closely examining external forces and perceived constraints (political, economic, social, and technological) and by analyzing internal strengths and weaknesses can an effective mission statement be formulated. A clearly formulated, broadly discussed and mutually accepted statement enables all parts of an organization to work toward common goals. Taken together, these can provide a focus for policy making and for management decisions of all types and all levels. The first question that must be addressed in the process of developing a mission statement is "What is the purpose of this organization?" After this has been answered, and the mission has been put into place in the strategic thinking of the organization, then quantitative and qualitative goals and objectives can be developed.

Of course, libraries and information centers are typically created with a mission of service. The New York State Library states as its mission: "The Library Development Team develops and improves the library ser-vices that all New Yorkers need for their lifelong learning and enjoyment."[28] The purpose of the National Library of Medicine is "to assist the advancement of the medical and related sciences, and to aid the dissemination and exchange of scientific and other information to the progress of medicine and to the public health."[29]

For public libraries, this mission has traditionally included education, information, and recreation or entertainment; and the library's services have emerged as a vehicle to accomplish a broader mission. In formulating goals, planners must go one step further by defining the overlap between the needs of the users and the physical and financial capabilities of the library or information center. This intersection is the foundation of the library's goals. Failure to identify concisely and correctly this common ground leads to the selection of goals—and later objectives and activities—that are unrelated and unrealistic, subject to false starts and ultimate failure. Likewise, it must be recognized that goals and objectives are likely to change over time and, therefore, must be viewed as flexible and changeable.

An organization's mission statement is often set forth in a charter, constitution and bylaws, annual report, or other authoritative pronouncements of the organization. It is the broad justification for the organization's existence. Although one might assume that the mission will not change, it does, sometimes subtly, sometimes dramatically. Consider the Baltimore County (Maryland) Library System. In 1977 its mission was "to make readily available to the greatest possible number of county residents the most wanted library materials of all kinds, and to serve as a point of access for any needed information." Five years later, the mission statement had been changed to, "To make readily available to Baltimore County residents library materials and information services proportionate to levels of demand and use, and to provide access to materials and information outside the library system." The system's latest mission statement is "to make readily available to Baltimore County residents library materials and information services in a cost-effective manner, proportionate to levels of demand and use, and to provide access to resources outside the library system."[30] To insure that the library responds appropriately to the changing environment, its mission should be reviewed periodically.

Organization-Wide Goals

> ⍟Some of the support in libraries for the human relations approach and the study of informal processes has its basis in the inherent difference of opinion between library managers and staff members over the type of organizational structure needed to achieve organizational goals.[31]
>
> —Duane Webster et al.,
> "Effecting Change in the Management of Libraries"

Goals are the organization's broad aspirations defined in operational terms, leading to measurable objectives or strategies and activities. Goals provide direction and produce effectiveness. They also provide a framework for future planning and help motivate individuals. Goals must be flexible and are subject to constant modification to reflect change. However, goals are not specific enough to be considered operational; objectives and activities quantify goals. They are the basis for development and measures against which the success or failure of goals can be determined. Goals are action oriented in that they cannot be merely stated; action must follow in the form of objectives, which specify means of achieving the goals. Often, two types of goals function in an organization—stated goals and real goals. Stated goals and real goals may be identical but often are different. If they are "real goals they will have an impact on the organization's policies, structure, operations and, in general, on the behavior of people."[32] The differences between stated goals and real goals are subtle and often financial. For instance, a library may want to offer bookmobile service (stated goal), but, if it does not adequately finance the operation, it cannot offer high-quality bookmobile service (real goal).

The New York State Library states its goals as:

1. All New Yorkers will have access to electronic doorway library services provided by libraries transformed by technology.

2. Libraries and library systems will provide high-quality, cost-effective services that meet the needs of their communities.

3. Public policy will acknowledge and support the roles of libraries in a learning society.

4. Libraries and archives will identify, preserve and make available information of enduring significance for the use of present and future generations.

5. The Library Development staff will provide high-quality, cost-effective services to their customers.

6. Library Development will have a supportive work environment for all staff.[33]

The University of Iowa Libraries state as their goals:

1. Information and instructional services are designed and delivered using various methodologies to meet current and changing information needs for a diverse university community in support of teaching, learning, research, and service.

2. Build local collections in all formats to ensure access to the most critical resources for teaching and research. Ensure access to information resources world-wide, both electronic and print, through licensing, enhanced connectivity, and consortia arrangements. Through the combination of on site resources and access to resources held elsewhere, support the full range of university programs and educational activities.

3. Recruit, develop and retain a diverse staff representing the range of knowledge, skills and talents required in a rapidly changing university environment.

4. State-of-the-art information technology is integrated into all aspects of library services, collections and operations to provide users the best possible access to information resources and services both on campus and world-wide.

5. Library staff seek to establish active partnerships with colleges, academic departments and programs in the development of new initiatives and in addressing problems of scholarly communication and publishing.

6. Continue focus on public outreach programs to increase the visibility of university libraries to numerous constituencies, and to expand access its resources for Iowa citizens.

7. Physical facilities provide efficient space for the housing and preservation of collections, workspace for staff and the provision of services in a technologically sophisticated environment.[34]

Specific Objectives and Strategies

Objectives can be conservative or expansive, but always should be stated in terms and conditions that stretch the enterprise. There is a real danger of setting objectives that are really hopes and not attainable ends or, on the other hand, so easily attainable that they are not challenging. In setting objectives, many things must be taken into account: the strengths of the library or information center, the limitations of the library or information center and how much can be accomplished with the financial and material resources available, and the objectives of the larger institution of which the library or information center is a part. Questions that must be addressed in the objective-setting exercise are:

- Is the objective suitable for this library or information center at this time?

- Does it take the organization in the direction it wants to go?

- Does it support the overall mission of the library or information center?

- Is it compatible and complementary with other objectives?

- Is it acceptable and understandable to the majority who will be charged with implementing it?

- Is it affordable for the organization?

- Is it measurable and achievable?

- Is it ambitious enough to be challenging?

The library or information center must be able to prove to both its staff and to the funding authority that the objectives are suitable, sustainable, and measurable. For example, one objective in a previous plan of the Montgomery County (Maryland) Library System was "By 1994, 85 percent of the residents of nursing homes, senior residential facilities, senior nutrition sites and facilities for the handicapped will be provided access to library materials and services through outreach to the facilities on a regularly scheduled basis."

The concomitant reasoning they noted at that time was that there were "approximately 102 facilities . . . housing and serving those in the elder community who may find it difficult or impossible to utilize regular library services and programs. . . . Approximately 78 percent of the more than 3,800 households in continuing care/sheltered housing facilities for seniors presently have access to library services and materials. . . . Residents of all nursing homes . . . presently have access to library materials. . . . Ninety percent of the clients of nutrition sites and adult day care centers have access to programs and materials and 56 percent of the . . . clients of senior centers have access to outreach services at these centers."[35]

Elements of the hierarchy of objectives involve:

- clients—who they are and who they are not;

- services—what services are needed, which should be added, and which deleted;

- personnel resources—what professional and support skills are needed to provide identified services;

- financial resources—what and where they are and how to maintain them; and

- community responsibilities—the library's obligations as a social institution.

Each objective relates to the others, and all are consistent and harmonious. There should be a maximum degree of compatibility among goals and objectives if the organization is to achieve its goals.[36] If an individual working in the organization does not see a relationship between his or her well-being and success (in regard to his or her own personal goals) and the well-being and success of the organization, then he or she is likely to have little motive to serve the objectives of the organization. It is also important to remember that many forces influence the process of planning and achieving goals; therefore, the process must be viewed from a number of perspectives. The three primary perspectives are:

1. environmental, that is, considering those constraints imposed on the organization by society in general;

2. organizational, that is, consideration of the organization as a system; and

3. individual, that is, the goals of the individuals working in the organization.

A balance must be achieved between what is realistic and obtainable and what is challenging and idealistic, but not necessarily completely attainable. The greatest problem in planning is bridging the gap between what is desirable (stated objectives) and what is possible (real objectives).

Unlike for-profit organizations, where the first objective is often to make the greatest profit, most libraries and other information centers have among their primary objectives socialization, that is, to pay adequate wages, to make the organization a good place in which to work, to provide a useful service, and to attract a competent staff. These information organizations, however, are responsible to higher authorities that may restrict those social objectives. Objectives can be forced upon libraries and information centers by the community, through social obligations, or by the employees through collective bargaining or other means. Just as profit and social objectives in business organizations can dictate opposing courses that force compromise, so in many information services organizations the individual's objectives and those of the organization as a whole can conflict and force compromise.

Specific objectives can be departmental or unit objectives, or short-range objectives of the whole organization. Most objectives are tangible or measurable, but others are not. For example, one objective may be to improve morale, but how can one measure morale? Nevertheless, objectives should be stated in terms of associations or activities that are in some way quantifiable and measurable.

Another challenge results from multiple service goals and related objectives combined with attempts to avoid any conflict in those activities. For example, when one examines the primary service goal of a university library, one must ask: Is the goal to provide needed curricular materials for students at the undergraduate level, or is it to provide materials that will allow faculty and graduate students to conduct research and advance the state of knowledge? Are they mutually exclusive? Can one be chosen over another? How does this relate to the mission of the organization?

Activities

At the lowest and very basic level, the elemental tasks are directly related to objectives and strategies, the specific activities that are required to achieve the objectives. They are usually short term, repetitive, measurable, and numerous at the operational level. They require effective policies and procedures to facilitate their achievement. Activities guide the everyday functioning of the organization, and in that sense are pragmatic and narrow.

This hierarchy of mission to goals to objectives to activities is illustrated in figure 2.8, taken from an earlier edition of the plan of the Montgomery County (Maryland) Public Library.

Fig. 2.8. Public library services plan for Montgomery County, Maryland.

Mission: To acquire, organize, provide access and offer guidance to a wide variety of information, materials and services which help to fulfill the intellectual, educational, social, cultural, community information, and recreational needs of all people in the County.

Goal: [Only one chosen as an illustration]
   5.   Improved reference service in all libraries through enhanced reference collections; improved access to reference materials in all formats and increase support of library users searching for information.

Objective: [Only one chosen as an illustration]
   5.2   By 1994 funding for reference materials will be increased by 25% in real dollars (adjusted for rises in costs of reference materials).

Rationale: Several factors, related to other initiatives ... and to the modern information environment, drive the need for expanded reference funding:

   • Expansion of services to target groups with more sophisticated information demands, such as consultants, entrepreneurs starting personal computer businesses, international exporters, public health educators, etc.

   • Need to locate a wider range of materials on these and other subjects in more locations around the County to improve user access.

   • Need to respond promptly to information needs identified in user studies.

   • Proliferation of new directories and other reference sources which are outcomes of electronic data storage and publishing. These are important products developed and marketed at higher prices by information entrepreneurs who regard information as a previously undervalued product.

   • The increasing availability of some information only in the electronic format.

Budget Implications:
   The FY '88 reference budget is $210,000. Twenty-five % of the $265,000 annual increment ... for the base materials budget in each of the 6 years of the plan would be dedicated to upgrading reference information. This would result in $1,312,500 additional being spent over the 6 years with a $375,000 allocation in year 6 and the same additional amount from year 6 on as a part of the base materials budget.

Obviously, because the planning process can be a costly proposition, improper selection or faulty specification of objectives wastes planning time and money, results in frustration, and renders the entire planning activity futile. Every library needs to spell out its own objectives, instead of relying on those of other organizations, because objectives determine the policy, planning, and organizational structure of the library. Objectives represent the end toward which other principles—organizing, staffing, and controlling—are aimed.

Once a strategic plan to achieve goals has been developed and objectives have been stated and approved, the individual strategies are assigned to one or more subordinate units of the organization for execution, and these units in turn assign activities to individual sections of the unit. Ideally, each unit executes several plans simultaneously, making consistent progress toward several objectives in keeping with the established priorities. In practice, this may not always work effectively. By nature, some people tend to invest more time in fulfilling objectives related to their own particular interests, thus losing sight of the priorities established for the unit. For example, the priority objective of a catalog department may be to catalog all current, incoming materials as quickly as possible. Other objectives (e.g., getting rid of a backlog or reclassifying portions of the already classified collection) may take priority with some staff members, so the department falls behind in achieving its primary objective. In addition, unforeseen circumstances, such as the loss of a key person, can jeopardize the achievement of objectives or can, at least, force major revisions or delays.

Unfortunately, many people carry out tasks; they do not achieve objectives. Some employees do not even know the objectives of an organization. Ask those people what justifies their positions and they will nearly always answer by listing the work they do, the tasks they perform, or the machines they control or supervise. These individuals are concerned with means and methods and may be unable to describe the goals and objectives. Perhaps the main benefit of setting goals and objectives is to provide a new way to look at those jobs; it concentrates thought and gives a sense of purpose and commitment. Organizations with clear goals and objectives tend to have higher staff morale. Understanding those goals and objectives and their environment and actively participating, is the best assurance of loyalty to objectives. By establishing written goals and objectives and communicating them to the staff, the organization encourages individuals to think through logical courses of action and provides a yardstick for decision making and ongoing activities. Such a planning exercise is the most effective way of measuring output for the organization.

Management by Objectives

One technique that can be used to supplement the planning process works specifically to merge organizational and individual goals and objectives in order to achieve greater success. Management by Objectives (MBO) has been informally applied in some libraries (though perhaps not consciously), to combine individual and institutional goal setting with the decision-making process. Much has been written on the technique of MBO, a process that has been in favor with industry and commerce for at least three decades. Some now believe that its time has passed, while others feel it is just coming into its own. It is a style of thinking that is still widespread and pervasive in both private and public organizations. Because its concepts are so closely aligned with those of strategic management, and because its focus for the future is on providing a framework for the management process, some discussion is warranted. For example, in an analysis of 70 studies on the use of MBO, it was found that the process has become more widely used in both government and business where the process is supported by top management.[37] MBO has seen its greatest success in for-profit organizations, but consider the following statement.

> MBO is a participative system of managing in which managers look ahead for improvements, think strategically, set performance stretch objectives at a beginning period, develop supporting plans, and give accountability for results at the end of the period.[38]
>
> —Paul Mali, *MBO Updated*

Although Management by Objectives allows one to direct oneself and one's work, it can also mean domination of one person by another. "Objectives are the basis of 'control' in the first sense; but they must never become the basis of 'control' in the second, for this would defeat their purpose. Indeed, one of the major contributions of management by objectives is that it enables us to substitute management by self-control for management by domination."[39]

Description of the technique has been further refined by George Odiorne, who defines it as a process whereby the superior and subordinate managers of an organization jointly identify its common goals, define each individual's major areas of responsibility in terms of the results expected, and use these measures as guides for operating the unit and assessing the contribution of each of its members.[40]

In essence, Management by Objectives means establishing objectives and approaching them as a team over a stated period of time. Objectives must be measurable, with time limits, and they must require specific and realistic action. Perhaps the two most important factors in this process are interactive goal setting and the performance appraisal. The interactive aspect identifies mutually agreed upon objectives for a person to pursue, making that person accountable for results. In true interactive sessions, both the supervisor and the employee give input to the goal setting and the appraisal. This follow-up requires open and free communication without fear of retaliation and without judgment, but with trust and respect. Some feel that these sessions can be "self-defeating over the long run because they are based on a reward-punishment psychology that serves to intensify the pressure on the individual."[41] Indeed, the process is a very delicate one that can improve with experience, but it is not a process based upon threat or intimidation.

Management by Objectives is perhaps the most evident example of participative management because it involves everyone, to an extent, in the management process. It can clarify responsibilities, strengthen planning and control, and establish better relationships between supervisors and other staff members. In this process, at the start of appraisal periods, supervisor and subordinates agree upon specific results to be obtained during this period; they establish what is to be done, how long it will take, and who is to do it. The process rests upon several premises:

1. Clearly stated objectives. If they are not clear, they should be clarified.

2. A succession of specific objectives. Benchmarks must be established to measure progress.

3. Delegation of specific objectives. Certain people should be responsible for accomplishing specific objectives.

4. Freedom to act. Subordinates should be given objectives and authority and then be charged with accomplishment of those objectives.

5. Verifiable objectives. To achieve objectives, it is best to quantify them. If they are nonquantifiable objectives, they may relate to quantifiable ones. For example, if one wants to reduce absenteeism by 50 percent, the reasons for absenteeism must be considered. If the reasons relate to morale, then morale must be improved.

6. Clear communication. This exists only when objectives are specific, are agreed upon by all parties, are budgeted, and are known by all individuals who have a reason for knowing.

7. Shared responsibility. Team effort is the key to management by objectives.

8. Personal accountability. Each person must be accountable for the achievement of his or her assigned objectives.

9. Improving management ability. Management is able to plan more objectively when these premises are accepted.

Management by Objectives occurs in phases: finding the objectives, setting the objectives, validating the objectives, implementing the objectives, and controlling and reporting the status of the objectives. Research studies have confirmed that the process does, indeed, improve communications, increase mutual understanding, improve planning, create positive attitudes toward the evaluation system, employ management abilities, and promote innovation within organizations that have used it.[42] Simply stated by Odiorne, MBO helps solve management problems by:

1. providing a means of measuring the true contributions of managerial and professional personnel.

2. defining the common goals of people and organizations and measuring individual contributions to them. It enhances the possibility of obtaining coordinated efforts and teamwork without eliminating personal risk taking.

3. providing solutions to the key problem of defining the major areas of responsibility for each person in the organization, including joint or shared responsibilities.

4. gearing processes to achieving the results desired, both for the organization as a whole and for the individual contributors.

5. eliminating the need for people to change their personalities as well as for appraising people on the basis of their personality traits.

6. providing a means of determining each manager's span of control.

7. offering an answer to the key question of salary administration, "How should we allocate pay increases from available funds, if we want to pay for results?"

8. aiding in identifying potential for advancement and in finding promotable people.[43]

Some libraries and information centers have explored this technique's potential for their operations.

In practicing MBO one must guard against making the individual's objectives too easy, making them too difficult, setting objectives that conflict with policy, or setting objectives that hold an individual accountable for something beyond his or her control. Also, some concern has been expressed as to whether there is a deterioration of motivation over time. Such deterioration is reflected in lack of participation by all members, stacks of paperwork, emphasis on quantitative aspects, and increased administrative concerns.[44]

Finally, it is important to distinguish between objectives and policy. Objectives emphasize aims and are stated as expectations; policies emphasize rules and are stated as instructions.

Policy Making

In many discourses, policy making and decision making are synonymous. In practice, however, policy making is a part of decision making. Policies emanate from the original decisions and become general statements or understandings that channel thinking in future decision making. They serve as guidelines for actions, particularly those of a repetitive nature, in order to create some sense of uniformity in the conduct of an organization. Policies can be viewed as contingency plans because they are based on decisions that set the course of the plan. Policies, while they are sometimes expressed in positive or mutual terms, are essentially limiting because they dictate courses of action and are aimed at preventing deviations from a set norm. They attempt to eliminate differences that sometimes result from personality conflicts or irrational forces. Policies can become effective tools for transferring decision making to lower levels in the organization, because, within the broad policy outline, individuals at all levels can be charged with making operational decisions. A good working definition of policy making might be "a verbal, written, or implied overall guide setting up boundaries that supply the general limits and direction in which managerial action will take place."[45]

Both policies and objectives are guides to thinking and action, but there are differences between them. Objectives, as already discussed, are end points of planning, while policies channel decisions along the way toward meeting those objectives, after objectives have been established. Another difference is that a policy is usually effective or operational the day it is formulated and continues to be in effect until it is revised or deleted. A policy, then, leads to the achievement of objectives and aids in the decision-making process. As mentioned before, policies can give guidance to all levels of the organization. For example, by adopting equal employment opportunity practices, an institution ensures that all qualified individuals are seriously and equally considered by all hiring units within the organization for any position vacancy. The policy does not dictate the choice of a particular individual but does eliminate one factor—discrimination—as an element in the final decision.

Policy making is not reserved for top management. Policies include, on the one hand, major policies involving all segments of the organization and, on the other hand, minor policies applicable only to a small segment of the organization. Many policies in libraries provide basic direction toward the achievement of stated goals, including policies relating to materials, personnel, equipment use, and money—more specifically, the acquisi- tion of materials, personnel appointment and promotion, equipment purchase and use, and program budgeting. Examples of library and information center policies might be:

1. All new staff will be rotated through all departments during their first year of employment (a staff-development policy) or

2. Library materials should present all sides of controversial issues (a materials selection policy).

Policy manuals usually enumerate an organization's policies in relation to goals and objectives. A policy manual is an important record and is invaluable as a decision-making guide and as a way of communicating within the organization. It is also a basic tool for indoctrinating new staff members and assuring some degree of uniformity in approaches or responses to issues. Of course, it also serves as a historical record of decisions made.

All libraries have policies, whether they are written or unwritten, sound or unsound, followed or not followed, understood or not understood, complete or incomplete. It is almost impossible to delegate authority and clarify relationships without policies, because one cannot carry out decisions without some kind of guideline. It is important to remember that policies can provide freedom as well as restrict it, and that there are as many cases of frustration within organizations about the lack of rules, regulations, procedures, and policies as there are about arbitrarily established ones. In the absence of policy, each case is resolved on its own merit, so consistency is lacking. Lack of policy means that the same question may be considered time after time, by a number of different individuals, in several units of the organization, with the result that energy is wasted, redundancy is established, conflicting decisions are made, and confusion develops. Policy ensures some degree of consistency in the operation. Just as with objectives, policies may be stated in the form of guiding principles (these being board, comprehensive, and basic), or may be specific or operational and deal with day-to-day activities.

Sources of Policy

Policies can be categorized according to their source as follows:

1. Originated policy. This type of policy is developed to guide the general operations of the library. Originated policies flow mainly from the objectives and are the main source of policy making within the organization. An example of an originated policy is the previously mentioned policy to adhere to the concept of equal employment opportunity.

2. Appealed policy. Superiors in their assigned areas of responsibility may need certain decisions, and the worker is required to take it through the chain of command, where a common law is established. This type of policy can cause tension because it forces a decision or policy, which, consequently, often does not have the thorough consideration that is required. To draw an extreme example, it may be the appealed policy of the catalog department to make no more than two subject headings for each monograph. That policy has a great effect on the reference department's ability to work with patrons. Oftentimes, appealed policies are made by snap decisions.

3. Implied policy. This type of policy is developed from actions that people see about them and believe to constitute policy. Usually, this type of policy is unwritten. For instance, repetitive actions, such as promotion from within, may be interpreted as policy. This may or may not be the case. Particularly in areas relating to personnel, staff must be informed so that misunderstandings do not arise. When implied policies are recognized, policies should be developed or other statements used to clarify the issue.

4. Externally imposed policy. These policies, which come through several channels, dictate the working of an institution but may be beyond its control. For example, local, state, and federal laws have a direct bearing on the policies that libraries may formulate. These laws may be general, such as those relating to destruction of public property (Malicious Damage Act 1861), or specific, such as those relating to copyright (Copyright Act 1976). When policies are being formulated, they must be checked for compliance with law before they can be finalized.

No matter what objectives are set for libraries and information centers, the objectives are subject to government regulation. In the case of public libraries in the United States, objectives must adhere to government policy on the local, state, and national levels. If, for instance, a local authority decides, for local economic reasons, to drastically reduce the library service hours to the point that the library no longer meets state standards for allocating funds to that library, such an action would likely be in conflict with its obligation and thus be illegal. Or, if a library replans its service points and closes a branch library, people living nearby may petition their representatives or other local officials, who may decide that such a policy does not secure an improvement and may prevent the library from carrying out its policy.

Laws governing information services often relate to finances. Standards for capital investment, percentage of budget spent on materials, qualifications of staff, and so forth are developed by library officials. Because this is an external control upon all public library spending, it necessarily affects the planning and administration of public libraries.

Effective Policy Making

Policies fall into two groups: those that deal with the managerial functions of planning, organizing, staffing, directing, and controlling; and those that deal with the functions of the enterprise, such as selection and development of resources, finance, personnel, and public relations. Both types of policies relate to the characteristic behavior of the library to achieve its objectives.

Several basic rules should be considered when policies are being formulated. Some of these may seem simplistic, mundane, and even redundant, but it is surprising how many organizations ignore these basics when they are formulating policy. To be most effective, policies should be reflective of the objectives and plans of the organization. These should complement each other and build on that common strength. For this reason, any policy should receive detailed consideration before being proposed and certainly before implementation. Characteristics of good policies would include being:

1. Reflective of the objectives and plans of the organization. These should dovetail so that each builds on the other. For this reason, any policy should receive detailed consideration before being proposed and certainly before implementation.

2. Consistent. This maintains efficiency. Again, the existence of contradicting policies dissipates desired effects.

3. Flexible. Policies must change as new needs arise. Many organizations adhere to out-of-date policies. On the other hand, a laissez-faire

approach to policy formulation and revision may lead to disillusionment on the part of those who are charged with carrying out the policies. Some degree of stability must be maintained. Policies should be controlled through regular and careful review. Although the application of policies requires judgment, violation of the policy under the guise of flexibility should be avoided.

4. Distinguished from rules and procedures. Rules and procedures are firm, while policies, as guides, allow some latitude.

5. Written. A clear, well-written policy helps information dissemination. Because many policies affect individuals who have not been involved in their formulation, the policies should be discussed and widely distributed through letters, memoranda, announcements, and policy manuals.

Stated policies have several advantages.

1. They are available to all in the same form.

2. They can be referred to, so that anyone who wishes can check the policy.

3. Misunderstandings can be referred to a particular set of words.

4. They indicate a basic honesty and integrity of the organization's intentions.

5. They can be readily disseminated to all who are affected by them.

6. They can be taught to new employees easily.

7. The process of writing forces managers to think more sharply about the policy, thus helping achieve further clarity.

8. They generate confidence of all persons in the leadership of top management and in the fact that everyone will be treated substantially the same under given conditions.[46]

Implementing Policy

Policies are carried out or enforced by procedures, rules, and regulations. Procedures are guides to action, and they are subordinate to policies. They establish a method of handling repetitive tasks or problems and may be thought of as means by which work is performed. Basically, procedures prescribe standardized methods of performing tasks (after the best way has been determined) to ensure uniformity and consistency. Greater efficiency in routine jobs can be achieved through procedures that identify the best way of getting the jobs done. Procedures tend to be chronological lists of what is to be done. Examples of procedures include a timetable for budget preparation, a sequence of steps to be followed in searching and ordering library materials, and interlibrary loan procedures. Procedures are helpful in routine decisions because they break down the process into steps.

The relationship between procedures and policies best can be indicated by an example. Library policy may grant employees a month's annual vacation. The procedures specify how to schedule holidays to avoid disruption of service, maintain records to assure each employee a holiday of the right length, and apply for the holiday.

Rules and regulations, constituting the simplest type of a plan, spell out a required course of action or conduct that must be followed. A rule prescribes a specific action for a given situation and creates uniformity of action. Rules may place positive limits (should), negative limits (should not), or value constraints (good or bad) on the behavior of individuals working in the institution or on individuals using the institution as a service. Rules ensure stable, consistent, and uniform behavior by individuals in accomplishing tasks, addressing personnel issues, and relating to both the internal and external environment. Like procedures, rules and regulations guide action, but they specify no time sequence. Like decisions, rules are guides, but they allow no discretion or initiative in their application. Examples of rules might be the prohibition of smoking in the library or information center or the fact that reference books do not circulate. Regulations also establish a course of action that is authoritative; failure to adhere to regulations can elicit discipline.

Decision Making

> Regardless of formal position in the organization, the librarian is an information processor—not only in the provision of services to the patrons but also as a decision-maker in the operation of the library. It is this second role of information processor to which attention must be drawn, for it is in this role that the librarian affects the decisions being made in the organization.[47]

> —Charles R. McClure,
> *Information for Academic Library Decision Making*

Some writers consider decision making synonymous with management.[48] If actions are to be taken, then decisions must be made. There is no doubt this is an important part of management, one of the basic planning principles. Selection from among alternatives is the core of planning.

According to Drucker, "a decision is a judgment. It is a choice between alternatives. It is rarely a choice between right and wrong. It is at best a choice between 'almost right' and 'probably wrong'—but much more often a choice between two courses of action neither of which is probably more nearly right than the other."[49] Decision making, therefore, complements planning because it involves choosing the best alternative for the future of the enterprise, and decisions with organization-wide implications are related specifically to the planning process. A decision must be made, with a course of action in mind, by choosing the alternative that one thinks is best. This is not necessarily the alternative that is best, because that can be determined only later. Of course, such a choice implies an awareness of alternatives and the important factors that need to be considered.

Decision making is a conscious choosing, and it is a much slower process than some would like to imagine. The stereotype of finger-snapping and button-pushing fades with systematic research and analysis. The decision-making process involves a blend of thinking, deciding, and acting; information is key to the process. Deliberation, evaluation, and thought must be brought into play. While many decisions are mundane, others are of unmeasured consequence and could change the library's or information center's course of action. An example of the latter is the decision to open a new branch library or to purchase a totally integrated online system for the library's or the information center's operation. Such decisions can be made only after long, thoughtful review, analysis, and discussion. The manager who has the ultimate responsibility must make a decision that will have a great impact on the operation of the library and on many people, both staff and patrons. Attention paid to the final act—the decision itself—obscures the fact that a number of steps and minor decisions were made along the way, and the announcement of the decision is only the final step.

Decision making at a formal level involves a series of scientific steps: defining the problem, analyzing it, establishing criteria by which it can be evaluated, identifying alternate solutions, selecting the "best" one, implementing it, and evaluating the results. The decision-making procedure can be divided into four phases:

1. Intelligence gathering. The environment inside and outside the organization is searched for conditions requiring a decision, and information is assembled with respect to those conditions.

2. Design. The available courses of action are determined and analyzed to determine their relative values as solutions to the decision problems that have been detected.

3. Choice. An available course of action, which is designed to convert the present, less-desirable situation into a future situation judged to be more desirable, is selected.

4.   Review. Past choices are assessed and new directions adjusted.[50]

These phases, of course, do not have clear-cut boundaries, or strict sequence.

Although this discussion is primarily about the steps in a major decision-making process, it is important to remember that everyone makes decisions every day and that most of these decisions are, to some degree, reached by the same process discussed here. Some organizational decision making, which was once reserved for the executive, is now being delegated to others in the organization. According to Drucker,

> decision making can no longer be confined to the very small group at the top. In one way or another almost every knowledge worker in an organization will either have to become a decision-maker himself or will at least have to be able to play an active, an intelligent, and an autonomous part in the decision-making process. What, in the past, has been a highly specialized function, discharged by a small and usually clearly defined organ—with the rest adapting within a mold of custom and usage—is rapidly becoming a normal if not an everyday task of every single unit in this new social institution, the large-scale knowledge organization. The ability to make effective decisions increasingly determines the ability of every knowledge worker, at least of those in responsible positions, to be effective altogether.[51]

One of the characteristics of an effective decision-maker appears to be "the ability to distinguish between problems for which existing procedures are appropriate and those for which new ground must be broken. It is ineffective and inefficient to deal with an exceptional problem as though it were routine, or a generic problem as though it were an exceptional case."[52]

Group Decision Making

The approach to decision making by groups is quite different from individual decision making, primarily because of group dynamics. However, group decision making should follow the same process if it is to be constructive. Although techniques of both decision making and participatory management are discussed elsewhere in this text, it is pertinent to discuss very briefly here the group decision process. Again, this concerns broad strategies and objectives that reflect organizational decisions. Simon points out that "almost no decision made in an organization is the task of a single individual."[53] Not everyone would agree. When Max Weber formulated the concept of bureaucracy with emphasis on the position rather than the person, he detailed the delegation of responsibility, channels of communication for decision making, and the need for specialization for decision-making purposes. His theory, for all intents, rejects interaction among subordinates for decision-making purposes. Those attitudes may be outdated, but certainly have not been abandoned. There are, nevertheless, several advantages to group decision making, including:

1. Group judgment. The old adage "two heads are better than one" applies here. Group deliberation is important in identifying alternative solutions to a problem.

2. Group authority. There is a great fear of allowing one person to have too much authority. Group decisions prevent this problem to an extent. However, it must be remembered that one person must ultimately answer for decisions that have been made. Thus, the role of leadership in the organization is not diminished but altered.

3. Communication. It is much easier to inform and receive input from all parts of the organization through a group. Also, if various interest groups have been represented during the process of making major decisions, there is less resistance to the decisions. Communication permits a wider participation in decision making and therefore can have some influence on employee motivation.

There are also distinct disadvantages to the group approach. As a cynic once wrote, a committee is a group of "unfits appointed by the incompetent to do the unnecessary." More realistically, disadvantages might be:

1. Cost. Group decision making requires a great deal of time, energy, and, therefore, money.

2. Compromise. Group decisions can be diluted to the least common denominator. Pressures of uniformity force compliance. There are two ways to view this. The major drawback may be that majority rules. The desirability of a consensus should not take precedence over critical evaluation in such a situation. On the other hand, a group can prevent an individual from going off the track by forcing him or her into line with the thinking of the rest of the group.

3. Indecision. There are delays in reaching a final decision because of the lengthy deliberations required. Groups are often accused of engaging in too much irrelevant talk and not enough concrete action.

4. Power. One individual usually emerges as a leader. This person may be in a position of influence in the organization. The authoritarian personality of an administrator can be used as a tactical weapon, so that the group process simply becomes one of minimizing opposition to an action that has already been decided on by the administrator. The cohesiveness of the group and the attitudes of one person toward another are important factors in the group process.

5. Authority. Groups are frequently used to make decisions that are beyond their authority. This can cause great delay and only enhances a feeling of frustration on the part of members, particularly if management rejects the group decision. The responsibility and authority of the group should be clearly set out at the beginning.

The democratic approach of group decision making improves morale, stresses the team approach, keeps individuals aware, and provides a forum for free discussion of ideas and thoughts. Traditionally, librarians have not demanded a greater voice in decision-making affairs because they have had an employee rather than a professional orientation. The higher a person is on the administrative scale, the less aware he or she is of the inadequate opportunities available for staff participation. This is an area of great discussion and disagreement in all types of organizations.

Steps and Factors in Decision Making

If the organization's goals are clear, the next important step in decision making is developing alternatives. This step is possible in almost all situations. Effective planning involves a search for these alternatives. If there is only one solution, management is powerless to devise alternatives, and no decision is required, although some adjustments may be necessary. In most cases, however, several alternatives exist.

Final selection of a course of action is a matter of weighing expected results against enterprise objectives. What is best for one segment is not necessarily best for the whole. Making only two subject entries in the catalog, for instance, is easier for the cataloging department but harder for the reference department. Choosing a course of action commits the entire enterprise to the chosen position.

The scientific approach to decision making requires that one first identify the problem. Once that has been done, the decision-maker must collect and analyze all data available on the problem. This includes intuition, opinion, and impression, in addition to concrete data. It may involve operations research. After all alternatives have been developed, one must select what appears to be the most appropriate alternative. Often, this alternative is then expressed as policy for the functioning of the organization. This selection process involves a great deal of risk taking as well as uncertainty, because it is only after the decision has been implemented that one can determine whether or not it was appropriate. The final step of implementation brings the decision into the control aspect of the organization.

> ℚ Participative management is not decision making by committee or by staff plebiscite. Good management requires that when all the facts have been gathered and analyzed and all the advice is in, the appropriate administrator has to make the decision and take responsibility for it. Knowing when and how to seek and take advantage of consultative advice and prior approval of decisions where appropriate is one of the most important managerial skills.[54]
>
> —Richard DeGennaro,
> "Library Administration and New Management Systems"

Several factors influence decision making for libraries and other information centers. Such things as population trends, educational achievement, user and nonuser needs, all point to the necessity of a community analysis before final decisions can be made on services to be offered by the library. Selection from among alternatives is made on the basis of the following:

1. Experience. In relying on one's experience, mistakes as well as accomplishments should act as guides. If experience is carefully analyzed and not blindly followed, it can be useful and appropriate.

2. Experimentation. This approach toward deciding among alternatives, although legitimate in many situations, is expensive where capital expenditures and personnel are concerned.

3. Research and analysis. Although this is the most general and effective technique used, it may be somewhat expensive. However, the approach is probably more beneficial and cheaper in the long run, particularly for large academic, public, and special libraries.

Another important factor in the decision-making process is the perceived level of importance of a particular decision. There are two basic types of decisions: a major one affecting the total organization and a lesser one, which has less effect on the overall organization but is nonetheless important. The routine decisions comprise as much as 90 percent of the decisions made in an organization. Most decisions of lesser importance do not require thorough analysis.

Politics is paramount in decision making, as is consideration of the human factor. Acceptance of change is essential to the success of a decision. Those who will be affected by the decision should be told early on—preferably, they should be involved in the decision from the beginning. The following suggestions may facilitate involvement in the decision-making process:

1. Distinguish big from little problems to avoid getting caught in a situation that is rapid-fire and not effective.

2. Rely on policy to settle routine problems, and subject the big problems to thorough analysis.

3. Delegate as many decisions as possible to the level of authority most qualified and most interested in handling the problem.

4. Avoid crisis decisions by planning ahead.

5. Don't expect to be right all the time; no one ever is.

Decision making is at the heart of any organization. The approach that the librarian and the information specialist take to decision making and to the involvement of others will determine the direction the library or information center will take in the future.

Conclusion

Planning is an analytical process that involves assessing the future, determining a desired mission for that future, creating objectives in the context of that future, developing alternative courses of action for such objectives, and selecting an appropriate agenda from among those alternatives that are priorities, and pursuing a detailed course of action.

Notes

1. Peter F. Drucker, *Management: Tasks, Responsibilities, Practices* (New York: Harper & Row, 1974), 121-22.

2. Harvard College Library, *Commitment to Renewal* (Cambridge, MA: Harvard College Library, 1992), 1.

3. Columbia University, "Detailed Organization Description of the Columbia University Libraries" (effective June 1973), 11.3.1. (Mimeograph, April 12, 1973.)

4. Duane E. Webster, *Library Management Review and Analysis Program: A Handbook for Guiding Change and Improvement in Research Library Management* (Washington, DC: Association of Research Libraries, 1973). Grady Morien et al., *Planning Process for Small Academic Libraries: An Assisted Self-study Manual* (Washington, DC: Association

of Research Libraries, 1980). Duane E. Webster, *Academic Library Development Program* (Washington, DC: Association of Research Libraries, 1977). Vernon E. Palmour et al., *Planning Process for Public Libraries* (Chicago: American Library Association, 1980). Charles R. McClure, *Planning and Role Setting for Public Libraries* (Chicago: American Library Association, 1987). Nancy Van House, *Output Measures for Public Libraries: A Manual* (Chicago: American Library Association, 1987). Nancy Van House et al., *Measuring Academic Library Performance: A Practical Approach* (Chicago: American Library Association, 1990). Paul Kantor, *Objective Performance Measures for Academic and Research Libraries* (Washington, DC: Association for Research Libraries, 1984). R. H. Orr, "Measuring the Goodness of Library Services: A General Framework for Considering Quantitative Measures," *Journal of Documentation* 29 (1973): 329-31. S. Easun, "Beginner's Guide to Efficiency Measurement: An Application of Data Envelopment Analysis to Selected School Libraries," *School Library Media Quarterly* 22, no. 2 (1994): 103-6. C. Guyonneau, "Performance Measures for ILL: An Evaluation," *Journal of Interlibrary Loan and Information Supply* 3 (1993): 101-26. K. Hendrickson, "Standards for University Libraries: Evaluation of Performance," *College & Research Libraries News* 50 (1989): 680-81.

5. R. M. Cyert and J. G. March, *A Behavioral Theory of the Firm* (Englewood Cliffs, NJ: Prentice-Hall, 1963), 111-12.

6. Bernard Taylor and John R. Sparkes, *Corporate Strategy and Planning* (New York: John Wiley, 1977), 3.

7. Henry Mintzberg, *The Rise and Fall of Strategic Planning* (New York: Prentice-Hall, 1994), 333.

8. Drucker, *Management*, 25.

9. Michael Hammer and James Champy, *Reengineering the Corporation* (New York: HarperBusiness, 1993), 3.

10. George Steiner, *Top Management Planning* (New York: Macmillan, 1969), 34.

11. Fred Luthans, *Introduction to Management: A Contingency Approach* (New York: McGraw-Hill, 1976), 95.

12. Edward R. Johnson, "Academic Library Planning, Self-Study, and Management Review," in *Planning for Library Services*, ed. Charles R. McClure (New York: Haworth Press, 1982), 72.

13. American Library Association, *Library Bill of Rights with Amendments* (adopted June 18, 1948). (Chicago: American Library Association).

14. Benjamin B. Tregue and John W. Zimmerman, *Top Management Strategy: What It Is and How to Make It Work* (New York: Simon & Schuster, 1980).

15. Emory University General Libraries, "Strategic Plan" (Atlanta, GA: Emory University, October 6, 1994, mimeographed).

16. The Free Library of Philadelphia, "Mission Statement" (Philadelphia, PA: The Free Library of Philadelphia, January 19, 1989, Internet).

17. Richard DeGennaro, "Shared Understanding," in *Harvard College Library 1995* (Cambridge, MA: The Harvard College Library, 1995), 1.

18.   Arthur Langley, "The Role of Formal Strategic Planning," *Long Range Planning* 21, no. 3 (1988): 48.

19.   Benjamin B. Tregue and John W. Zimmerman, "Strategic Thinking," *Management Review* 68 (February 1979): 10-11.

20.   Richard Cyert, "Designing a Creative Organization," in *Handbook for Creative Managers* (New York: McGraw-Hill, 1988), 186.

21.   An example is academic libraries, where the following current standards exist: "Standards for University Libraries," *College & Research Library News* 40 and *College & Research Libraries* 39, no. 2 (April 1978): 89-99; revised 1989. "Standards for College Libraries 1985," *College & Research Libraries News* 46, no. 5 (May 1985): 241-52; revised 1995. "Guidelines for Two-Year College Learning Resource Programs (Revised)," *College & Research Libraries News Part 1* 43, no. 1 (January 1982): 5-10; *Part 2* 43, no. 2 (February 1982): 45-49. "Standards for Community, Junior and Technical College Learning Resources Programs," *College & Research Libraries News* 55, no. 1 (January 1994). "Information Power: Building Partnerships for Learning" (draft), American Association of School Libraries, 1997.

22.   Robert D. Stueart, "Long-Range Planning in U.S. Public Libraries," in *Public Libraries Today and Tomorrow: Approaches to Their Goals and Management*, ed. H. Ernestus and H. D. Weger (Boston Spa, England: British Library Research and Development Department, 1986), 40.

23.   Quoted in David P. Snyder and Gregg Edwards, *Future Forces* (Washington, DC: Foundation of the American Society of Association Executives, 1984), 1.

24.   Leonard S. Silk and M. Louise Curley, *A Primer on Business Forecasting* (New York: Random House, 1970), 3-4.

25.   Becker and Hayes, *LCM—The Library Costing Model* (Sherman Oaks, CA: Becker and Hayes, 1993).

26.   Emory University Libraries, "Strategic Plan" (Atlanta, GA: Emory University, 1996).

27.   Denver Public Library, "Mission and Values" (Denver, CO: Denver Public Library, 1997, Internet).

28.   New York State Library, New York State Education Department, "Improving Library Services for All: A Strategic Plan for the Division of Library Development" (Albany, NY: New York State Library, October 1996, Internet).

29.   Public Law 941, Section 371, U.S. Code Annotated, 1982, Title 42, S.275. See "National Library of Medicine," in *American Library Law*, 5th ed. (Chicago: American Library Association, 1983), 55.

30.   Eleanor Jo Rodger and Vernon E. Palmour, *Baltimore County Public Library Long-Range Plan II, 1983-88* (Towson, MD: Baltimore County Public Library, 1983), 1.

31.   Duane Webster et al., "Effecting Change in the Management of Libraries: The MRAP Program," in *Coping with Change* (Washington, DC: Association of Research Libraries, 1973), 42.

32. Amitai Etzioni, "The Organization Goal: Master or Servant," in *Modern Organization* (Englewood Cliffs, NJ: Prentice-Hall, 1964), 7.

33. New York State Library, "Improving Library Services for All," p. 2.

34. The University of Iowa Libraries, "Strategic Plan 1996-2000" (Iowa City, IA: University of Iowa Libraries, December 2, 1997).

35. "Public Services Plan for Public Libraries in Montgomery County, MD, FY 83-88" (Montgomery County Government, Rockville, MD, May 1982), 4, 6.

36. Fremont E. Kast and James E. Rosenzweig, *Organization and Management: A Systems Approach* (New York: McGraw-Hill, 1974), 158-59.

37. Robert Rodgers and John E. Hunter, "A Foundation of Good Management Practices in Government: Management by Objectives," *Public Administration Review* 52 (January-February 1992): 27-39.

38. Paul Mali, *MBO Updated* (New York: John Wiley, 1986), 47.

39. Stephen J. Carroll Jr. and Henry L. Tosi, *Management by Objectives* (New York: Macmillan, 1973), 3.

40. George S. Odiorne, *Management by Objectives* (New York: Fearon-Pitman, 1965), 55-56.

41. Harry Levinson, "Management by Whose Objectives," *Harvard Business Review* 48 (July-August 1970): 134.

42. Stephen J. Carroll Jr. and Henry L. Tosi, "Goal Characteristics and Personality Factors in a Management-by-Objectives Program," *Administrative Science Quarterly* 15, no. 3 (1970): 295-301.

43. Odiorne, *Management by Objectives,* 55.

44. John M. Ivancevich, "A Longitudinal Assessment of Management by Objectives," *Administrative Science Quarterly* 17 (March 1972): 127.

45. M. Valliant Higginson, "Putting Policies in Context," in *Business Policy,* ed. Alfred Gross and Walter Gross (New York: Ronald Press, 1967), 230.

46. Dalton E. McFarland, "Policy Administration," in *Business Policy,* ed. Alfred Gross and Walter Gross (New York: Ronald Press, 1967), 230.

47. Charles R. McClure, *Information for Academic Library Decision Making* (Westport, CT: Greenwood, 1980), 5.

48. Herbert A. Simon, *The New Science of Management Decision,* 2d ed. (New York: Macmillan, 1966), 143.

49. Peter F. Drucker, *The Effective Executive* (New York: Harper & Row, 1967), 143.

50. Simon, *The New Science of Management Decision,* 39.

51. Drucker, *The Effective Executive,* 162.

52. Jerry W. Koehler et al., *Organizational Communication* (New York: Holt, Rinehart & Winston, 1976), 218.

53. Herbert A. Simon, *Administrative Behavior* (New York: Macmillan, 1957), 133.

54. Richard DeGennaro, "Library Administration and New Management Systems," *Library Journal* 103, no. 22 (December 15, 1978): 2480.

Readings

Ansoff, H. Igor. *Implanting Strategic Management.* 2d ed. Englewood Cliffs, NJ: Prentice-Hall, 1990.

Anthony, Robert N., J. Deardon, and V. Govindarajan. *Management Control Systems.* 7th ed. Homewood, IL: Irwin, 1992.

Asantewa, Doris. *Strategic Planning Basics for Special Libraries.* Washington, DC: Special Libraries Association, 1992.

Beck, Arthur C., and Ellis D. Hillman. *Positive Management Practices: Bringing Out the Best in Organizations and People.* San Francisco: Jossey-Bass, 1986.

Beer, Stafford. *How Many Grapes Went into the Wine: Stafford Beer on the Art and Science of Holistic Management.* New York: John Wiley, 1994.

Benveniste, Guy. *Mastering the Politics of Planning.* San Francisco: Jossey-Bass, 1989.

Best, M. J. *Linear Programming: An Introduction.* Englewood Cliffs, NJ: Prentice-Hall, 1985.

Blasingame, Ralph, and Robert L. Goldberg. *Planning, Another View.* Philadelphia: Drexel University College of Information Studies, 1987.

Bryson, John M. *Strategic Planning for Public and Nonprofit Organizations.* San Francisco: Jossey-Bass, 1995.

Certo, Samuel C., and J. P. Peter. *Strategic Management: Concepts and Applications.* New York: McGraw-Hill, 1991.

Clement, Richard W., ed. *Strategic Planning in ARL Libraries SPEC Kit no. 210.* Washington, DC: Association of Research Libraries, 1995.

Corrall, Sheila. *Strategic Planning for Library and Information Services.* London: ASLIB, 1994.

Davidson, Mike. *The Transformation of Management.* Boston: Butterworth-Heinemann, 1996.

Feiring, B. R. *Linear Programming: An Introduction.* Beverly Hills, CA: Sage Publications, 1986.

Galliers, Robert. *Strategic Information Management.* Oxford, UK: Butterworth-Heinemann, 1994.

Gardner, James R., R. Rachlin, and H. W. A. Sweeny. *Handbook of Strategic Planning.* New York: John Wiley, 1986.

Georgantzas, N. C., and W. Acar. *Scenario-Driven Planning.* Westport, CT: Quorum Books, 1995.

Goldberg, Beverly. *Dynamic Planning: The Act of Managing Beyond Tomorrow.* New York: Oxford University Press, 1994.

Gordon, Gilbert, and I. Pressman. *Quantitative Decision Making for Business.* 2d ed. Englewood Cliffs, NJ: Prentice-Hall, 1983.

Grant, John H., and W. R. King. *The Logic of Strategic Planning.* Boston: Little, Brown, 1982.

Hall, Owen P. *Complete Models for Operations Management.* Reading, MA: Addison-Wesley, 1989.

Hamburg, Morris et al. *Library Planning and Decision-Making Systems.* Cambridge, MA: MIT Press, 1974.

Hamdy, A. Taha. *Operations Research: An Introduction.* New York: Macmillan, 1988.

Hatten, K. J., and M. L. Hatten. *Strategic Management: Analysis and Action.* Englewood Cliffs, NJ: Prentice-Hall, 1987.

Kearns, Kevin P. *Managing for Accountability.* San Francisco, CA: Jossey-Bass, 1996.

Koteen, Jack. *Strategic Management in Public and Nonprofit Organizations.* New York: Praeger, 1989.

Locke, Elvin H., and Gary P. Latham. *Goal Setting: A Motivational Technique That Works.* Englewood Cliffs, NJ: Prentice-Hall, 1984.

Macdonald, Charles R. *MBO Can Work!* New York: McGraw-Hill, 1982.

Majone, Giandomenico. *Evidence, Argument and Persuasion in the Policy Process.* New Haven, CT: Yale University Press, 1989.

Makridakas, Spyros G. *Forecasting, Planning and Strategy for the 21st Century.* New York: Free Press, 1990.

Mali, Paul. *MBO Updated.* New York: John Wiley, 1986.

Migliore, P. Henry et al., ed. *Strategic Planning for Not-for-Profit Organizations.* New York: Haworth Press, 1994.

Mintzberg, Henry. *The Rise and Fall of Strategic Planning.* New York: Prentice-Hall, 1994.

Molz, Kathleen Redmond. *Library Planning and Policy Making: The Legacy of the Public and Private Sectors.* Metuchen, NJ: Scarecrow Press, 1990.

Oster, Sharon M. *Strategic Management for Non-Profit Organizations.* New York: Oxford University Press, 1995.

Renfro, William L. *Issues Management in Strategic Planning.* Westport, CT: Quorum Books, 1993.

Richards, Max D. *Setting Strategic Goals and Objectives.* 2d ed. St. Paul, MN: West, 1986.

Riggs, Donald E. *Strategic Planning for Library Managers.* Phoenix, AZ: Oryx Press, 1984.

Schneider, Karl. *Expert Systems and Computer Aids to Decision Making, 1970-85.* Beltsville, MD: National Agricultural Library, 1986.

Thompson, Arthur A., and A. J. Strickland III. *Strategic Management: Concepts and Cases.* 4th ed. Homewood, IL: Irwin, 1987.

Thompson, Christine E. *Decision Support Systems: A Bibliography.* Monticello, IL: Vance Bibliographies, 1985.

Watstein, S. B. et al., comp. *Formal Planning in College Libraries.* Chicago: American Library Association, 1994.

Zaleznik, Abraham. *The Management Mystique.* New York: Harper & Row, 1989.

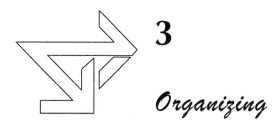

3

Organizing

*In order to be successful, organizations must have capabilities
that allow them to coordinate and focus behavior in ways
that are tuned to the marketplace and produce
high levels of performance—ways that differentiate
them from their competitors. Every organization
must understand what capabilities it needs
to compete . . . and then develop them
by creating the appropriate
organizational designs and
management systems.*[1]

—Edward E. Lawler III,
From the Ground Up

The planning process described in the previous chapter defines goals and objectives. After these are set, management's next function is to design an organizational structure that will facilitate the achievement of those goals and objectives. Organizing involves determining the specific activities necessary to accomplish the planned goals, grouping the activities into a logical framework or structure, assigning these activities to specific positions and people, and providing a means for coordinating the efforts of individuals and groups.[2]

Organizing divides an organization into smaller, more manageable units and makes the work done in each unit compatible with that done in the others. Organizing can be thought of as a bridge connecting the objectives developed in planning to the specific means for their accomplishment.[3]

Organizing has long been central to the study of management. The classical writers in the field of management provided more guidelines and principles in relation to organizing than to any other managerial function. These classical writers viewed an organizational structure as a lasting entity. Their overall perception was that organizations were stable structures, almost always arranged in hierarchical fashion, with the power flowing in an orderly fashion from the individuals at the top of the hierarchy to those below. As Henry Mintzberg has written:

> It probably would not be an exaggeration to claim that the vast majority of everything that has been written about management and organization over the course of this century . . . has had as its model, usually implicitly, [this] form of organization. With its dominant vertical hierarchy, sharp divisions of labor, concentration on standardization, obsession with control, and of course, appreciation of staff functions in general and planning in particular [this] type has always constituted the "one best way" of management literature.[4]

One of the most striking changes in management in the past decades has been a rethinking of organizational structure. Much of this rethinking has been forced on managers by rapid changes in the environment, especially increasing foreign competition and the growing importance of computerized information in all types of organizations. The traditional thinking about organizing has been transformed also by the introduction of a number of "*re*-words"—*reengineering, restructuring, reinvention,* and *redesign.*[5] The old conventions about organizational stability have been challenged and discarded in many corporations. Organizations have cut the size of their workforces: in an attempt to become more efficient and save money they have downsized or "rightsized." Hierarchies have been flattened and broadened, and more flexible organizations have arisen. The new model of organization being touted by management experts is flexible and adaptable to change, has relatively few levels of formal hierarchy, and has loose boundaries among functions and units.[6]

> In the initial shock of adjusting to sharply increased competition, the fat and happy must learn to become lean and mean. Across the length and breadth of the U.S. industrial sector, increased import penetration . . . sparked an all-out war on costs. After three decades of almost uninterrupted growth in revenues, profits, and employment, U.S. industrial firms—en masse—were forced to bite the bullet of downsizing and restructuring.[7]
>
> —Andrew Wilson,
> "U.S. Firms Restructure and Revitalize"

Not surprisingly, most of the reengineering and restructuring of organizations has occurred in the corporate world, the sector that usually leads the way in organizational transformation. Publicly supported organizations have been slower to change and move away from the traditional organizational structures. Although some libraries and other information centers have begun to reshape and restructure, as a whole they have not been as radically altered as organizations in the private sector. For instance, a recent study of large research libraries found the reorganization changes "incremental rather than dramatic."[8] However, even in the corporate world there is much indecision about reorganization and the best type of structure. As Johansen and Swigart write: "The organizational model of the sixties is clearly inadequate, and a comprehensive model has yet to appear for the nineties. Many organizations are running blind. We have outlived the usefulness of models from the industrial era but don't yet have robust organizational models for the information era."[9]

It is certainly true that managers in all types of libraries, just as managers in other types of organizations, are considering possible restructuring. Many of the same forces that have resulted in the reshaping of other types of organizations have also affected libraries and information centers: increased automation, reduction in budgets, changing information needs and expectations of users, and the need for staff to have more autonomy and control over their work.[10] As a result of these pressures, organizational changes have occurred in a number of libraries and in most cases have resulted in flatter, more flexible structures. Many more libraries, however, have not changed their overall organizational structures.

> Business organizations are changing, whether they want to or not. The changes are chaotic—the experience from inside or close to a large corporation, as well as the feeling inside your stomach. The pyramids of corporate strength have flattened into a web of organizational ambiguity. Individual employees no longer have a sturdy structure to climb. Instead, planning a career is more like crawling out on a webbing of rope, grasping for stability that comes and goes quickly.[11]
>
> —Robert Johansen and Rob Swigart,
> *Upsizing the Individual in the Downsized Organization*

Very few libraries have actually *reengineered*, which is defined as "the fundamental rethinking and radical redesign of business processes to achieve drastic improvements in performance."[12] But in truth, there are very few business corporations that have reengineered in the real sense of the term. Reengineering requires that managers totally reconsider all the processes involved in meeting an organization's goals and objectives and restructure the organization as if they were beginning it afresh. True re-engineering means completely discarding the old organizational structure and starting all over—it is not for the faint of heart. Instead, most libraries that have reorganized have done so by keeping at least some of the previous structure while making incremental changes in departments and subunits.

> &I have long believed that there is no ideal library organization, and that a finite number of possible permutations exists, each with the potential to be effective in a given situation.[13]
>
> —Joanne R. Euster et al.,
> "Reorganizing for a Changing Information World"

Libraries and information centers are currently organized in a variety of ways, ranging from very flat to traditional hierarchical organizations. Although libraries and information centers may have many different structures, each may be appropriate; having different structures does not necessarily mean that some are right and some aren't. As this chapter will show, there is no optimum way to organize and no consistent prescription for the best type of organizational structure. Although the trend now is toward flatter structures, it is not true that they are always superior to more hierarchical ones. Traditional hierarchies work best in some situations, while flatter structures are more suitable in others. As in so many other areas of management, the best organizational structure depends on the circumstances in a specific case.

Organizational theorists have moved away from a prescriptive approach and now agree that there is no one best answer. They urge the organization to think about what it hopes to accomplish and to adopt the type of organizational structure that allows it to best achieve its goals. The question then becomes, "which organization design performs better in a particular market and location, and which design best enhances the company's core competencies. . . . The executive's operating focus becomes how to create congruency—the fit among all organizational components consistent to the chosen organization design—so that the organization is the most efficient."[14]

> &Organizations are made up of living people and processes, not things. Their survival depends on how they respond to changes in the external environment. Flexibility is essential. Rigid structures do not survive major turbulence.[15]
>
> —Robert Johansen and Rob Swigart,
> *Upsizing the Individual in the Downsized Organization*

In summary, organizing is "a process by which the manager brings order out of chaos, removes conflicts between people over work and responsibility, and establishes an environment suitable for teamwork."[16] In this chapter, the component pieces of the organizing process are examined. Ways in which the organization is broken apart (specialization) as well as the ways in which the organization is brought back together (coordination) will be discussed. Various aspects of organizing, covering the *why*, *how*, and *when*—why organizing is important, how to choose the most appropriate structure, and when reorganization should be considered—are examined. The classic theories of organization are covered in addition to more contemporary views on the topic. Finally, the different types of organizational structures that libraries and other information agencies have adopted are examined.

Getting Started with Organizing

One of the most important aspects of organization is choosing the design of the enterprise, both its structure and the allocation of the jobs. As long as the work to be accomplished in an enterprise can be done by one person, there is little need to organize. But as soon as an enterprise grows so that more than one worker is necessary, decisions must be made about its organization.

As managers move up the hierarchy, and/or as the size of their organization grows, they become more concerned with the issues of organizational design. . . . Managers are concerned with three related goals when they make design decisions. 1) To create an organization design that provides a permanent setting in which managers can influence individuals to do their particular jobs. 2) To achieve a pattern of collaborative effort among individual employees, which is necessary for successful operations. 3) To create an organization that is cost effective.[17]

Because they are usually small, most organizations need little structure when they start up. For example, when Steve Jobs and Steve Wozniak began the Apple Computer Company in a garage in 1976, they probably gave little thought to formal organizational structure. When organizations are small, there is less need for organizational structure because decisions can be made by just a few people and communication can be very informal. But, if an organization is successful and grows larger the need for a formal structure becomes more critical. As Apple Computer expanded, its managers needed to think about how to organize the corporation so it could achieve its goals and objectives. Today, Apple's organization reflects the larger, more complex corporation it has become.

Library and information agencies reflect the same increasing complexity of organization as they grow larger. For example, consider the case of a small, special library in a fast-growing corporation. When the library is first established, one librarian may be sufficient to perform all the tasks associated with operating the library, including acquisitions, cataloging, reference, interlibrary loan, and online searching. But as the parent corporation grows larger and the demand for information supplied by the library increases, more employees are needed. Now decisions must be made about the organization of that library. The expanded library and its new employees could be structured in many ways. The task of the manager is to try to establish the most effective and efficient structure. It is possible that each employee could do a portion of all the tasks that need to be done, with each one spending some time doing acquisition, reference, cataloging, and so forth. More likely, though, the work will be divided in such a way that each employee will specialize, at least to some extent, in one or more of the tasks that have to be performed.

Since the publication of Adam Smith's *The Wealth of Nations* more than 200 years ago, it has been recognized that division of labor leads to greater efficiency. Smith believed that a nation's wealth could be increased if organizations used a high degree of worker specialization. He described one factory in which pins were produced. In this factory, 10 workers produced as many as 48,000 pins a day. The task of making a pin was subdivided into a series of smaller tasks, such as straightening the wire and cutting it. If each worker had been working alone to make the whole pin alone, he could produce only about 20 pins a day.[18] So, specialization usually leads to more efficiency in jobs, but as will be discussed in chapters 4 and 5, too much specialization often results in jobs that are boring and dissatisfying to the employee. Specialization is more often found in larger organizations; in smaller ones, employees often have to perform many types of functions.

In the case of the corporate library described above, it is likely that the library organizer would decide that each employee should specialize to some extent. In that case, the manager would divide the tasks to be performed, and the tasks would be allocated so that one employee would be in charge of acquisitions, two would focus on cataloging, two would work in reference services, one would perform online searches, and so on. Probably, there would also be one employee accountable for the operation of the entire library. One of that person's responsibilities would be to coordinate all the tasks that have to be done to be sure that all processes work together and all objectives are accomplished. That person would be the library director, the manager who makes the ultimate decisions about the structuring of the organization.

The restructuring of this library illustrates two key concepts in organization: specialization and coordination. When more than one person is working toward an objective, each worker must know what part to do to avoid confusion and duplication of effort. No matter how precisely the work is divided, the workers' efforts will not mesh exactly unless some means of coordination is provided. As Henry Mintzberg wrote,

> Every human activity—from the making of pots to the placing of a man on the moon—gives rise to two fundamental and opposing requirements: the *division of labor* into various tasks to be performed and the *coordination* of these tasks to accomplish the activity. The structure of an organization can be defined simply as the sum total of the ways in which it divides its labor into distinct tasks and then achieves coordination among them.[19]

Every organization must decide how it wants to divide its tasks or specialize; this specialization involves breaking the whole organization into parts. Then the organization must decide how to integrate all the specialized parts to create a whole product or service. The latter goal is achieved by coordinating.

What an Organization Is

The development of organizations is inevitable in any complex culture because of the limitations of individuals. When a single person cannot do all the work that needs to be done, there is no choice but to organize and to use more people to accomplish the task. There are many types of organizations, and they vary greatly in size and in purpose. Although they differ in many ways, the local Girl Scout troop, the neighborhood garden club, and IBM are all organizations.

> An organization is a human group, composed of specialists, working together on a common task. Unlike society, community, or family—the traditional social aggregates—an organization is purposefully designed and grounded neither in the psychological nature of human beings nor in biological necessity. Yet, while a human creation, it is meant to endure—not perhaps forever, but for a considerable period of time.[20]
>
> —Peter Drucker,
> *Post-Capitalist Society*

Throughout most of human history, organizations have played a much less important role in people's lives than they do now. For instance, over the past 200 years, the United States has changed from a country where almost all workers were self-employed, either as farmers or independent craftspeople, into one in which almost all workers are employed by organizations. Even as recently as the turn of the century, farmers constituted over one-third of the total U.S. workforce.[21] Today, most people spend their work life as one employee among many working in an organization.

Organizations exist "to make ordinary human beings perform better than they seem capable of, to bring out whatever strength there is in its members, and to use each [member's] strength to help all the other members perform."[22] Organizations are, therefore, groups of individuals joined together to accomplish some objective. Organizations are designed to overcome individual limitations.

But organizations are more than an aggregation of individuals: Organizations have characteristics of their own, over and above the characteristics of the people who make them up. For example, organizations have a distinct structure; they have rules and norms that have developed over time; they have a life cycle that goes beyond the lives of individuals; and they usually have goals, policies, procedures, and practices. They exist in an environment that affects many of these characteristics. They are likely engaged in processing some kind of input and turning it into an output. They interact with other organizations, and they have to change internally to keep up with external pressures.[23]

Organizational Culture

Each organization tends to develop its own organizational, or corporate, culture, as norms of the organization arise and become manifest in employee behavior. In the corporate world, many organizations have very strong cultures. Wal-Mart, for example, has developed a culture based on the belief that its founder Sam Walton's thriftiness, hard work, and dedication to customers is the source of the company's success. IBM has a strong corporate culture that is very different from that at Tandem Computer. Organizations with a strong culture are viewed by outsiders as having a certain style or way of doing things.[24]

Most libraries have their own culture. For instance, in some, the employees dress in a businesslike manner; the men wear coats and ties and the women wear tailored suits and dresses. In others, the employees dress in a much more casual manner. In some libraries, the workers tend to socialize a great deal off the job, while in others there is little interaction outside of work hours. In some libraries, the director is always addressed formally using a title, such as Dr. Brown or Ms. Smith. In other libraries, everyone is on a first-name basis. The ways in which workers dress, social-ize, and interact with one another are just a few examples of organizational culture.

> ❧ The organization itself has an invisible quality—a certain style, a character, a way of doing things—that may be more powerful than the dictates of any one person or any formal system. To understand the soul of the organization requires that we travel below the charts, rule books, machines, and buildings into the underground world of corporate cultures.[25]

> —R. H. Kilmann, "Corporate Culture"

Organizational culture is defined as the "assumptions that a group dis-covers it has as it learns to cope with problems of external adaption and internal integration." *External adaption* refers to how the organization finds a niche in and copes with the external environment. *Internal integra-tion* is concerned with establishing and maintaining effective working rela-tions among members of the organization. In both of these categories, the assumptions that have worked well are taught to new members of the group as the correct way to perceive, think, and feel in relation to those issues.[26] In other words, the culture reflects the values of the organization. The organization's culture is usually created and perpetuated by the organi-zation's top management, which "not only creates the rational and tangible aspects of organizations, such as structure and technology, but also is the creator of symbols, ideologies, language, beliefs, rituals and myths."[27]

One of the first things that newly hired employees learn is "the way things are done here," including information about the organization's his-tory, its cast of characters, and expectations about employee behavior. Often when employees are unhappy in a job it is because there is not a good fit between the organization's culture and what the employee had ex-pected. In many cases, when this mismatch occurs employees resign from their jobs or are asked to leave because they cannot conform to the culture.

Employees are always happier when they can accept the culture of the organization in which they work, and organizations look for this fit when filling positions. They do this because an organization's culture is largely maintained through recruiting employees who fit into the culture. In addition to hiring individuals they think will fit into the culture, man-agers reinforce the organizational culture by (1) what they pay attention to; (2) the way they react to critical incidents and crises; (3) how they allo-cate rewards; (4) the way they carry out role modeling and coaching; (5) what methods they use for selection, promotion, and removal; and (6) their various organizational rites, ceremonies, and stories.[28]

If an organization wishes to change its organizational culture, it has to restructure all of the factors listed above. Obviously, it is not easy to change the culture in an organization because it is usually deeply ingrained in the employees and managers. Organizational culture is often the cause of inflexibility in organizations. Employees are resistant to change because they have "always done it that way." However, some organizations, such as Toyota, have consciously shaped a corporate culture that welcomes change.[29]

Formal and Informal Organizations

Organizations may be classified as formal or informal. A formal organization is legally constituted or decreed by those in authority. This is the organization as it is supposed to function, based on the deliberate assignment of tasks, functions, and authority relationships. The formal organization is the set of official, standardized work relationships. An informal organization, on the other hand, is more loosely organized and flexible. It is often created spontaneously. Informal organizations can exist independent of formal organizations; for instance, four people who gather to play bridge constitute an informal organization. However, many informal organizations are found within the confines of a formal organization. After the formal organization has been established, informal organizations arise naturally within its framework. The unofficial relationships within a work group constitute the informal organization.

Informal organizations are never found on the organization chart, but they often have a profound impact on the formal organization. Classical management principles usually ignored the existence of informal organizations, and many managers still underestimate the importance of these informal ties. For the individual who is employed by an organization, both the formal and informal relationships affect his or her organizational role.

Libraries as Organizations

This chapter focuses on formal organizations. Libraries are one type of formal organization; most libraries are not-for-profit, service organizations, with special organizational characteristics. As Lowell Martin has pointed out, libraries:

- are service agencies, not profit-making firms.

- purvey information, not more tangible services or products.

- perform functions both of supply and guidance, a combination that in the medical field is shared among the doctor's office, the hospital, and the pharmacy.

- provide professional service without, in most cases, having a personal and continuous client relationship.

- for all their general acceptance, are currently marked by ambiguous goals rather than clear-cut objectives.

- during their long history, have accumulated set conceptions of function and method that make for rigid structure and resistance to change.

- respond both to resources and to clientele in a dual and sometimes conflicting orientation, with some staff characterized as resource-minded and others as people-minded.

- function as auxiliaries to larger enterprises, such as universities, schools, and municipalities, and not as independent entities.

- because of their auxiliary role, are subject to external pressures from political bodies, faculties, and users.

- are staffed in the higher echelons by personnel with graduate training, making for a highly educated core staff.

- are administered by professionals who are promoted from the service ranks, not by career managers.

- seek identity and domain within a host of communication and information sources in the community at large and in their parent organization.[30]

Although libraries and information centers are distinct types of organizations, they share many characteristics with other types of organizations. In this chapter, libraries and information centers will be the focus of attention, but the theories and principles discussed are the same used in all other types of organizations.

Organizational Structure

The terms *organization* and *organizational structure* are often used interchangeably, but more precise definitions are available. The organization is the group of individuals joined to achieve an objective. An organizational structure (sometimes called an organizational design) results from the organizing process and is the system of relations, formally prescribed and informally developed, that governs the activities of people who are dependent on each other for accomplishment of common objectives.[31]

Because the structure of organizations is created by people, it should in no way be considered permanent, fixed, or sacred. Traditionally, many managers have been reluctant to alter an organizational structure once it has been established. This may be due to fear of change or failure to recognize that new activities necessitate new or modified organizational structures. It has been said that most of the organizations existing today were created to meet goals and objectives that no longer exist for those organizations. For managers to continue to use an old organizational structure to achieve new goals and objectives results in inefficiency, duplication of endeavor, and confusion. In a period when there is little competition or when changes in the outside environment are occurring slowly, it is possible to get by with an outdated organizational structure, but when competition becomes more intense and the environment more turbulent, an outdated structure will lead to problems.

> ⟪Are you organized for yesterday rather than today? Are you organized for the kind of small, cozy family operation you were, and now you've grown from a four-room boarding house into a six-hundred-room hotel without any change? When the noise level rises, it's a sign of discomfort. Your organization structure and the reality of your operation are not congruent anymore. Then you need a change in your structure.[32]
>
> —Peter F. Drucker,
> *Managing the Non-Profit Organization*

It is not easy to develop an organizational structure that provides for the efficient achievement of planned goals and objectives. And, as organizational structures get larger and involve more people, more complex problems are encountered. The organizational structure must provide for the identification and grouping of similar or related activities necessary for achieving the organization's goals and objectives; it must permit the assignment of these activities to appropriate units of the emerging organization. It must provide for the coordination of activities under a manager and the delegation of authority and responsibility necessary for the manager to carry out the assigned activities.

Specialization: Departmentalization

An organization divides the total tasks to be done (or specializes) in two ways. The first is by establishing horizontal specializations, which result in the creation of various departments, each performing specific tasks. The second is by establishing vertical differentiation, or a hierarchy of positions.

Vertical differentiation involves structuring authority, power, accountability, and responsibility in an organization.

An organization is structured horizontally by identifying and grouping similar or related activities or tasks into subunits or departments. To identify similar or related tasks sounds simple, but it becomes complex when the tasks are examined to determine how they contribute to the organization's goals and objectives. Grouping tasks creates blocks of activity-oriented tasks and people-oriented tasks. How the blocks are placed in relation to one another will indicate the true goals and objectives of the organization.

Blocks of activity tasks, such as cataloging a book or acquiring materials, put primary emphasis on process, procedure, or technique. These tasks can vary from the most routine, requiring little skill, to very complex tasks, requiring extensive ability and knowledge as well as conformity with a process, procedure, or technique. People-oriented tasks, which place primary emphasis on human relationships, require the ability to communicate, to guide or direct, and to motivate other individuals.

Most of the older forms of organizations put primary emphasis on activity-oriented tasks. Since World War II, however, it has been recognized that people-oriented tasks fulfill very important roles in any organization. Examples of routine activity-oriented tasks in a library are shelving books or copy cataloging; complex activity-oriented tasks might include the selection of books in accordance with a book-selection policy or the development of Internet-based user instruction modules. People-oriented tasks might include the relationship of the reference librarian to the library user, the attitude of the supervisor to subordinates, or the ability of the library director to work with officials in government or academic institutions.

Having identified blocks of tasks, the managers designing an organization must place them in a logical order. The manager must answer the questions "What blocks should be put together or kept apart?" and "What is the proper relationship of the blocks?" Some of the blocks will be of primary importance, others will be secondary.

According to Drucker, it is not as important to identify all tasks that are required in an organization as it is to identify the key tasks. He proposes that an organization design start with the following questions: In what area is excellence required to obtain the company's objectives? In what areas would lack of performance endanger the results, if not the survival, of the enterprise? He recommends, in short, that libraries ask what the organization is for and why it exists, and build on that basis.[33] These are questions all organizations, including libraries, need to ask and have answered before organizing.

&Organizations are like elephants—they both learn through conditioning. Trainers shackle young elephants with heavy chains to deeply embedded stakes. In that way the elephant learns to stay in its place. Older elephants never try to leave even though they have the strength to pull the stake and move beyond. . . . Like powerful elephants, many companies are bound by earlier conditioned constraints. "We've always done it this way" is as limiting to any organization progress as the unattached chain around the elephant's foot. Success ties you to the past. The very factors that produced today's success often create tomorrow's failures.[34]

—James A. Belasco,
Teaching the Elephant to Dance

In a similar vein, other management experts urge organizations to ask, "What business are you in?" They point to the plight of the American railroad companies, which almost became extinct because they thought they were in the business of trains, not realizing that they were actually in the transportation business. Most libraries and information centers now realize that they are in the information business, and that they have competitors in the private sector that did not exist before. Libraries and information centers have had to redefine themselves, and this redefinition will eventually require a change in the structure of the organization. Libraries and information centers are in the midst of this redefinition, and some have changed their structures to reflect it.

Parts of an Organization

Organization design can be seen as the putting together of a fairly standardized set of building blocks; it is a process similar to building a house. Although houses may have many types of design, ranging from traditional colonial to modern contemporary, and although their sizes may range from small cottages to large mansions, almost all houses share common characteristics. They will all have a foundation, a roof, certain essential rooms, and ways to provide services such as electricity and water. Organizations are designed in a similar fashion. Although the variety and number of blocks will vary with the size and the type of institution, with pieces that can be put together in different ways, all organizational structures have a great deal in common. Managers who are attempting to organize (or reorganize) are, metaphorically speaking, the architects of the structure—they are shaping the space to meet the needs and aspirations of the organization.[35]

So, most organizations contain the same basic parts. Mintzberg has categorized the five basic elements of organizations as:

- a *strategic apex*, which consists of the organization's top management and is responsible for the overall functioning of the organization.

- the *middle line*, which is composed of the mid-level managers who coordinate the activities of the various units. They serve to link the operating core to the strategic apex.

- the *operating core*, which is made up of the workers who carry out the mission of the organization.

- the *technostructure*, which consists of those units that provide the organization with technical expertise.

- the *support staff*, which is composed of the workers who provide the organization with expertise in areas such as labor relations or personnel.[36]

These components are illustrated in figure 3.1.

Fig. 3.1. Mintzberg's model of the organization is made up of five components. From *Structuring of Organizations: A Synthesis of the Research* by Mintzberg, ©1979. Reprinted by permission of Prentice-Hall, Inc., Upper Saddle River, NJ.

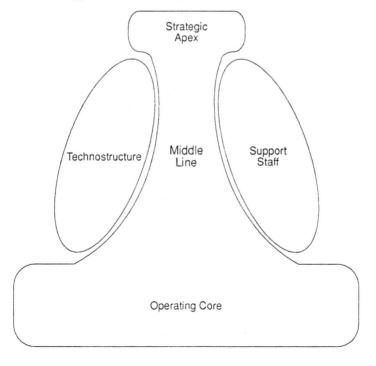

In a large library, the director and the assistant and associate directors form the strategic apex. The heads of the various departments make up the middle line. Employees in units such as library systems and original cataloging comprise the technostructure, while employees in units such as personnel and public relations constitute the support staff. The largest group, the operating core, consists of the employees who work in areas such as circulation and reference. They are the ones carrying out the organization's mission of linking people to information. Although some small organizations do not contain all of Mintzberg's categories, most larger ones do, although the size of each component in relation to the others varies according to factors such as type and complexity of endeavor, age of the organization, and its size.

Methods of Departmentalization

Business and industry have generally used six methods to establish departments: numbers, function, territory, product, customer, and process or equipment. Libraries and other information agencies have used many of the same methods. In addition, libraries have developed two other methods to establish departments: subject and form of resources. In both businesses and libraries, these methods are used in varying combinations to produce a hybrid structure. Each method of departmentalization is discussed below.

Numbers. The concept of establishing departments by number is used primarily in the military, where a designated number of troops make up a squad, a platoon, or a regiment. Only in a few situations do libraries use this as a basis for organization—for example, a library might organize by number when moving from one location to another. A designated number of individuals would be assigned to the moving process according to the method of moving, the distance, the items to be moved, and the timetable for completing the move. This is usually a temporary organizational structure for a library.

Function. In business, the most common organizational design is the functional structure. In libraries, too, this method is extensively used. The functions of circulation, reference, acquisition, cataloging, and management, to name but a few, historically have been the basis of library organization. The grouping of necessary library activities has resulted in these functional categories.

In some of the organizational patterns that have emerged in the last 50 years, a number of these functions have been combined in one department with subdepartments performing related functions. A good example is the emergence of the major functional department of technical services, which includes many units that once were autonomous functional departments.

Order or acquisitions departments, catalog departments, serials departments, binding departments, and book processing departments, previously
autonomous, are now combined because their activities are related to the
organization's end goal of acquiring and organizing library resources.

Functional design has a number of advantages. It groups specialists
with similar backgrounds and interests. It also ensures that higher organizational levels will be aware of the contributions and the needs of the various
subunits of the organization. There are three disadvantages of functional
division. First, it may lead to competition between various departments,
for example, competition for resources or disagreements over the most
appropriate procedures. In some libraries, the reference and cataloging departments may disagree about the best classification or subject headings
for a particular book. Second, workers in functional settings may lose sight
of the end product of the whole organization, especially when workers are
distanced from the ultimate users of the product. Finally, this organizational design is not so effective if the organization has units in different locations. The functional design appears to work best in organizations that
do not need close collaboration among the functional departments.

Territory. In industries that operate over a wide geographic area, all
activities in a designated geographic territory are commonly grouped together and placed under the direction of a manager. This structure permits
the industries to adapt to local situations as far as the local labor market,
local needs and problems, and local production problems are concerned.
Libraries also use this principle of territory or area in their organizational
structure. For instance, public libraries have always been very concerned
about the location of their central facility and the areas to be served by
their branch libraries, bookmobiles, and storefront libraries. Academic libraries that have branches—such as a science library, architecture library,
or education library—are concerned that these facilities be in the area
where the appropriate clientele will be located.

The primary advantage of this type of organization for libraries is
that the individual units can be located close to their users, can get to
know their needs better, and, it is hoped, can serve them better. Territorial
organization also provides a training ground for managers, because it gives
a manager a chance to work relatively autonomously as the manager of a
smaller unit that is geographically separated from the central organization.
It is not uncommon for a librarian who has been the head of a branch library to be promoted to the head of the library system.

The biggest disadvantage of territorial organization is that it increases
the difficulty of coordination and communication within the organization. In
addition, rivalries often crop up between the different locations. Many large
public libraries hard hit by funding cuts have had to make difficult decisions
about whether it is better to maintain the quality of the central collection

or to maintain service to various neighborhoods through the branches. Finally, territorial organization usually leads to duplication, for example, in resources like standard reference books.

One of the unanswered questions pertaining to library organizational structure is the degree of geographic centralization that should prevail. Typically, library administrators favor a more centralized organization because of the tight control and budgetary advantages associated with that design. On the other hand, users typically prefer a more decentralized system because of its convenience and more personalized service (in spite of the special problems of users working in interdisciplinary areas). Some of the arguments against decentralization have been weakened by the increasing importance of information technology and the advent of new methods of document storage and retrieval that lessen some of the costs involved in duplication of material in decentralized locations. A library that uses an online catalog and online reference and bibliographical services would find it less expensive to maintain a decentralized collection than a library that uses print materials exclusively.

Product. Large industries use this method of organization because it allows for specialization. Organization by product is particularly useful in diversified industries in which production of one product is sufficiently large to employ fully specialized facilities. In such cases, departmentalization by product allows a product manager complete control over all functions related to that product, including profit responsibility. For instance, the operating divisions of one of the world's largest corporations, General Motors, are organized along product lines.

This form of organization is used infrequently in libraries. Although the product of a print shop (a printed bibliography or brochure), or a product of the systems office (such as the library's Web site) might be considered a product, in almost every case, this product is a minor part of the total operation of the library.

Customer. Businesses, especially retail stores, use this structure to appeal to the needs and desires of clearly defined customer groups. So do libraries. Since the late 1800s, special children's sections have been one of the most used sections in public libraries. Public libraries also have aimed their services at other customer groups, such as young adults or business users. Academic libraries have used this structure in establishing undergraduate libraries.

The advantage of this type of departmentalization is that it allows libraries and information centers to meet the special and widely varying needs of users. The disadvantages are similar to those involved in territorial departmentalization. Coordination among departments is difficult, and competition among various departments, especially for resources, may arise. In addition, when budgets get tight, services to special groups may be eliminated.

Some organizations have decided that service to some customers may best be handled in a more general manner. For example, many public libraries have eliminated their young adult departments. In some large universities, an undergraduate library was first established and then later eliminated because it was felt that undergraduates could be better served by the main library.

Process or Equipment. Industry uses this structure when large installations are required, for example, a smelting plant or a steel mill. Libraries have used this method, on a much smaller scale, when dealing with equipment. Libraries that operate a book bindery centralize all the specialized, heavy binding equipment in one place. Also, this method has been used for centralizing smaller equipment, such as printing equipment, microform readers, phonograph players, and VCRs. There is a trend in school media centers and some public libraries to distribute this type of equipment throughout the library and to disregard this method of organization.

In a recent article, Sweeney criticizes the traditional functional departmentalization of libraries and suggests that they need to focus on process, not function.

> Reengineering a library requires major changes in library work processes. Most libraries are hierarchy and department oriented, not process oriented. Libraries are structured with many departments such as cataloging, circulation and reference. The notion of work processes is not typically taught in library and information science schools nor is it prevalent in practice.[37]

Sweeney suggests that functional departmentalization leads to fragmentation and low customer satisfaction because no one department owns the entire process. Instead, he advocates that libraries should be organized to increase customer satisfaction. In his opinion, customers would be better satisfied if libraries were organized around processes—a collection of activities that takes one or more kinds of input and creates an output that is of value to a customer.[38] Team and matrix organization, discussed later in this chapter, do provide more attention to process, but to date, process is not a widely used method of departmentalization.

Subject. Large public and academic libraries use this method extensively. It provides for more in-depth reference service and reader guidance, and it requires a high degree of subject knowledge on the part of the staff. There is no pattern of subjects included in a subject department and no set number of subject departments. In academic libraries, subject departments are usually broad in scope and include all related subjects in areas like humanities, social sciences, or science. In large public libraries, subject departments such as business, fine arts, and local history are common.

There are definite advantages of subject departments. All materials dealing with one topic are gathered together, which is convenient for users. The librarians working with this material usually have special training in the subject matter. The disadvantages include the increased cost of the necessary duplication of material and the hiring of specialized personnel. Each department must be staffed, even when usage is low. One reference librarian might be sufficient to handle all reference inquiries at a central desk when demand is low; but if there are four subject-area reference desks, four reference librarians are required, even if there are few inquiries. In addition, as has been frequently pointed out, although subject divisions are convenient for users working strictly within a subject field, users who are pursuing interdisciplinary topics spread across subject lines must go to many subject departments to find the materials they need.

Form of Resources. Many libraries have used format, or the form in which resources are issued, as a basis for organization, especially as the quantity of nonbook and nonprint material has increased. It is not unusual to find separate map, microform, audiovisual, periodicals, online services, electronic resources, and documents departments in a library. Many of these specialized forms present special problems in acquisition, storage, handling, or organization. Often, librarians working in format-based departments handle all functions relating to the department's resources, including functions that are normally performed centrally. For instance, a government documents department may order, process, provide reference service, and circulate all government documents. Format-based departments are most useful for patrons seeking one type of resource, for instance, audiovisual materials. More commonly, however, users seek information on specific topics, and they may easily miss relevant materials that are housed in various format-based departments.

Summary. Only in the most specialized library would a single organizational method be used. A large public library, for example, generally has a circulation department (function), subject department (combining several functions), branch libraries (territory), children's services (customer), business services (customer), a print shop (equipment), document collections (form), and several others.

There is no one right way to establish departments in an organization. There are advantages and disadvantages associated with each method; a manager interested in organization should be aware of both the strengths and the disadvantages. Also, as stated previously, no organizational structure, no matter how good, is intended to last forever. Institutions change, and the organizational structure must change to reflect new situations. Managers need to look first at the tasks that need to be accomplished, the people involved in accomplishing them, the users being served, and the pertinent external and environmental factors, and then design a suitable departmental organization. Often, employees feel threatened by any change in organizational structure; managers should communicate the reasons for changes and provide reassurance to employees who need it.

> ℚ People are anxious about organizational structure because it defines their position, and in fact, has a large impact on their power and privileges. The issue thus becomes highly political, with each person typically supporting the structure that most benefits him or her. . . . The stakes in structuring decisions have been particularly high in the past because restructuring was relatively infrequent. People feared they would be placed in a permanent, or close to permanent position. Lately, as companies more frequently restructure in response to more rapid environmental and strategic change, the stakes seem lower, the battles less intense, and companies somewhat more supple organizationally.[39]
>
> —Benson P. Shapiro, "Functional Integration"

Departmental Patterns of the Future

For several decades writers have speculated about the type of libraries and information centers that will exist in the future. Most of these writers have expected increased decentralization. More than fifteen years ago, Hugh Atkinson predicted that the academic library of the future would be decentralized.[40] He felt the "ideal library is one with one or two librarians, one or two library clerks, a handful of student assistants, a homogeneous identifiable clientele, and a collection large enough to suit that clientele."[41] In his view, the emergence of an increasing number of smaller, decentralized units would require a different administrative structure, with the central administrator serving as a coordinator rather than a supervisor; this setting would demand an extraordinarily talented administrative staff to avoid conflict.

About the same time, Charles Martell proposed restructuring the library into small, client-centered work groups, with librarians operating at all points where the library interacts with its user groups. Each member of the work groups would perform a number of library functions: advanced reference, development of the collection, client instruction, original cataloging, and other forms of information service.[42] The client-centered organizations provide an opportunity for teamwork, greater work variety, and the promise of an improvement in the quality of service.[43]

These early advocates of decentralization were thinking in terms of the decentralization of the library as a physical entity. Today, we have moved away from thinking of libraries just as places and realize that libraries of the future will contain elements of "bricks, books, and bytes."[44] Much has been written about the virtual library and the library without walls. This type of library would not be a physical entity, and the storage function traditionally performed by libraries would be eliminated because all information would be available via computer technology.

It is unlikely that material in paper form will disappear any time in the near future. Libraries as physical places will continue to exist, but they will likely be vastly different from those of today. For instance, academic libraries could have small branch libraries containing just a few books and journals scattered throughout the campus; these branch libraries would provide most access to information electronically. Students and faculty would also have access to electronic resources from their dormitory rooms, offices, or homes. Public libraries could be much more decentralized with small branches or kiosks in government offices, businesses, shopping malls, or other locations. With computer technology, the branches would not have to own a large number of materials, but the librarian could have needed material available via a computer workstation and could respond to users' needs upon request. Public library patrons who own computers would have access to materials from their homes.

New technologies will doubtless have a major impact on the departmental patterns of all types of libraries and information centers, but at this point, one can only speculate about what their effects will be. It seems likely, however, that automation will permit libraries and information centers of the future to be more decentralized and thus provide their users with the geographically dispersed, individualized service they have always preferred. It also seems likely that efforts to introduce more flexibility into libraries and information centers, including the use of cross-functional teams, will lead to libraries and information centers where the barriers between departments are much less fixed. There will likely be more frequent changes in library structure, and workers will become more used to working in organizations that are periodically reshaped to fit new needs. In the libraries and information centers of the future, it will be even more important for managers to closely observe the organizational structure of the library to see whether it still is adequate to achieve its goals and objectives.

Specialization: The Hierarchy

Within the structure of an organization, specialization exists in two dimensions. We have just discussed the specialization found on the horizontal axis—the grouping of tasks in departments and subunits. The vertical axis contains a different type of specialization—the structuring of authority (see fig. 3.2). In organizations, authority is the degree of discretion conferred on subordinates that makes it possible for them to use their judgment in making decisions and issuing instructions. A manager is assigned to each department or subunit within an organization. Each manager has a measure of responsibility and authority, delegated by his or her superior. The need for such delegation is obvious; if managers are responsible for the accomplishment of designated tasks and the supervision of employees, they must have the authority to guarantee efficient performance. The vertical hierarchy provides a channel through which authority flows from top management down to the managers of subunits. It also provides a means to coordinate the efforts of many individuals performing a variety of tasks. The concept of a vertical hierarchy is central to the classic theories of organizing. Now that so many organization are using teams, encouraging horizontal communication, and instituting multiple reporting patterns, the vertical hierarchy may be less critical than it used to be. Nonetheless, it is important to understand this concept even if many organizations are de-emphasizing its importance.

Fig. 3.2. Vertical and horizontal specialization within libraries.

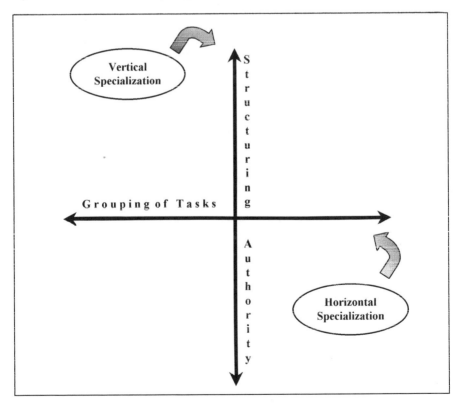

The Scalar Principle

As departments and subdepartments are assigned various tasks, primary and secondary units of the organization emerge. Primary organizational departments have numerous tasks and broad responsibilities; secondary or subdepartments have specific tasks and limited responsibility. For example, a copy catalog unit would be a subdepartment of a cataloging department. A subdepartment's tasks contribute to the fulfillment of the responsibilities of the primary department. The manager of the primary department supervises the manager of the subdepartment to assure compliance with the needs of the primary department. Authority flows from the primary to the secondary manager.

The scalar principle requires that there be final, ultimate authority and that lines of authority descend to every subordinate position. The clearer the line of authority, the more effective the organizational performance and communication. Henri Fayol described the scalar principle as

> the chain of supervisors ranging from the ultimate authority to the lowest ranks. The line of authority is the route followed—via every link in the chain—by all communications which start from or go to the ultimate authority. This path is dictated both by the need for some transmission and by the principle of unity of command, but it is not always the swiftest. It is even at times disastrously lengthy in large concerns, notably in governmental ones.[45]

A clear understanding of the scalar principle by each subordinate is necessary for an organization to function effectively. Subordinates must know to whom and for what they are responsible, and the parameters of each manager's authority are clear.

The vertical hierarchy develops as a result of the ranking of organizational units. A scalar hierarchy may be illustrated as a pyramid, with the ultimate authority at the apex and authority fanning out as it flows down. The positions at the top of the pyramid deal with broader tasks and responsibilities, those at the bottom with more specific tasks and responsibilities (see fig. 3.3). While the vertical hierarchy may remain stable over a period of time, tasks and responsibilities may shift as managers and supervisors delegate.

Delegation is the transfer of authority within closely prescribed limits. In an effective organization, the position holding ultimate authority delegates authority to subordinate managers. The delegation of authority to subordinates does not relieve the ultimate authority of responsibility; a manager is responsible for the actions of subordinates, even if authority has been delegated. A manager can delegate to subordinates almost anything for which that manager has responsibility. Of course, managers cannot delegate all authority without abdicating the managerial role. This is rarely a problem, however. Most managers delegate too little; some clutch tenaciously at authority and dislike delegating anything.

Fig. 3.3. The flow of authority within a traditional organization.

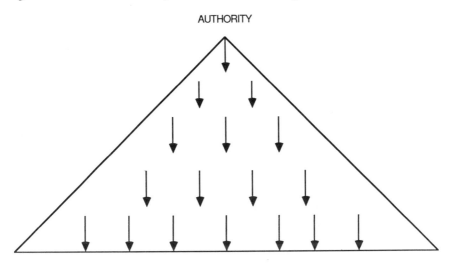

AUTHORITY

The process of delegation involves determining the expected results, assigning tasks, delegating authority for accomplishing the tasks, and holding people responsible for the accomplishment of tasks. The delegation process should never be practiced only in part, but it often is. Too often managers give subordinates the responsibility to perform designated activities, but withhold the authority to accomplish them. Many managers find it difficult to delegate adequate authority, because they fear that a subordinate might make a mistake or perform poorly. In addition, some managers feel that they are not doing their jobs unless they make all of the decisions, even the smaller ones that subordinates could easily make. These managers spend a disproportionate amount of time on minor decisions, not realizing that, by doing so, they are taking time and attention away from the more important decisions that only they can make.

> ⚸ Delegation without authority is empty. Before delegating think carefully whether you are willing to permit work to be done without your direct oversight or review. Too much review, especially of professionals, breeds apathy, dependency, and passive resistance, and destroys motivation.[46]

> —Allen B. Veaner,
> *Academic Librarianship in a Transformational Age*

Effective managers have learned to delegate. They are willing to let go of some of their authority and trust their subordinates. They know that subordinates sometimes make mistakes, and they are willing to take the risk because they realize that delegation is necessary in any organization. In addition, effective managers always remember that responsibility cannot be delegated without authority. A subordinate given responsibility without authority probably will be unable to function efficiently.

In describing the departmentalization process in organizations, the issues of centralization and decentralization were discussed. These same issues, although in a different form, are also relevant to a discussion of hierarchy. In the context of the vertical hierarchy of an organization, centralization and decentralization do not refer to geographic dispersal but to the dispersal of authority for decision making. In highly centralized organizations, authority is concentrated in the highest echelons of the hierarchy; almost all decisions are made by those at the top. In the traditional organization, the authority was highly centralized in the hands of top managers. These types of organizations have been termed *command and control* organizations because they were structured to centralize both the command and control of the organization in the ranks of top management. It was assumed that whoever was in command would also tightly control the organization.

In contrast, in decentralized organizations the authority to make decisions is pushed down in the organizational structure. As institutions become larger and more complex, there is a tendency toward decentralization. Centralization and decentralization can best be envisioned as two ends of a continuum. Organizations marked by a high degree of retention of power, duties, and authority by top management are centralized; those marked by a high degree of delegation of duties, power, and authority at lower levels of the organization are decentralized.[47] Decentralized organizations are often described as "participative," because they allow for greater employee participation in decision making (see chapter 5). Most organizations lie between the two extremes of the continuum.

Both centralization and decentralization offer advantages.[48] The major advantage of centralization is that it offers the tightest means of coordinating decision making in the organization. Managers have a great deal of control over the decisions that are made because only a small number of managers are permitted to make them.

As mentioned earlier, many of today's organizations are moving away from a command and control configuration toward a more decentralized structure. The advantages of decentralization are several. First, the decisions to be made in many organizations are so numerous that if they are centralized the manager may be overwhelmed by the amount of decision making that needs to be done.

Mintzberg warns against centralization of decision making. He has written that

> Perhaps the most common error committed in organizational design has been the centralization of decision making in the face of cognitive limitation. The top managers, empowered to design the structure, see errors committed below and believe that they can do better, either because they believe themselves smarter or because they believe they can more easily coordinate decisions. Unfortunately, in complex conditions, this inevitably leads to a state known as "information overload": the more information the brain tries to receive, the less the total amount that actually gets through.[49]

These managers become overwhelmed by too much information and too many decisions to be made, and the organization becomes paralyzed by their inaction.

> Almost everyone agrees that the command-and-control corporate model will not carry us into the twenty-first century. In a world of increasing interdependence and rapid change, it is no longer possible to figure it out from the top. Nor, as today's CEOs keep discovering, is it possible to *command* people to make the profound systemic changes needed. . . . Increasingly, successful organizations are building competitive advantage through less controlling and more learning—that is, continually creating and sharing new knowledge.[50]
>
> —Peter M. Senge,
> "Communities of Leaders and Learners"

A second advantage of decentralization is that it allows organizations to respond quickly to local conditions. Because the transmission of information for decision making takes time, a decentralized organization is able to make more timely decisions.

A final advantage of decentralization is that it serves as a stimulus to motivation. An organization that wishes to attract and retain creative and intelligent people is better able to do so when it permits them considerable power to make decisions.

The idea of decentralization is contrary to the classical concept of hierarchy, which centralizes all authority in the primary administrator. However, some degree of decentralization is practiced by almost all modern organizations.

Most large organizations have cut back the number of middle managers, resulting in a flatter, more decentralized structure. Some have actually slashed these intermediate layers of management. In 1993, the Center for the Study of American Business (CSAB) surveyed 132 manufacturing executives from a variety of large manufacturing firms. More than 50 percent reported significant structural change over the past five years, and most of these changes involved reshaping the organization to cut down the number of layers and eliminate middle managers. As one respondent to the survey stated, "I think we have seen substantial changes in structure. Phalanxes of middle management have been removed."[51] The managers reported that this restructuring was done for two reasons: (1) to cut costs, and (2) to improve and decentralize decision making by pushing it down the hierarchy.

Much of the flattening of structures has been permitted by the introduction of information technology. Technology has the potential to increase top-down control and to demotivate and deskill jobs, but if it is used to provide employees with information needed for decisions, it can empower employees. Information technology, telecommunications combined with databases and computational programs, makes more reliable information available much more quickly than it ever was before to both top managers and those who work at lower layers in an organization.[52] Hierarchies were an effective method of coordinating interdependent behavior of many people by creating fewer interfaces, but "now thousands can communicate quickly through computer conferencing. . . . 'Groupware' and 'organizationware' can aid in the formation of consensus for action."[53] The new information technologies are making it possible for new forms of organizations to develop.

Now top managers can receive up-to-the minute information on operations via their computers—information that was once collected and interpreted by middle managers. For this reason some experts have argued that information technology may lead to greater centralization. In their view, middle managers, who in the past often served primarily as information collectors and routine decision makers, are being replaced by information technology systems.

> ◊ The computer is smashing the pyramid. The technology of the computer is doing the kinds of jobs that middle managers used to do. Cuts in middle management have ranged from a low of 10 percent to a high of 40 percent. Corporations are experimenting with new structures to replace the structures that used to house middle management.[54]
>
> —John Naisbitt and Patricia Aburdene,
> *Re-inventing the Corporation*

This viewpoint is disputed by other experts, who feel that management information systems by their very nature will be insufficient to provide top managers with the kind of information they need for decision making.[55] Perhaps these systems would be inadequate if the managers attempted to centralize all decision making, but with the move toward decentralization of decision making, information technology is a tool that can be used to share information both up and down the organizational ladder. In organizations such as libraries and information centers, where there are a number of highly educated and skilled workers, it is likely that technology will play a key role in permitting further decentralization of decision making.

Unity of Command

A classical management principle that provides clarity in the vertical hierarchy is that of unity of command. The organizational structure should guarantee that each employee has one supervisor who makes assignments and assesses the success of the employee in completing those assignments. However, in many organizations employees have several supervisors. In libraries, this is often true of the clerical staff and shelvers; in many large libraries, subject bibliographers are responsible to both the head of reference and the head of technical services. An employee with more than one supervisor is placed in the awkward position of determining whose work to do first, how to do the work, and which instructions to follow. Unity of command protects the employee from such undesirable situations. As modern organizations have become more complex, theorists have realized that employees are often subject to multiple influences. When faced with conflicting pressures, the employee should have a single supervisor who can resolve the conflict. In addition, job descriptions should clearly spell out the worker's duties and the amount of time to be spent on each.

Span of Control

Just as employees should not be accountable to too many supervisors, managers should not be responsible for too many employees. Span of control (sometimes called span of management) refers to the number of people or activities a manager can effectively manage. When a manager supervises a large number of employees, that manager is said to have a *wide* span of control, whereas one who supervises a small number is said to have a *narrow* span of control. When the number of subordinates exceeds the span of control of a single manager, something must be done to reduce their number. Managers usually solve the problem by grouping some of the jobs together and placing an individual in charge of each of the groups. The manager then deals primarily with the individuals in charge of the groups rather than with all of the subordinates. Obviously, span of control is closely related to how many levels exist in an organization's hierarchy. When there is a broad span of control, there are fewer managers, and the organization tends to be flatter.

> ⚗ The prime benefits of flat organizations are what we call their "self-defense" properties. That is, *none* of us is smart enough to keep our hands out of our subordinates' business. But if the span is wide (at least twice as wide as you think wise is a good rule of thumb), then you simply don't have enough hours to interfere, though most of us try desperately to do so at first. Flat structure, in a word, automatically breeds ownership, whether you like it or not.[56]
>
> —Tom Peters and Nancy Austin,
> *A Passion for Excellence*

There is no set number of subordinates that constitutes the ideal span of control, although some management experts have proposed a maximum number.[57] Recent research shows that the size of an effective span of control varies widely, depending on the type of organization and the type of activity being supervised. Managers have moved away from trying to specify the "ideal" span of control to considering which is most appropriate to a specific situation.

One of the criteria used to determine the number of people a manager can adequately manage is the number and variety of tasks being managed. If the activities of the units assigned to one manager are similar, the span of control can be increased. If the activities vary extensively and require thorough knowledge, the span of control should be decreased. One must consider what knowledge the manager must have to do an adequate job; the broader and more detailed the required knowledge, the fewer units should be assigned.

Another criterion used to determine span of control is the amount of time available to be spent in communication. Time is a critical element in many enterprises. A manager who has several subordinates must reduce the time spent supervising each. Thus, it will be necessary for the manager with a large number of subordinates to spend more time in the initial training of a new supervisor, to give assignments in broad terms of goals or objectives to be achieved, and to delegate authority so that the supervisors may manage their personnel. If the span of control is wide and the manager fails to function as described, time will be consumed by frequent conferences, daily meetings, and repetitive instruction.

In institutions that are encountering rapid rates of change, the span of control must be narrow. There would not be time to react to rapid changes if a manager had a large number of subordinates. For example, during World War II, when General Dwight D. Eisenhower was supreme commander of the Allied Expeditionary Forces, he had a narrow span of control—only three immediate line subordinates. More routine situations allow a wider span of control.

When many organizational units report to one manager, a flat or horizontal organization is created, and a wide span of control prevails. There are few levels of operation in a flat organization. Figure 3.5 shows only two levels of operation—the director and the manager of each unit to which specific activities have been assigned. But the scope of knowledge required of the director is extensive indeed. When a manager has many subordinates, supervision of each unit is likely to be minimal. In organizations with narrow spans of management, a tall, vertical organization is created. Figure 3.4 shows a vertical organization with four levels of operation. Each supervisor's span of control is narrow—in this organization the director has direct supervision only over 2 people—a great reduction from the 12 positions shown in figure 3.5.

Fig. 3.4. A vertical organization chart (figures in parentheses indicate level according to authority lines).

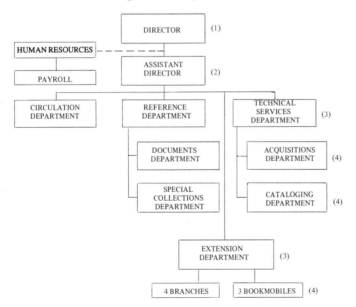

Fig. 3.5. A flat organization chart.

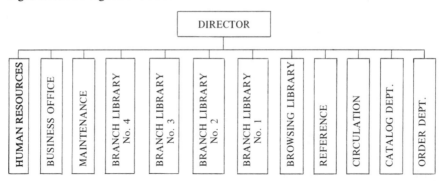

As would be expected, both narrow and wide spans of control have advantages and disadvantages. A narrow span of control offers tight control and close supervision; frees managers to think of future matters, because they are not burdened with an excessive number of present problems; and provides managers of lower quality the chance to perform effectively because they manage fewer and more highly specialized people and activities. If one contrasts the amount of time the director with the narrow span of control (see fig. 3.4) spends in supervising with the director with the wide span of control (see fig. 3.5), one can see how there should be more time available for planning and thinking about the "big picture." However, a narrow span of control requires a larger number of managers, which can be costly, and adds complexity to the organization's communication and coordination processes. On the other hand, a wide span of control, in which the manager is unable to exercise close supervision, may promote maturity of subordinates by allowing them to make more decisions on their own. In addition, a wide span of control requires fewer managers; this reduces costs and simplifies communication and coordination. The disadvantages of a wide span of control are that managers are unable to exercise tight control and supervision, and, in general, higher-quality and more costly employees are needed, because they have large jobs and must act independently.

> ☙By now you may be asking, what is the right number of levels of management for an organization? How many individuals should report to a single manager? Unfortunately, there are no simple answers to these questions. . . . I have seen some managers work effectively with a hundred individuals reporting to them, and I have seen others for whom twenty is too many. The correct number has a great deal to do with a manager's skills, the complexity of the work, and the organization's ability to develop self-managing teams.[58]
>
> —Edward E. Lawler III,
> *From the Ground Up*

As discussed before, a number of organizations have become flattened by eliminating entire layers—especially middle management layers—both because they believe that a flatter organization enables people to make better decisions by putting decision making closer to the actual problems and because a structure with fewer middle managers is less costly to run. Many American firms have cut layers in response to the greater profitability of their foreign competitors who utilize a flatter corporate structure. For instance, General Motors has had as many as 22 layers between its top executive and the lowest workers, Ford has had seventeen, while Toyota has had only seven.[59] The past decade has seen a general interest by GM, Ford, and other companies in flattening structures and removing layers.

This movement reverses the pattern of the recent past when organizations have tended to add layers of management to provide tighter control. For instance, over the last 50 years, many libraries introduced a new layer of administration to avoid a too-wide span of control. As recently as the 1940s, almost all libraries, regardless of size, were organized along departmental lines. Work was apportioned among various departments—circulation, reference, and cataloging, for example—and all department heads reported to the library director. As libraries grew, the number of departments grew also, until the span of control was so wide that either the administration began to break down or the library director became so involved in operational duties that no time was left for broader responsibilities, such as planning or cultivating institutional relationships. Large libraries tried various ways of reorganizing, but by the early 1950s, most adopted a bifurcated organizational structure based on a division of library functions into technical services and readers' services. An assistant or associate library director in charge of each area reported to the director. In that way, the director's span of control was decreased. Although this bifurcated pattern of organizations remains in place in many large libraries, it is being replaced in some by more decentralized structures where the director's span of control is wider.

> Along with bigness comes complexity, unfortunately. And most big companies respond to complexity in kind, by designing complex systems and structures. They then hire more staff to keep track of all this complexity and that's where the mistake begins. The solution doesn't go well with the nature of people in an organization, in which things need to be kept reasonably simple if the unit is truly to pull together.[60]
>
> —Thomas J. Peters and Robert H. Waterman Jr.,
> *In Search of Excellence*

The concept of span of control is important. It demonstrates that there is a limit to the number of persons an individual can effectively manage. The optimal width of the span of control depends on a number of circumstances, including the variety of activities assigned, the rate of change, and the amount of time a manager must give each subordinate.

Line and Staff Positions

An important but sometimes confusing authority relationship in any organization is that of *line* and *staff* positions. The concept of line and staff has been used for a good many years, but it still causes friction and difficulty. Line positions are responsible and accountable for the organization's primary objectives. Staff positions provide advice, support, and service to the line positions. Line and staff are also distinguished by their decision-making authority. Because line positions are responsible for accomplishing the organization's primary objectives, they have final authority to make decisions. Staff positions, on the other hand, provide suggestions and advice for the line positions but cannot, theoretically, make decisions for the line positions. As the old saying goes, "Line tells; staff sells." The staff must convince the line managers to adopt their suggestions. By maintaining final decision-making authority in the line positions, an organization seeks to keep authority for decision making in the positions accountable for results and to preserve a clear chain of command from the top to the bottom of the organization.

As libraries have grown in size and complexity, they have relied more heavily on staff positions to provide support, advice, and information. Many libraries now have a number of staff positions dealing with public relations, systems, personnel, planning, fund-raising, and budgeting. These staff positions are held by individuals skilled in specific functions who provide the facts and information needed by the decision makers. A library human resources office, for example, may be responsible for receiving applications, interviewing applicants, maintaining personnel files, and recommending promotion or transfer. But, generally, the human resources director does not have the authority to make human resources decisions. For instance, the human resources department facilitates the search for a new department head, but the actual decision about whom to hire is made by someone else—most likely by the library director. Only individuals in the line position—the authority position—make these kinds of decisions. Although the head of the human resources department serves in a staff position for the entire library, he or she would at the same time have a line position within the human resources department and make decisions relating to its operation.

&Finally, the best GMs [general managers] use staff people well and expect them to make positive contributions, not to nitpick or "*gotcha*." They appoint strong functional leaders (not line-manager rejects, politicians, or tired old pros) who can provide innovative, idea-driven leadership (not just ask good questions) and can transfer ideas across the organization. As a result, line managers respect and use the staff instead of writing unfriendly memos or playing unproductive political games.[61]

—Andrall E. Pearson,
"Six Basics for General Managers"

Conflicts often develop between line and staff personnel, usually where there are unclear notions of duties and authority. If staff employees do not understand their role in the organization, they will be frustrated and confused. On the other hand, if line managers continually disregard the advice of the staff, fearing that staff members may undermine the line manager's position and authority, the staff will be underutilized and its expertise wasted. Managers to whom staff employees report should be sure that authority relationships are understood and should encourage line personnel to listen to staff and keep them fully informed so that staff positions can play their intended role of offering support and advice.

Coordination and Integration

Division of work, or specialization, is one important task in setting up an organization, but it is equally important to make provisions for coordination. As mentioned earlier, every organization must specialize by dividing the tasks to be done and also must coordinate or integrate these activi- ties, bringing together all the individual job efforts to achieve a particular objective.

It is sometimes hard for a manager to strike the right balance between too much and too little coordination between departments. If there is too little, each department will focus inward on its own responsibilities. There will be too little attention given to the organization's overall objectives and likely there will be both duplications and omissions in what is done because of the lack of the overall "big picture" view. At the same time, too much coordinating can lead to departments getting in each other's way and little getting accomplished. Sometimes in libraries you hear the complaint that librarians spend all their time in committee meetings and hence do not have time to do their "real" work. While this is almost always an exaggeration, it is true that in all types of organizations a great deal of time is consumed by committees and meetings. These are good methods of achieving coordination and integration among units, but if allowed to proliferate uncontrolled they can take far too much time away from the real work of the organization. So managers need to strive to maintain a balance between specialization and coordination.

Coordinating Mechanisms

There are a number of ways that coordination can be achieved. The vertical hierarchy is the chief means of providing coordination and integration, because the power and accountability associated with the hierarchy help ensure that all parts of the organization work compatibly with one another. The planning techniques discussed in chapter 2 provide another means of coordinating. Policies, procedures, and rules provide guidance for members of the organization. When organizational members follow agreed-upon guidelines, they are more likely to perform in a manner that is consistent with overall goals. In similar fashion, the organizational manual serves as a coordinating mechanism by specifying the activities that are to be conducted in each unit. The functional statements in the manual are designed to ensure that all work is covered and that the separation of the overall duties and functions provides the mix necessary to achieve organizational objectives. Committees provide another means of coordination among specialized units because they often draw members from various parts of the organization and because they encourage communication and participation in decision making. Staff positions, because they provide assistance and advice to managers throughout an organization, also promote coordination.

Michael McCaskey points out that the more highly differentiated or specialized an organization, the more difficult it is to coordinate.

> The manager/designer must resist differentiating the organization radically—the greater the differences between the units, the harder it is for them to coordinate activities with each other. . . . [W]hen an organization is highly differentiated people have to spend more effort translating and appreciating the framework of people in different units. Most people think in their own terms and it takes an increased effort to move into another's frame of reference. The chances for misunderstandings increase in a highly differentiated organization.[62]

To encourage ease of coordination, the structure should be kept as simple as possible. Structures that are too complex and have too many reporting patterns do not make the priorities clear and, for that reason, cause the organization to lose focus on what it is really trying to accomplish.[63]

 The simplest organizational structure that will do the job is the best one. What makes an organizational structure "good" are the problems it does not create. The simpler the structure, the less that can go wrong.[64]

—Peter F. Drucker,
Management: Tasks, Responsibilities, Practices

Peters and Waterman found that successful companies usually maintain a basic simplicity of form. In their words, "making an organization work has everything to do with keeping things understandable for the tens or hundreds of thousands who must make things happen. And that means keeping things simple."[65] Simplicity in form aids in coordination.

Mintzberg provides another viewpoint on coordination. He identifies five mechanisms that explain the fundamental ways organizations coordinate their work. These five mechanisms—mutual adjustment, direct supervision, and standardization of work processes, outputs, and skills—provide the means to hold the organization together.

Mutual adjustment means informal communication. Because it is such a simple mechanism, mutual adjustment is the coordinating mechanism used in the simplest of organizations, for example, in a small library with a limited number of employees. Where there are just a few workers there is no need for elaborate hierarchy, and direct communication among all workers is unimpeded. Hence, informal communication permits the coordination of activities without use of a more elaborate mechanism. And as will be discussed later, mutual adjustment is also used by the most complex of organizations, where sophisticated problem-solvers facing extremely complicated situations must communicate informally to accomplish their work.

In *direct supervision* one individual takes responsibility for the work of others, issuing instructions to them, and monitoring their actions. In a library that has individual departments, mutual adjustment does not suffice to coordinate work. A hierarchy in which, as Mintzberg says, "one brain coordinates several hands,"[66] needs to be established.

Mintzberg's remaining methods of coordination involve standardization. With standardization, coordination is achieved before the work is undertaken. In a sense, standardization incorporates coordination into the design of the work; this reduces the need for external coordinating mechanisms.

Standardization of work processes occurs when the content of specific jobs is specified and programmed, that is, the processes are standardized to a high degree. Supervisors overseeing such workers have little need to coordinate because a high degree of specificity is built into the jobs that are to be performed. The classic case of this type of standardization is found on assembly lines where workers perform highly specified tasks.

Standardization of outputs occurs when the results of the work, for example the dimensions of the product or the performance, are specified. Certain outputs are standardized in libraries and information centers; for instance, the order of records in a catalog is usually standardized by means of a tool like the ALA filing rules.

Where neither the work nor its outputs can be standardized, some coordination is attained by "standardizing" the worker. *Standardization of skills* occurs when the training required to perform the work is specified. In most libraries and information centers, an ALA-accredited master's degree is required for entry-level professional positions. Although curricula differ among schools of library and information science, it is assumed that a person who has earned an accredited MLS has acquired the initial skills and knowledge needed to be a professional librarian.

Mintzberg sees the five coordinating mechanisms as a continuum; as organizational work becomes more complicated, the means of coordination shifts from mutual adjustment to direct supervision, to standardization of work processes, to standardization of outputs, and, finally, to standardization of skills. As mentioned previously, the most complex organizations revert to the beginning of the continuum and use the coordinating device of *mutual adjustment*.

> Finally, the most complex organizations engage sophisticated specialists, especially in their support staffs, and require them to combine their efforts in project teams coordinated by mutual adjustment. This results in the *adhocracy* configuration, in which line and staff as well as a number of other distinctions tend to break down.[67]

> —Henry Mintzberg,
> "Organizational Design: Fashion or Fit?"

Consider the organization charged with putting a man on the moon for the first time. The project requires an incredibly elaborate division of labor, with thousands of specialists doing specific jobs. At the outset, no one can be sure exactly what needs to be done; that knowledge develops as the work unfolds. In the final analysis, despite the use of other coordinating mechanisms, the success of the undertaking depends primarily on the ability of the specialists to adapt to each other along the uncharted route.[68]

Although organizations may favor one coordinating mechanism, no organization relies on a single one, and most mix all five. At the least, a certain amount of mutual adjustment and direct supervision is always required, no matter what the reliance on standards. Libraries and information centers use all five of the coordinating mechanisms.

Managers should remember the importance of coordination. It serves as the glue that permits the various units of the organization to move together toward the achievement of organizational objectives. The larger and more complex an organization becomes, the more those coordinating mechanisms are needed.

Organization Charts

A useful aid for visualizing the horizontal and vertical differentiation within an organization is the organization chart. An organization chart is a graphic presentation of the organizational structure. Although it includes staff units, its primary function is to show how lines of authority link departments.

Lines of authority are usually represented on organization charts by solid lines. Lines that show staff organizational units are usually represented by broken lines. Formal communication follows the lines of organizational units and authority. Informal lines of communication are not shown on the traditional organization chart.

On an organization chart, authority flows down and out; it does not return to the point of origination. For example, in figure 3.6, the main line of authority flows from the director down to the assistant director and from that position down and out to the three functional departments. The business office is supervised by the director only. Authority flows from the director down to the assistant director and continues down and out to the business office, where it stops. In other words, in this library the assistant director "reports" to the director, as does the head of the business department. The heads of the circulation, reference, and technical services departments "report" to the assistant director. Understanding that authority flows out and stops is very important in interpreting organization charts. The business office has no authority over the assistant director or the other organizational units shown in the figure.

In the library represented in figure 3.7, the director has authority over the human resources office. Because the human resources office performs a staff function, this authority is depicted with a broken line. The human resources office serves in an advisory capacity to the director and to all other units of the organization, without authority over any unit. However, the human resources office, in its internal operation, has line authority in that it supervises the payroll functions.

Some of the blocks in figures 3.6 and 3.7 seem to represent individuals (e.g., director and assistant director), while others represent functions (e.g., circulation, reference, and technical services). The blocks that represent functions include all assigned activities and a manager. The blocks that seem to represent individuals actually represent all the activities assigned to that position. For the director, activities include the direct supervision of the business office in figure 3.6 and the human resources office in figure 3.7. In addition, both charts assume that the director will perform activities such as planning; working with outside groups, organizations, and individuals (such as the public library board or, in a university library, the vice-president for academic affairs); and evaluating library services. In both charts, the assistant director is responsible for day-to-day supervision of the three operating units, but other activities are also assigned to this position. Although it may appear that a unit of the organization structure is designated by an individual's title, one must recognize that the organizational block includes all the activities of that position.

Fig. 3.6. Organization chart showing authority lines.

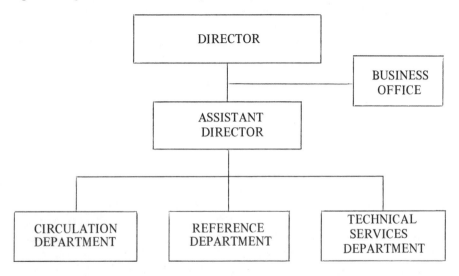

Not many organizations are as simple as those represented by figure 3.6 and figure 3.7. Some are very complex. Various means have been developed to show the authority relationship of one unit to another, and some organizational charts are very complex and, because of their size, sometimes confusing. It is commonly believed that the higher on the chart the unit appears, the greater is its status and authority, and, occasionally, the organizational status of a unit is misunderstood because of its location on the organization chart. The importance of an organizational unit is not determined by its position on the organizational chart but by the line of authority and the number of managers that authority passes through before reaching the final authority. Following the line of authority in figure 3.4 reveals that the assistant director provides immediate supervision to circulation, reference, and technical services. It is apparent that these organizational units are important, because they are placed rather high on the organization chart. But what of extension—the unit that provides service outside the central building? It is shown low on the chart. Analyzing the authority line reveals that extension is equal in status, rank, and importance to the other three units. Extension reports to the same position—the assistant director—as do circulation, reference, and technical services.

Fig. 3.7. Line and staff organizational units.

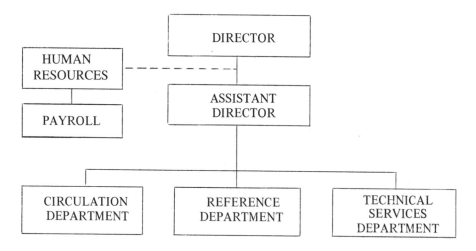

The organizational charts in figure 3.4 through figure 3.7 are traditional. They are based on the hierarchical concept and are designed to show the relationship of one organizational unit to another through lines of authority. A few organizations, although structured traditionally, depict their structure in a nontraditional organization chart. Figure 3.8 is an example of this type of chart. This doughnut model consists of a series of concentric circles, each of which shows a different level of operation. Top administrators are shown in the center, and successive circles represent the various levels of the organization. This is not a different organizational structure but a different way of showing that structure.

Organization charts can be used to define and describe channels of authority, communication, and information flow. They can be used to show the status or rank of members of the organization, and the span of control of each supervisor can be readily detected. Developing an organization chart helps the manager identify problems or inconsistencies in the organization, such as the assignment of unrelated or dissimilar activities to a unit.

&Organizations don't have tops and bottoms. These are just misguided metaphors. What organizations really have are the outer people, connected to the world, and the inner ones, disconnected from it as well as so many so-called middle managers, who are desperately trying to connect the inner and outer people to each other.[69]

—Henry Mintzberg,
"Musings on Management"

Fig. 3.8. Organization chart presented as a "doughnut."

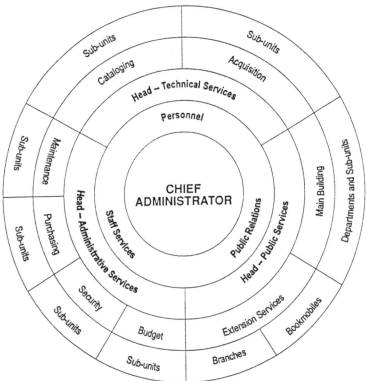

Every library, regardless of size, should have an up-to-date organization chart. It should be available to all staff to help them understand relationships within the library. But it must be understood that an organization chart, a static model of a dynamic process, is limited in what it can do. It shows division of work into components; who is (supposed to be) whose boss; the nature of the work performed by each component; and the grouping of components on the levels of management in terms of successive layers of superiors and subordinates. It does not show the importance or status of the organizational units, the degree of responsibility and authority exercised by positions on the same management level, clear distinctions between line and staff, all channels of communication and contact (only the formal ones are shown), all key links or relationships in the total organizational network, and the informal organization that is a logical and necessary extension of the formal structure.[70]

Appendix B includes organization charts from several libraries, including several that have recently reorganized. Analysis of the charts indicates that the principles of organizing are sometimes violated. On some of the charts, some positions have two or three supervisors. The span of control of some supervisors is larger on some of the charts than is usually recommended. An organization chart reflects local situations that may be historical or may represent the desire and intent of the top administrator, regardless of the general principles of organizational design.

Types of Formal Organizations

Organizations can be of many types and structures. Recently, in response to competitors who have taken away market share, many of the largest corporations, such as General Motors and IBM, have modified their organizational structure. It is widely recognized that no one structure is suitable to all organizations, and factors such as growth, competition, technology, and environmental uncertainty have to be considered in choosing a structure.

> ☙ This is a world in which there are now many more choices about organizational alternatives (forms) than there have been in the recent past. It is also a world in which technological alternatives are many and the variations are proliferating. It is probably going to require some form of "organization design skill" to achieve a good fit between the organizational and technical alternatives available.[71]
>
> —Harvey F. Kolodny,
> "Some Characteristics of Organizational Designs
> in New/High Technology Firms"

Nonetheless, some types of organizations are very common. In the modern world, most large organizations, including libraries, are structured as bureaucracies. In this next section, the traits and characteristics of bureaucracies are described, and some of the criticisms of bureaucracies as structures are discussed. Then some alternatives to the bureaucratic structure are introduced.

Bureaucracies

" 'Bureaucracy' is a dirty word. . . . It suggests rigid rules and regulations . . . impersonality, resistance to change. Yet every organization of any significant size is bureaucraticized to some degree."[72] The term *bureaucracy* is used often in a derogatory fashion, with a connotation of cumbersome structure, red tape, and over-organization, but the term has a different origin.

Bureaucracies were first described in the early part of the twentieth century by Max Weber, a German sociologist trained in law, economics, history, and philosophy. His perceptive and incisive theoretical analysis of the principles of bureaucracies is undoubtedly one of the most important statements on formal organizations; it has had a profound influence on almost all subsequent thinking and research in the field.[73]

Weber created the concept of bureaucracy as a model for use in his analysis of organized industrial society. He attempted to construct a model of a perfectly rational organization; one that would perform its job with maximum efficiency. Basing his model on reasoning rather than on empirical evidence, Weber described the characteristics of this ideal administrative framework as follows:

- Impersonal and formal conduct. Because personality and emotional-based relationships interfere with rationality, nepotism and favoritism not related to performance should be eliminated.

- Employment and promotion on the basis of technical competence and performance. Using these criteria ensures that the best-qualified people will pursue a career in the organization and remain loyal to it.

- Systematic specialization of labor and specification of responsibilities. All of the work necessary to accomplish the tasks of the organization should be divided into specific areas of competence, with each employee and supervisor having authority over his or her functions and not interfering with the conduct of others' jobs.

- A well-ordered system of rules and procedures that regulates the conduct of work. These rules serve (a) to standardize operations and decisions, (b) as receptacles of past learning, and (c) to protect incumbents and ensure equality of treatment. The learning of rules represents much of the technical competence of incumbents, because the rules tell them what decisions to make and when to make them.

- Hierarchy of positions such that each position is controlled by a higher one. The hierarchy of authority is impersonal, based on rules, and the superior position is held by the individual having greater expertise. In this way, compliance with rules and coordination is systematically ensured.

- Complete separation of the property and affairs of the organization from the personal property and affairs of the incumbents. This serves to prevent the demands and interests of personal affairs from interfering with the rational, impersonal conduct of the business of the organization.[74]

Weber's concept of bureaucracy is the basis for much influential thought and investigation into organizations. His work brings together a large number of the concepts already discussed in this chapter—division of labor, horizontal specialization, hierarchy of authority, and standardization of work processes. The organization of a typical library includes many characteristics of bureaucracy. Almost all libraries are marked by the hierarchical structure, a large number of rules (ranging from cataloging and filing rules to circulation rules), the demands of technical competence, and the systematic specialization of labor.

> The hierarchical kind of organization we call bureaucracy did not emerge accidentally. It is the only form of organization that can enable a company to employ a large number of people and yet preserve unambiguous accountability for the work they do. And that is why, despite all its problems, it has so doggedly persisted.[75]
>
> —Elliot Jaques, "In Praise of Hierarchy"

Since Weber formulated his ideas concerning bureaucracies, many critics have written about the dysfunctional aspects of bureaucracies. A great deal of this criticism of bureaucracy focuses on the internal workings of the organization, especially the unintended consequences of control through rules.[76] Other criticism centers on the relationship of the bureaucratic organization to its environment, and the tendency of the traditional bureaucracy to largely ignore the outside world. This criticism considers the bureaucratic organizational model flawed because it treats the organization as if it were a closed system unaffected by the uncertainties of environment.[77] Other criticism faults the bureaucratic model for being overly mechanical and ignoring individual and group behaviors in organizations.[78]

    €[Functional bureaucracies] breed dependence and passivity. In a functional organization, there is a natural tendency for conflicts to get kicked upstairs. People get too accustomed to sitting on their hands and waiting for a decision to come down from above. Well, sometimes the decision does come down. But sometimes it doesn't, and even when it does, often it comes too late, because market conditions have already changed or a more nimble competitor has gotten there first. Or maybe the decision is simply wrong—because the person making it is too far from the customer.[79]

—Robert Howard,
"The CEO as Organizational Architect"

    In stable environments, changes occur slowly. For organizations, stable environments mean that customer needs change slowly, and thus, organizations are under little pressure to change their established methods. In a stable environment, organizations handle information that is largely predictable. Carefully developed plans can be made in advance, and exceptions are so few that there is time for upper level decision-makers to decide what to do.

    The rules and procedures characteristic of bureaucracies work best in a stable environment. Indeed, bureaucracies seem to be the best-tailored, most efficient organizations for stable environments. The rapid changes taking place in today's environment cause many to question the stability that is an integral part of the bureaucratic model. Organizations that exist in unstable environments encounter change frequently. They must be adaptable and flexible. Long lists of policies and rules cannot be relied upon; circumstances change too quickly for decisions to be adequately covered by rules. As technology evolves rapidly, frequent product and service changes result from both the changing needs of customers and the pressure of competitors. Bureaucracies are less efficient in a turbulent environment than in a stable environment because they lack the ability to adapt easily to change. Bureaucracies lack this ability because they "are geared to stable environments; they are performance structures designed to perfect programs for contingencies that can be predicted, not problem solving ones designed to create new programs for needs that have never been encountered."[80]

    €Hierarchy is an approach to organization that is beginning to lose its once unquestioned authority where it exists in its most extreme form; in multilevel hierarchy, which gives rise to multilevel bureaucracy, and absolute hierarchy, where all work is determined by downward assignment and where peers play no part in distributing work among themselves. History has imposed these forms of organization upon us. They will be displaced only if we find something better.[81]

—Meredith Belbin,
The Coming Shape of Organizations

Although the bureaucracy is the most common form of organizational structure, there are other forms. In observing 20 English and Scottish firms, Tom Burns and G. M. Stalker identified two types of organizations, the mechanistic and the organic.[82] Bureaucracies represent the mechanistic organizational structure. Mechanistic organizational structures are shaped in the traditional, pyramidal pattern of organization. This type of organization is designed to be like a machine, hence the name. "People are conceived of as parts performing specific tasks. As employees leave, other parts can be slipped into their places. Someone at the top is the designer, defining what the parts will be and how they will fit together."[83]

Burns and Stalker found that the mechanistic, or bureaucratic, structure worked best for organizations that perform many routine tasks and operate in a stable environment; mechanistic structures were not successful in organizations that were required to adjust to environmental changes.

Organic Systems

The organic organization's structure is completely different from the mechanistic organization. This structure is based on a biological metaphor, and the objective in designing such a system is to leave it open to the environment so it can respond to new opportunities. The organic form is appropriate to changing conditions that constantly give rise to fresh problems and unforeseen requirements for action. Organic structures are more appropriate than bureaucracies for today's better educated workers, who seek greater freedom in their work. An organic structure is characterized by:

- an emphasis on lateral and horizontal flows of communication within the organization;

- organizational influence based largely on the authority of knowledge rather than an individual's position in the structure;

- members of the organization tending to have a systemwide orientation rather than narrow, departmental views;

- job definitions that are less precise and more flexible and duties that change as new problems and challenges are confronted; and

- a commitment by many members to professional standards developed by groups outside the formal organization. For instance, engineers may identify as strongly with their professional societies as they do with the firms for which they work.[84]

In almost every respect, the organic institution is the opposite of the classical bureaucracy. Bureaucracies emphasize standardization and formal relations; organic structures are marked by loose, informal working relations, and problems are worked out as needs arise.

> ❧ Organizations used to be perceived as gigantic pieces of engineering with largely interchangeable human parts. We talked of their structures and their systems, of inputs and outputs, of control devices and managing them, as if the whole was one large factory. Today the language is not that of engineering but of politics with talk of cultures and networks, or teams and coalitions, of influence or power rather than control, of leadership not management.[85]
>
> —Charles Handy, *The Age of Unreason*

Burns and Stalker are careful to emphasize that while organic systems are "not hierarchic in the same sense as are mechanistic, they remain stratified." Positions are differentiated according to seniority, that is, greater expertise. The lead in joint decisions is frequently taken by seniors, but it is an essential presumption of the organic system that the lead, or the authority, is taken by those who show themselves most informed and capable. The location of authority is settled by consensus.[86]

Organic structures are further marked by workers' commitment to the organization, a blurring of the distinction between the formal and informal organization, and the development of shared beliefs about the values and goals of the organization. However, because of the departure from the familiar clear and fixed hierarchical structure, many managers feel uncomfortable in organic organizations. In many ways, it is harder to be a manager in an organic system than in a bureaucracy, because most of the certainties associated with a stable hierarchy do not exist in the organic system. Much more ambiguity is associated with the organic pattern of organizing, and managers must be able to tolerate that ambiguity.

> ❧ Executives who have good interpersonal skills, are comfortable with delegating, and enjoy the intellectual challenge of a healthy debate, favor flatter more participative designs. Executives who have a high need for control, a genius for

detail, and a strong ability to organize prefer hierarchical, closely managed configurations. Debates among the differing styles are often endless and pointless, for the argument regresses into one of personal preference.[87]

—Miles H. Overholt,
"Flexible Organizations"

Mechanistic and organic systems are on the extreme ends of a continuum. A small group of scientists working in a laboratory represents an organic structure; a highly structured factory producing a standard product for a stable market represents a mechanistic one. Most institutions fall somewhere between these two extremes. And, an organization can contain both organic and mechanistic units. Burns and Stalker characterized whole organizations as mechanistic or organic, but Lawrence and Lorsch found these descriptions more accurately described units within an organization.[88]

Few libraries are structured as pure organic systems. Some small, special libraries come close to this model, as do small academic libraries that have adopted a collegial system of organization similar to that used in academic departments.[89] In the collegial system, instead of a single final authority position, a group of individuals participate in making decisions that affect the whole organization. The collegial pattern has been used successfully in some small libraries, but the large number of professional and nonprofessional employees in most libraries make this form of organization impossible.

> ‽Traditionally, libraries have been organized along hierarchical lines, internally structured according to function. In this structure responsibility for decision making is placed with the head of the library, and authority diminishes with descending levels of the organizational pyramid. While this organization has its advantages, it is prone to becoming an uncompromising bureaucracy. Too often it results in poor communication, organizational stratification, stifled initiative, and bureaucratic overstaffing. . . . Lack of coordination within and between departments and competition among units over priorities, resources, and means to attain library objectives increase the likelihood of conflict and misunderstanding between organizational units. Divided by factional interests, staff members focus on their own narrow domains. . . . In a stable environment, this structure has managed to function effectively. However, it is clearly ill equipped to face the challenges of the electronic information age.[90]

—Susan Jacobson, "Reorganization"

Because of their size, the technology they use, and the services they perform, most libraries and information centers are still organized bureaucratically. But as libraries "have been criticized for their inability to keep up with social and individual expectations and their failure to change quickly enough to meet competitive challenges,"[91] they have begun to search for new forms of organizational structure. There is a growing acceptance of the fact that the traditional hierarchical system needs to be modified. As Michael Gorman writes:

> Hierarchies are not hospitable to creativity and self-fulfillment. Such structures are inimical to the open and flexible nature of library work . . . other negative characteristics of hierarchical library organizations are their innate internal rigidity and uniformity within substructures. . . . Beyond such examples, there is the enormous difficulty of carrying out change within the hierarchical structure. The hierarchy is inherently resistant to internal chance and *must* be replaced by an open structure of clusters of staff interacting with each other in a multidimensional and innovative manner.[92]

There is a widespread belief that the adoption of new technologies will inevitably lead to radical changes in the organizational structures of libraries. It is interesting that there has been so much speculation about the impact of technology with so little demonstrable change. A recent examination of the organization charts of today's libraries did not reflect radical changes in the way libraries are organized; the introduction of technology has not affected the basic, bureaucratic structure.[93] Instead, the structure of libraries has changed in a way that is not reflected on the organizational chart. Rather than completely restructuring, libraries and information centers are becoming more hybrid in structure by organizing some departments more organically than others, or by employing "overlays," or modifications imposed on the basic bureaucratic organizational structure.[94] The pyramid remains largely intact, but modifications are in place.

> I don't mean, in these reflections to disparage the hierarchy unduly. It worked for us, and in many ways it still does, since we in truth have not departed that far from it. It may not feel that way, but, realistically, I can say that we have a long way to go yet.[95]
>
> —John Lubans,
> "I Ain't No Cowboy, I Just Found This Hat"

Modifications to Bureaucracies

Libraries rely heavily on various types of coordinating positions and temporary groups to deal with increasing complexity, but, in most cases, these modifications are superimposed upon the traditional bureaucratic structure. Modifications may be traditional, such as committees, or innovative, such as quality circles; they may be permanent, such as matrix organizations, or more transitory, such as temporary task forces. But in libraries and information centers of all types, the hierarchical structures are being modified by a number of means. A discussion of some of these modifications follows.

Matrix Organizational Structure. One of the significant innovations in organizational design is the matrix organizational structure. In task forces or project management, types of organization discussed later, group members are withdrawn from their departments and temporarily assigned to the project manager. For the duration of the project, group members have a reporting responsibility to both the project manager and their department supervisor. In matrix management, dual assignments become part of the permanent organizational pattern. Matrix management represents an attempt to retain the advantages of functional specialization while adding the project management's advantage of improved coordination.[96]

Aerospace firms were the first to use the matrix structure by experimenting with organizational structures that combined project management with functional departmentation. Functional departments continued to exist in the traditional vertical hierarchy, but project management was superimposed over those departments as a horizontal overlay; hence the name matrix.[97]

The matrix is a fairly complex structure that violates many management principles, especially the principle of unity of command. Although many businesses, including banks and insurance and chemical companies, use a matrix organizational pattern, it is still not common. One reason that this type of structure has not been more widely adopted is that it is often confusing: The simple chain of command is replaced by multiple authority relationships, and managers need to function as team leaders rather than as traditional managers.[98] People working in such an environment need to be able to tolerate a great deal of ambiguity. As two library managers wrote, matrix management is "difficult to implement. It runs against our cultural bias, and it is sufficiently complex and ambiguous that it requires virtually constant monitoring to keep it running well. Most of us have lived in hierarchical organizations all of our lives, and it is difficult for us to even visualize, much less adapt to, another form of organization."[99]

&⟋In practice, however, the matrix proved all but unmanageable. Dual reporting led to conflict and confusion; the proliferation of channels created information logjams as a proliferation of committees and reports bogged down the organization; and overlapping responsibilities produced turf battles and a loss of accountability.[100]

—Christopher A. Bartlett and Sumantra Ghoshal,
"Matrix Management"

One of the few published accounts of matrix management in libraries describes the experience of San Francisco State University. This library was looking for a way to increase organizational effectiveness, particularly in reference services and collection development. After considering the options, the library decided to adopt a matrix management organization. Program coordinators were chosen for the various services provided by the readers services division: user education, online, reference, and collection development. Librarians working in the readers services division had a dual reporting responsibility to the assistant director for public services and to the program coordinator of their specific service unit.[101] The organizational structure of the division is illustrated in figure 3.9.

A number of corporations have experimented with and then eliminated the matrix management organizational pattern because of its complexity and lack of clear-cut authority lines. At the present, this type of organizational structure is not found in its pure form in many libraries, although some have adopted modifications of it, either as an overall organizational structure or in specific units of the library.

Committees. One of the most common modifications to libraries' hierarchical structure is committees. Committees are especially useful when a process does not fall within the domain of any one chain of command, so a committee consisting of representatives from all the units involved is established. Standing committees often deal with ongoing issues such as staff development, automation, and personnel. Ad hoc, or temporary, committees are formed as required. For instance, many libraries use search committees in the hiring process. The power held by committees varies from library to library. In some libraries and information centers, committees have the authority to establish policy; in others, they play an advisory role.

Committees provide a means to bring a wide variety of knowledge and experience to bear on a topic. They also are useful in obtaining commitment to policies and decisions. However, committees are often slow to act, and they are costly because of the time required of participants. All of the advantages and disadvantages of group decision making discussed in chapter 2 pertain to decision making by committees.

Fig. 3.9. A matrix organizational structure. From Joanne Euster and Peter Haikalis, "A Matrix Model of Organization," in *Academic Libraries: Myths and Realities, Proceedings of the Third Annual ACRL Conference* (Chicago: American Library Association, 1984). Reprinted with permission of American Library Association.

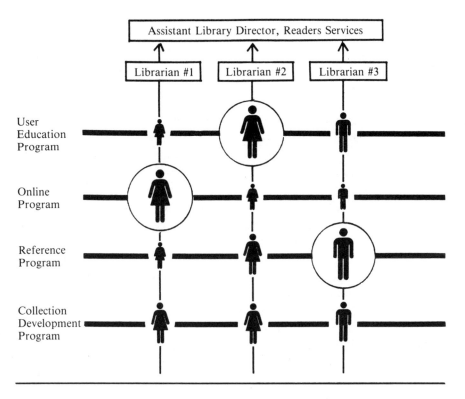

A Schematic of Matrix Organization
for the Readers Services Division of the
San Francisco State University

 Individual librarian and/or Program Coordinator interaction with the Division Head

Relationship of individual librarian participation to various divisional programs

 Individual librarian and/or Program Coordinator interaction with peers and/or other Program Coordinators

Circled figure represents Program Coordinator

 Size of figure represents librarian time commitment to specific program

Task Force or Project Management. Task forces are similar to committees, except that their assignment is generally full-time rather than part-time, that is, employees leave their primary jobs to devote all their time to the task force. A task force has a specific, temporary task to perform, and when the task is completed the members of the group return to their primary jobs. Task forces are particularly valuable when the undertaking is a one-time task that has a broad scope and specific, definable results; is unfamiliar or lacks precedent; calls for a high degree of interdependence among the tasks; and involves a high stake for the task force in the successful completion of the project.[102] In libraries and information centers, task forces are often called upon to deal with new, unfamiliar, or involved projects, such as the reclassification of a library collection or the installation of a new online catalog.

The term *project management* is used to describe the structure of an organization that often creates groups to work on special projects. Project management uses temporary groups to work on specific projects; after completion of the project, the members of the group either return to their primary jobs or are assigned to another project group.

Quality Circles. Quality circles are not committees or task forces but small groups of employees that meet regularly and voluntarily to recommend solutions to quality and productivity problems. Quality circles make recommendations only; it is up to management to implement them. Quality circles allow employees greater control over their working conditions and, because they permit line employees greater opportunities for decision making, they increase decentralization. Without a commitment from management, however, quality circles cannot succeed.

Generally, 6 to 12 volunteers from the same work area make up the circle. The members receive appropriate training, usually from a facilitator who is a specially trained member of management. The facilitator helps ensure that the circles run smoothly. Typically, the circles meet for four hours a month during the work day. Members of the group choose the work-related problems they wish to solve.[103]

The quality circle concept was imported from Japan and has received widespread acceptance in the United States. It has been estimated that more than 90 percent of the Fortune 500 companies have had such programs.[104] Some libraries and information centers have instituted quality circles; for instance, quality circles at some branches of the Chicago Public Library have been reported to be very successful. They "have tackled both large, complex problems and small, nagging ones. In all cases, their objectives have been to make their work easier or more rewarding."[105] Other reported experiences with quality circles have been less successful.

The popularity of quality circles appears to be fading somewhat. The results of quality circles in the business environment seem to be mixed.

Most quality circles make their greatest contributions shortly after their formation, and sustaining successes over a longer period of time demands considerable effort.[106]

Like any other management device, quality circles do not work well in every setting. It is unrealistic to expect that a technique that is highly successful in one type of organization or national culture will be successful in another. There has to be a fit between the quality circles and the rest of the organization. Because a number of participants are needed to make up the circles, medium-size and large libraries seem to be the most appropriate settings for quality circles, and some libraries are experimenting with them. However, not enough libraries have reported their results to allow judgments about the overall success rate of quality circles in library settings (see chapter 5 for more information on quality circles).

Self-Managing Teams. If interest in the use of quality circles has waned, there has been an increased interest in the use of teams in the workplace. The team approach is a shift from groups being managed to groups that manage themselves. When a number of employees work as a group to perform related tasks, it is possible to redesign the overall work, not as a set of individual jobs but as a shared group task. A number of American companies, including General Motors, Exxon, Proctor and Gamble, Citibank, General Foods, and Prudential Insurance have used relatively autonomous or self-managing work teams in office or manufacturing settings.[107] Self-managing or autonomous teams take over many of the functions traditionally reserved for managers, including determining their own work schedules and job assignments.

> ⍉ The major difference between self-directed work teams and their predecessors, such as quality circles, is that team direction isn't a program but a profound change in how companies do business. It involves using the collective brainpower of all employees as a competitive strategy, empowering them with the responsibility for all functions of the business.[108]
>
> —Jana Schilder,
> "Work Teams Boost Productivity"

Some people have questioned how the use of teams differs from the use of committees, which have been utilized by libraries of all types for many years. There are in fact distinct differences between teams and committees. Committees are marked by the following characteristics:

1. Members are appointed by administration.

2. Leadership is usually appointed.

3. They have a specific charge and are result oriented.

4. Agendas are set with the charge.

5. Broad participation is not required.

On the other hand, teams are marked by these characteristics:

1. Members are those "who do the work."

2. Leadership is chosen by the team.

3. They are process oriented.

4. Agendas are set by the team.

5. Everyone participates.[109]

One of the first libraries to use self-managing teams was Yale, where the technical services department adopted the approach in 1989. The model was chosen to create a work environment in which staff would

1. assume personal responsibility for the results of their performance;

2. continuously monitor their performance;

3. take the initiative to correct any deficiencies or problems;

4. seek the resources, guidance, or help they need to perform effectively; and

5. take the initiative to help others improve their performance after having met their own responsibilities.[110]

The Yale technical services department was reorganized into four departments: processing services, database management, preservation, and systems. Each of the departments has a department head, and the departments are structured into a number of teams, each having a team leader. The teams consist of 4 to 12 members and include both librarians and support staff. It is reported that the experience so far has been positive. "Staff at all levels are actively engaged in problem solving and are contributing in new and different ways. Some teams are already aggressively pursuing changes to work flow in order to operate more effectively. Morale appears to be at a high level; the general atmosphere within technical services is positive and upbeat. Perhaps most astounding is that productivity has already increased."[111] These results are encouraging, indeed.

> ✑ By stressing self-directed teams, big firms, within their own button-down, command/control, committee-ridden organizations, are trying to re-create the same kind of creative tension that exists in small, independent firms. In doing

so, they are trying to reduce what could be described as *internal transactions costs*—all the additions to costs caused by excessive bureaucracy, oversight and central direction, and by poor communications across functions, between business groups, or among people at different levels of the organization.[112]

—Andrew Wilson,
"U.S. Firms Restructure and Revitalize"

Many other libraries have begun to use teams in all types of departments, sometimes as a part of a Total Quality Management (TQM) strategy and sometimes not (see chapter 5 for more information about the use of teams in TQM). While some of these libraries, such as the ones at Clemson, Duke, or the University of Arizona, have used the team approach for the entire library, others use teams only in a few departments.[113] Figures 3.10 and 3.11 show how the organizational chart of the Clemson University libraries changed with the implementation of a team approach to organization.

Fig. 3.10. Clemson University Library organization prior to reorganization. Reproduced with permission of Clemson University Library.

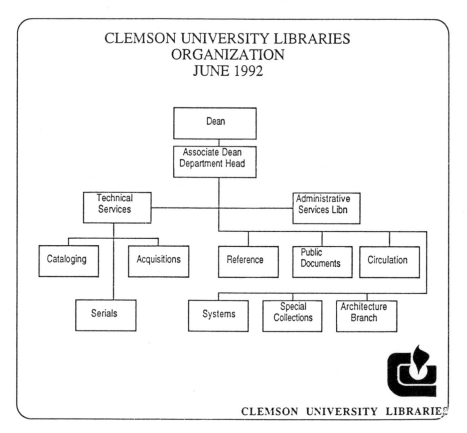

Fig. 3.11. Clemson University Library organization after reorganization. Reproduced with permission of Clemson University Library.

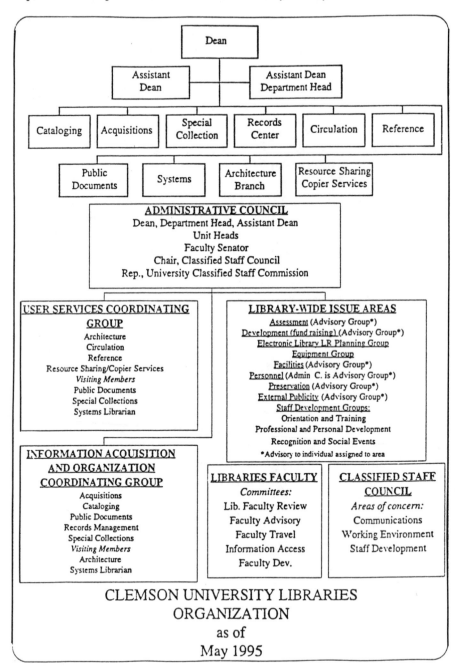

The role of a manager changes when teams or work groups are used. In an organization that uses teams, the core behaviors of a manager are developing the talents and skills of the team members, getting them excited about the mission of the team, and fostering effective working relations. Five skills needed in a team leader are those of:

1. developing self-motivated staff capable of setting their own goals and evaluating their own efforts;

2. helping diverse members of the team learn to generate and implement their own ideas;

3. developing teams that manage their own daily work;

4. championing cross-functional effort to improve quality, productivity, and service; and

5. anticipating, initiating, and responding to changes caused by forces outside the organization.[114]

Work teams are gaining increasing popularity in library settings, and they provide yet another way to provide greater decentralization within the hierarchical structure. As all of the accounts of organizations that have switched to the team approach note, it is not an easy or a fast process. The hierarchical approach, with all of its deficiencies, is one that both managers and employees are most familiar with, and sometimes the old certainties look very alluring. As one manager noted, "At times the old way of doing things beckons to us like a pair of old and comfortable shoes," but, he goes on to add that, "by and large we have been able to make good progress toward a goal of self-managing teams."[115] It is important for any library considering teams to understand that a team-based organization means undergoing a radical change in organizational culture, and that the process is neither fast nor easy.

Making Changes

&Library conferences and library journals are abuzz with talk of paradigm shifts . . . the non-library . . . the library without walls . . . the library as electronic switching center . . . and on and on. Meanwhile, most librarians get on with the essential daily tasks, involved in incorporating new technologies into existing services; maintaining and improving existing collections; and generally making real if unspectacular progress in the face of financial adversity.[116]

—Walt Crawford and Michael Gorman,
Future Libraries: Dreams, Madness, and Reality

Although there are as yet few signs of radical reorganization of libraries, librarians in all types of libraries and information centers are thinking about it and trying to devise the structures that allow them to reach their goals most successfully. Most libraries are considering ways to flatten the structure and make the organization more flexible and responsive. These changes are being considered while the library is "getting on with essential daily tasks." Any reorganization is of course complicated because "current services must be maintained while the infrastructure is being built to support the information needs of the 21st century."[117]

If a library is considering reorganization, what steps should it undergo in its transformation? The first thing is to realize that a significant change in structure will most likely be difficult and time-consuming. It is easy to discuss organizational change in the abstract, but when it comes to implementation, change is usually more difficult than expected.

> ᘓIn my opinion, organization structure is so important to the future of our libraries that it is often worth undertaking the complicated three- to five-year process of changing a library's basic character if its existing structure is at odds with contemporary needs for change.[118]
>
> —Jerry D. Campbell,
> "Building an Effectiveness Pyramid for
> Leading Successful Organizational Transformation"

In a recent study of large research libraries that had undergone reorganization or restructuring, Hewitt found that there were four major factors precipitating it. These reasons are similar to those found in other types of organizations. They are:

1. A need for organizational flexibility.

2. A need for a stronger external and client-centered orientation.

3. A need to provide for more staff empowerment and work satisfaction.

4. A need to improve management processes, such as communication, coordination, and planning.[119]

A number of accounts of library structure reorganization have appeared in the recent literature. These reorganization attempts vary in the way they were carried out, and most resulted in different types of restructuring. But there are some common elements found in most successful efforts to change. Overholt has summarized these steps as follows:

1. Determine and select the organizational design that best matches the organization's strategy;

2. assess whether the organization's employees can work well in the preferred design; and

3. then develop a plan for how to move the organization from the current configuration to the new one.[120]

The first step then is to decide what type of structure is needed. Peter Drucker, who has written so much about organizational structure, provides three ways to determine the type of structure necessary for a specific organization: (1) activities analysis, (2) decision analysis, and (3) relations analysis.[121] The activities analysis requires the manager to perform a detailed and thorough analysis of activities so that it can be determined what work has to be performed, what activities belong together, and where the activities should be placed in the organizational structure. The decision analysis identifies the kinds of decisions that are needed, where in the structure of the organization they should be made, and the degree of involvement of each manager in the decision-making process. The relations analysis emphasizes the relationships among the units of the organizational structure and the responsibilities of each manager to the various units as well as the responsibilities of the various units to each manager. After performing these three analyses, a manager would have information to be used in determining the structure needed for the organization.

Therefore, planning for the type of structure chosen is important. Analyses such as the ones Drucker proposes would be helpful in gathering information about the type of structure to be implemented. Often other data, especially on use and satisfaction, are gathered. Managers interested in implementing change in an organization's structure should learn as much as possible from reading on the topic and talking to others who have implemented change, but the structure chosen for a particular organization should be based on that organization's specific needs, and not chosen because a certain type of organization structure is being implemented elsewhere. Some libraries and information centers have used consultants in this planning process, and others have done it with planning committees drawn from library employees.

      Perhaps the library personnel who have to make the greatest changes and who will face the most difficulties in the transformation of the library are library administrators. The roles of the director, assistant directors, and department heads must change from managers, controllers, directors of activities, deciders and evaluators to leaders, coaches and facilitators. All these administrators must be willing to give up a great deal of decision-making authority and become much more comfortable with being challenged, having to explain, not having the last say, and living with ambiguity and uncertainty.[122]

—Carla J. Stoffle et al., "Choosing Our Futures"

    The second step in any structural change is a consideration of whether the employees will be able to work well in the proposed new structure. One part of this consideration concerns the personal style of the organization's managers. Not all present-day managers adjust well to a flatter, less bureaucratic style of organization. They learned to manage in the command and control mode, and they feel more comfortable using that style. If a library is considering drastic changes to its structure, it needs to consider whether this new structure will be congruent with the present managers' styles. If not, it will likely fail unless the structural changes are adopted in tandem with other changes, such as changes in management personnel or providing in-depth training to managers in how to manage in the new environment.

> One of the reasons that the traditional command-and-control approach has been so effective in the past and is so hard to change in the present is precisely that its elements reinforce each other. Leaders for example are trained and selected to behave in a hierarchical manner. Status symbols reinforce their authority, pay plans reward them for moving up hierarchies and staff support and information flows allow them to coordinate and make decisions more effectively than anyone else. Movement away from this model requires not just a change in their behavior but a change in how the organization is designed, managed and structured.[123]

It is not just top-level managers, however, who will likely need help in adjusting to a new structure. Many lower level staff and middle managers may also find the adjustment difficult. Staff development needs to be provided to all employees to ready them for the new organizational structure. Much attention has to be paid to the human side of the organization.

It cannot be stressed too much that different types of structures will demand different types of management expertise and different types of employee skills. Inevitably there will be both managers and employees who will not be effective or comfortable in a newly restructured organization. These individuals will either have to be retrained and made comfortable or be replaced; any planning for change must take these needs into account. As the director of one library that has reorganized wrote:

> The key to making the reorganization work is staff education and training. This point cannot be overemphasized. Moreover, educational efforts must target all staff, including management. The staff needs to learn how to participate in the new organization. . . . Not only do staff members need to acquire new knowledge and skills, but, also their attitudes and philosophies must be reexamined and refined.[124]

The staff development and training required to bring about organizational transformation successfully, both in the planning and implementation phases, requires a large amount of monetary and time investment.

The third step is to develop the strategy for moving from the current configuration of the organization to the new configuration. This is the implementation stage of the process. Recently published accounts of how certain libraries and information centers have approached restructuring can provide some insights into strategies being employed.

The accounts of successful restructuring have all included a great deal of employee input. Unless employees understand the reasons for the change and "buy into" the change proposed, it is unlikely to be effective. Staff members must understand the concepts underlying the new structure to ensure their full participation.

There is a critical need throughout the entire process, beginning from inception, for effective communication. This communication needs to be both external—for the library is usually a part of a larger organization that needs to be informed about the proposed changes—and internal. Organizational communication will be discussed in chapter 5, but it should be noted here that if employees are not kept well informed of proposed changes, rumors will be rampant. Changes in organizational structures can be very threatening; good communication keeps everyone informed about proposed changes and helps to alleviate employee anxiety.

Almost all the descriptions of organization transformation in libraries and other settings have stressed the time and effort involved in the process, with most commenting that it took longer than they had anticipated to implement. It is also not an inexpensive undertaking.

The process has been expensive. It has taken an enormous amount of time, in total length and in staff weeks. It has required consistency and constancy of vision over a span of several years. Sometimes it also has required, uncomfortably, that we remain flexible and adaptable and that we recognize that ambiguity is an ongoing part of our organization life, not an occasional problem to be eradicated. Would we do it again? Most emphatically *yes*.[125]

Finally, a method of assessment has to be built into the process so it can be determined whether the new structure is successful in carrying out the organization's goals and objectives. This assessment should attempt to pinpoint the things that are working well and the things that still need to be changed. In most of these settings, the reorganization is viewed as an iterative process. Typically, everything does not work well with the first reorganization attempt; some things need to be fine-tuned and mistakes need to be corrected. Once greater flexibility is built into the system, it will be easier to face future changes and to view any restructuring process as an evolutionary one.

In summary, any structural reorganization requires effort and cannot be implemented quickly. Mistakes will be made in the process, and there will be many times in the course of the process when almost everyone will wonder why they ever wanted to consider reorganization. It is important to reward small successes along the way and to keep employees focused on the expected results of the reorganization. It should be encouraging to any organization that feels itself mired in structural change to look to the published reports of libraries that have finished the initial stages of reorganization. Almost all report greater productivity, increased flexibility, better communication, and improved decision making.

The Library Organization of the Future

&We have tried to incorporate technology into the library, a little bit here and a lot there, but have often done so in response to external pressure. What we have not done is to look at the library as a whole and determine if its present configuration is appropriate to the goals and objectives it must meet. . . . The library's organization has changed little if at all in more than a century. The information explosion has increased the library's size but has not changed its organization.[126]

—Ann E. Prentice,
"Jobs and Changes in the Technological Age"

Libraries and information centers, like all other institutions, are feeling their way toward a new organizational structure. They are moving, slowly, away from rigid hierarchies to more organic forms of organization. The move is appropriate, because there has often been tension in libraries between the professional status of many of their employees and the bureaucratic organizational form.

More and more, the tendency in libraries and information centers is to allow decisions to be made at the levels in the organization where the most information about the decisions exists. This is contrary to practice in the typical bureaucracy, where decisions and the information needed to make them are pushed up the hierarchy to a top manager.

Overlays to the hierarchy attempt to bring together people who have the necessary information, and let them make the decisions that will affect them. The effect is to create groups that can focus on problems, projects, or products better than the traditional hierarchy can. These overlays allow the organization to cut across departmental lines and to decentralize decision making. They make the organization more flexible.[127] Although the organizational charts may still appear fairly hierarchical, these organizations have begun the metamorphosis into a new type of organization.

> ᘓ Whatever the risks or advantages of alternatives to hierarchy, the fact is that few models are in existence in libraries at present.[128]
>
> —Joanne R. Euster, "The New Hierarchy"

Because of their size, the large number of routine tasks performed, and the type of product they produce, it is doubtful that many libraries will ever adapt a strictly organic organizational form, although some small libraries and some subunits within larger libraries may. Most libraries and information centers probably will continue to experiment with modifications and expansions or overlays that will permit some decentralization of decision making and some measure of hierarchical control. At the present time, the most innovative structural changes appear to be occurring in libraries that are creating a strong team culture within a somewhat flattened hierarchy. But this is certainly not the only possible approach. There will be a long period of time in which librarians experiment with new organizational models, and some failures can be expected. Because libraries and information centers differ in so many ways, no one organizational structure will suffice for all. And, for most libraries, there will need to be different types of organizational structures within the larger whole.

&. Even within the same organization there is no one or best way to design operations. For example, would anyone seriously contend that you want the management of your accounts receivable "organized" in the same way with the same amount of control as a team working on developing software for an artificial intelligence (AI) system? I certainly hope not. In one case, there is a clear need for tight control and adherence to procedures, whereas the other situation begs for unbridled creativity.[129]

—Clifford Haka, "Organizational Design"

So, libraries like other types of organizations are moving away from the strictly mechanistic, hierarchical organization to another form of organization. They are moving at different speeds, and they are adopting different types of organizational structures, but they are in the process of changing and becoming "post-hierarchical."

The post-hierarchical library is a flattened structure, unlimited by the traditional hierarchy, anti-bureaucratic, with empowered cross-functional teams, fewer people, constant learning, and redefined and re-engineered work processes focused on customer service. The purpose of the post-hierarchical library is to increase user satisfaction with reduced resources and more staff empowerment.[130]

Libraries and information centers are beginning to experiment with new forms of organizational structures. There will not be just one successful model but a number of different models. The design of an organization should be contingent upon the environment in which it operates, the tasks the employees must perform in this environment to achieve the organization's objectives, and the characteristics of the employees.[131] Each library will need to discover what works best for it, which organizational structure is most effective and efficient in allowing the organization to achieve its purposes and reach its objectives.

Regardless of the structure chosen, it must be one that will facilitate flexibility and change. The age of the rigid, unchanging organizational structure is over, and organizations must be ready to change their forms to meet changing conditions and needs. At the same time, there must be a core of stability built into the structure because no organization or its employees can function effectively if there is frequent complete restructuring. As Peters and Waterman observe, "The excellent companies, as we've seen, do make better use of task forces, project centers, and other ad hoc devices to make things happen. The excellent companies also appear to be reorganizing all of the time. They are; but most of the reorganization takes place around the edges. The fundamental form rarely changes that much."[132] In their view, the best organizations have found a way to build stability into the structure but at the same time have incorporated organizational features that allow innovation and responsiveness to the external environment. Libraries and information centers that have maintained the traditional hierarchical structure modified with various overlays are attempting to achieve the same objectives.

Like everything else, management trends change over time. Right now the flat organizational structure is in fashion. Some experts confidently predict that the age of bureaucracies is finished and that hierarchical structures are doomed,[133] but others take a different viewpoint. David Fagiano, president of the American Management Association, recently wrote, "As we have with most management concepts . . . we have driven the dismantling of traditional corporate structure to Luddite proportions. Each time we reach this point, momentum shifts, and the pendulum of change begins to swing back toward a more centrist position."[134] Fagiano predicts that the recent trend toward flatter structures will inevitably reverse and that hierarchical business structures will return to favor soon.[135]

What we should learn from the pendulum swing of management trends of all types is that there is not just one answer to any problem, and that it is a mistake to adopt any management trend, dealing with organizing or anything else, without seeing whether that answer suits the circumstances of a particular organization. The rush to flatten structures has taught us a great deal, and in certain types of organizations, flatter structures will provide more efficiency and effectiveness. However, flattening is not the only or necessarily the best approach to use in fashioning every organization's structure. Each organization must consider its own needs and design a structure to allow it to achieve its objectives.

Conclusion

Each organization must be structured to achieve its goals and objectives. The organizational structure must allow workers to specialize, while coordinating and integrating the activities of those workers at the same time. Although organizing is one of the most important managerial functions, it must be remembered that it is not an end in itself but merely a means to allow the organization to reach its objectives. The design principles discussed in this chapter are tools, which are:

> neither good nor bad in themselves. They can be used properly or improperly; and that is all. To obtain the greatest possible simplicity and the greatest "fit," organization design has to start out with a clear focus on *key activities* needed to produce *key results*.

They have to be structured and positioned in the simplest possible design. Above all, the architect of the organization needs to keep in mind the purpose of the organization he [or she] is designing.

Organization is a means to an end rather than an end itself. Sound structure is a prerequisite to organizational health but it is not health itself. The test of healthy business is not the beauty, clarity, or perfection of its organization structure. *It is the performance of people.*[136]

Organizational structures fail if they do not encourage workers to perform at their highest levels. As many experts have noted, too much reengineering and reorganization can result in a demoralized workforce, especially when the employees do not understand or have little input into the organizational changes. From the employees' point of view, it can appear that the organizational structure is far more important than the people who work there. In many of the reengineered structures, reorganization and downsizing have resulted in many workers losing their jobs and in feelings of instability and overwork among those who remain. At the same time, the managers in these restructured organizations are stressing the importance of their employees and touting the importance of "the performance of people." As a recent article in *Fortune* magazine states, workers are being asked to accept two contradictory statements:

You're expendable. We don't want to fire you, but we will if we have to. Competition is brutal, so we must redesign the way we work to do more with less. Sorry, that's just the way it is. And one more thing—you're invaluable. Your devotion to our customer is the salvation of this company. We're depending on you to be innovative, risk-taking, and committed to our goals.[137]

An organization's structure is important, but it is never more important than its employees. So, while libraries and other types of organizations search for better, more efficient structures, they must keep in mind that the effectiveness of the structure depends primarily on the performance of the people working there.

Today the most successful companies are those where top executives recognize the need to manage the new environmental and competitive demands by focusing less on the quest for an ideal structure and more on developing the abilities, behavior, and performance of individual managers.[138]

The next two chapters will focus on the organization's employees and will discuss the managerial functions of staffing and directing. They will discuss how to deal with the important and challenging area of human resources.

Notes

1.   Edward E. Lawler III, *From the Ground Up: Six Principles for Building the New Logic Corporation* (San Francisco: Jossey-Bass, 1996), 12-13.

2.   Herbert G. Hicks and C. Ray Gullett, *Management*, 4th ed. (New York: McGraw-Hill, 1981), 321.

3.   Ibid.

4.   Henry Mintzberg, *The Rise and Fall of Strategic Planning: Reconceiving Roles for Planning, Plans and Planners* (New York: Free Press, 1994), 399.

5.   Robert Johansen and Rob Swigart, *Upsizing the Individual in the Downsized Organization: Managing in the Wake of Reengineering, Globalization, and Overwhelming Technological Change* (Reading, MA: Addison-Wesley, 1994), xi.

6.   Rosabeth Moss Kanter, Barry A. Stein, and Todd D. Jick, *The Challenge of Organizational Change: How Companies Experience It and Leaders Guide It* (New York: Free Press, 1992), 3.

7.   Andrew Wilson, "U.S. Firms Restructure and Revitalize," in *The Dynamic American Firm*, ed. Kenneth Chilton et al. (Boston: Kluwer Academic Publishers, 1996), 153.

8.   Joanne D. Eustis and Donald J. Kenney, *Library Reorganization and Restructuring* (SPEC Kit, 215) (Washington, DC: Association of Research Libraries, 1996).

9.   Johansen and Swigart, *Upsizing the Individual in the Downsized Organization*, 13.

10.   Joe A. Hewitt, "What's Wrong with Library Organization? Factors Leading to Restructuring in Research Libraries," *North Carolina Libraries* 55, no.1 (Spring 1997): 3.

11.   Johansen and Swigart, *Upsizing the Individual in the Downsized Organization*, x.

12.   Michael Hammer and James Champy, *Reengineering the Corporation: A Manifesto for Business Revolution* (New York: HarperBusiness, 1993).

13.   Joanne R. Euster et al., "Reorganizing for a Changing Information World," *Library Administration and Management* 11, no. 2 (Spring 1997): 103.

14.   Miles H. Overholt, "Flexible Organizations: Using Organizational Design as a Competitive Advantage," *Human Resources Planning* 20, no. 1 (1997): 23.

15.   Johansen and Swigart, *Upsizing the Individual in the Downsized Organization*, 12.

16.   Harold Koontz and Cyril O'Donnell, *Principles of Management: An Analysis of Managerial Functions*, 4th ed. (New York: McGraw-Hill, 1968), 239.

17.   Jay Lorsch, "Organizational Design," in *Managing People and Organizations*, ed. John J. Gabarro (Boston: Harvard Business School Publications, 1992), 313-14.

18.   Jay R. Galbraith, *Organization Design* (Reading, MA: Addison-Wesley, 1977), 13.

19.   Henry Mintzberg, *The Structuring of Organizations: A Synthesis of the Research* (Englewood Cliffs, NJ: Prentice-Hall, 1979), 13.

20.   Peter F. Drucker, *Post-Capitalist Society* (New York: HarperBusiness, 1993), 48.

21.   John Naisbitt, *Megatrends: Ten New Directions Transforming Our Lives* (New York: Warner Books, 1982), 14.

22.   Peter F. Drucker, *Management: Tasks, Responsibilities, Practices* (New York: Harper & Row, 1974), 455.

23.   John H. Jackson and Cyril P. Morgan, *Organization Theory: A Macro Perspective for Management* (Englewood Cliffs, NJ: Prentice-Hall, 1978), 3.

24.   John P. Kotter and James L. Heskett, *Corporate Culture and Performance* (New York: Free Press, 1992), 15-18.

25.   R. H. Kilmann, "Corporate Culture," *Psychology Today* 28 (April 1995): 63.

26.   Edgar H. Schein, "Organizational Culture," *American Psychologist* 45 (February 1990): 111.

27.   Andrew Pettigrew, "The Creation of Organizational Cultures" (Paper presented to the Joint EIASM-Dansk Management Center Research Seminar, Copenhagen, 18 May 1976), 11 (Quoted in Thomas J. Peters and Robert H. Waterman Jr., *In Search of Excellence: Lessons from America's Best-Run Companies* [New York: Harper & Row, 1982], 104).

28.   Edgar Schein, *Organizational Culture and Leadership* (San Francisco: Jossey-Bass, 1992): 228-53.

29.   A. Taylor, "Why Toyota Keeps Getting Better and Better and Better," *Fortune* 122 (November 19, 1990): 66-79.

30.   Lowell A. Martin, *Organizational Structure of Libraries* (Lanham, MD: Scarecrow Press, 1996), 12-13.

31.   Howard M. Carlisle, *Management: Concepts and Situations* (Chicago: Science Research Associates, 1976), 331.

32.   Peter F. Drucker, *Managing the Non-Profit Organization* (New York: HarperCollins, 1990), 114-15.

33.   Drucker, *Management*, 530.

34.   James A. Belasco, *Teaching the Elephant to Dance: Empowering Change in Your Organization* (New York: Crown, 1990), 2.

35.   Robert Howard, "The CEO as Organizational Architect: An Interview with Xerox's Paul Allaire," *Harvard Business Review* 70 (September-October, 1992): 120-21.

36.   Henry Mintzberg, "Organization Design: Fashion or Fit?" *Harvard Business Review* 59 (January-February 1981): 103.

37.   Richard T. Sweeney, "Leadership in the Post-Hierarchical Library," *Library Trends* 43, no. 1 (Summer 1994): 67.

38.   Ibid.

39.   Benson P. Shapiro, "Functional Integration: Getting All the Troops to Work Together," in *Managing People and Organizations*, ed. John J. Gabarro, 358-59.

40.   Hugh C. Atkinson, "The Impact of New Technology on Library Organization," in *The Bowker Annual of Library & Book Trade Information*, 29th ed. (New York: R. R. Bowker, 1984), 113, 114.

41.   Ibid., 114.

42.   Charles R. Martell Jr., *The Client-Centered Academic Library: An Organizational Model* (Westport, CT: Greenwood, 1983), 67.

43.   For a description of how a library instituted a client-centered approach to organization, see Claudine Arnold Jenda, "Management of Professional Time and Multiple Responsibilities in a Subject-Centered Academic Library," *Library Administration and Management* 8, no. 2 (Spring 1994): 97-108.

44.   *Books, Bricks, and Bytes: Daedalus* 125, no. 4 (Fall 1996).

45.   Henri Fayol, *General and Industrial Administration* (New York: Pitman, 1949), 14.

46.   Allen B. Veaner, *Academic Librarianship in a Transformational Age* (Boston: G. K. Hall, 1990), 129.

47.   Hicks and Gullett, *Management*, 350.

48.   Mintzberg, *The Structuring of Organizations*, 181-213.

49.   Ibid., 183.

50.   Peter M. Senge, "Communities of Leaders and Learners," *Harvard Business Review* 75, no. 5 (September-October 1997): 30-31.

51.   Kenneth Chilton, "American Manufacturers Respond to the Global Marketplace," in *The Dynamic American Firm,* ed. Kenneth Chilton et al., 174.

52.   Ibid., 166.

53.   Jay R. Galbraith and Edward E. Lawler III and Associates, *Organizing for the Future* (San Francisco: Jossey-Bass, 1993), 8.

54.   John Naisbitt and Patricia Aburdene, *Re-inventing the Corporation* (New York: Warner Books, 1985), 5-6.

55.   Mintzberg, *The Structuring of Organizations*, 342-44.

56.   Tom Peters and Nancy Austin, *A Passion for Excellence: The Leadership Difference* (New York: Random House, 1985), 317.

57.   See, for example, Lyndall Urwick, "The Manager's Span of Control," *Harvard Business Review* 34 (May-June 1956): 41.

58.   Lawler, *From the Ground Up,* 90.

59.   J. B. Treece, "Will GM Learn from Its Own Role Models?" *Business Week* (December 10, 1990): 62-64.

60.   Peters and Waterman, *In Search of Excellence*, 306.

61.   Andrall E. Pearson, "Six Basics for General Managers," in *The Craft of General Management,* ed. Joseph L. Bower (Boston: Harvard Business School Publications, 1991), 17.

62.   Michael B. McCaskey, "An Introduction to Organizational Design," *California Management Review* 17 (Winter 1974): 13-20.

63.   Peters and Waterman, *In Search of Excellence*, 307.

64.   Drucker, *Management*, 601.

65.   Peters and Waterman, *In Search of Excellence*, 306.

66.   Mintzberg, *The Structuring of Organizations*, 4.

67.   Mintzberg, "Organizational Design: Fashion or Fit?" 103.

68.   Ibid., 3.

69.   Henry Mintzberg, "Musings on Management," *Harvard Business Review* 74, no. 4 (July-August 1996): 61.

70.   Harold Steiglitz, "What's Not on the Organization Chart," *The Conference Board RECORD* 1 (November 1964): 7-10.

71.   Harvey F. Kolodny, "Some Characteristics of Organizational Designs in New/High Technology Firms," in *Organizational Issues in High Technology Management*, ed. Luis R. Gomez-Mejia and Michael W. Lawless (Greenwich, CT: JAI Press, 1990), 174.

72.   Charles Perrow, *Organizational Analysis: A Sociological Review* (Belmont, CA: Wadsworth, 1970), 50.

73.   Peter M. Blau and W. Richard Scott, *Formal Organizations* (San Francisco: Chandler, 1962), 27.

74.   Jackson and Morgan, *Organization Theory*, 77.

75.   Elliot Jaques, "In Praise of Hierarchy," *Harvard Business Review* 68 (January-February 1990): 127.

76.   See, for example, Robert K. Merton, "Bureaucratic Structure and Personality," *Social Forces* 18 (May 1940): 560-68; Philip Selznick, *TVA and the Grass Roots* (Berkeley, CA: University of California Press, 1969); Alvin W. Gouldner, *Patterns of Industrial Bureaucracy* (New York: Free Press, 1954).

77.   See, for instance, James D. Thompson, *Organizations in Action: Social Science Bases of Administrative Theory* (New York: McGraw-Hill, 1967).

78.   Warren G. Bennis, *Changing Organizations: Essays on the Development of Human Organization* (New York: McGraw-Hill, 1966); Rensis Likert, *The Human Organization: Its Management and Value* (New York: McGraw-Hill, 1967).

79.   Howard, "The CEO as Organizational Architect," 110.

80.   Mintzberg, *The Structuring of Organizations*, 375.

81.   Meredith Belbin, *The Coming Shape of Organizations* (Oxford: Butterworth-Heinemann, 1996), vi.

82.   Tom Burns and G. M. Stalker, *The Management of Innovation* (London: Tavistock, 1966), 119-20.

83.   McCaskey, "An Introduction to Organizational Design," 14.

84. Burns and Stalker, *The Management of Innovation*, 122.

85. Charles Handy, *The Age of Unreason* (Boston: Harvard Business School Press, 1989), 89.

86. Burns and Stalker, *The Management of Innovation*, 122.

87. Overholt, "Flexible Organizations," 23.

88. Paul R. Lawrence and Jay W. Lorsch, *Organization and Environment: Managing Differentiation and Integration* (Boston: Graduate School of Business Administration, Harvard University, 1967).

89. Joan Bechtel, "Collegial Management Breeds Success," *American Libraries* 12 (November 1981): 605-7.

90. Susan Jacobson, "Reorganization: Premises, Processes and Pitfalls," *Bulletin of the Medical Library Association* 82, no. 4 (October 1994): 370.

91. R. Euster and Peter D. Haikalis, "A Matrix Model of Organization for a University Public Services Division," in *Academic Libraries: Myths and Realities* (Chicago: American Library Association, 1984), 357.

92. Michael Gorman, "The Organization of Libraries in the Light of Automation," *Advances in Library Automation and Networking*, vol. 1 (Greenwich, CT: JAI Press, 1987): 160-61.

93. Ann De Klerk and Joanne R. Euster, "Technology and Organizational Metamorphoses," *Library Trends* 37 (Spring 1989): 467.

94. Ibid., 464.

95. John Lubans, "I Ain't No Cowboy, I Just Found This Hat: Confessions of an Administrator in an Organization of Self-Managing Teams," *Library Administration and Management* 10, no. 1 (Winter 1996): 37.

96. Jackson and Morgan, *Organization Theory*, 152.

97. Carlisle, *Management: Concepts and Situations*, 373.

98. Alex Bloss and Don Lanier, "The Library Department Head in the Context of Matrix Management and Reengineering," *College & Research Libraries* 58, no. 6 (November 1997): 499-508.

99. Euster and Haikalis, "A Matrix Model of Organization," 359-60.

100. Christopher A. Bartlett and Sumantra Ghoshal, "Matrix Management: Not a Structure, A Frame of Mind," *Harvard Business Review* 68 (July-August 1990): 139.

101. Euster and Haikalis, "A Matrix Model of Organization," 359-60.

102. John M. Stewart, "Making Project Management Work," *Business Horizons* 8 (Fall 1965): 54-68.

103. Edward E. Lawler and Susan A. Mohrman, "Quality Circles After the Fad," *Harvard Business Review* 63 (January-February 1985): 64-85.

104. Ibid., 64-71.

105. Joan S. Segal and Tamiye Trejo-Meehan, "Quality Circles: Some Theory and Two Experiences," *Library Administration and Management* 4 (Winter 1989): 19.

106. E. E. Adam, "Quality Circle Performance," *Journal of Management* 17, no. 1 (1991): 25-39.

107. David R. Hampton, *Management* (New York: McGraw-Hill, 1986), 391.

108. Jana Schilder, "Work Teams Boost Productivity," *Personnel Journal* 71 (February 1992): 69.

109. Rush G. Miller and Beverly Stearns, "Quality Management for Today's Academic Library," *College & Research Libraries News*, 55 (July/August 1994): 408.

110. Gerald R. Lowell and Maureen Sullivan, "Self Management in Technical Services: The Yale Experience," *Library Administration and Management* 4 (Winter 1989): 20.

111. Lowell and Sullivan, "Self Management in Technical Services," 23.

112. Wilson, "U.S. Firms Restructure and Revitalize," 159.

113. See, for example, Joseph F. Boykin Jr. and Deborah Babel, "Reorganizing the Clemson University Library," *The Journal of Academic Librarianship* 19, no. 2 (May 1993): 94-96; Joanne R. Euster et al., "Reorganizing for a Changing Information World," *Library Administration and Management* 11, no. 2 (Spring 1997): 103-14; Joan Giesecke, "Reorganizations: An Interview with the Staff from the University of Arizona Libraries," *Library Administration and Management* 8, no. 4 (Fall 1994): 196-99; Susan Jacobson, "Reorganization: Premises, Processes and Pitfalls," *Bulletin of the Medical Library Association* 82, no. 4 (October 1994): 369-74; John Lubans, "I Ain't No Cowboy, I Just Found This Hat: Confessions of an Administrator in an Organization of Self-Managing Teams," *Library Administration and Management* 10, no. 1 (Winter 1996): 28-40; Nancy Markle Stanley and Lynne Branche-Brown, "Reorganizing Acquisitions at the Pennsylvania State University Libraries: From Work Units to Teams," *Library Acquisitions: Practice and Theory* 19, no. 4 (1995): 417-25.

114. Maureen Sullivan, "The Changing Role of the Middle Manager in Research Libraries," *Library Trends* 41, no. 4 (Fall 1992): 275-76.

115. Lubans, "I Ain't No Cowboy, I Just Found This Hat," 37.

116. Walt Crawford and Michael Gorman, *Future Libraries: Dreams, Madness, and Reality* (Chicago: American Library Association, 1995), 123.

117. Eustis and Kenney, *Library Reorganization and Restructuring*, 2.

118. Jerry D. Campbell, "Building an Effectiveness Pyramid for Leading Successful Organizational Transformation," *Library Administration and Management* 10, no. 2 (Spring 1996): 86.

119. Hewitt, "What's Wrong with Library Organization?" 6.

120. Overholt, "Flexible Organizations," 24.

121. Peter F. Drucker, *The Practice of Management* (New York: Harper & Row, 1954), 195-201.

122. Carla J. Stoffle, Robert Renaud, and Jerilyn R. Veldof, "Choosing Our Futures," *College & Research Libraries* 57, no. 3 (May 1996): 223.

123. Lawler, *From the Ground Up,* 17.

124. Jacobson, "Reorganization," 373.

125. Euster et al., "Reorganizing for a Changing Information World," 105.

126. Ann E. Prentice, "Jobs and Changes in the Technological Age," *Journal of Library Administration* 13, nos. 1-2 (1990): 52.

127. Jackson and Morgan, *Organization Theory,* 148-49.

128. Joanne R. Euster, "The New Hierarchy: Where's the Boss?" *Library Journal* 115 (May 1, 1990): 43.

129. Clifford Haka, "Organizational Design: Is There an Answer?" *Library Administration and Management* 10, no. 2 (Spring 1996): 75.

130. Sweeney, "Leadership in the Post-Hierarchical Library," 62.

131. Lorsch, "Organizational Design," 315.

132. Peters and Waterman, *In Search of Excellence,* 311.

133. See, for example, Tom Peters, *Liberation Management: Necessary Disorganization for the Nanosecond Nineties* (New York: Alfred A. Knopf, 1992).

134. David Fagiano, "Pendulum Swings Back," *Management Review* 86, no. 8 (September 1997): 5.

135. Ibid.

136. Drucker, *Management,* 602.

137. Brian O'Reilly, "The New Deal: What Companies and Employees Owe One Another, *Fortune* 129 (June 13, 1994): 44.

138. Bartlett and Ghoshal, "Matrix Management," 138.

Readings

Belbin, Meredith. *The Coming Shape of Organization.* Oxford, UK: Butterworth-Heinemann, 1996.

Burns, Tom, and G. M. Stalker. *The Management of Innovation.* London: Tavistock, 1966.

Chilton, Kenneth, Murray Weidenbaum, and Robert Batterson. *The Dynamic American Firm.* Boston: Kluwer Academic Publishers, 1996.

Deevy, Edward. *Creating the Resilient Organization.* Englewood Cliffs, NJ: Prentice-Hall, 1995.

Drucker, Peter F. *Managing the Non-Profit Organization.* New York: HarperCollins, 1990.

Eustis, Joanne D., and Donald J. Kenney. *Library Reorganization and Restructuring* (SPEC Kit, 215),Washington, DC: Association of Research Libraries, 1996.

Galbraith, Jay R., and Edward E. Lawler III and Associates. *Organizing for the Future: The New Logic for Managing Complex Organizations.* San Francisco: Jossey-Bass, 1993.

Gomez-Meija, Luis R., and Michael W. Lawless, eds. *Organizational Issues in High Technology Management.* Greenwich, CT: JAI Press, 1990.

Hackman, J. Richard, and Greg R. Oldham. *Work Redesign.* Reading, MA: Addison-Wesley, 1980.

Hammer, Michael, and James Champy. *Reengineering the Corporation: A Manifesto for Business Revolution.* New York: HarperBusiness, 1993.

Handy, Charles. *The Age of Unreason.* Boston: Harvard Business School Press, 1989.

Howard, Jennifer, and Laurence Miller. *Team Management: Creating Systems and Skills for a Team-Based Organization.* Atlanta, GA: Miller Howard, 1994.

Kanter, Rosabeth Moss, Barry A. Stein, and Todd D. Jick. *The Challenge of Organizational Change: How Companies Experience It and Leaders Guide It.* New York: Free Press, 1992.

Kotter, John P., and James L. Heskett. *Corporate Culture and Performance.* New York: The Free Press, 1992.

Lawler, Edward E. III. *From the Ground Up: Six Principles for Building the New Logic Corporation.* San Francisco: Jossey-Bass, 1996.

Martin, Lowell A. *Organizational Structure of Libraries.* Rev. ed. Lanham, MD: Scarecrow Press, 1996.

Mintzberg, Henry. *The Structuring of Organizations: A Synthesis of the Research.* Englewood Cliffs, NJ: Prentice-Hall, 1979.

Naisbitt, John, and Patricia Aburdene. *Re-inventing the Corporation.* New York: Warner Books, 1985.

Osborne, David, and Ted Gaebler. *Reinventing Government: How the Entrepreneurial Spirit Is Transforming the Public Sector.* Reading: MA: Addison-Wesley, 1993.

Pearson, Gordon. *The Competitive Organization: Management for Organizational Excellence.* London: McGraw-Hill, 1992.

Peters, Thomas J., and Robert H. Waterman Jr. *In Search of Excellence: Lessons from America's Best Run Companies.* New York: Harper & Row, 1982.

Peters, Tom. *Thriving on Chaos: Handbook for a Management Revolution.* New York: Alfred A. Knopf, 1987.

Schein, Edgar H. *Organizational Culture and Leadership.* 2d ed. San Francisco: Jossey-Bass, 1992.

4

Staffing

*Digital information libraries have human resource requirements
that are only now beginning to come clear.*[1]

—Peter R. Young,
"Librarianship: A Changing Profession"

Organizations could not exist without people. To a large extent, an organization's employees are the key to its success or failure. Even in highly automated settings, people are required to coordinate and control the automated functions. And while libraries and other information agencies are becoming more automated, they are still highly labor intensive organizations, with most of them devoting between 50 and 60 percent of their budgets to employee costs. In such labor-intensive organizations, the human resources are especially critical to success, because almost everything else in the organization depends on them. A library can have an outstanding collection of print and electronic materials, access to a wealth of online resources, cutting-edge automated systems, and an award-winning building, but if it does not have a well-trained, competent staff, the patrons using the library will not be served effectively. Thus, in libraries and information centers as in most other organizations, one of the manager's most critical functions is to provide the human resources needed to carry out the functions of the organization.

The function of staffing encompasses all the tasks associated with obtaining and retaining the human resources of an organization. These tasks include recruitment, selection, training, evaluation, compensation, and development of employees. Until recently, all of these staffing functions were termed "personnel management," but in recent years that term has been replaced with another—"human resources management." Although the two phrases are still sometimes used synonymously, human resources management has been the favored term since 1989, when the American Society for Personnel Administration (ASPA) voted to change its name to the Society for Human Resources Management (SHRM). The name change was symbolic of the expanding role that human resources, another term for an organization's employees, play in the modern workplace. Employees are no longer looked upon just as "costs" to the organization; instead they are "resources," just as the budget and the physical plant are resources. All resources are important, but good human resources are the greatest asset an organization can have.

> &The organization which treats people as assets, requiring maintenance, love and investment can behave quite differently from the organization which looks upon them as costs, to be reduced whenever and wherever possible.[2]
>
> —Charles Handy, *The Age of Unreason*

As a result of this change in outlook, the role of human resources specialists has been redefined. In most organizations human resources specialists have moved away from being considered paper-pushing, clerical workers to being thought of as a strategic part of management. Today they spend a large part of their time matching organizational problems with human resource solutions, demonstrating the impact that human resources have on the "bottom line" of the organization.[3] In almost all modern organizations, there is a realization that the organization is the people who work there. Hence those specialists who work with employees are recognized as an essential part of the organization.

Some large libraries and information centers have specially trained individuals who work exclusively on the staffing aspects of management. These individuals, usually called human resources or personnel directors, are responsible for directing the human resource functions. Other information centers or special libraries located within larger organizations use the human resources services of the parent organization. In a large organization, the human resources department consists of a director (and possibly other professional level workers) and support staff members who perform the clerical functions. In libraries, the human resources or personnel directors sometimes have MLS degrees, with additional coursework and experience in human resources management, but often this person is not a librarian.

Many libraries and information agencies, however, are too small to have one person who is a full-time human resources or personnel specialist. Instead, the director usually performs the top-level staffing functions that relate to the entire organization. But in every library, even in those large enough to have a human resources department, all managers, from directors down to first-line supervisors, are involved in staffing functions. For instance, many librarians have supervisory responsibility over others, and human resources management comes with that responsibility because the training and evaluation of library employees are usually performed within a specific department by an employee's immediate supervisor. Although the degree of responsibility for human resources increases as a manager moves up the hierarchy, staffing is a basic task for every manager. For that reason, the principles of good human resources management should be widely understood throughout the organization.

The need for human resources skills usually appears early in a manager's career, and some librarians never have an opportunity to learn effective human resources management before they must practice it. Many new librarians in their first positions are called upon to supervise other workers, oftentimes workers with a great deal more seniority than themselves.

Usually, one of the most challenging—and sometimes frustrating—aspects of every manager's job is dealing with people-related problems. Because no organization is static, the people in it and the problems associated with it change. Often, no sooner is one personnel problem solved, than another develops. And, it is crucial to remember that each person is different. Some managers proceed on the mistaken notion that everyone can be treated identically, but every employee is unique, and often techniques that have worked well with one employee will not be effective in dealing with another. So, although it is relatively easy to learn the basic principles of staffing, managing employees is a never-ending challenge.

> It is possible to spend countless hours reviewing the so-called newer theories of personnel management. Heavily influenced by the "Japanese Mystique" of "quality production" from "quality staff," these theories (and the practices they preach) are instructive and often useful. But it is the universality and timeliness of some old fashioned notions about sound personnel management practices that still matter most.[4]
>
> —David Bender,
> "Improving Personnel Management Through Evaluation"

Managing human resources has become more complex in the last few decades for a number of reasons. One of the reasons is the increasing diversity of the workforce: As it becomes less homogenous, a manager has to learn to deal with people from many different backgrounds. The American workforce is being transformed from a group composed largely of white males into one in which the majority of workers will be women, African

Americans, Hispanics, or employees who have recently immigrated from another country. This diversity provides organizations with great opportunities, but diversity can also present problems unless managers understand the needs of these new workers and accept the challenge of managing a heterogeneous workforce.

Another reason for the increasing complexity of personnel management centers around the expectations of most contemporary workers, especially well-educated employees. These employees expect to have jobs that are meaningful and that provide opportunities for promotion and career advancement. No longer are most employees content to remain in dead-end jobs where they have no input in the decisions that affect them and their jobs. Most managers realize that autocratic management is not an effective way of dealing with most of today's employees. Instead, managers who wish to have productive employees must empower workers, and the library profession is seeking ways to do this by decentralizing decision making and increasing employees' control over their work environment. According to Maureen Sullivan, administrators need to focus "on empowering others by encouraging self-responsibility and shared responsibility in the enterprise. . . . This empowerment represents a shift away from a dependent relationship to one of interdependence."[5]

Still another factor changing the nature of managing people in libraries and information centers is automation. In the past two decades, automation has restructured many library jobs, created others, and eliminated still others. Automation brings many benefits for library employees and users; at the same time, it complicates the jobs of managers and employees. Some employees find it difficult to adapt to new electronic technologies. In some organizations, technology is used to monitor the amount of work that employees perform, which many employees view as an invasion of their privacy. In addition to psychic stress, automation can also produce physical problems, often caused by the repetitive motions involved in using keyboards for long periods of time. Some employees develop technology-related ailments, such as carpal tunnel syndrome or back and neck injuries. Managers have had to become more knowledgeable about the potential and pitfalls of technology and its impact on employees.[6]

> New forms of technology inevitably change the ways people are mobilized to work as well as the kinds of skills and behavior that are critical for productivity. These changes are rarely born without pain and conflict—nor do they emerge exactly as planners envision them. Instead, new concepts of work organizations and behavior emerge from an interaction between the demands of a new technology, its social organization, and the

responses of the men and women who must work with the new technological systems.[7]

—Shoshana Zuboff,
"New Worlds of Computer-Mediated Work"

It is not just technology that is restructuring jobs. Many of the hierarchical organizational patterns are also being modified. Instead of a group of workers reporting to one supervisor, in many types of organizations the workforce is now structured into teams that to a large extent manage themselves. Team organization brings benefits to workers, but it also presents new challenges to managers.

In addition, many organizations have downsized and become smaller. In many cases, fewer employees are employed doing more work. Other organizations are relying more heavily on part-time or temporary workers. Organizations that are in the process of downsizing, are handling the same amount of work with a "leaner and meaner" employee pool, or have a large number of temporary employees provide additional complexities to human resources managers.

Finally, the job of the manager has become more complicated because of the growing number of external regulations, especially those from state and federal governments. The purpose of these regulations is to make organizations safer and more equitable. External regulations are not new; laws relating to pay, safety, and labor relations have been in place for decades. However, the number of regulations with which organizations must comply has increased, and managers dealing with people need to be knowledgeable about the various, often complex, regulations that pertain to their employees.

The ways in which organizations manage their employees have changed greatly because the fundamental principles of human resource management have changed. According to Michael Armstrong, following are the principles of modern human resource management:

1. People are the most important assets an organization has, and their effective management is the key to success.

2. Organizational success is most likely to be achieved if the human resources policies and practices are linked with and make contributions to the achievement of the organization's objectives and strategic plans.

3. The organization's cultures and values will exert a major influence on the achievement of excellence, and this culture must be managed so that the values are accepted and acted upon by employees.

4. Continuous effort is required to encourage all individuals in the organization to work together with a sense of common purpose.[8]

> ☒ Most human resource planning in American corporations has played second fiddle to other business decisions—judgments are made and human resources follow. But this condition is changing fast. There is now little doubt that human resources is achieving parity. . . . People are becoming a fundamental factor in corporate vitality and survival.[9]
>
> —Robert W. Goddard, "Work Force 2000"

This chapter provides an overview of the staffing function in libraries and information centers. The first part of the chapter describes the different types of staff found in a typical library and provides information about the organizational framework of various types of jobs that must be established before an organization can hire a staff. The central sections of the chapter focus on the staffing functions that relate directly to individuals holding jobs within an organization. These functions include hiring, training, evaluating, compensating, and disciplining employees. The chapter concludes with an examination of some of the external issues, especially legal issues and unionization, that have had a major impact on staffing in libraries.

Types of Staff

The staff of most libraries and information centers is composed of a diverse group of employees with various levels of education and responsibility. As libraries and information centers have incorporated more technology into their processes, the type of staff employed has necessarily become more varied. Professional librarians almost always constitute the smallest group of library employees. Typically, these librarians have earned at least one graduate degree, that is, a master's degree in library or information science, but some of them hold a second master's degree in a subject field or a doctorate. The professional staff works at the predominantly intellectual and nonroutine tasks, those requiring "a special background and education on the basis of which library needs are identified, problems are analyzed, goals are set, and original and creative solutions are formulated for them, integrating theory into practice, and planning, organizing, communicating, and administering successful programs of service to users of the library's materials and services."[10] Professional librarians serve in leadership roles, directing the total organization and the various departments and subunits. They also provide the expertise needed to fulfill the information needs of the library's patrons.

> ⚕[N]o professional should do a task which can be per-
> formed by a paraprofessional, no paraprofessional should do
> a task which can be performed by a clerical staff member,
> [and] no human being should do a task which can be per-
> formed by a machine.[11]

—Michael Gorman,
"The Academic Library in the Year 2001"

The support staff consists of workers with a wide range of skills, from paraprofessional to clerical. The support staff is usually the largest group of full-time employees in a library, and the activities of these employees cover a wide range of essential duties, including the tasks of entering, coding, and verifying bibliographic data; maintaining book funds; ordering; circulating materials; claiming serials; filing; and copy cataloging. The routine operations in most departments are handled by the support staff. The educational background of these workers varies widely. Some may have only a high school diploma, but many have a bachelor's degree, and some have graduate degrees of various kinds.

In the past decade especially, libraries have needed both librarians and support staff with a strong technology background. Many libraries and information centers now employ specialists to work specifically with technology, for instance to manage the library's local area network. These technology specialists are sometimes professional librarians, but often these employees do not have an MLS degree.

Libraries usually employ a large number of part-time employees. Part-time employees, such as pages in public libraries and student assistants in academic libraries, work at easily learned, repetitive tasks such as retrieving items from the stacks or shelving returned books. Because these workers typically work for only a limited period of time, they require a great deal of training and supervision in proportion to the number of hours they work.

As mentioned earlier, libraries are labor-intensive organizations, and, traditionally, the largest part of their budgets has been devoted to staff. In the past the traditional rule of thumb for dividing library budgets was 60 percent for personnel, 30 percent for materials, and 10 percent for other expenses. This budget ratio is rapidly being discarded. Many libraries are now confronted with no-growth or shrinking budgets while costs for library automation and library materials are climbing rapidly. A number of libraries have tried to reduce the size of their staffs to cut the cost of their human resources component. Like private corporations, libraries have become "leaner and meaner" organizations. Some feel that for libraries to remain viable still larger changes must be made. For instance, Jerry Campbell advocates that research libraries "reverse the current standard in budget ratios. The new look should be 33 percent for staff, 50 percent for materials/access, and 17 percent for 'other.' "[12] A change of this magnitude will be difficult to implement without an accompanying reduction in service and a loss of employee morale.

Nonetheless, libraries and information centers, like other organizations, must strive to improve their productivity. Many libraries and information centers are turning to part-time and contract workers in an attempt to achieve more flexibility and to save money. A recent survey showed that over 20 percent of 1995 MLS graduates are working in part-time or temporary positions.[13] Other libraries and information centers are employing contract workers to work on temporary assignments. Some others have employed contract workers to perform janitorial and groundskeeping services. Others have outsourced certain functions, including core functions such as cataloging, to outside agencies. The term *outsourcing* refers to purchasing from an outside source certain services or goods that an organization previously provided or produced for itself. All of these new methods of getting work done with different types of workers have the possibility of presenting problems to a manager. There is often a potential clash of attitudes about values and service between the permanent staff and these more temporary workers.[14] Long-term contract workers, hired as a cost-cutting measure to do basically the same job as regular employees but without being paid benefits, often resent the dual standard of compensation.[15] Libraries, like other organizations, must become more productive, but managers must realize that these economizing measures can make both their own work and their employees' lives more difficult.

Despite all of these attempts to downsize the number of employees,[16] the results have not produced significantly lower percentages of the library budget being devoted to staff. Public libraries still devote over 65 percent of their budgets to staff.[17] In the last statistics available from 1992, academic libraries reported a lower percentage of their budget, 51.78 percent, was spent on salaries and wages.[18] Compare this to when automation was first introduced into libraries, and it was predicted that the number of employees would decline as a result. This has not proven to be true. To date, library automation has done more to change the nature of jobs in the library than to cut the number of people needed to provide effective library service. In many cases, the introduction of automation has increased the demands for the services provided by libraries and information centers, and in fact has resulted in a need to add additional staff to meet the needs of users.

> ⌖Librarians of electronic information find their job now a radically restructured one—they must consciously construct human attention structures rather than assemble a collection of books according to commonly accepted rules. They have,

perhaps unwillingly, found themselves transported from the ancillary margin of the human sciences to their center. If this is so—and can it be doubted?—how should we train librarians, much less plan the buildings where they will work?[19]

—Richard A. Lanham, *The Electronic Word*

One of the most difficult issues that library administrators continue to face is matching the appropriate level of work to the appropriate type of employee. For many years, professional librarians for at least part of their working day engaged in tasks that did not require a professional background. This was especially true in small libraries, because in many small libraries the only employee was a professional librarian. During the 1930s and early 1940s, it was not uncommon to find libraries in which 50 percent or more of the total staff was classified as professional librarians. In the past few decades, the tasks that professional librarians perform have become more clearly demarcated from those done by other staff members, and, in many cases, tasks that previously had been done by professionals have been transferred to members of the support staff. These transfers have been made possible by the increase in the number of staff members in most libraries and by the introduction of new technologies. Today, in most libraries, the ratio is usually one professional librarian to three support staff members, and, in some libraries, the proportion of professional to support staff is even smaller. As library technology advances, it may be feasible to turn over still more functions to support staff, and the ratio of professional to nonprofessional may decrease even further.

The movement of task oriented work from the professional staff to the support staff has been under way for at least a generation and has been well documented. The shift illustrates an important social aspect of the "technological imperative" in that once a technology is applied to carry out very complex, routine mental work, that work is driven downward in the work hierarchy, away from professionals whose work then expands to comprehend new and more challenging responsibilities, such as those librarians now carry out. Thus in losing a "job," the librarians acquired a much more clearly definable professional responsibility. The change has provided magnificent professional enrichment opportunities for librarians and has similarly enriched the jobs of support staff.[20]

—Allen B. Veaner, "Librarians"

The last comprehensive attempt to clarify desirable staffing patterns in libraries was the 1976 "Library Education and Personnel Utilization" (LEPU) statement. Even though many parts of the statement are now outdated, it still has relevance because it recognizes (1) that skills other than those of librarianship are needed in libraries and (2) that nonlibrarians must have equal recognition in both the professional and support ranks. To accomplish this goal, the document recommends that libraries establish a dual career lattice that allows both librarians and nonlibrarian specialists to advance in their chosen careers. (See fig. 4.1.)

In addition to recognizing the importance of specialists, LEPU recommends that librarians be permitted to advance within an organization without becoming administrators. In many libraries, promotion and advancement are possible only when the employee assumes greater supervisory responsibility. However, there is a great need for administrators to recognize and financially reward the important role that nonadministrative librarians play. The LEPU statement advocates that there "are many areas of special knowledge within librarianship which are equally important [as administration] and to which equal recognition in prestige and salary should be given. Highly qualified persons with specialist responsibilities in some aspects of librarianship—archives, bibliography, reference, for example—should be eligible for advanced status and financial rewards without being forced to abandon for administrative responsibilities their areas of major competence."[21]

Although the LEPU statement was produced more than 20 years ago, most libraries and information centers have yet to deal successfully with some of its recommendations. Many libraries, despite the influx of nonlibrarian specialists, have yet to adopt dual career lattices to allow these nonlibrarians to advance, and most libraries still need to develop organizational patterns that will allow employees to advance in salary and in professional rank without becoming administrators.

Staffing patterns in libraries have been changed and complicated by the changes that technology has brought to the work environment. Most large libraries now employ a number of automation specialists—some of these specialists have library degrees, others do not. Largely as a result of automation, tasks that were once assigned solely to professional librarians have drifted downward and almost all tasks performed in libraries are more complex and intellectually demanding than before. The strict demarcation that was once observed in most libraries between support staff and professional librarians has eroded as virtually all employees of libraries have become knowledge workers.[22] As Allen Veaner has written, "Work classifications schemes have not fully caught up with this new reality; the once-easy bipolar division of staff into librarians and support personnel has become uncertain and subject to much questioning."[23] Some of the many job classifications of support personnel can be seen in table 4.1.

Fig. 4.1. Dual career lattices. From "Library Education and Personnel Utilization" (Chicago: American Library Association, 1976), p. 4. Reprinted by permission of the American Library Association.

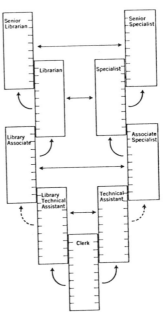

If one thinks of Career *Lattices* rather than Career *Ladders*, the flexibility intended by the Policy Statement may be better visualized. The movement among staff responsibilities, for example, is not necessarily directly up, but often may be lateral to increased responsibilities of equal importance. Each category embodies a number of promotional steps within it, as indicated by the gradation markings on each bar. The top of any category overlaps in responsibility and salary the next higher category.

Table 4.1—Types of Support Staff

The types of support workers employed in libraries and information agencies have increased, reflecting the changing and varied responsibilities of the support staff in today's libraries. The titles listed below were collected in a recent survey of support staff classifications.[24]

Delivery Worker	Applications Systems Analyst	Human Resources Specialist
Development Associate	Systems Specialist	LA Specialist/Coordinator
TV Repair Supervisor	Public Information Officer	Photographer
Curatorial Assistant	Business Coordinator	Fiscal Officer
Learning Disabilities Specialist	Graphic Design Specialist	Adult Literacy Specialist
Bookmobile Driver	Marketing Specialist	Volunteer Resources
Gallery Manager	Electronic Technician	Network Specialist

The library profession has not come up with a uniform model addressing the types of staffing patterns. Libraries and librarians need to look at the necessary qualifications for all levels of library work and hire a workforce that has qualifications matching those needed. Some groups, for instance the Special Libraries Association, have issued guidelines on the competencies needed by practitioners in a particular type of setting.[25]

Although the LEPU statement provides a general framework to be used in considering staffing needs and utilization, perhaps the fact that it has not been revised in over 20 years indicates that one set of guidelines is no longer sufficient to meet the complexity of staffing the modern information center.[26]

Charles Handy has suggested that the organizations of the future will be "shamrock" organizations, made up of three different groups of workers: "groups with different expectations, managed differently, paid differently, organized differently."[27] The first leaf of the shamrock is the core workers, the permanent employees who are essential to the organization. This core group is becoming smaller in all types of organizations. Work is increasingly being done by workers in the two other leaves: the contract workers and the part-time and temporary workers. Although these other groups of workers have always existed, what is different today is the relative sizes of the three groups.

> It happened because it had to. The bad years of the late 1970s and early 1980s forced organizations to make significant reductions in their manpower, most of whom were still full time employees. The threat of economic disaster forced them, in other words, to cut back their cores. When times improved, managers were not going to be caught the same way twice; they did not expand the core but went instead to the other two leaves.[28]

Libraries and information centers, like other types of organizations, are increasingly relying on a smaller core group with a reliance on part-time workers and outsourcing. They are employing an increasing number of support staff to perform diverse duties. And while the old patterns of staffing are disappearing, the patterns of the future are not yet clear.

The Organizational Framework for Staffing

> ✍As technology is added to the organization, it is often in addition to existing activities as in the case of online searching. New tasks are added to existing job descriptions or new jobs such as online librarian are created. The old tasks and old jobs may or may not go away. . . . [We] need to review

the workflow, review jobs and determine how each task contributes to the overall objective.[29]

—Ann E. Prentice,
"Jobs and Changes in the Technological Age"

Organizations are formed and jobs are created when the overall task of the organization is too large for any one individual. Libraries, like all organizations, are networks of interacting components. Jobs are the individual building blocks upon which the organization is built.

Although the terms *job*, *position*, and *occupation* are often used interchangeably, each has a distinct definition in human resource terminology. A *position* is a collection of tasks and responsibilities that constitute the total work assignment of one person. Thus, there are as many different positions in an organization as there are people employed there. The Slavic language cataloger in a large academic library holds a position as does the bookmobile driver in a public library. A *job*, on the other hand, is a group of positions that generally involve the same responsibilities, knowledge, duties, and skills. Many employees, all performing slightly different work, may be classified under the same job title. A library may employ many catalogers, all of whom have different responsibilities but whose duties are similar enough to be classified in the same job group. An *occupation* is defined as a general class of job found in a number of different organizations, for example, librarianship is considered to be an occupation.

A job should always be a planned entity consisting of assigned tasks that require similar or related skills, knowledge, or ability. Ideally, jobs should never be created haphazardly at the whim of an employee or to suit the special knowledge or ability of a particular individual. Instead, jobs should be carefully designed to ensure maximum organizational effectiveness. It is the responsibility of the library administration to identify the tasks that are to be included in a job. The tasks should be similar or related. All the tasks to be accomplished by a specific job should require approximately the same level of education. One task should not be so excessively complex that extensive education is required, while another is so simple that it could be performed by an individual with much less education. Further, the tasks assigned to any one job should require comparable experience. Some tasks can be performed only after extensive experience, while others can be executed by novices. And last, tasks assigned to a job should require comparable responsibility. Some tasks have end responsibility, which means that there is no review of what is done. The action of the individual in a job having end responsibility is final. Such end responsibility is frequently found in reference services, book selection, and top administration. Other jobs require little or no end responsibility. Work is reviewed. Revisers in a catalog department may have end responsibility, while the catalogers whose work is revised have no end responsibility. To summarize, a well-defined job has assigned to it tasks that are (1) comparable in the amount of education required, (2) comparable in the amount of experience required, and (3) comparable in the degree of responsibility required.

It was long a principle of job design that all the tasks that comprised a job should, if possible, be related to the accomplishment of a single function, process, or program, or should be related to the same subject field or type of material. In large institutions, this was easily accomplished; in small institutions, however, workers often had to work at multiple tasks. Although in terms of specialization, the assignment of a single function, process, or program to a job makes sense in terms of efficiency, it can be carried too far. There is now a much greater interest in jobs that allow workers to practice multiple skills. This new interest reflects a growing belief that to make a job too narrow may, in many cases, be detrimental to workers and managers. To increase flexibility within organizations, jobs are now being designed to take advantage of multiple skills. More organizations are encouraging cross training, that is, having employees learn techniques for jobs other than their own so that if the need arose, there would be additional employees who would know how to get a specific job done. Workers are being encouraged to work both with and across other functions and units.

This flexibility and broadening of job responsibilities is a change in the way that jobs have traditionally been structured. The allotment of narrow, specialized portions of a large task to specific workers is known as division of labor. Adam Smith, in *The Wealth of Nations* (1776), first wrote about the benefits of division of labor. When each job consists primarily of a few simple, repetitive tasks, the skill level and training required for performing that job are low.

In the United States during most of this century, the scientific management principles popularized by Frederick W. Taylor and the Detroit style of mass production introduced by Henry Ford heavily influenced the thinking of individuals who designed jobs. There was widespread acceptance of the principle of dividing tasks into small component units and having each worker responsible for just a small portion of the overall task. This type of job design promoted efficiency and ease of training. More recently, there has been a realization that this approach to job design disregards the psychological nature of the worker and often leads to worker dissatisfaction and alienation. Often workers who perform one small task over and over begin to feel like cogs in a machine. Now, many industries are trying to provide job enrichment by redesigning jobs so they comprise a wider variety of tasks and more responsibility. In addition, in the spirit of continuous improvement, all organizations, including libraries and information centers, are rethinking the design of jobs in an attempt to find better ways of accomplishing the objectives of the organization.

> &Job enrichment will not be a one-time proposition, but a continuous management function. . . . The argument for job enrichment can be summed up quite simply: if you have employees on the job, use them. If you can't use them on the job, get rid of them, via automation or selecting someone with lesser ability. If you can't use them and you can't get rid of them, you will have a motivation problem.[30]
>
> —Frederick Herzberg, "One More Time"

Although few library jobs were ever as narrow and confining as those on an assembly line, the principle of job enrichment is especially important in organizations like libraries and information centers. The educational level of most of the employees in a library is typically quite high, and well-educated workers are usually seeking jobs that are intellectually challenging. A job should not be so restrictive that assigned tasks are quickly mastered and soon become dull, monotonous, and boring. Instead, the scope of a job should be large enough to challenge and encourage employees to grow in skills, knowledge, and abilities. Some jobs in libraries must be performed according to prescribed procedures to maintain uniformity or because of standardized methodologies. These jobs are generally low in the hierarchy. Nevertheless, even at this level, the employee should be given every opportunity to be creative, to exercise initiative, and to vary the routines, as long as the established standards are maintained. The "judicious expansion" of certain jobs leads to higher productivity, lower absenteeism, and increased job satisfaction, whereas routine and repetitive tasks discourage initiative and tend to produce apathetic and uncommitted workers.[31]

Technology has had the greatest impact on lower-level jobs where work is routine, with less of an effect on higher-level jobs where decision making is concentrated. Just adding technology to a job function does not in itself make the job more interesting. In fact, information technology can lead to de-skilling when the computer takes decision making away from an employee and "makes it possible to formalize the skills and know-how intrinsic to a job and integrate them into a computer program."[32] To further complicate things, sometimes lower-level employees feel that technology is forced upon them by managers who themselves are not using a great deal of technology in their own jobs.[33]

A recent study of paraprofessional technical services positions found that the introduction of technology had changed the positions over time

primarily by changing the tools by which the work is done. It had done little to add autonomy, authority, and decision making to the positions.[34]

It is not easy to redesign jobs to make them more fulfilling to workers, and some workers resist job enrichment. Although the buzzword now
in all types of organizations is *empowerment*, it must be remembered that
there are some workers who do not want to be empowered.

> People work in organizations for many reasons: to earn a
> paycheck, to get away from home, to contribute to society, to
> make friends, to master particular skills, to get recognition and
> the like. Some people even come to work because they enjoy
> being told what to do, or they feel most secure in a structured,
> well-ordered environment, or they get satisfaction out of doing
> one thing well, over and over. In other words, not all people
> want to be empowered to make their own decisions, and
> assuming that they do can create dysfunction.[35]
>
> —Ron Ashkenas et al.,
> *The Boundaryless Organization*

A basic rule for human resources management is to match the individual to the job, with workers who do not want autonomy and empowerment not being forced to accept them. Nonetheless, the talents of great
numbers of workers are underutilized at the present time, and it benefits
both the worker and the organization to create jobs that allow employees
to work up to their full potential. If libraries want their employees to be innovative and responsible, they must provide jobs that give employees an
opportunity to develop these factors.

Hackman and Oldham have proposed a model that identifies five
core job dimensions essential to job enrichment. These dimensions are:

- Skill variety. The extent to which a job requires a number of different
  activities using a number of skills and talents.

- Task identity. The extent to which a job requires completing a whole
  piece of work from beginning to end.

- Task significance. The worker's view of the importance of the job.

- Autonomy. The extent to which employees have the freedom to plan,
  schedule, and carry out their jobs as desired.

- Feedback. The extent to which a job allows the employee to have
  information about the effectiveness of their performance.

As figure 4.2 illustrates, these core job characteristics lead to critical psychological states that allow the worker to experience the meaningfulness of the work, the responsibility for the outcome of the work, and the knowledge of the actual results of the work. These psychological states affect an employee's feeling of motivation, quality of work performed, and satisfaction with work, and they lead to low absenteeism and turnover.[36]

Fig. 4.2. Hackman and Oldham's core job characteristics.

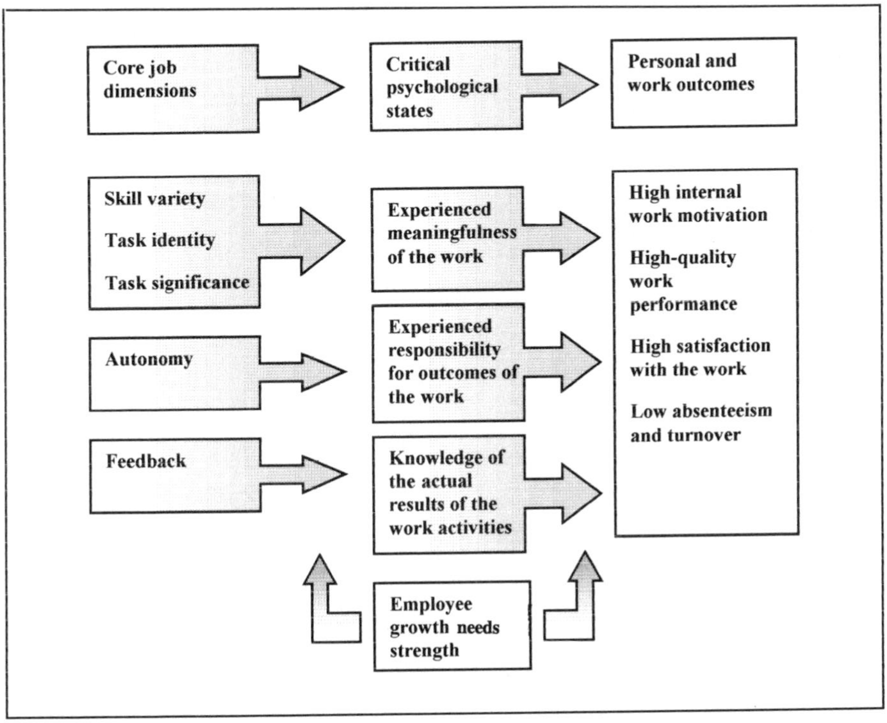

Despite a great deal of interest in the area of job design, no new model has arisen to replace the Hackman and Oldham job characteristics model.[37]

Job design continues to be a dominant area of interest for theorists and researchers. . . . Jobs are the window through which individuals perceive, experience, and contribute to organizations. Similarly, jobs are also the window through which organizations direct the work of individuals in productive ways, assess their value to the organization and undertake efforts to motivate their behavior.[38]

Just as organizations are changing, so are the jobs within organizations. Managers need to look at the jobs in the organization and see if they are designed in a way that balances the need for efficiency with the need for a more enriched job to ensure employee motivation. Since the Hackman and Oldham model has been found to be an effective way of understanding job design, jobs should be designed as much as possible to provide the core elements of job variety, autonomy, task significance and identity, and feedback.

Job Descriptions

After a job has been established, the next step is to write a job description that specifies the duties associated with that job, the relationship of the job to other units of the institution, and the personal characteristics, such as education, skill, and experience, required to perform the job. Today, most government agencies and private industries require job descriptions for all employees. Job descriptions vary from organization to organization, but generally contain the following elements:

1. *Job identification.* This section of the description typically includes the job title, line number, and department.

2. *Job summary.* This section of the job description provides a description of the major responsibilities and provides a justification for the existence of the job.

3. *Job activities and procedures.* This section includes a description of the tasks performed by the incumbent in the job, sometimes including the percentage of the job that is devoted to each of the tasks. There should be clear delineation of what the duties and responsibilities of the job are, although some flexibility often is inserted by the use of a phrase such as "and other duties on occasion as assigned." The enumeration of the job's activities and procedures is the most important part of the job description. This enumeration identifies for the employee the exact tasks for which he or she will be responsible. It also indicates to the supervisor those tasks that require training, supervision, or task evaluation. Without this section of the job description, neither the employee nor the supervisor knows what the employee is expected to do. The tasks assigned should, of course, be comparable in the amount of education, experience, and responsibility required and should demand similar or related skills, knowledge, and abilities.

4. *Relationship of the job to the total institution.* This section states the title of the person to whom the incumbent reports, the number of employees or the organizational unit supervised by this job, and the internal and external relationships required by the job.

5. *Job requirements*. Job requirements are established by each organization and identify the minimum acceptable qualifications required for an employee to perform the job. Requirements often include amount of education; amount of experience; and special skills, knowledge, or abilities demanded. All job requirements should be necessary for the successful performance of the job. For some jobs, requirements are set unrealistically high, which artificially restricts the pool of possible applicants. Sometimes, job specifications reflect what the organization would like to have and not what is necessary to perform the job effectively. Job specifications (for example, an educational requirement such as a college degree) that are not essential for successful job performance are invalid and may violate Title VII of the 1964 Civil Rights Act.

Job descriptions fulfill several important administrative and human resources needs. A job description may be used in recruiting new employees. Not only does the recruiter know exactly the capabilities for which to search, but the candidate also knows exactly what would be expected if the job were accepted. For this reason, the job description always should be made available to applicants for their study and review. After an individual has been hired, the job description becomes the basis for determining training needs and identifying tasks that require special effort before the employee can perform them well. Later, the job description becomes the basis for formal performance appraisal. Job descriptions are also used to evaluate job worth to aid in developing a compensation structure. Appendix C includes examples of job descriptions.

Job Analysis

In principle, a job should be stable over time. Once the job has been defined and the characteristics necessary to perform it have been specified, the job should not be appreciably changed by the incumbents holding the job or by different situations. In reality, though, jobs are dynamic and often change considerably over time. New machinery or equipment may be introduced. Departments or even entire libraries may be reorganized. Changing technology may alter the skill requirements necessary for a job. In libraries, for instance, the job of cataloger has changed greatly since the introduction of the bibliographic utilities. Thus, it is important to remember that job descriptions and specifications must be kept up-to-date to ensure that they still describe the activities and characteristics of that job.

&Job categories change constantly in an evolving economy. Once all telephone calls were made through an operator. . . . Today there are comparatively few telephone operators, even though the volume of calls is greater than ever. Automation has taken over.[39]

—Bill Gates, *The Road Ahead*

Because all jobs change over time and because employees, by emphasizing or deemphasizing certain portions of their jobs, can produce drastic changes in the job, all organizations should occasionally perform a job analysis. The job analysis allows the institution to gather information about what is actually being done by employees holding specific jobs. A variety of methods may be employed for a job analysis. Some of the most common include direct observation of the job, interviews, written questionnaires, or asking employees to record what they do on a job through a daily log or diary. Each of these methods has its advantages and disadvantages. It is beneficial to acquire data using more than one method to make sure that sufficient information is gathered. The results of the job analysis can be useful in writing new job descriptions, in specifying the skills and abilities needed by workers holding the job, and in determining the appropriate compensation for that job. A job analysis can also indicate when a job needs to be redesigned.

Sometimes employees feel threatened by a job analysis, but in most cases the data provided by the analysis allows an organization to effectively manage its human resources and to provide better training, performance evaluation, and promotion and compensation opportunities.

&The quality of job analysis is also very important to the employee. The job is where the employee and the organization come together. The job is the domain of the employee and is an expression of the employee. It is that segment of the organization which the employee controls and manages. The employee will know when work is not well understood and managed. The employee will conclude and rightly so, that the organization does not value his/her work when it does not accurately analyze and manage that work.[40]

—James P. Clifford,
"Manage Work Better to
Better Manage Human Resources"

Because a complete job analysis of all positions is not only time-consuming but demands extensive expertise, complete analyses are not performed regularly in libraries. When they are, library administrators often call in special human resources or management consultants to help accomplish the analysis. Another approach found in some libraries is to use the human resources department of the parent institution to perform the analysis. For example, the human resources department of a municipal or county government or of a college or university might assist in designing and carrying out the job analysis program.

To keep jobs up-to-date between complete analyses, supervisors should report any significant changes in the makeup of tasks in their units. Some institutions conduct periodic audits of the jobs in every department. The audit involves checking the tasks that are actually being performed against the ones specified on the job description. When discrepancies are found, either changes are made in the work habits of the employee, if certain essential tasks are not being carried out, or changes are made in the job description, so that it will reflect the changes that have occurred in the job for legitimate reasons (for example, the introduction of new equipment or technology).

Job Evaluation

After jobs have been designed and accurate job descriptions written, all the jobs within the organization are arranged in hierarchical order. An attempt is made to enumerate the requirements of each job and its contribution to the organization and then to classify it according to importance. Skill, education, experience, and the amount of end responsibility are common criteria used in making this evaluation. A number of methods can be used to assign jobs to ranked categories.

Some organizations use the point method. These organizations develop a quantitative point scale that identifies the factors involved in a job and assign weights to the factors. The higher the number of points, the higher the job is in the hierarchy. Other organizations use a factor system, which is calculated by comparing jobs one with another and also by subdividing jobs into factors that have dollar values attached to them. The factor method is similar to the point method but with a monetary scale in place of a point scale.

Two nonquantitative systems are widely used for evaluating jobs. Simple ranking systems compare actual positions to one another to create a ranked hierarchy. The job classification system defines classes of jobs on the basis of duties, skills, abilities, responsibilities, and other job-related qualities. The jobs are grouped into classes arranged in a hierarchy. Regardless of the system used, it is always the job that is classified, not the employee holding the job.

The hierarchically arranged jobs are divided into various groups, which vary from library to library. Usually, all professional librarian positions fall into one group; library assistants or paraprofessionals into another; and library technicians, clerks, and custodians into still others. Within each group there will be hierarchical levels based upon the experience, education, and responsibility associated with each job. A job title is assigned to each level, usually modified by the use of a numeral. Jobs requiring the same level of education, experience, and responsibility are given the same title, although the tasks associated with each may be different. Both an experienced reference librarian and an experienced cataloger could be classified as Librarian III. Figure 4.3 shows a hierarchy of professional library positions.

Fig. 4.3. A hierarchy of professional level jobs.

Job Title	Education	Experience	End Responsibility
Librarian IV	MLIS from an accredited LIS school plus an Advanced Certificate	10 years' with 3 years in supervisory positions	Final responsibility for the operation of the institution
Librarian III	MLIS from an accredited LIS school plus subject specialization	5 years of professional experience	Under general supervision and according to policies, end responsibility for a department
Librarian II	MLIS from an accredited LIS school	2 years of professional experience	Under general supervision and according to policies, responsible for a unit of a department
Librarian I	MLIS from an accredited LIS school	0 years of experience	Under general supervision and according to policies, performs assigned task

The same procedure is used for all other job groups. A hierarchy for clerical level jobs is shown in figure 4.4. There is no standard for the number of levels in each group. In larger institutions there may be many, in smaller ones only a few.

Fig. 4.4. A hierarchy of clerical level jobs.

Job Title	Education	Experience	End Responsibility
Clerk III	High school plus business school graduate	3 years of experience	Under general supervision, end responsibility for payroll
Clerk II	High school plus some business school	2 years of experience	Under general supervision, end responsibility for verifying invoices
Clerk I	High school diploma	0 years of experience	Under close supervision, perform assigned tasks

If a library uses the dual career lattices recommended by LEPU, it will have two lattices, one for the nonprofessional and professional librarians and another for nonlibrarian specialists. Specialists are placed at the same level of the hierarchy as librarians if their education, experience, and end responsibilities are comparable. A library using a dual career lattice would have a classification like that illustrated in figure 4.1.

Recruitment and Hiring

Recruitment involves seeking and attracting a pool of applicants from which qualified candidates for a vacant position can be chosen. When librarians recruit candidates, they need to consider the labor market. In most libraries, support staff positions are filled from the local labor market. Openings are advertised only in local publications, and almost all support staff positions are filled by individuals already living in the area. On the other hand, in many libraries candidates for professional vacancies come from the national labor market. Almost all libraries and information centers recruit top administrators nationally. In these cases, libraries and information centers advertise in national periodicals, such as *American Libraries, Library Journal,* or *The Chronicle of Higher Education,* in the hope of attracting a large number of well-qualified applicants.

The Internet is changing the way that open positions are being advertised. The classified sections of many newspapers and specialized publications are available on various Web sites. For instance, *The Chronicle of*

Higher Education's position openings can be seen at http://www.chron-icle.merit.edu/.ads/.links.html. There are also sites specifically devoted to employment advertisements where job seekers can search job openings by category. Some organizations, including libraries, publicize open positions on their own Web sites. Many libraries post positions to be filled on specific list-serves that are apt to be read by people with the appropriate background for and interest in the job vacancy. Advertising on the Internet is advantageous to both the organization with the open position and the job seeker because it usually provides access to information about positions to individuals who might not see the printed ad, especially if it appeared in a regional newspaper that the job seeker did not usually read.[41] The cost is generally lower also.

Because libraries serve a multicultural clientele, most libraries try to hire a culturally diverse staff. These efforts sometimes are unsuccessful, especially at the professional level. Despite attempts to increase the number of minorities in the profession, minorities are still underrepresented. In 1994-1995, only 4.24 percent of the graduates of ALA accredited programs were African American, 2.17 percent were Hispanic, 3.44 percent were Asian/Pacific Islander, and .16 percent were American Indian, percentages far below the representations of these groups in society.[42] In the Association of Research Libraries (ARL) libraries in 1996-1997, minority librarians made up 15.7 percent of the total librarians.[43] In an attempt to increase the number of minorities in libraries, libraries and schools of library and information science have tried a number of approaches. Some have introduced undergraduate internship programs designed to bring more minorities into the profession. Others have established minority intern programs to attract new MLS graduates. Other libraries have instituted diversity plans to coordinate their efforts to produce a more diverse workforce.

> ॐ Women, Hispanics, Asian Americans, African Americans, Native Americans—these groups and others outside the mainstream of corporate America don't bring with them just their "insider information." They bring different, important, and competitively relevant knowledge and perspectives about how to do work—how to design processes, reach goals, frame tasks, create effective teams, communicate ideas and lead. When allowed to do so. . . . [a diverse work force] can help companies grow and improve by challenging basic assumptions about an organization's functions, strategies, operations, practices and procedures.[44]
>
> —David A. Thomas and Robin J. Ely,
> "Making Differences Matter:
> A New Paradigm for Managing Diversity"

Despite these efforts, the profession has been relatively unsuccessful in attracting minorities to the field. Librarianship must compete with more lucrative professions, and, not surprisingly, often comes in second in terms of attracting minority entrants. Despite the difficulties, at each hiring opportunity managers should make an effort to attract qualified minority applications to diversify their workforce.

Applicants for a job often include both internal candidates, individuals already employed by the organization who are seeking job transfers or promotions, and external candidates, individuals from outside the organization. There are advantages and disadvantages associated with both the external and internal recruiting of personnel. The first advantage of recruiting external candidates is the larger pool of talent that can be tapped. The second advantage is that new employees bring fresh insights and perspectives to the organization. The major disadvantage to external recruiting is that filling a position with an external candidate generally takes a longer time and is more expensive than filling it with an internal candidate. It also takes a longer time for an employee hired from the outside to become oriented to the organization, because the new employee must acquire familiarity with the people, procedures, and special characteristics of a new organization.

The biggest advantage of filling positions with internal candidates is that it usually fosters high morale. Employees in organizations that have a policy of promotion from within have an additional incentive for good performance, because they know they will be considered for a promotion when openings occur. Another advantage of recruiting from within is that mnagement can more accurately appraise the suitability of the candidate. The internal candidate is a known factor, while the external candidate is less well known; therefore, there is less risk in the selection and placement of an internal candidate. There are, however, inherent problems and limitations of always relying on internal promotion. Probably the most dangerous is organizational inbreeding. When all subordinates have been employed by the same organization, they all may know just one way of doing things. When these subordinates are promoted, they tend to perpetuate what they have seen done in the past, and the organization may not be exposed to new ideas and innovation. In general, the best policy is probably filling the majority of vacancies from within when there are fully qualified individuals to assume these positions. But, it is also wise to fill at least some high-level positions by outsiders to inject new ideas into the organization.

Selection refers to the process of actually choosing the individual who will most likely perform the job successfully. The fundamental goal of selection is to achieve a good fit between the qualifications of the applicant and the requirements of the position. Successful matching of an applicant to a position is very important, because failures are not only costly to the persons hired but also to the organization. If the match is bad, corrective measures, such as training, transfer, demotion, or termination of employment, are often required.

The time spent in selecting the right person for a position is time well spent. Oftentimes, organizations do not realize the large investment of scarce organizational resources that may be committed to each new employee. A decade ago, Constance Corey studied the investment her library would make in a new entry-level librarian who would stay in the job for 25 years. She estimated that the investment would be in excess of $1 million, conservatively estimated, without including office furnishings, training, travel expenses, moving costs, or even the cost of recruitment itself.[45] With inflation, that figure would be even larger today. Since such a large sum of resources is associated with each new hire, it is wise to ensure that the best applicant is selected for each position. This has always been important, but is even more so now, when a slow job market means little turnover in library staffs. If the right candidate cannot be found the first time, it is better to readvertise the position and try again than to hire someone who may not be able to do the job.

One selection tool used more frequently in private corporations than in libraries is the assessment center. Assessment centers use comprehensive standardized procedures to make human resources decisions, primarily about hiring and promotion. Multiple assessment procedures, such as job simulations and situational exercises, are used to evaluate individuals. Trained management evaluators assess each individual's performance in exercises like discussion groups, in-basket exercises, and presentations, and then make recommendations about the candidate's strengths and potential. Assessment centers have been shown to have a high degree of accuracy in predicting success in the job, and the techniques have been accepted by the Equal Employment Opportunities Commission (EEOC) as a valid, racially blind method of selecting personnel.[46] Assessment centers are becoming more prevalent in the public sector, and some libraries are beginning to make use of this technique.[47]

Each organization should have a well-designed selection system. Typically, the selection process includes application forms, applicant testing, personal interviews, verification of past performance and background, and hiring.

Application Forms. Libraries often use standard application forms for vacant positions. In some cases, a cover letter and a resume are substituted for the application form. The application form is used by the employer to gain written information about the candidate. The typical application form contains questions that identify the applicant, such as name, address, and telephone number; questions about an individual's education and work experience; and questions related to the specific requirements of the job or the organization. The employer receiving an application form must ensure that the applicant has the experience and the education needed for the job. The employer looks for steady progress in experience and asks questions about unexplained gaps in the work history. Information on the application form allows tentative judgments to be made about an applicant's suitability for a position; it also screens out obviously unqualified candidates.

Applicant Testing. Some libraries use tests to see if an applicant possesses the skills needed for a specific job. These tests are most useful when the job requires certain skills that can be easily tested. For instance, a typist might be given a typing test to ensure that the applicant's speed and accuracy are satisfactory. The most useful tests are a sample of the work itself or a task that closely resembles the work and requires the same skills and aptitudes. If a test is used for selection, the EEOC requires that the employer establish the validity and reliability of the test.

Job Interview. When the pool of candidates has been narrowed down, the most promising applicants are invited for an interview. Sometimes, libraries initially interview candidates by telephone, but, in most cases, telephone interviews are used to narrow a pool of candidates and to choose those who will be invited for a personal interview. The job interview is the single most important tool in the selection process. Although many employers do not use tests in selecting employees, very few do not interview job candidates. In many libraries, multiple interviews are held, thus allowing a wider participation in the selection process.

The purpose of the interview is to supplement information obtained through other sources. The interviewer uses this opportunity to find out more about the applicant's technical and professional knowledge, experience, and personal characteristics. The applicant finds the interview useful to learn more about the job itself, to clear up any uncertainties about the position or the organization, and to be introduced to the staff that he or she would work with if hired.

The sole focus of the interview should be job requirements, and questions should be designed to provide information about an individual's suitability for the job that is being filled. It is important to remember that all questions asked during an interview should be job-related. The EEOC has forbidden the use of interview questions that are not related to job requirements. Candidates may not be asked questions about race, religion, gender, national origin, age, or handicaps. Specific questions that are prohibited are listed in table 4.2.

Table 4.2— Permitted and Prohibited Questions in Employment Interviews

Topic	Permitted	Prohibited
Marital status	None	Are you married? Are you planning to get married? What does your spouse do? Do you have children?
Sexual Orientation	None	Do you live alone?
National origin	None	Where were you born?
Citizenship	Do you have a legal right to work in the U.S.?	Are you a U.S. citizen?
Religion	None	Do you go to church? Synagogue?
Disabilities	None	Do you have any health problems? Any disabilities?
Criminal History	Have you ever been convicted of a crime?	Have you ever been arrested?
Age	None	How old are you?[48]

Interviewing is a skill that can be improved with practice. To start, the interviewer should prepare for the interview. He or she should be familiar with the information provided by the candidate on the application form. The interviewer should plan an outline of questions to be asked and specify the information that he or she is trying to obtain. The same basic questions should be asked of all individuals being interviewed for a specific position. The interviewer should also arrange a place for the interview that will be private and free of interruptions.

&Since the establishment of Affirmative Action, it has been universal practice to compile a uniform list of key questions for all candidates. Even if there were no legal requirement, a consistent instrument applied to all candidates would be the most sensible, rational course in recruiting, and a definite aid to minimizing bias.[49]

—Allen B. Veaner,
Academic Librarianship in a Transformational Age

One of the first rules of interviewing is to put the applicant at ease. A relaxed applicant will display a more normal behavior pattern than a tense applicant. The candidate should be encouraged to talk, but the interviewer must maintain control of the interview and remember that the objective is to gather information that will aid in the selection process. Too often, interviewers spend an excessive amount of time discussing the organization and the position and never obtain from the applicant the information needed to make a good hiring decision. The best interview is one in which the applicant does most of the talking.

The interviewer must listen carefully and note pertinent facts. He or she should refrain from excessive notetaking, however, because it will inhibit the applicant. Questions should be phrased correctly. Open-ended questions elicit the best answers because they force a candidate to think through a situation. The interviewer should avoid leading questions, that is, questions that signal the desired answer. Instead of asking, "You wouldn't object to weekend work, would you?" ask, "How would you feel about working weekends?" The interviewer should never be judgmental. By refraining from expressing disbelief or shock at a candidate's response, the interviewer encourages the person to reveal failures as well as successes. As soon as the interview is over, the interviewer should record his or her impressions about the applicant. If this is delayed, valuable information and impressions about the applicant will be forgotten.

Background Verification. At some point, either before or after the interview, an employer will want to verify information provided by the candidate by contacting references and previous employers. Most jobs require that the applicant list references: personal, school, or past employers. Personal references are unreliable, because few applicants would list a person who would not give a highly favorable reference. If the applicant has a work history, previous employers are the most valuable source of information. An applicant should give written permission to have references checked before the individuals listed as references are contacted.

Reference checking is frequently conducted by telephone. It is felt that individuals provide more frank and specific information on the telephone than in writing. Some organizations, however, divulge information about past employees only in writing, and the amount and type of information provided varies from organization to organization. Usually, a prospective employer is able to verify the accuracy of the information the applicant provides, such as position held, last salary, supervisory responsibilities, and reasons for leaving. The prospective employer may also ask whether the previous employer would be willing to rehire the employee and why. Although previous or present supervisors usually provide accurate assessments, sometimes they may give a better recommendation than the applicant deserves—either because they would like to see that applicant leave his or her present place of employment, or because they do not feel comfortable giving negative information about individuals. The reference checkers should probe and follow up if they feel that the person giving the reference is hesitant or not responding to the questions being asked.

The same set of basic questions should be asked of all references about all candidates. Only questions relating to an applicant's job performance should be asked. Even if references are checked on the telephone, the prospective employer should also ask to have a written reference so that there will be written documentation if an employment decision is challenged.

If an applicant does not list supervisors from recent jobs as references, a prospective employer might want to contact them anyway. Very few applicants falsify their credentials, but it is always wise to verify the information given. If a particular educational background is required, the applicant's school record should be confirmed. A person's job history might be verified by calling the organizations listed to ensure that the person has indeed worked there. The investigation into an applicant's background is sometimes overlooked by prospective employers. It costs little in either time or money and is generally worth the effort.

Hiring. The last step in the selection process is choosing the individual who will be hired to fill the vacant position. In some libraries, many people contribute to the final decision, especially for professional positions. Search committees, which are commonly used in academic and other types of libraries, are one way of allowing peer involvement in the selection process. The search committee usually recommends a ranked list of finalists for the position, then an administrator usually makes the final choice. In some libraries and information centers, the director always makes the final decision; in others, the immediate supervisor is allowed to choose, subject to the approval of higher management. If the appropriate information has been gathered and if the four selection steps have been performed effectively, the likelihood of making a good decision is quite good; the applicant's qualifications will match the job requirements, and the fit should be successful.

If good hiring practices are not followed, an organization may be plagued by a high level of turnover in its staff. While turnover can have many causes, one of the most common is job dissatisfaction. While a certain amount of turnover is healthy, and allows organization to bring in employees with new ideas and experiences, excessive turnover can be detrimental. It is costly because an employee has to be replaced, and a new one has to be retrained. A great deal of turnover also can threaten morale in an organization because the remaining employees feel that there is a lack of continuity and that the organization is in a constant state of change. An excessive amount of turnover should be a warning to a library to carefully examine its hiring and recruitment practices.

Training and Staff Development

Almost all practicing librarians have some assigned responsibilities that involve training other employees. The trainee may be a shelver, a beginning clerical employee, or another professional. As a professional librarian assumes a greater role as manager, training will become a major responsibility.

Training can be as limited as instructing an individual in specific steps that are essential for achieving a coordinated, uniform product. Or, training can be as broad as presenting the philosophies and techniques essential to make a community analysis. Here, the term covers the gamut from how to why, that is, instructing an individual not only how to do a job but also why an assigned job is important. An employee who performs a task without understanding why it is important and how it fits into the endeavor of the institution will perform perfunctorily at best. If the employee understands and appreciates why a job is assigned, the task will be performed more efficiently.

In a library, as in any institution, there are many levels of training. Some training is received by everyone; other parts of the training program are more individualized. Although training is expensive in terms of the time it takes, it is false economy to try to minimize it. Over a period of time, the cost to the institution is returned in quality performance.

The first type of training typically received is an orientation. After an employee has been hired, he or she needs a general orientation to the organization. Usually, if a number of new employees come in at about the same time, a general orientation meeting is held. This general orientation for all employees provides information that all employees need, regardless of level or place of employment within the institution. Perhaps some of the information was transmitted during the selection process, but it is wise to reinforce that knowledge. A general orientation usually includes two basic areas: general information and the goals, objectives, and philosophies of the organization.

The general information part of the orientation covers rules and policies applicable to all employees, including information concerning pay periods, how vacation and sick leave are accumulated and how they can be used, requirements for reporting illness, and the use of time clocks. Many libraries have specific ways of answering telephone calls, such as requiring that the name of the library or department and the individual's name be given. The reason for this requirement is explained. Some libraries require employees to wear name tags. Again, the reason for this is given. The overall policies that affect all employees are interpreted in a way that makes the new employee a part of the organization and sympathetic with its general requirements.

> ᛒ[M]ore often than not, after the new employee is chosen, the contract is signed, and the beginning work date is set, the people involved in the hiring process wipe their brows (with a muttered "Thank goodness that slot is filled!"), and move back into the flow of business as usual without making adequate preparations for their newly appointed librarian.[50]
>
> —Dorothy E. Jones,
> "I'd Like You to Meet Our New Librarian"

Each employee, regardless of level or place of employment in the institution, needs to know its overall goals, objectives, and basic service philosophies. The director should make the presentation on these topics, not only because he or she best knows the philosophies, goals, and objectives of the institution, but also because the new employee is impressed and more readily accepts such information when it comes from the chief administrator. New employees who receive a careful introduction to policies and procedures will more easily assume a productive role in the organization.

Although some libraries still treat orientation sessions in a casual manner, others have given careful thought to what should be included. For instance, figure 4.5 illustrates the checklist used by Kent State University in its orientation for new employees. The form asks for signatures of all the individuals involved to ensure accountability.[51]

As soon as a new employee reports for work, the immediate supervisor begins training in the specific tasks of the job. Occasionally, this training is given by the person leaving the job, but the practice of having the incumbent train the new employee is risky, particularly if the departing employee has been a problem. The practice perpetuates the departing employee's work habits and patterns, and it frequently establishes attitudes and opinions toward the supervisor, the department, and the organization. For these reasons, it is recommended that the immediate supervisor be in charge of training new employees.

There are many ways of training. The worst way is to verbally describe in a few minutes the tasks to be performed. The new employee, already uneasy by being in a new environment with new responsibilities, probably will hear little of the supervisor's remarks. Some employees are able to observe other employees, figure out the job from the job description, or learn the job on their own, in spite of the supervisor. Others fail, and their failure is the fault of the supervisor.

Fig. 4.5. Checklist for new employees: what every new libraries/media services employee should know. From Shelley L. Rogers, "Orientation for New Library Employees: A Checklist," *Library Administration and Management* 8, no. 4 (Fall 1994): 213-17. Reprinted with permission of the American Library Association.

What Every New Libraries/Media Services Employee Should Know
C H E C K L I S T

√ DIRECTOR OF STAFF SERVICES discusses:

I. Introduction to Kent State University and Libraries/Media Services

DATE

- University ID card
- Parking permit
- Map of campus; tour of especially relevant offices, such as Personnel
- Tours: department, main library, branch libraries, regional libraries as appropriate
- Introductions to staff
- Promotional materials about University services and organizations (e.g., Wellness Center, physical fitness facilities, Audio Visual Services, Professional Women of Kent State University)
- Copies of undergraduate and/or graduate catalogs

DATE

- Community information: what does Kent offer ... Portage and Summit Counties ... greater Akron/ Cleveland metropolitan areas ... Ohio
- Library circulation policies
- When the library operates
- List of University paid holidays
- Keys and getting into the building outside of normal work schedule
- Completion of *Confidential Vital Information Record*
- Safety manual
- University/corporate perks (e.g., Sea World, Sam's Club, American Express card)

II. Personnel Policies and Procedures

DATE

- Breaks: length, frequency, where allowed physically, coordination with co-workers, etc.
- Lunch/dinner, including bringing food into the library
- Flextime availability
- Calling supervisor, forms to fill out for sick leave, vacation, leave of absence
- Court leave
- Use of radios and radio/headphones on the job
- Making/receiving personal telephone calls
- Dress codes
- Attending classes, completing class assignments

DATE

- Changing one's regular schedule
- Attendance at University and library functions and meetings, such as May 4 Remembrance, Women's Day events, etc.
- Timecards
- Professional development: meetings, conferences, seminars; travel reimbursement
- Pay raises
- Promotions
- Exiting the University
- Faculty issues: reappointment, tenure, sabbatical, faculty committees, mentors, library liaison program, use of research leave, exit interviews

III. Information About the Job and the Organization

DATE

- Information about the relationship with the supervisor, including: chain of command; administering discipline/ rewards; performance evaluations; communicating with supervisor, including what supervisor needs to know and what is confidential
- Information about relationships with co-workers: when and how to discuss mutual interests and concerns; what to tell the supervisor
- Information about relationships with supervisees: policies as for supervisors above

DATE

- L/MS personnel structure: organizational charts, personnel rosters, descriptions of committees, how to become involved
- L/MS communication methods: memo writing protocol, telephone protocol, availability of committee reports, *Local Data Record, Inside, Matrix, Connect,* other publications and reports, communicating with others
- List of L/MS telephone numbers
- List of radio stations to tune in if snow might close down University operations

Director of Staff Services sign-off:

New Employee sign-off:

continued

Fig. 4.5 (continued)

✓ SUPERVISOR discusses:

	DATE		DATE
• Training information: how long is training period, when reviewed, who reviews performance, when is a decision about employment binding, implications with respect to layoffs	_____	• Getting into the department outside of regular working hours	_____
• Job description/outline of job responsibilities	_____	• Relationship with supervisor: the chain of command, expectations of the supervisor, departmental meetings, how to request other meetings, when and how to discuss issues and concerns	_____
• Procedures manuals: personal copy or knowledge of ready availability	_____	• If new employee supervises others, the supervisor may make recommendations on how the new employee should relate with supervisees	_____
• When the department operates	_____	• Word processing: availability of computers and software for on and off the job	_____
• Work schedules of co-workers and supervisor	_____	• Supplies and equipment: when and how to request	_____
• Personal schedule: regular working hours, timeliness	_____		

Supervisor sign-off: _____

New Employee sign-off: _____

✓ PERSONNEL – STAFF BENEFITS OFFICE discusses:

	DATE		DATE
• Benefits: tuition waiver, insurance (life, medical, dental), retirement, travel reimbursement	_____	• Explanation of Benefits Fest	_____

Personnel Office sign-off: _____

New Employee sign-off: _____

Training must be carefully planned. The following principles guide a good trainer:

1. Teach the simple tasks first.
2. Break down the task into its basic components.
3. Teach only the correct procedures.
4. Keep teaching cycles short, and reinforce them with practice.
5. Develop skills through repetition.
6. Motivate the trainee.

A library's responsibility for training and education does not end when a new employee is properly trained for his or her position. Periodically, following the initial orientation, the institution provides continuing training programs for new employees and for selected groups of employees.

New employees need more orientation to the institution than that provided by the general orientation; they also need an understanding of the responsibilities of the various organizational units of the library. Units, such as the human resources office, the public information office, and various subject or functional departments, are described so that employees see their role in the total organization. These training sessions are usually conducted by the manager of the unit being discussed. Using visual presentations and permitting extensive discussion and questions makes such sessions productive.

Training for new employees continues for a long time as these new hires become socialized into the organization's culture, with its norms for acceptable and unacceptable behavior. These new employees will look to more senior staff members to serve as role models. When faced with a gap in knowledge, they will usually turn to more senior employees to act as teacher or coach. Experienced staff play a vital role in helping new employees make an effective transition to a new setting.[52]

Staff Development

> Any organization develops people; it has no choice. It either helps them grow or it stunts them. It either forms them or it deforms them.[53]
>
> —Peter F. Drucker,
> *Managing the Non-Profit Organization*

It is not only new employees who need continuing education. Employees who enter libraries and information centers with the best educational preparation need continual updating to stay current. The rapid changes taking place in all types of libraries compel them to attach new importance to staff development and continuing education. This continuing education can be offered in various ways. On a recurring basis, as specific training needs are identified, selected groups of employees might receive training in specific topics, such as how to conduct good performance evaluation interviews, how to prepare performance evaluation reports, how to prepare departmental budget recommendations, or how to do task analysis for job description revisions. These training sessions, which concern all units of the organization, may be conducted by a specialist within the institution or by an authority brought into the institution for this purpose.

The training programs described so far are developed and presented by the institution. In addition, many training and educational programs exist outside the institution; these should be available to employees. Attendance at local, regional, and national conferences and workshops provides opportunities for employee development and growth. But, at the present time, when the roles and responsibilities of librarians of all types are changing, more structured forms of training or education must be available. Many institutions provide tuition funds for employees who take formal courses that are job-related. The need to take courses beyond the first professional degree increases as library operations become more complex. Some librarians may need extensive retraining to prepare them to work with a new computer system or to prepare them for new positions in other parts of the library. The fear of automation still encountered in a few librarians might be lessened if they knew that systematic plans were being made to retrain individuals displaced by automation.

Many organizations of all types have begun to view managers and supervisors as "coaches" for the employees they supervise. Like a good coach, a supervisor should act as a role model, help the employee set realistic goals, give feedback on performance, provide suggestions on how to improve, and provide reinforcement and encouragement. The supervisor and the employee should not view themselves as adversaries. Instead, they are on the same team, each trying to improve the overall performance of the organization.

Lois Jennings suggests that libraries are in a period of such rapid growth that their long-term success depends on "regrowing" their current staffs to enable them to make the transition from the end of one era in library services to the start of another. In Jennings' view, regrowing occurs on two fronts. First the staff must develop the understanding necessary for the library to become a different type of organization. Second, the staff must believe in the knowledge that they already possess as information professionals and reassess how they will reorient that knowledge to respond to changing client needs. Staff must let go of old ways of applying their skills and develop confidence in their ability to move beyond the comfort zone of established pattern. Although this type of growth is partly the responsibility of the individual as a professional, fostering the conditions for this growth requires leadership from the top.[54]

Peter Senge advocates that all organizations must be transformed into "learning organizations." Learning organizations are those where "people continually expand their capacity to create the results they truly desire, where new and expansive patterns of things are nurtured, where collective aspiration is set free and where people are continually learning how to learn together."[55] Senge contends that most modern organizations have learning disabilities—fundamental problems in the way jobs and organizations are structured that result in organizations learning poorly. He recommends that organizations adopt specific tools or disciplines that will help them learn better. These disciplines are:

- Systems thinking. Individuals understand the whole system and not just separate parts.

- Personal mastery. Individuals continually clarify and deepen their personal vision, focus their energies, develop patience, and see reality objectively.

- Mental models.

- Building shared vision. The leader's vision is transmitted and shared by all employees.

- Team learning.[56]

No library is exempt from change, and every library, regardless of size or type, needs a planned staff development program. Such activities are not haphazardly scheduled but are organized on a structured continuum. Such programs provide the means by which employees can grow on the job and pre pare to advance as opportunities become available. Good staff development programs contribute to employees' career development; through such programs, employers can identify potential supervisors and prepare them for that responsibility. Human resources are too valuable for any institution to fail to invest in the training programs that the times require.[57]

Mentoring

Mentoring is a specialized form of career development. Although mentoring has always existed in organizations of all types, only in the last few decades has the importance of this process been recognized. There has been a growing interest in mentoring, and a large number of articles and books about it have appeared recently in both the professional and popular press. The reason for this interest is the clear link between career success and having a mentor. Many studies provide evidence of this link; their findings are fairly consistent in stating that very few individuals advance to the top administrative ranks in an organization without the help of a mentor.[58]

Today, the term *mentor* is used to describe an influential person who significantly helps another, usually younger person, reach his or her major goals. A mentor is a person who oversees the career and development of another person. Michael Zey, in *The Mentor Connection*, identifies four functions of mentoring: teaching, psychological counseling and emotional support, organizational intervention, and sponsoring. The context and meaning of the term is adjusted slightly by each mentor and protégé. No two mentoring experiences are exactly alike, because no two people or set of organizational circumstances are exactly alike.[59]

The need for the mentor varies at different points in the protégé's career, and the things a mentor does for a protégé also differ. A new employee needs a mentor to help him or her learn more about the details of the job and the organization. As he or she becomes more technically competent and begins to ascend the organizational ladder, the need for teaching might be less important than the need for emotional support. When the appropriate times for promotion and advancement occur, the mentor can be most helpful by providing organizational intervention and sponsoring the protégé.

The advantages to the protégé are clear. But, as mentoring involves a considerable investment on the part of the mentor, it may be hard to understand what causes individuals to serve in such a capacity. Most mentors do not enter into such a relationship from altruism alone. The benefits are almost always mutual, and the mentoring role is almost always professionally rewarding. Sometimes, the mentor receives job assistance from the protégé and secures a valuable ally within the organization. In addition, the mentoring procedure causes the mentor to reexamine the day-to-day workings of the organization, which usually causes the mentor to learn more about the organization. Often, the protégé can serve as a sounding board for the mentor's ideas.

> ✍ Mentoring is a complex subject. There are advantages and disadvantages to the practice. Obviously, those in the organization who don't have mentors may resent those who do. . . . [I]f one wishes to continue to advance, developing a network that includes a mentor greatly enhances the probability of success.[60]
>
> —Joseph Berk and Susan Berk,
> *Managing Effectively*

A protégé who succeeds can make a mentor look very good. One of the responsibilities of present-day management is developing talent. The protégé validates the mentor's worth to the organization. Having protégés who can help perform the mentor's job shows the mentor to be a highly productive manager who knows how to delegate well. The mentor also gains a reputation as an individual who is able to spot and develop new talent. And, as a protégé advances, the mentor not only shares in the glory but builds up a strong network of past and present protégés. Finally, many mentors derive great personal pleasure out of the process. They enjoy teaching and feel a sense of personal gratification as the protégé's career advances. They are pleased to see the continuity of their own work carried on by the protégé.

The benefits of mentoring spill over to the organization. These benefits include properly socialized employees, integrated workers, and a smoothly functioning managerial team. Mentoring is almost always a three-way beneficial process. The benefits of mentoring are illustrated in figure 4.6.

There are more individuals who would like to have mentors than those who actually have them. Some organizations have established formal mentoring programs where new employees are provided a mentor. These programs sometimes succeed, but mentoring relationships that arise spontaneously usually are more successful, because both the mentor and the protégé see the value of each other without being forced into a relationship. With most library employees now having access to electronic mail, some mentors are now off-site and advise through e-mail.[61] Mentoring relationships, both formal and informal, should be encouraged by organizations as a means of career development and growth.

Fig. 4.6. Benefits provided by mentoring. From Michael G. Zey. *The Mentor Connection: Strategic Alliances in Corporate Life.* New Brunswick, NJ: Transaction Publishers, 1990. Reprinted with permission.

The Mutual Benefits Model

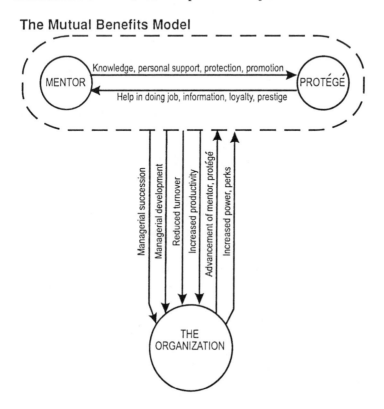

Plateauing and Burnout

The heightened interest in mentoring is natural, considering the demographic realities of our time. Members of the baby boom generation, having first experienced crowded elementary and secondary schools, then crowded colleges and dorms, and, fierce competition for entry-level jobs after graduation, are finally reaching the age where they expect to assume occupational positions of authority and responsibility. Instead, they face yet another shortage—this time, a shortage of higher level administrative positions. Because most industries are not expanding, there is a surplus of qualified managers, most of whom would like to advance in their careers. These individuals eagerly seek mentors in the hope of attaining an inside track on career success.[62]

> ℚAlthough virtually all employees' careers will stall somewhere short of the top, their growth within their job need not stop. The real difficulty will be keeping these plateaued employees contributing when they can no longer be stimulated by the promise of a promotion or a new career opportunity. Fortunately, there are ways to reinvigorate their work, to challenge them, and to keep the spark alive. People do not leave their organization because of lack of promotion, but because of lack of growth.[63]
>
> —Barbara A. DeLon,
> "Keeping Plateaued Performers Motivated"

Most organizations, including libraries and information centers, are now in either a nongrowth or a downsizing mode. Well-qualified employees find their career advancement blocked, because there are no openings in the positions directly above them and, even worse, many of these positions are held by individuals who are only slightly older than the employee who is seeking advancement, so there is little likelihood the position will be available before retirement. This phenomenon, which is called plateauing, is of great interest to managers, because many plateaued workers are frustrated, depressed, and nonproductive. Plateauing can occur in two ways. Structural plateauing occurs when an individual is no longer promoted within the organization; content plateauing means that a job has become routine, and no challenging tasks are added to it.[64] Both types of plateauing result in employees who are stuck and no longer stimulated by promise of promotions or new job content.

A special type of plateauing is sometimes referred to as the glass ceiling. The glass ceiling is an invisible barrier that prevents women and minorities from ascending the institutional hierarchy. Although in the past two decades, women and minorities have made significant progress into lower- and middle-management levels, neither are represented in upper management in proportion to their numbers in the general population. A recent Department of Labor study shows that the glass ceiling is real, not a product of disgruntled employees' imaginations.[65]

> ⚘Women complain about glass ceilings. They can see what goes on up there, at the so-called top; they just cannot easily get through. . . . But worse still may be the concrete floors. Too many managers can't even see what is going on at the ground level of their organizations, where the products are made and customers served [presumably]. This suggests that we need more than *transparency* in management. We need to smash up the ceilings and bust down the floors as well as break through the walls so that people can work together in that one big circle.[66]
>
> —Henry Mintzberg, "Musings on Management"

Although some employees accept plateauing as an inevitable part of a career, others do not. Supervisors often find that personnel problems such as irritation with fellow employees and intolerance of bureaucracy develop more frequently with plateaued employees than others. In addition, organizations can lose valuable workers who seek employment elsewhere when they feel that they are "stuck" in a no-promotion situation.[67]

Table 4.3—Human Resources Practices That Foster Successful Plateauing
Performance Management
1) Fight negative stereotyping with accurate appraisals
2) Ask around to appreciate fully how employees contribute
Training
1) Train for the future, not for advancement
2) Train everyone to contribute, not just the fast trackers
Career Development and Staffing
1) Broaden opportunities to grow on the job
2) Remove roadblocks to lateral and downward moves
3) Help employees identify new challenges
Compensation
1) Pay employees for performance, knowledge, or teamwork
2) Look beyond financial compensation
3) Check to see if your perks send the right messages
Human Resources Planning
1) Determine how many employees are plateaued
2) Determine what proportion of plateaued employees are successful[68]

Managers can use a number of strategies, including those listed in table 4.3, to help employees overcome the stress of plateauing. These strategies include job enrichment, lateral transfers, restructuring organizations to make them more horizontal so that decision-making power increases in the lower ranks, and educating employees about plateauing so that they will be prepared for periods of stagnation in their career development.[69] Employees can be encouraged to take advantage of mentoring and networking opportunities to offer career support and possibilities for change. Managers of libraries, as well as other organizations, should attempt to find ways to make jobs interesting and keep workers' enthusiasm alive, if they want to maintain the effectiveness of employees whose careers have become plateaued. To crack the glass ceiling, managers should encourage women and minorities to apply for promotions, as openings occur.

Job-Related Stress

&Many information professionals, fresh from graduate school, enter their first job filled with enthusiasm, eager to make a difference and to help people meet their information needs. . . . New librarians are not on the job for long, however, before they realize that their own needs and expectations do not always match the needs and expectations of their organization or their clients. Workloads are often too heavy for the time allotted; staff are expected to perform many jobs simultaneously; positive feedback, from either clients or the organization, is usually scarce. . . . Many organizations don't give staff a chance for input into their own destinies. These are some of the chronic stresses that can turn enthusiasm into stagnation, frustration, and eventually, apathy.[70]

—Mary Haack, John W. Jones, and Tina Roose,
"Occupational Stress Among Librarians"

Employees in all types of organizations are susceptible to stress. Stress can be the result of either mental or physical strain. Although libraries are sometimes considered to be stress-free environments, they are not, and library employees can be subjected to various sources of mental and physical stress, ranging from burnout to carpal tunnel syndrome.

Today more employees in all types of organizations, including libraries and information centers, are reporting feeling stress or tension as a result of their jobs. Without a doubt, among librarians part of the cause of this stress is the increasing rate of change within the profession. Librarians, now more than ever, are being asked to master new methods and technologies required for doing their jobs. Organizational change of all types, if too rapid and frequent, may result in stress. Some librarians feel the stress of what is known as role conflict when different groups of people hold different views about how that employee should behave. Oftentimes in libraries and information centers, there is tension between the professional and support staff when roles are blurred and changing.[71] In addition, in many libraries the effect of downsizing has resulted in a smaller number of employees doing the same amount of work.

Although it has been commonly thought that managers feel more stress than lower-level employees, recent research has shown that is not true. For example, a study of 270,000 male employees at a large corporation found that the rate of coronary disease increased at successively lower levels of the organizations. It is thought that top-level executives feel less stress because they have greater control and predictability over their work than employees at lower levels.[72] The more control employees have over their own work and the more information they have about possible changes that will occur, the less likely they are to feel job-related stress.

Stress may be evidenced in a number of ways including absenteeism, irritability, tardiness, and inability to perform well. Of course, not all stress-related disorders are caused by workplace stress; many employees have stresses caused by off-the-job factors, such as family problems, but the job of the manager is to help identify the cause of the stress and try to eliminate it if it is resulting from the job.

> Stress is not something "out there" or inherent in "stressful" things or situations. Rather stress is within a person—i.e., a response. The source of the demand or challenge is referred to as a "stressor." A stressor . . . for one person may cause a completely different response in another.[73]
>
> —Charles A. Bunge,
> "Stress in the Library Workplace"

Burnout is a specific type of stress-induced condition that affects individuals engaged in "people" work. Burnout results from emotional strain and the stress of interpersonal contact, especially from dealing with people who are having problems. Individuals suffering from burnout typically experience exhaustion, both physical and emotional; a negative shift in the way they respond to other people; and a loss of self-esteem.[74] The number of librarians suffering from the effects of stress or burnout is increasing as a result of working in such an ever-changing environment.

Remedies for burnout can be found at two levels. At the personal level, employees should structure their lives outside of work to give them a sense of comfort and control. Employees should pursue an active life outside of the work environment. The managerial responsibilities for aiding workers with burnout include knowing the symptoms of burnout and making workers familiar with them, holding staff meetings that can be used for staff support, and fostering a sense of teamwork among the staff. If staffing patterns permit, managers may also restructure jobs so that librarians do not spend as much time with patrons or revise schedules to shorten periods of time spent at public services desks. Workshops in stress management or time management can also be useful.[75]

It is important to try to prevent burnout, because it is rarely confined to one worker. "If one worker complains of the work environment and/or questions the worth, rewards, or necessity of his or her work, it is sure to have some effect on co-workers."[76] To keep burnout from spreading, managers need to recognize the symptoms and prevent it whenever possible.

> ⌖ There is a great discontinuity in the working lives of librarians of all kinds today. On the one hand, there are the omnipresent pressures of staffing services, maintaining libraries and their services, simply making sure that materials are acquired, catalogued, checked out and checked in—in short, the common task, the daily round that makes a library *work*. On the other hand, there are the futuristic dreams and nightmares—the feeling that somehow, some time soon, everything will be changed. Small wonder that so many librarians want to give up on the daily grind and trust in, or fear the electronic Wizard of Oz.[77]
>
> —Walt Crawford and Michael Gorman,
> *Future Libraries: Dreams, Madness and Reality*

Another type of stress being found more commonly in libraries today is physical stress, usually resulting from the use of computers. Now that computers are used as a tool by almost every category of workers in a library, more and more employees are suffering from a condition known as repetitive strain injury—most frequently carpal tunnel syndrome. Carpal tunnel syndrome has been common for a long time in employees working in factories who perform the same motion repetitively throughout the day. Now the same condition is appearing in libraries and information centers where staff spend a large part of the day working on computer keyboards. Repetitive keyboarding can lead to carpal tunnel syndrome.

One recent survey found that 3.1 percent of staff in ARL libraries are affected by carpal tunnel syndrome.[78] Libraries and information centers have undertaken to prevent and provide relief for carpal tunnel syndrome by purchasing ergonomic chairs, workstations, and keyboards. Other libraries and information centers have instituted more frequent breaks, increased the types of activities within a job, started exercise sessions, and provided training in attempts to alleviate and prevent carpal tunnel syndrome. Because the use of computers will continue to be an essential function in the work life of most library employees, managers of all types need to be mindful of this physical stress to prevent the development of more cases of carpal tunnel syndrome among employees.

Carpal tunnel syndrome seems to be the most harmful result of using computers. Although a few years ago there was concern about radiation resulting from video display terminals (VDTs), studies have shown that the radiation produced by computer terminals of all types is slight. More common complaints are of eye strain, back and neck pain, and body fatigue, which probably result from sitting in one position for too long. Again, good ergonomic practices, such as proper positioning of monitors, supportive chairs, good lighting, adequate ventilation, and more frequent breaks from working on the computer can alleviate many of these complaints.

Today's workers are demanding a more healthful environment in which to work, and most managers are trying to provide such a workplace. Most libraries today are smoke-free, so nonsmokers are not exposed to secondhand smoke. Many libraries encourage employees to participate in exercise programs or other "wellness" programs. Employee Assistance Programs have been instituted at a number of organizations to provide help for employees with various types of personal problems such as alcoholism or drug use. Managers realize that it is cost-effective to invest in the health of employees as healthier employees are more productive than those who are suffering from physical or mental conditions. Eliminating as much mental and physical stress as possible from the workplace is a win-win situation for employees and employers.

Evaluation: Performance Appraisals

A formal review is more than once-a-year paperwork and more even than a "people program." It is a way to link performance with corporate strategy. Because a review provides the occasion to open the books and share information, it can be a powerful idea generator and a rich source of improvement. Take the time to do it right.[79]

—Nancy K. Austin,
"Updating the Performance Review"

Performance appraisal is the systematic evaluation of an individual employee's job-related strengths and weaknesses. In all types of organizations, employees have to be evaluated. Some workers are better than others at specific jobs. Some workers take the initiative and carry through an assignment with little supervision. Others may be unreliable or must always be closely supervised to ensure the successful completion of a project. When decisions have to be made about pay increases or promotions, the supervisor must have a way to distinguish the excellent performers from the mediocre. Before systematic performance appraisals were developed, those decisions were often made on the basis of supervisors' subjective, spur-of-the-moment impressions. A systematic, written performance appraisal system provides a sounder method of distinguishing among the performances of employees.

Not every management expert advocates performance appraisal. For instance, W. Edwards Deming claimed that performance appraisal is one of the seven deadly diseases afflicting Western management.[80] He states that

> what is wrong is that the performance appraisal or merit rating focuses on the end product . . . not on leadership to help people. . . . Merit rating rewards people that do well in the system. It does not reward attempts to improve the system. . . . Moreover a merit system is meaningless as a predictor of performance. . . . Traditional appraisal systems increase the variability of performance. The trouble lies in the implied preciseness of rating systems. . . . One of the main effects of evaluation of performance is nourishment of short-term thinking and short-term performance.[81]

However, Deming is in the minority in his view. Most managers, although they realize that performance appraisals are not perfect tools, are advocates of their value.[82]

As a result of other changes in the organization, there has been a shift in some organizations in the focus of evaluations. Especially in team-based organizations, there has been a move to see the supervisor as more of a coach than a boss. If the supervisor is functioning as a coach, the feedback to the employee is continuous throughout the year. Even in these types of organizations formal performance assessments may still only be done once a year, but there should be no surprises. Learning theory suggests that immediate feedback helps learners increase their performance. All employees need feedback more than once a year, and good supervisors provide it. Usually, the frequent feedback is done on a more informal, spontaneous fashion, while the annual evaluation is done in a more formal, structured manner.

Judging another's performance is usually difficult, and often both supervisors and subordinates feel ambivalent about performance appraisal. Some writers have likened appraisals to paying taxes. They are something that managers are obligated to do but would like to avoid. Although most employees want feedback on how they are doing, they would prefer feedback that is consistent with their image of themselves as good performers.[83]

Formal performance assessments have two main objectives. The first objective of a performance appraisal is to determine how well an employee performs on the job. The second objective is to help an employee know how well he or she is doing, so that if improvement needs to be made, the employee knows in what area performance is falling short. Thus, performance appraisal can be used to encourage the growth and development of an individual worker. To achieve the second objective, the evaluation of an employee's performance must be communicated to the individual. Without this transfer of information and the development of a remedial process or plan, the employee cannot be expected to achieve improvement or redirection in performance.

Most managers regard performance appraisals as useful tools with several important functions. A good performance appraisal system can serve as a basis for human resources decisions relating to promotion, demotion, and termination of employees. It facilitates the promotion of outstanding workers and the weeding out or transfer of poor performers. Systematic, written assessment of a worker by a number of raters over a period of time helps make these decisions reasonable and sound. Performance appraisal also can serve as the basis for wage and salary treatment. Many organizations relate at least some decisions about the size and frequency of pay increases to an employee's performance appraisal rating. If properly conducted, the performance appraisal will give every level of management a better understanding of the individual worker's capabilities and potential. The entire appraisal process can facilitate understanding between supervisors and employees. Performance appraisal provides concrete feedback to employees that allows them to improve their performance by making them aware of weaknesses and how to correct them.

So, appraisals aid in creating and maintaining a satisfactory level of performance by employees. The performance appraisal process should help employees establish personal goals that will enable them to grow and develop and that, in turn, will further the goals of the institution. In addition, performance appraisals can serve as information gathering tools that provide data to be used in determining both organizational and individual training needs.

Good performance appraisal systems are careful to make a distinction between the variations of employee performance caused by the employee's shortcomings and those caused by inadequacies of the organization. For instance, the best employee cannot be productive if there is a problem with getting materials—a cataloger cannot catalog if there is a backlog in acquisitions that prevents the books getting to the cataloging department. An appraiser must be careful to never blame the deficiencies of the organization on the individual employee.

> One of the problems attributed to appraisal is that it can inappropriately attribute variation in performance to the individual employee rather than to problems at the higher organizations level. The effect of this is to shift the blame for problems onto individuals rather than to examine and act upon what is wrong with the organization. Consequently, badly conducted appraisals can jeopardize morale, adversely affect teamwork, and leave an individual feeling unfairly criticized.[84]

> —Brendan McDonagh, "Appraising Appraisals"

Each organization determines when performance appraisals will be administered. There should be a definite schedule, and the schedule should be public knowledge. Performance appraisals are most commonly done on a yearly basis. Ideally, though, performance appraisals would be done frequently enough to let employees know if their performance is satisfactory and, if not, the steps that need to be taken for improvement. For some employees, this cannot be accomplished solely through an annual performance appraisal. It is recommended that informal performance appraisals be done several times a year to supplement the formal annual appraisal.

New employees need more frequent appraisals than do long-established workers. In most organizations, new staff members serve a probationary period before permanent appointment is made. That probationary period may vary from a few months for clerical positions to up to one year for professional positions. A performance rating should be administered at the end of the probationary period, but a good supervisor will review the job description and the quality of job performance with the new employee several times during the probationary period.

After the probationary period, performance appraisals are administered on a recurring basis. Some institutions schedule all employee evaluations at the same time. This practice permits the supervisor to most easily compare the performance of all subordinates. But grouping all the appraisals presents drawbacks. Supervisors with a large number of appraisals to complete can be overwhelmed, resulting in poorly prepared performance evaluations. Not enough time is allowed for thoughtful, careful evaluation. To avoid overload, some institutions do performance evaluations on each anniversary of the employee's appointment to permanent status. This time-table distributes the workload over the entire year and permits careful judgments to be made.

Who should do the appraisals? By far, the most common practice in libraries and information centers, as in other institutions, is to have the immediate supervisors evaluate the performance of their subordinates. The immediate supervisor has the greatest opportunity to observe the subordinate and, thus, is most familiar with that employee's performance. Because the supervisor is accountable for the successful operation of his or her unit, it is appropriate that the supervisor have authority over human resources administration affecting that unit.

Although the custom of having the immediate supervisor evaluate subordinates is most common, other types of evaluations replace or supplement this practice in some institutions. Peer ratings are used to evaluate some professional librarians, primarily academic ones. Because many academic librarians have faculty status, those librarians have adopted the same type of peer review of performance that is used for most faculty members in institutions of higher education. Professional librarians interact with one another and are usually familiar with each other's work. In addition, many elements of the librarian's work, particularly at the departmental level, require cooperative work. Thus, they should be good judges of each other's performance.[85]

In some organizations, employees are allowed to appraise the performance of their immediate supervisor. Considerable trust and openness are necessary to make this type of appraisal successful, and, in most cases, subordinates do not assess their bosses without guaranteed anonymity. When subordinates do evaluate their superiors, the appraisals are not used to determine pay raises; often, employee appraisals are not seen by anyone but the managers. Instead, these evaluations serve primarily as a tool for the guided self-development of the manager and as a means of giving employees a way to express their opinions. Several studies of upward evaluations have shown that usually staff feel supervisors have used the upward evaluations and improved as a result.[86]

Upward evaluations provide supervisors with information that can be used to improve performance and thus can be very useful. But, because inaccurate and inadequate information gathered about a supervisor could lead to a distorted view of the supervisor's performance and thus potentially could lead to legal challenges, it is important that a formal process be developed and a valid and reliable instrument used.[87]

A few organizations are experimenting with what is termed *360-degree* or *multirater* feedback, a process where an employee's performance is assessed through confidential feedback from a variety of sources, including direct reports, managers, peers, internal and external customers, and the individual employee. This 360-degree process allows a employee to get feedback on facets of performance that are often overlooked in a traditional top-down performance assessment. This practice, which has been adopted more frequently in Great Britain than the United States, yields valuable data, but it can be very threatening to individual managers.[88]

Some organizations permit employee self-evaluation. Employees can usually give an accurate picture of their own strengths and weaknesses. If an employee is accurate in identifying strengths and weaknesses, the supervisor only has to confirm and help the employees set goals to improve the weaknesses. Individuals are much less defensive if they themselves have pointed out their shortcomings instead of having those shortcomings pointed out by their manager. But, unfortunately, not all employees are able to evaluate themselves accurately, and there is often low agreement between the employee's evaluation and that of the supervisor.[89] Employee self-appraisal is most useful in employee development and identifying training needs. If self-appraisal is used as part of employee evaluation, it is almost always used in conjunction with another type of appraisal.

Whatever type of performance appraisal program is instituted, it must be strongly supported by senior management. Senior management must orient and train supervisors in systematic evaluation and convince them of its value. Management must also give supervisors sufficient time to carry out the appraisals. Most supervisors dislike the process of evaluating their employees and, in particular, try to avoid discussing deficiencies with the employee. Unless the upper echelons of management indicate their support, the program likely will be ineffective.

One of the major challenges of performance appraisal is establishing the standards of performance against which an employee's work is judged. Standards that need to be established usually fall clearly into three categories:

1. *Quality-quantity standards.* How well does the employee perform the various tasks in the job description, and how much of each task is actually accomplished?

2. *Desired-effect standards.* Is work complete, accurate, and performed on time, benefiting the goals and objectives of the institution and users? Are sound data gathered as a basis for judgment and decisions?

3. *Manner of performance standards.* Is the work accomplished in cooperation with others, without friction? Can the employee adapt to new programs or processes?[90]

Because no two supervisors interpret these standards in exactly the same way, top management must define the standards. This is sometimes done by issuing a performance evaluation manual to be used by supervisors in evaluation. If supervisors interpret standards differently or give greater weight to one standard over another, inequity in evaluation from department to department will result.

Problems in Rating

Because appraisals are carried out by humans, they are subject to a number of weaknesses and errors. The most common errors found in performance appraisal are:

1. *The halo effect.* Supervisors often let the rating they assign to one characteristic unduly influence their rating on all factors. For example, if a supervisor thinks an employee is outstanding in one area, the supervisor gives that employee excellent ratings on all the factors being evaluated. One way to minimize the halo effect is to have the supervisor evaluate all subordinates on the same factor before going on to the next.

2. *Prejudice and partiality.* Sometimes a supervisor allows personal feelings about a subordinates to affect the rating given to that subordinate. It is a serious error for a supervisor to let personal likes and dislikes interfere with evaluating an employee's work performance. In addition, is it not only an error of judgment but a constitutional violation to consider race, creed, color, religion, politics, nationality, or gender in evaluating work performance.

3. *Leniency or strictness.* When some raters are extremely lenient and some are extremely strict, employees working at the same level of performance receive vastly different ratings depending on their supervisor. Some supervisors give all their subordinates relatively high ratings because they do not want to face any resentment or disappointment that might result from lower ratings. This leniency causes all the ratings to be so close to the top of the scale that they are worthless to management and unfair to the really good employees. The error also creates an unrealistic feeling of success when improvement in performance may be badly needed and often possible. Less common but equally damaging is the practice of giving low ratings to all employees. Sometimes these overly strict raters have artificially high standards that few subordinates can ever achieve. Both of these errors are caused by the subjectivity of the ranking process, and both can be alleviated, to some extent, by careful training of the evaluators.

4. *Central tendency.* Some appraisers are reluctant to use either the high or low extremes of the rating scale and cluster all their ratings about the center. On a normal distribution curve more people will be rated closer to the mean than to any other point on the scale. However, when all ratings are clustered at the center, most of the value of the systematic performance appraisal is lost.

5. *Contrast.* This error occurs when the supervisor does not measure the work the employee has actually done but measures what he or she thinks the employee has the potential to achieve.

6. *Association.* Sometimes raters with a number of evaluations to complete rate factors at the same level merely because they follow each other on the page. This may also happen when the supervisor is tired or bored and tries to make hurried judgments without all the facts.

7. *Recency.* This is the error of a rater who appraises only the work the employee has done in the recent past, rather than the work done over the entire period of time covered by the appraisal.

A number of techniques can reduce errors in performance appraisal. As mentioned earlier, training can reduce errors. Some errors can be lessened by keeping good records of employee performance. Errors can also be reduced if supervisors have input into the type of appraisal system that is used. If raters have participated in developing the system, they will use it more effectively. Finally, errors can be minimized if the organization's top management makes it clearly understood that all supervisors are to take performance appraisal very seriously. Not only should good appraisals be expected, they should be rewarded. When the organization not only expects good appraisals but systematically rewards supervisors who carefully and conscientiously perform those appraisals, it lays the foundation for an effective system of performance evaluation.

Methods of Performance Appraisal

There are no standard methods of performance appraisal, and there is no method that works best in all settings. Instead, there are a number of effective methods that can be used. Institutions do not have to select a single method, but generally one method or combination of methods is agreed upon for the entire institution. The method used may be that used by the parent institution, as in the case of a library that is part of a larger municipal or academic system. Some examples of performance appraisals forms are presented in appendix D.

If the library is free to select its own method, staff committees may have input into selecting the method. In larger libraries and information centers, the human resources office often plays a key role in the selection and development of the method used. The performance appraisal methods most commonly used are essays, ranking, forced distribution, graphic ratings scales, and the behaviorally anchored rating scale. Management by objectives also provides a means of performance appraisal (see chapter 2). Regardless of the type of instrument used, all factors being assessed should be job-related.

In the *essay* method, the rater describes an individual's performance in a written narrative. The essay can be unstructured, but, usually, the rater is asked to respond to general questions relating to the employee's job knowledge, strengths and weaknesses, and promotion potential. The major drawback of essays is that their length and content may vary and consistency is hard to achieve. The rater's writing ability may also affect the appraisal. An employee might receive a comparatively poor rating because the rater does not write well. Essays are most effective when they are combined with some other appraisal technique.

Several *ranking* systems are used in employee appraisal. Using the simple ranking method, the supervisor ranks the employees from highest to lowest—from best employee to worst. In alternative ranking, the supervisor first chooses the best and the poorest performers. Then the next-best and the next-poorest performers are chosen, alternating from top to bottom, until all employees have been ranked. The paired comparison method is an organized way of comparing each employee with every other employee, one at a time. The advantage of the ranking system is its simplicity. The major disadvantages are that it does not reveal the degree of difference between persons in adjacent ranks, and individuals with the same performance rating must be given separate ranks. In addition, it is difficult to compare various groups of employees, because the ones ranked highest in one unit may not be as good as those ranked highest in another unit.

A common problem with rating scales is that too many people are rated on the high end of the scale. The forced distribution rating system is designed to prevent this clustering. Forced distribution requires the rater to compare the performance of employees and to place a certain percentage of employees at various performance intervals. Usually, a supervisor must allocate 10 percent to the highest category and 10 percent to the lowest, with the other employees proportionately assigned as follows:

10%	20%	40%	20%	10%
Lowest	Below Average	Average	Above Average	Best

This method assumes that the performance in a group of employees is distributed according to a normal curve. In many units, this assumption may be untrue. The forced distribution method is most difficult to use when evaluating a small number of people.

The *graphic rating scale* is the most commonly used method of performance appraisal in libraries and information centers. The rater evaluates the employee on factors such as quantity of work, dependability, initiative, job knowledge, and accuracy. Some organizations use a very simple form, with the factor being evaluated listed and defined, followed by a multiple-choice format for the rating. The supervisor indicates the rating of the employee for each factor by placing a mark on the horizontal line, as shown below.

Accuracy is the correctness of work performed.

Poor	Fair	Average	Good	Excellent

It is very difficult for supervisors to agree on the meaning of *average, fair,* or *excellent.* No matter how much training supervisors receive, these terms will be interpreted differently by different individuals.

In recent years, most institutions have improved the graphic rating scale by eliminating such terms as poor, fair, and excellent. In their place, a short phrase is used to describe the different levels of performance. The most difficult part of developing these new scales is to provide a short phrase that cannot be misinterpreted, thus assuring comparable interpretations by various supervisors. Using this type of form, accuracy might be evaluated as follows:

Accuracy is the correctness of work duties performed.

Makes frequent errors	Careless, often makes errors	Usually accurate. Only makes average number of errors.	Requires little supervision. Is exact and precise most of the time.	Requires absolute minimum of supervision. Is almost always accurate.

It does not make any difference how many levels of an element are defined; generally four or five are given, as in the example above. The fact that graphic rating scales require relatively little time to construct and administer doubtlessly contributes to their popularity. Graphic rating scales also force an evaluator to consider several dimensions of performance, and they are standardized and comparable across individuals. Their biggest drawback is that they are susceptible to errors such as halo, central tendency, or leniency. In addition, all rating scales tend to look backward, judging an employee performance over the period of time being assessed instead of helping the employee set goals for improvement.

Behaviorally anchored rating scales (BARS) were developed to correct some of the deficiencies in the graphic rating scale. BARS are relatively new and are not yet found in many libraries and information centers.[91] In developing BARS, the active participation of job holders and supervisors helps to identify key job dimensions and areas of responsibility. Each job is likely to have several job dimensions and separate scales for each. The anchors are specific, written descriptions of actual job behaviors that supervisors agree represent specific levels of performance. To carry out a performance appraisal using BARS requires the rater to read through the list of anchors on each scale (i.e., for each job behavior) until the anchor that best describe the employee's job behavior are identified. The scale value opposite the anchor is checked. The evaluation is obtained by combining the scale values chosen for each job dimension. BARS take more time to develop than graphic rating scales, and a separate form must be developed for each job. The use of BARS can help reduce error, if good behavioral statements are provided as anchors. Also, because BARS are developed with the participation of managers and job holders, the likelihood is higher that this appraisal method will be accepted. Figure 4.7 shows a BARS that was designed to evaluate the job dimension of project planning, which is a function of many managerial positions.

The Performance Appraisal Review

Institutions structure the performance appraisal review process in various ways, but some elements are common to almost all reviews. First, the office that is responsible for distributing evaluation forms to supervisors distributes the appropriate forms. The office that has this responsibility varies according to the size of the organization. A human resources office, the library director's office, or an administrative assistant's office might be responsible. That office identifies the individual whose performance is to be evaluated, the department in which the job is located, the name of the person responsible for completing the form, and the date the form is due back in the initiating office.

Fig. 4.7. A behaviorally anchored rating scale. From "Developing Behavior-ially-Anchored Rating Scales (BARS)," by C. E. Schneier and R. W. Beatty, August 1979. Reprinted from the August 1979 issue of *Personnel Administra-tor.* Reprinted with the permission of *HRMagazine* published by the Society for Human Resource Management, Alexandria, Va.

Scale values	Anchors
7 [ ] Excellent	Develops a comprehensive project plan, documents it well, obtains required approval, and distributes the plan to all concerned.
6 [ ] Very good	Plans, communicates, and observes milestones; states week by week where the project stands relative to plans. Maintains up-to-date charts of project accomplishments and backlogs and uses these to optimize any schedule modifications required.
	Experiences occasional minor operational problems, but communicates effectively.
5 [ ] Good	Lays out all the parts of a job and schedules each part; seeks to beat schedule and will allow for slack.
	Satisfies customers' time constraints; time and cost over-runs occur infrequently.
4 [ ] Average	Makes a list of due dates and revises them as the project progresses, usually adding unforeseen events; insti-gates frequent customer complaints.
	May have a sound plan, but does not keep track of mile-stones; does not report slippages in schedule or other problems as they occur.
3 [ ] Below average	Plans are poorly defined, unrealistic time schedules are common.
	Cannot plan more than a day or two ahead, has no con-cept of a realistic project due date.
2 [ ] Very poor	Has no plan or schedule of work segments to be per-formed.
	Does little or no planning for project assignments.
1 [ ] Unacceptable	Seldom, if ever, completes project because of lack of planning and does not seem to care.
	Fails consistently due to lack of planning and does not in-quire about how to improve.

The person who received the form then needs to evaluate the employee's performance. As mentioned earlier, the rater is most commonly the em-ployee's immediate supervisor, who is supposed to know the most about the job and the employee being evaluated. It is the rater's responsibility to com-plete the form thoughtfully and carefully. Usually, it is wise for the rater to base judgments on notes or a diary kept over a period of time. The rater must have proof of evaluations given, particularly negative evaluations. The rater must consider the employee's work from the last period of rating to the cur-rent time; evaluation should not be based solely on what happened recently.

The rater must not be afraid to give a negative rating. With today's emphasis on accountability, it is the rater's responsibility to be accurate and truthful in the evaluation of an employee's performance. Not infrequently, a rater rates an employee as adequate or good, but requests the employee's discharge or transfer a few months later. If the employee's performance is bad, say so, but have proof.

Sometimes, a rater is consciously or unconsciously prejudiced against an employee. Prejudice arises not only from race or creed, but also from color of hair, personality, sexual preference, physical characteristics, or other factors. In order to make sure that no prejudice or bias influences an evaluation, the rating should be reviewed by the supervisor's supervisor—the next person in the hierarchy. Together the rater and his or her supervisor should review the proposed performance evaluation and come to a consensus on the accuracy of the evaluation.

After the evaluation form is complete, the rater must share the results with the employee. This information is usually provided in a performance appraisal interview. Conducting the performance appraisal interview is probably the most difficult part of the process—at least, it is the part most dreaded by employees and supervisors. Some well-defined steps should be taken to prepare for the interview. To prepare the employee, the supervisor should make an appointment with the employee and make the purpose of the appointment clear. Before the meeting is held, the supervisor should give the employee the completed performance appraisal form. The employee should have at least 24 hours to review the evaluation of his or her work and to consider its fairness and appropriateness. In addition the supervisor must prepare for the meeting. The supervisor might examine previous performance appraisals to review the employee's progress. Certainly, the supervisor will plan the meeting's structure. Accomplishing these two steps eliminates two of the most prevalent errors in performance appraisal interviews. First, the employee has time to study the appraisal, instead of being suddenly handed an appraisal without time to think about it. Second, the supervisor plans the meeting, instead of calling it on impulse in an attempt to get it out of the way.

> Thou shalt treat employees as adults and with respect, and not lose sight of the fact that they are people, not just human resources. . . . The surest way for a business to fail is to suggest, through its actions or statements, that people are nothing more than useful commodities. As managers, we must never forget that we are dealing with people—real human beings who deserve to be treated with fairness, honesty, and respect.[92]
>
> —Kent E. Romanoff,
> "The Ten Commandments of
> Performance Management"

Because of the sensitivity of this interview, the supervisor must establish as informal an atmosphere as possible. Frequently, supervisors move away from their desks to an area with more informal furniture, because the supervisor's desk, a symbol of authority, functions as a barrier and a psychological obstacle to many workers. The supervisor should employ techniques of good interviewing (see pp. 189-91). He or she should ask questions or make comments that encourage the employee to talk. The supervisor should not lecture the employee. If the employee is encouraged to talk, the discussion will naturally center on the performance appraisal. The employee has the opportunity to express concern or approval of the appraisal and the supervisor can explain why certain elements were rated as they were.

In this interview, the supervisor's objectives are to identify problems the employee has in performing any assigned tasks; to plan methods or procedures by which these problems might be resolved; to determine the employee's general level of satisfaction with the job, the institution, and the working environment; and to help the employee plan personal programs and activities that will make him or her more effective in the job or that will help him or her prepare for advancement. The last objective is particularly important. Together, the employee and the supervisor are establishing current and long-range goals for the employee. After mutual agreement, the goals are recorded on the performance evaluation form; at the next evaluation interview, progress toward the goals is measured. By signing a performance evaluation form, the employee indicates acceptance of the evaluation and proposed goals.

Of course, not all interviews go smoothly. In some cases, the supervisor may have to demote or terminate an employee. The supervisor should be able to anticipate when such action might be necessary and be prepared. Previous and current performance appraisals, as well as the known attitude and behavior of the employee, provide indications that difficulty might be encountered. The wise supervisor is seldom caught unprepared for any direction the interview takes.

Performance appraisal is a necessary though difficult part of human resources administration. The rationale is that if employees are told where their performance is deficient, they will take steps to improve it. But, as Saul Gellerman points out, this is an oversimplification. "It would be more accurate to say that most [people] would want to correct the deficiencies in their performance if they agreed that they were deficient and if there appeared to be enough advantage in correcting them to justify the effort."[93] Difficulties in communication and lack of trust are the reasons performance appraisal frequently results in resentment and tension between the supervisor and the employee.

Granted, performance appraisal may be an imperfect tool of human resources administration. If it is viewed as a tool of second- or third-level supervisors, it loses its clout and encourages strife. But if it is given strong support from top-level management, and if it uses objective standards for evaluation, it helps employees understand where they stand—and that is something all employees want to know.

Discipline and Grievances

At one time or another, almost every manager has to deal with an employee who fails to comply with the requirements of the job or the organization. That employee's supervisor may need to invoke some sort of disciplinary procedure to resolve the problem. Conversely, sometimes, an employee has a complaint about the organization or its management. In that case, the employee may need to use the grievance procedure to resolve the problem.

Discipline is the action taken by an organization against an employee when that employee's performance has deteriorated to the point where action is necessary or when that employee has violated an institutional rule. Discipline is a communication to employees that they need to change their behavior to come up to established standards. Discipline may need to be adminis- tered for reasons ranging from excessive absenteeism to theft. Discipline is one of the most challenging areas in dealing with employees. The supervisor must be aware of the dual objectives of discipline: preserving the interests of the organization and protecting the rights of the individual.

Most organizations have formal policies and procedures for handling discipline. It has been estimated that only about 5 percent of employees ever need discipline; the vast majority are good workers who want to do the right thing.[94] But the policies and procedures must be in place to deal with the few that do need them. Before establishing disciplinary procedures, each institution must develop rules and regulations governing employee performance and must take measures to ensure that these rules and regulations are clearly understood by each employee. If an employee violates a rule or work standard, discipli- nary action is taken. Before this is done, however, it should be established that the poor performance is not caused by external factors such as poor training, supervision, or inadequate equipment.

Disciplinary actions take various forms, depending on the nature and frequency of the offending behavior. Most organizations employ what is known as progressive discipline, which provides for a series of steps before dismissal so that an employee will have the opportunity to correct the un- desirable behavior. The mildest disciplinary action is the simple oral warn- ing. The penalties escalate to an oral warning noted in the employee's personnel record, then to a written warning, then to suspension without

pay for varying lengths of time, and finally, to the harshest penalty, discharge from the job. In the case of gross misconduct, such as assault on a
supervisor or theft, however, an employee can be dismissed without going
through all the steps. To prevent possible litigation, documentation should
be kept at each step of the process.

> ⁕Management has the responsibility for building an organ-
> izational climate of preventive discipline. In doing so, it
> makes its standards known and understood. If employees do
> not know what standards they are expected to uphold, their
> conduct is likely to be erratic or misdirected. Employees are
> more likely to support standards that they have helped create.
> . . . They usually want to know the reasons behind a standard
> so that it will make sense to them.[95]
>
> —Keith Davis and John W. Newstrom,
> *Human Behavior at Work*

To administer discipline effectively, the penalties must be imposed
consistently and fairly and with advance warning. Many human resources
experts refer to the "red-hot stove" method of administering discipline.
When someone touches a red-hot stove, the discipline is immediate, given
with warning, consistent, and impersonal. The best disciplinary systems
have these characteristics. Discipline should be carried out impersonally,
without a feeling of animosity on the part of the supervisor. A supervisor
should never hesitate to use discipline when necessary but should always remember that discipline is not intended to humiliate an employee but to
correct a problem or modify job behavior. Discipline should be administered privately and in a calm manner. The supervisor should encourage
two-way communication and allow the employee to speak. A follow-up
plan for improving behavior should be agreed upon. If possible the interview should end on a positive note so that the employee can believe that
the supervisor and organization want him or her to succeed.[96]

No one likes to administer discipline, but if handled properly, a disciplinary system can be an effective tool in handling job-related employee
problems. In addition to the individual being disciplined, discipline may
prevent others from acting in a similar fashion, assure others that inappropriate behavior will not be tolerated, and communicate the manager's commitment to a high standard of conduct.[97]

When none of the discipline procedures are effective, a manager may
have to discharge an employee. *Firing* is the term that is usually used for a
for-cause dismissal. An employee who has committed a major transgres-
sion, such as stealing, gross insubordination, or the like, would be fired.

Termination results from an employee's failure to meet job expectations after a reasonable amount of time.[98] Discharging an employee is never easy, but the process must be handled correctly, because the mishandling of terminations is a major cause of employee lawsuits. Documentation is important in all human resources decisions but especially important in the case of terminations. All evidence supporting the need for termination should be available in case of litigation.[99] Managers should treat the employee with respect and understand how traumatic it is to lose a job for whatever reason. At the same time, however, it is the duty of a manager to remove poorly performing employees before they affect the morale of other workers and impede the work being done in the unit.

> Employee response to the news of a job loss may run the gamut from passive acceptance or relief to emotional outburst to lawsuits or tragic acts of violence. However, you as a manager must remember that care and compassion can go a long way toward mitigating the negative consequences of a discharge.[100]
>
> —Miriam Rothman, "Employee Termination"

Discipline is concerned with the problems organizations have with employees. A grievance system, on the other hand, provides a method for employees to deal with problems they have with supervisors or with the organization. A grievance is any dissatisfaction relating to one's employment that is brought to the attention of an organization's management. Grievance procedures are found in both unionized and nonunionized organizations, but the procedure is apt to be more formal and well-defined in unionized situations.

Often, in nonunionized institutions, the open-door policy is used to solve employee grievances. This policy is based on the assumption that when supervisors encourage employees to come to their office voluntarily at any time to discuss problems and complaints, they will feel free to do so. But this assumption is not completely sound. The open-door policy works only when the supervisor has been able to instill in employees a feeling of trust. Employees must feel that any problem or complaint will be objectively heard and fairly resolved and that the supervisor will not hold it against them or consider them troublemakers. The open-door policy works when the supervisor is skilled in human relations and is sensitive to employee needs and feelings. The open-door policy gives the supervisor an opportunity to explain why a certain action was taken and to resolve the complaint or grievance through direct communication.

The open-door policy, while it can operate in a unionized organization, is more likely to function in a nonunionized organization. In the absence of a union contract, the supervisor has more freedom and more options to resolve problems. Factual problems are probably the easiest to resolve, because they involve working conditions, hours of work, or changes in the procedures of a job. Problems involving feelings or emotions are much more difficult to handle. Here, the supervisor must constantly ask "Why does the employee feel this way?" The answer will depend on the supervisor's understanding of people.

In a unionized institution, the collective bargaining agreement establishes the procedures to be used for handling employee complaints. The grievance procedure goes through certain steps outlined in the union contract. In general, the first step is for the aggrieved employee to meet with his or her union steward, who is the union representative for that employee's unit. The employee and the union steward discuss the grievance and together bring the grievance to the grievant's supervisor. If a mutually satisfactory solution cannot be reached at this stage, the grievance is put in writing, and the process is continued with the next level of management. If the problem still is not resolved, higher management and the human resources department usually become involved. If a solution to the grievance cannot be arrived at in the organization, the grievant can request arbitration, a process by which both the employer and the union representing the employee agree to settle the dispute through an outside, neutral third party. The decision made by the arbitrator is binding on all parties involved.

It is essential that organizations have a written, public grievance procedure. In a unionized organization, this procedure is part of the union contract. In a nonunionized organization, management must see that such procedures are established. A grievance procedure defines: the manner in which grievances are filed (written or oral), to whom the grievance is submitted, how the grievance proceeds through the organization's hierarchy, where decisions about the grievance can be made, and the final point of decision. Usually, the procedures identify actions that aggrieved employees can take if they are not satisfied with the final decision.

Grievance procedures are ways of removing the employee from the direct and complete control of the immediate supervisor. Grievance procedures may discipline supervisors and act as guarantees to employees. They exist to assure employees that justice is available when they have a legitimate complaint against the organization.

Compensation: Salary Administration

The ultimate aim of salary administration is to arrive at an equitable system of compensating employees for the work they perform. Unlike many corporations, which operate for profit and often provide annual bonuses, stock options, or other special incentives to reward employees, most libraries and information centers offer only salaries and fringe benefits.

Most libraries differentiate between wages and salaries. *Wages* refers to compensation of employees whose pay is calculated according to the number of hours worked each week, and *salary* refers to compensation that is uniform from one pay period to the next. Wages are usually reported as being so much per hour, while salaries are reported in terms of so much per year.

Two other terms are used to describe the two kinds of workers. Wage-earning employees are often referred to as *nonexempt* personnel. Generally, nonexempt employees work in nonsupervisory positions and are covered by the Fair Labor Standards Act. Nonexempt employees must be paid "time-and-a-half" (the hourly wage multiplied by 1.5) for overtime work. Salaried workers are often referred to as *exempt* personnel. Exempt employees are usually managerial or professional employees who are exempt from the Fair Labor Standards Act. Employers are not required to pay such employees overtime regardless of the number of hours worked.

Both wages and salaries comes from the same general pool. Most libraries receive the bulk of their salary monies from the institution to which they are attached. For public libraries, this funding comes from the municipality, the county, or other political structure. Academic libraries receive their funds from the parent educational institution, as do school media centers. Special libraries draw their funding from their parent institution. In addition, a few libraries receive a smaller amount of personnel funds from endowments, federal or foundation grants, or, very occasionally, from earned income. Funds received from federal or foundation grants are allocated to specific projects or programs on a temporary basis; such funding is often called *soft* money.

Private businesses and institutions are not required to make public the wages or salaries of any individual or group of employees. Indeed, in many industries, salary information is a closely kept secret. The justification for salary secrecy is to prevent discontent among employees. Most public institutions, on the other hand, are required to make salary information available to anyone. In some states the salaries of state employees are printed in the newspaper as a matter of public record.

Some employees dislike having salaries disclosed, because they may feel strongly that the amount of money they earn indicates their worth as an individual. Sometimes public disclosure of salaries may lead to envy and a loss of morale. On the other hand, open disclosure of salaries is thought to curb favoritism and to lessen pay discrimination among employees. Many human resources specialists feel that, if possible, a compromise between the two positions is best. An organization should disclose the pay ranges for various jobs within the organization but not reveal what any particular individual is earning.

> ℚ Compensation systems in the United States historically have been influenced by the culture of individualism and competition. One's pay not only meets one's physical needs, but is a major measure of personal achievement and esteem.[101]
>
> —Paul F. Buller, Nancy K. Napier, and
> Glenn M. McEvoy,
> "Popular Prescriptions"

In libraries, a salary administration program consists of three parts: the determination of what salary to pay, the development of a salary scale, and the process of awarding salary increases.

Determination of Salary

All institutions that pay personnel for services rendered must determine what is a fair and equitable compensation for the education, experience, and responsibility required in the job. A job that requires more of each of these three criteria should receive more pay than a job that requires less. The determination of the salary associated with any job should be directly related to the job evaluation (see pp. 207-21). In general, the higher the job is evaluated, the higher the salary.

Institutions that wish to recruit and retain highly qualified personnel must offer salaries that are competitive in the job market. Individuals who have specialized education, who have demonstrated capability resulting from successful work experience, and who are willing to accept responsibility are always in demand. Thus, the compensation must be adequate to attract them. While money may not be the most important motivator for some people, it is still very important to most. Institutions that strive to obtain and retain the best people will usually offer salaries higher than institutions that will accept lower performance and anticipate turnover.

The question of fair pay generally involves two general issues: (1) internal equity, or what the employee is paid compared to what other employees in the same organization are paid; and (2) external equity, or what the employee is paid compared to what employees in other organizations are paid for performing similar jobs. If organizations are to avoid dissatisfaction about pay, employees must be convinced that both internal and external equity exist. Pay dissatisfaction can have a negative influence on the employee's work. Edward Lawler illustrates the results of pay dissatisfaction among employees. (See fig. 4.8.) Employees who are dissatisfied about pay not only desire more compensation, but find their jobs less attractive as well. The consequences of these two conditions are detrimental to the organization as well as the employee.[102]

Fig. 4.8. Model of consequences of pay dissatisfaction. From E. E. Lawler III, *Pay and Organizational Effectiveness* (New York: McGraw-Hill, 1971). Reprinted with permission of Edward E. Lawler III.

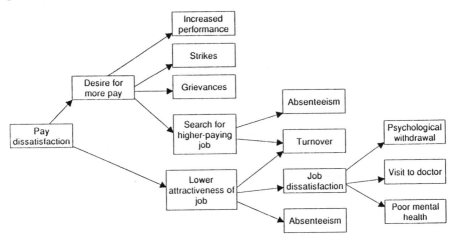

In general, the salaries of professional librarians are competitive nationally, although there are sometimes regional and local conditions that affect salaries. In large metropolitan centers, such as New York City or San Francisco, the cost of living is greater than in smaller communities. Factors of this nature affect the level of salary offered. The annual report of professional salaries received by current graduates of accredited schools of library and information science (LIS), usually published in an October issue of *Library Journal*,[103] shows the regional variation of beginning salaries as well as the national average and median salaries. It must be remembered that this information is provided for only beginning or entry-level positions.

The entry-level position is the only position for which the job requirements can be accurately described. Although there are some exceptions, the entry-level position generally requires five or six years of education beyond the secondary school, with the years of education culminating in graduation from an accredited LIS school; no professional experience; and minimal or moderate end responsibility in job performance. The requirements of other levels of professional positions vary from institution to institution. Thus, many institutions use the entry-level salary as the basis of their salary scale and build upon it to compensate more experienced employees.

In addition to the *Library Journal* survey, there are several ways to gather information on entry-level salaries as well as on the salaries of other professional levels. Every two years, the Special Library Association conducts an in-depth survey of its members, which is reported in *Special Libraries*. The American Library Association periodically reports information about salaries in *American Libraries*. The Association of Research Libraries publishes an annual salary survey. Some state libraries issue salary data for all libraries in that state. An institution may wish to gather this data conducting a salary survey or by simply evaluating salaries offered in advertisements in professional periodicals. Regardless of the method used, great care must be taken to assure that all the data gathered apply to positions that have the same job requirements.

Salaries for library positions other than those held by professional librarians usually are determined by the going rate of pay in the community in which the library is located. A national overview of salaries for library support staff is published on an irregular basis by *Library Mosaics*.[104] Information concerning local salaries can be obtained from agencies and institutions, such as the school system, local government, employment agencies, or chamber of commerce. If desired, a library can conduct a salary survey within a community. Of course, careful attention must be paid to the requirements of each job to be sure that the employee receives adequate compensation for the required education, experience, and responsibility.

Information technology has altered the jobs of most librarians, and often the job classifications and the pay scales have lagged in recognizing these changes. In many organizations the tasks that librarians perform are similar to those performed by computer or systems workers, but because they are classified differently, these people are paid less.

> Despite growing confluence in the use of information technologies, performance of seemingly comparable work, and sometimes strong administrative connections in such organizations, institution policies (as reflected in classification and compensation systems) appear not to be keeping pace with changes in actual job content. The job streams or "families" with their differing evaluation structures, pay scales and benefit status that have been in existence for decades have not been adjusted to take into account the significant alterations occurring at the working levels on campus.[105]
>
> —Anne Woodsworth and Teresa Maylone,
> *Reinvesting in the Information Job Family*

If libraries and information centers wish to attract the most talented employees, efforts must be made to be sure that the salary offered to their employees is as attractive as that offered to employees performing similar functions working elsewhere.

Development of a Salary Scale

A salary scale establishes the amount of money that will be paid for the accomplishment of duties designated in the job description. The scale has a minimum and a maximum amount that will be paid for that job. The minimum represents the beginning or entry-level salary and the maximum amount should indicate the value of the job to the institution when it is performed with maximum efficiency and thoroughness. The difference between the minimum and the maximum are steps on the salary scale that designate salary increases awarded the employee as proficiency increases or as experience is gained. After an employee has reached the top step of a grade, the only way he or she can receive a pay increase is by moving to a higher range.

Each library has to develop its own salary scale, but such scales are influenced by many external factors. For instance, there are numerous constraints on how these scales can be developed. Federal and state laws concerning minimum wage put a floor under the compensation of the lowest paid employees. In 1998, the federal minimum wage was $5.15 per hour. The existence of a union contract may affect how employees are paid. The salaries paid in competing institutions influence the salary scale. Finally, the law of supply and demand plays a part; employees in high-demand specialties may have to be paid more than employees with more common expertise.

The establishment of the salary scale is closely linked to the process of job evaluation (see pp. 207-21). Regardless of which method of job evaluation has been used (for instance, the factor method or the classification method), the ultimate objective is to ascertain the correct rate of pay for all jobs and the relationship in terms of salary between all jobs in the organization.

Although some institutions have salary scales that do not overlap, it is much more common for the ranges of adjacent pay grades to overlap. The use of an overlapping pay scale allows an outstanding performer in a lower grade to make a higher salary than a below-average worker in a higher grade. In a like fashion, an experienced worker in a lower grade would make a higher salary than a beginning worker in a higher grade.

In administering a salary scale, some common-sense principles should be kept in mind. First, there should be equal pay for equal work. If two jobs have equal requirements in terms of education, experience, and responsibility, the pay should be the same. Of course, this does not prevent having a salary range with individuals at different steps within the range. Second, employees are not required to enter a salary scale at the first step.

Most institutions recognize previous related work experience, and allow a new employee to enter higher on the scale. Third, if an employee is promoted from one rank to another, for instance, from Librarian I to Librarian II, the employee should not be forced to take a pay cut if the beginning salary of Librarian II is lower than the salary the employee earned as Librarian I. Instead, the employee should be given a somewhat higher salary to compensate him or her for assuming more responsibility.

Salary Increases

Three common methods of determining salary increases in libraries and information centers are length of service, merit, or some combination of length of service and merit. Length of service equates increased pay with seniority. The underlying assumption is that an organization should recognize the fact that an experienced worker is more valuable than an inexperienced one. Librarians working in public schools usually have pay schedules with predetermined steps; with each year of experience, the librarians advance a step on the salary scale. Often, public employees receive a uniform salary increase, for example, a 5 percent increase, and all employees receive the same percentage increase. This is a way of rewarding seniority. Every employee who completes another year of employment receives the same percentage increase.

The merit system is based on the concept that salary increases should be awarded only for quality performance. In any organization, it is obvious that some workers contribute more than others. Merit pay allows the organization to reward the employees who work the hardest and who are the most valuable. It is presumed that merit pay will encourage all employees to perform more efficiently in the hopes of receiving a larger pay increase.

There are drawbacks to each of these methods. The automatic increase, though easy to administer, does not allow the organization to reward exceptional performers. The merit system is much more difficult to administer, and it is almost impossible to construct a plan of merit increases that will please all employees. Supervisors are often accused of using merit systems to reward their favorite employees. Because all merit systems are at least partially based on subjective judgment, they are difficult to construct. The merit system also presents problems when many employees receive no pay increase at all. During periods of high inflation, employees who are given no salary increase are seriously affected by a loss of spending power. Automatic "Cost of Living Adjustments" (COLAS), which are found in some industrial union contracts, are provided by very few libraries. So if employers do not give some kind of across-the-board raise to all employees, workers will not be able to maintain the same standard of living from year to year.

Most libraries use some combination of merit and seniority to award pay increases. All employees may be awarded a certain amount of money for a pay raise, with that amount increased if their job performance is meritorious. If a merit system is used, it should be carefully designed, well publicized, and closely related to employees' performance appraisals.

Regardless of whether the salary program is based on service, merit, or a combination, most libraries do not limit an employee's movements on the salary scale to just one step at a time. For outstanding service and major contributions to the organization, an employee might be moved two or more steps on the salary scale at one time.

Recognition and Rewards

Individuals working in libraries rarely receive the monetary nonsalary rewards, such as stock options, that are available to employees in the private sector. Nonetheless, many libraries have tried to structure some no-cost or low-cost way to reward employees and to show that they are appreciated. For instance, the Duke University Library has had an Employee Recognition Program in place for several years to recognize outstanding employees. Other organizations have tried to devise much broader recognition systems. For instance, at the library of the University of Wisconsin–Eau Claire, each employee is given a blank award certificate to give to any university employee for either an especially meritorious action or for excellence sustained over time. This type of award fits well with the Total Quality Management principle that states to each employee, "If you see a problem, you own it," as these awards clearly tell an employee, "If you see great performance, recognize it."[106]

Employee recognition programs usually are successful, because employees are motivated by recognition. People who feel appreciated identify with the organization and are more productive than those who do not feel appreciated. Managers of successful reward systems must be sure that rewards are tied to the organization's needs, the reward system is flexible and fair, rewards are publicized and if appropriate presented in a public forum, and the timing is right. It is best to schedule frequent reward presentations so employees receive the reward soon after the achievement being recognized.[107]

> ℵ Good leaders need to make sure that each member of the unit . . . realizes that his or her work is respected and appreciated by the administrator, by the parent body, and by his or her coworkers. This does not mean that administrators should spend their days going around patting everyone on the back. It does mean, however, that administrators are responsible for communicating appreciation for work done well.[108]
>
> —Joan M. Bechtel,
> "Leadership Lessons Learned from
> Managing and Being Managed"

In *A Passion for Excellence*, Peters and Austin argue for the value of celebrations in organizations. In their opinion, the best organizations make conscious efforts to publicly reward good performance by applause and celebrations. Although many reward programs are expensive to implement, others cost very little. Some managers find it difficult to design meaningful awards for jobs that cannot be measured in quantifiable terms. Peters and Austin suggest that "the people closest to the job know the job best, and its impact on others, so have them specify the standards for achieving the award."[109] Celebrations and awards can be effective morale boosters and increase productivity and quality.

Fringe Benefits

A major portion of employees' compensation package consists of fringe benefits. The number and variety of benefits provided by libraries and information centers for their employees has grown over the years to the point where items of this nature represent a major factor in total compensation. Because of the importance of benefits as a part of compensation, some employers have stopped using the word *fringe* when referring to benefits.

The package of benefits offered to employees is determined by the individual library or by the library's parent institution. Some benefits are required by federal or state law, and, in unionized institutions, some are mandated as part of a collective bargaining agreement. Federal and state regulations apply to almost all workers in the United States. Among the benefits required by these laws are Social Security, unemployment insurance, and worker's compensation. Unemployment insurance and worker's compensation are financed solely by employer contributions. Social Security is financed by equal contributions from employer and employee. The amount of Social Security tax has increased rapidly over the years. In 1937, the combined employer-employee tax rate was 2 percent on a maximum of $3,000 in earnings. In 1997, the combined rate was 15.3 percent.[110] For many low-paid employees, contributions to Social Security are larger than their federal income tax.

In addition to benefits mandated by federal or state law, organizations provide many types of employee benefits. For some of the benefits, the employer pays the full cost, and for others, the employee pays a portion of the cost. In private industry, a recent trend is the use of flexible, or cafeteria, plans, which allow employees some discretion in choosing the specific elements of their benefit program from a range of options. This approach allows employees to tailor a program to their needs. For example, an employee who is covered by a spouse's health insurance plan might forgo the health insurance option and instead select a larger amount of life insurance. To date, however, few public institutions provide such cafeteria plans.[111] The benefits most commonly found in libraries include group insurance policies, paid time off, retirement plans, employee assistance programs, and miscellaneous benefits, such as job sharing.

Most libraries provide several types of group insurance plans. Medical insurance, often including major medical coverage of catastrophic illness, is a benefit provided by most organizations. The cost of medical insurance has escalated in the past few years, and some organizations have shifted more of the cost of this insurance onto the employee. More organizations are now mandating the use of health maintenance organizations (HMOs) by their employees in an attempt to control the cost of medical insurance. In addition to health insurance, many organizations provide both group life insurance and disability insurance; the latter tides employees over during periods of disability caused by sickness or accident. Dental insurance is provided by some libraries. The payment for these types of insurance varies; in some libraries, the institution pays the full cost, but, more commonly, the employee pays a portion of the cost, especially for coverage of dependents.

Paid time off includes holidays, vacations, and various types of leave. It is also standard practice in many organizations to pay employees for rest periods and lunch breaks.

Employee retirement plans are pension or retirement plans offered by most libraries and information centers in addition to Social Security. Commonly, both the employer and employee make contributions to the plan.

Many employees are offered access to Employees Assistance Programs (EAPS). These programs provide assessment and referral for employees who have problems with depression, family dissension, substance abuse, and financial or legal problems. At one time, employees with personal problems were fired if these problems got in the way of work performance. Many organizations now provide EAPS to help employees work through these problems and improve work performance.

Librarians may be offered a wide variety of other benefits, depending on where they work. Some of these monetary benefits include travel and moving expenses, tuition refunds, and access to subsidized daycare.

A nonmonetary benefit found more and more in libraries and information centers is the alternative work schedule. Instead of requiring all employees to work the same hours, alternative work schedules, such as flextime or the compressed workweek, allow employees some freedom in choosing the hours and days they work. This flexibility, of course, can be granted only if appropriate provision is made to cover service to users and supervisory and training responsibilities. Before instituting any type of alternative work schedule, administrators should develop clear plans of action, with targeted jobs tested in advance to determine the likely effects of the new schedule.

A few libraries and information centers have instituted the practice of job sharing. Job sharing splits one job between two individuals. Usually, the salary is shared; benefits, such as medical insurance, are sometimes pro-rated, but, in the best cases, both employees receive benefits. Both flextime and job sharing are attractive to employees with small children because it enables them to spend more time with the children. Other employees also find these options beneficial; their existence sometimes allows organizations to keep valuable employees they would otherwise lose. But as mentioned earlier, organizations are now relying more heavily on part-time workers than ever before and as a result many employees work fewer hours per week than they would prefer. Although the employing organization may find it beneficial, this type of arrangement cannot be considered a benefit to the employee.

> A life cycle view of an employee means that the corporate culture responds to an employee's changing needs throughout that employee's life, recognizing in a fundamental way that the employee's personal life strongly influences his or her effectiveness at work, and that the corporation must play an active role in alleviating some of the external pressures.[112]

> —Charlene Marmer Solomon,
> "Twenty-Four Hour Employees"

Many employees take their benefits for granted, not realizing that benefits are a sizable part of the total labor cost of any organization. Fringe benefits add significantly to the salary of an employee because of the contributions made by the employer. On a percentage basis, the cost of benefits has increased substantially in recent years. The *Statistical Abstract of the United States* reports that, for all domestic industries in 1995, the total cost of all benefits was more than 28 percent of total annual wages.[113]

Both employers and employees gain from a well-designed and well-administered benefits program, despite its cost. In considering a benefit program, a manager must carefully study each element of the program to deter- mine its future financial impact on the institution. After determining that the program is needed and desired by the employees, the manager must carefully define the program and establish the policies and procedures necessary to assure its fair and equitable implementation. Finally, the manager should communicate information about the benefits package to all employees, to inform them what is available, when they are eligible, and what procedures are involved in obtaining benefits. Supervisors should be able to speak knowledgeably about the entire benefits package, because many employees turn to their immediate supervisors for information of this type.

Comparable Worth

In the 1980s, the issue of comparable worth began to draw much attention. At the heart of this issue is the fact that many occupations in our society are segregated by gender; men are heavily concentrated in certain types of occupations, and women are concentrated in others. At the same time, women who work are, on the average, paid less than men who work. In 1994, the median earning of women who worked full time were 72 percent of the earnings of men who worked full time ($22,205 to 30,854).[114] Part of this disparity can be attributed to the fact that the occupations in which women are concentrated pay less than occupations in which men are concentrated. Because librarianship is a profession that is approximately 80 percent female, salaries of both male and female librarians are adversely affected. The Equal Pay Act, passed in 1963, made it illegal to pay one gender less than the other for doing substantially the same work on jobs under similar working conditions requiring equivalent skills, effort, and responsibilities. It is clearly illegal to pay different wages to men and women in substantially equal jobs.

Advocates of comparable worth say the concept of equal pay for equal work should be broadened to include equal pay for comparable work. For example, a job in a profession dominated by women, such as librarianship, which requires a certain level of education and experience, should pay the same salary as a job in a profession dominated by men, such as engineering, if that job requires comparable (but not identical) education and work experience. Comparable worth is based not on jobs being the same but being comparable, based on a comparison of the intrinsic worth or difficulty of that job in comparison to other jobs in that organization or community. Proponents of comparable worth base their claims on Title VII of the Civil Rights Act, which, in a broader fashion than the Equal Rights Act, forbids discrimination in compensation.

The EEOC in 1977 contracted with the National Academy of Sciences to conduct studies and an analysis of comparable worth. The final report concludes:

> The committee is convinced by the evidence, taken together, that women are systematically underpaid. Policies designed to promote equal access to all employment opportunities will affect the underpayment of women workers only slowly. Equal access to employment opportunities may be expected to be more effective for those who have invested less in skills than for those who have invested more. . . . For these reasons the committee believes that the strategy of "comparable worth" merits consideration as an alternative policy. . . . The viability of a strategy of paying jobs in accordance with their "worth" requires, first, that an appropriate

mechanism, other than current market wage rates, can be found to measure the relative worth of jobs to an employer, and, second, that wages commensurate with worth can be set and paid for by the employer.[115]

That passage points out two of the main problems with instituting comparable worth: the difficulty of establishing the mechanism to measure the worth of jobs and the sizable increase in labor cost to employers. There is still a great deal of controversy concerning comparable worth, and perspectives on the topic differ widely, even among librarians. Recent court decisions indicate the courts will not require employers to implement comparable worth policies nor find them liable of discrimination for using market values in setting salaries. But nothing prohibits an employer from adopting comparable worth standards. There is no doubt that employees in many fields, especially those employed by state or local governments, will continue to press to have comparable worth issues addressed.

Human Resources Policies and Procedures

Throughout this chapter, much has been written about personnel policies and procedures. The importance of both types of documents cannot be overemphasized. The development of policies and procedures is an integral part of the staffing function of libraries and information centers.

Every library should have a set of human resources policies. A policy is a statement of action that commits management to a definite plan or course of action. Policies (for example, those pertaining to hiring and promotion) play an important role in every organization. They are used as guidelines for decision making. By reducing ad hoc decision making, human resources policies lead to greater consistency and continuity in an organization.

Clearly defined policies are essential to an effective human resources program. The employees need to understand, through written policy statements, topics such as what the human resources program is, how it operates, why salaries are administered in a particular way, how and when performance appraisal will take place, and what benefits are available.

Even in larger libraries and information centers with specialized human resources departments, the formulation of policy usually is the responsibility of the library director. In all types of libraries, the director should establish policy with input from others. The preparation of policy statements should be an opportunity for involvement of other groups. A group of supervisors or staff members might recommend the establishment or modification of a policy. Discussing, evaluating, and writing the policy statement can encourage the participation of the groups that will be affected by it.

An effective set of human resources policies serves a number of functions. First, the formulation of such policies requires library management to think through the needs of both employees and the organization. Second, such policies provide consistent treatment for all employees. Because each supervisor follows the same policies, the equal treatment of each employee is assured. Clearly stated policies minimize both favoritism and discrimination. Third, such policies assure continuity of action, even during periods when managers or supervisors change. New managers have a written standard to follow, and policy remains stable. Employees need not endure vacillations in policies when supervisors resign or retire.

A human resources policy may be broad. For instance, "The X Library does not discriminate against any employee on the basis of age, gender, race, religion, age or national origin." Policies may also be narrow. For instance, "All employees are entitled to four weeks of paid vacation each year." It must be remembered that a policy is a general statement of intent and does not spell out the exact methods by which it will be implemented. That function is accomplished by the procedure. A procedure provides the methods for carrying out a policy. It sets forth the steps that are essential to accomplish a particular result. A library will have procedures as to how vacation times will be allotted or how equal opportunity will be assured.

In addition to policies and procedures, organizations also have rules. A rule is defined as a law, regulation, or prescribed guide for conduct or behavior. Rules can be considered minimum standards of conduct that apply to a group of people. Rules apply uniformly to the group concerned. Libraries, like all other institutions, must have rules. Examples of rules are the number of hours to be worked each day or how many absences an employee can have. Rules serve to ensure predictability of behavior so that the organization can achieve its goals and function without undue disruption.

Obviously, the policies, procedures, and rules of an organization should be written down. If they exist only in the mind of the director, they fail to serve the purposes for which they are developed. But, they must be more than written; they must be communicated to and understood by all employees. Policies locked in the director's desk are just as ineffective as those that are unwritten.

How are policies, procedures, and rules communicated through an organization? First, special care must be taken to communicate these documents to supervisors, so that they can administer them equitably and uniformly. Often, organizations have special training sessions to acquaint supervisors with policies or to periodically review them. Nonsupervisory employees commonly learn about the policies, procedures, and rules through the employee's handbook, which is usually given to each new employee during orientation.

The information contained in the handbook should be followed up with oral explanation, and any changes in policies, procedures, or rules should be communicated and explained by the employee's immediate supervisor.

External Impacts on Staffing

All of the subjects discussed so far relate to specific internal staffing functions found in libraries and information centers of all types. There are, however, two broader external forces that have had a profound impact on human resources work in many libraries and information centers. These issues are (1) legal protections for employees, and (2) unionization.

Legal Protections

The number of federal and state regulations relating to the staffing function of management has increased over the past decades, and today, virtually every human resource function from hiring to firing is affected by these regulations. These regulations have provided workers with more legal protection—especially in the area of equal employment. Nonetheless, there are still some areas where employees have very few rights. Almost every employee not covered by a collective bargaining contract or civil or state service rules is at risk for dismissal because of the *employment at will* principle that permits either party to an employment contract to cancel it at will. Although legislation protects workers from firing for such reasons as age, gender, national origin, or disability, workers not covered by either collective bargaining or civil service regulations have few legal remedies to combat being fired or discharged.

There are other areas where workers have limited protection. Although the right to free speech is guaranteed by the First Amendment to the U.S. Constitution, managers in the private sector can legally discipline workers who say something damaging about the corporation or its practices. The right to privacy is another area where employees, especially those in the private sector, do not have clear protections.

Privacy issues have become a growing concern for workers with the growth of electronic technologies of all types. For instance, although the Electronic Communications Privacy Act of 1986 prohibits outside interception of electronic mail by a third party, the act does not affect inside interception, and unless an individual organization has a policy prohibiting it, employers can read their staff's e-mail, listen in on telephone conversations, install small video cameras anywhere, and can search employees' lockers and desks. The use of electronic surveillance is growing, as more and more organizations monitor people using personal computers by counting keystrokes and mistakes.[116] On the whole, these new monitoring technologies are considered to be extensions of managerial prerogatives, and employees currently have few legal tools to combat them.[117]

Obviously, this electronic monitoring can be beneficial if it can prevent or disclose misconduct, or if supervisors use it in training to give constructive feedback to help an individual worker improve. But studies have shown that employees who know that they are monitored are more likely to be highly dissatisfied and to suffer from conditions such as fatigue and hostility.

Suggestions for reform on electronic monitoring have come from many sources, and the proposed reforms almost all advocate that employers do the following: monitor in the open, monitor only relevant activities, monitor only periodically, and encourage employee participation in setting up the monitoring standards and practices.[118] Employers have the right to monitor employees' communications and activities but should take care that such monitoring is only used when necessary. Employees should be familiar with and understand the policies relating to surveillance and monitoring.

Another challenging legal issue in the workplace is that of random testing for the use of drugs. Many employees feel that drug testing is a violation of privacy, but in most states, employers of all types have the right to screen employees for drug and alcohol use. These types of tests are often mandatory for certain positions, such as airline pilot.

Although the rights of employees are better protected now than in the past, there are still areas where few protections exist. Because the employment at will rule allows employers the right to discharge workers for any cause, employees who wish to keep a job sometimes are subjected to practices in the workplace that they feel violate their privacy. Many of these privacy issues are particularly resented by workers, causing mistrust and ill feelings on the job. The rights of both employers and employees need to be balanced. Supervisors should strive, as much as possible, to show respect for employees' privacy and dignity, even when they are not legally obliged to do so.

Equal Employment Opportunities

Many of the legal protections enjoyed by workers are found in the area of equal employment opportunity (EEO). Equal employment opportunity refers to the right of all people to be hired and to advance in a job on the basis of merit or ability. Discrimination against protected classes of people in any aspect of employment is now prohibited by law in the United States.

Before the passage of equal employment opportunity laws, employers were able to hire, promote, or fire whomever they wished. Today, women, racial minorities, older workers, and people with disabilities have acquired substantial employment rights under law. The equal employment opportunity laws have exerted a profound influence on the American labor scene. Staffing functions, such as hiring, interviewing, testing, training, promoting, appraising, disciplining, and compensating, have been affected by equal employment opportunity law.

In almost every situation, there will be more candidates for a job opening or a promotion than there are openings and promotions available—it is almost always necessary to select some candidates instead of others. The preference of one candidate over another is permitted as long as the preference is based upon what can be shown to be job-related criteria.

> ⚘ Ignoring *any* source of talent and motivation will unduly restrict a company.[119]

> —Rosabeth Moss Kanter,
> "Men and Women of the Corporation Revisited"

The laws that influence human resources activities are too numerous to discuss comprehensively in this section. Instead, only the highlights of the legal framework and the impact of the laws will be presented. Readers who are interested in this area should turn to a more complete treatment for more information.[120]

Civil Rights Act of 1964. Although federal laws prohibiting discrimination against certain groups of employees go back more than one hundred years to the Civil Rights Acts of 1866 and 1871, the biggest impetus to equal employment opportunity came with the passage of the Civil Rights Act of 1964, which President Lyndon Johnson signed into law. Title VII of that act prohibits discrimination based on race, color, religion, sex, or national origin in all employment practices, including hiring, firing, promotion, compensation, and other conditions or privileges of employment. The primary aim of the legislation is to make overt discrimination actionable in all phases of employment. The act does not guarantee that women and minorities must be hired for vacant positions or promoted within a library, rather, it requires that they be fairly considered and neither excluded nor hindered because of race, sex, religion, or national origin.

Title VII has been interpreted in the courts many times since passage of the act. Court decisions have established that an employer's practices are discriminatory if they affect any one of the groups protected by Title VII in an adverse manner, even if the employer had no intention to discriminate. The Supreme Court, in the landmark *Griggs v. Duke Power Company*, stated:

The objective of Congress in the enactment of Title VII is plain from the language of the statute. It is to achieve equality of employment opportunity and to remove barriers that have operated in the past to favor an identifiable group of white employees over other employees. Under the Act, practices, procedures, or tests neutral on their face, or even neutral in terms of intent cannot be maintained if they operate to "freeze" the status quo of prior discriminatory practice. . . . Congress did not intend by Title VII, however to guarantee to every person a job regardless of qualifications. In short, the Act does not command that any person be hired simply because he was formerly the subject of discrimination, or because he is a member of a minority group. Discriminatory preference for any group, minority or majority, is precisely and only what Congress has proscribed. What is required by Congress is the removal of artificial, arbitrary, and unnecessary barriers to employment when the barriers operate invidiously to discriminate on the basis of racial or other impermissible classification.[121]

Griggs v. Duke Power Company was based on a Duke Power policy that required certain categories of employees to have high school diplomas and certain test scores on two tests. In a class action suit brought against Duke Power Company, black employees argued that these practices were contrary to Title VII because a higher percentage of blacks did not have high school diplomas and failed the required tests. The suit also argued that neither of these requirements were necessary for successful job performance. In 1971, the Supreme Court ruled unanimously for the black employees, stating that if an employment practice cannot be shown to be related to job performance, it is prohibited under Title VII. It is the effect of an employment practice, not its intent, that determines if it is discriminatory.

It is against the law for any organization to have policies and practices that have an adverse impact on any protected groups, unless that organization can demonstrate that those policies and practices are justified by business necessity. Business necessity has been narrowly interpreted to mean that the employer must show overriding evidence that a discriminatory practice is essential to the safe and efficient operation of the firm. Once a plaintiff shows a prima facie case of discrimination by demonstrating adverse impact upon any protected group, the burden of proof falls on the organization to justify its employment policy or practice.

Title VII as amended by the Equal Opportunity Employment Act of 1972 covers all private employers of 15 or more people, all private and public educational institutions, state and local government, employment agencies, labor unions, and apprenticeship and training programs. Thus, most libraries in the United States are covered by Title VII. It is enforced by the EEOC, a five-member, independent agency appointed for a five-year term by the president, with the advice and consent of the Congress. The EEOC investigates discrimination complaints and develops guidelines to enforce Title VII.

It is sometimes forgotten how much the civil rights rulings have changed the entire field of human resource management. For just one example of the change, see the job advertisements listed in table 4.4. These advertisements were printed in *Library Journal* in 1959 before the advent of civil rights protection for job applicants. Advertisers were free to look for applicants of a specific gender or age.

Table 4.4—Job Advertisements Before Civil Rights Legislation

- Stymied in your present job? Want to broaden your experience? Like to work in a brand-new building under ideal conditions? Insist on liberal fringe benefits? Want faculty status? If so, and you are a male, you may be interested in the position of Assistant Cataloger. . . .

- Circulation-Reference Librarian needed immediately for active modern library in progressive community with 20,000. Real opportunity for young woman with initiative. . . .

- Assistant Director. Male. Newly enlarged public library in historic. . . .

- Position in small college for young woman interested in cataloging and general reference. . . .

- Cataloger (Assistant Librarian) needed for small, midwestern liberal arts college. MA, MS, in librarianship. or M.Lbn. desired. Either young female or male (preferred). . . .

- Cataloger (half time or less) Reference, rank of assistant librarian, faculty status, needed by small midwestern university. Woman under 40. . . .

- Director, Male, Challenging opportunity in fast-growing Long Island Suburb of 40,000. New air-conditioned building.

- Assistant librarian, Responsibility for main library service in a city-county. . . . Man or woman under forty.

Taken from the classified advertising sections in the January 15 and July 1959 issues of *Library Journal.*

Civil Rights Act of 1991. In November 1991, President George Bush signed into law the Civil Rights Act of 1991. This act was enacted in response to a number of Supreme Court decisions that limited the enforcement of

Title VII and created a heavier burden for plaintiffs. The Civil Rights Act of 1991 reverses seven Supreme Court decisions; it creates rights to compensatory and punitive damages, including the right to jury trial, for individuals who are the victims of intentional discrimination as defined by Title VII of the Civil Rights Act of 1964 and the Americans with Disabilities Act. There are caps on both the compensatory and punitive damages, except for racial discrimination; these caps are based not on the seriousness of the discrimination but on the size of the employer's workforce.

Executive Order 11246 and Affirmative Action. Executive Order 11246 was issued by President Lyndon Johnson in 1965 and was amended by Executive Order 11375 in 1967. The most significant action of this order is the section that requires government contractors to have a written plan of affirmative action to remedy the effects of past discrimination. Any organization that holds a government contract of a certain size is required to have a written affirmative action plan. Many other institutions have voluntarily produced such plans.[122] The Office of Federal Contract Compliance Programs (OFCCP) of the Department of Labor administers the order.

Affirmative action refers to a set of specific procedures designed to ensure an equitable distribution of women and minorities within an institution. Despite the belief of some, affirmative action does not require fixed quotas, preferential hiring, or the employment of unqualified people. Affirmative action does require an organization to determine whether there are fewer minorities and women working in particular jobs in the organization than would reasonably be expected by their availability in the workforce and to establish goals and timetables for remedying any underutilization that might be identified.[123]

The EEOC leaves little room for doubt about what it expects of employers. The most important measure of an affirmative action program is its results. Extensive efforts to develop procedures, analyses, data collection systems, and report forms, and to file written policy statements, are meaningless, unless they result in measurable, yearly improvements in hiring, training, and promotion of minorities and females in all parts of the organization.[124]

Despite the impact of affirmative action legislation over the past three decades, both the federal and state commitment to affirmative action seems to be weakening, and the future of affirmative action is unclear. Opponents of affirmative action have two major objections to it. They either argue that it has worked so well that it is no longer needed, or that it is a means of reverse discrimination against individuals who are not in the preferred classes, and thus it favors women and minorities at the expense of more qualified white males.[125]

Opponents to affirmative action have scored a number of recent successes. For instance, in 1996 California's voters passed a referendum banning gender or race preferences in state hiring. Some recent Supreme Court rulings, such as *Adarand Constructors v. Pena*, have narrowed the scope of affirmative action. In that case the Court did not reject affirmative action programs but said that they must be subject to a rigorous standard of judicial review, known as strict scrutiny, that puts the burden on the government to show that a program being challenged is constitutional.[126] President Bill Clinton is said to support a "mend, don't end" policy toward affirmative action, but all affirmative action programs are under increasing scrutiny, and their future is uncertain.

Additional Equal Opportunity Legislation. The Equal Pay Act of 1963 requires all employees to provide equal pay to men and women who perform work that is similar in skill, effort, responsibility, and is performed under similar working conditions. The only disparity permitted in payment of wages is when such disparity is the result of a seniority system, a merit system, a system that measures earning by quantity or quality of production, and a differential based on any factor other than sex. The law is administered by the EEOC.

The Age Discrimination in Employment Act prohibits age discrimination against persons who have reached the age of 40 in hiring, discharge, retirement, pay, and conditions and privileges of employment decisions. This act is also administered by the EEOC. Until recently, individuals over the age of 70 were excluded from protection; Congress has removed that restriction. The major effect of the amendment has been the removal of a mandatory retirement age in almost all occupational fields except for individuals such as police officers, firefighters, and airline pilots.

One of the most sweeping pieces of civil rights legislation, the Americans with Disabilities Act (ADA), was passed in 1990. The legislation bars discrimination against individuals who have disabilities. A person is considered disabled if he or she has a physical or mental impairment that substantially limits one or more of life's major activities, has a record of such an impairment, or is regarded as having such an impairment.[127] The definition of disability is very inclusive; it is estimated that as many as 43 million people may be covered by the act. The provisions of the act dealing with employment became effective in July 1992 for both public and private employers with 25 employees or more. The provisions of the ADA are more extensive than those of the earlier Vocational Rehabilitation Act of 1973, which applied to government contractors, agencies of the federal government, and other programs and activities that receive federal funds. Almost all human resources practices are covered by the ADA, including application, testing, hiring, assignment, evaluation, disciplinary actions, training, promotion, medical examinations, compensation, leave, benefits, layoff, recall, and termination.

&❧ The ADA was not written to provide unlimited opportunities for those labeled "disabled." Instead it was written as a means to provide the disabled with equal access to all those parts of life that others have had the opportunity to enjoy for centuries.[128]

—Teri R. Switzer,
"The ADA: Creating Positive Awareness and Attitudes"

Employers have the following legal obligations under the ADA:

1. An employer must not deny a job to a disabled person if the person is qualified and able to perform the essential functions of the job, with or without reasonable accommodation.

2. If a disabled person is otherwise qualified but unable to perform an essential function without accommodation, the employer must make the accommodation, unless that would cause the employer undue hardship.

3. An employer does not have to lower existing performance standards if the standards are job related and applied uniformly to all employees and applicants for the job.

4. Qualification standards that screen out or tend to screen out individuals on the basis of disability must be job related and consistent with business necessity.

5. Any test or other procedure used to evaluate the qualifications of applicants must reflect the skills and abilities of an individual rather than the impaired sensory, manual, or speaking skills, unless those are the job-related abilities the test is attempting to measure.[129]

To prevent litigation, all employers should examine their practices to be sure they are in compliance with the ADA. In addition, supervisors and nondisabled workers should be informed about the act and its implications. All employees will have to become better educated and more sensitive about people with disabilities. Policies should be in place and managers should provide education about disabilities such as AIDS that produce concern on the part of other employees.[130] Employers and coworkers will be seeing types of workers in the workplace they are not used to seeing. Staff need to be trained and made to feel comfortable about working with disabled individuals of all types—both as coworkers and as library patrons.

The Family and Medical Leave Act (FMLA) became effective in August 1993. This legislation was established so that workers could take time off from jobs to attend to sick children, parents, or their own illnesses.

The FMLA requires covered employers to provide up to 12 weeks unpaid, job-protected leave to employees for events including childbirth, adoption, their own serious health problems, or those of a close family member. This legislation recognizes that employees have responsibilities outside of work and that sometimes the family needs of the employee must take precedence over those of the employer. With the passage of FMLA, workers no longer have to choose between their jobs or taking time off to care for an ailing family member or themselves. As with any other benefit, the organization should have a clear policy on FMLA, covering the rights of employees to take leave, the steps necessary in requesting leave, and the medical certification required when leave is taken. Supervisors need to be familiar with the organization's FMLA policy, and employees should be informed of their rights.[131]

Sexual Harassment

A relatively new area of federal regulation is that of sexual harassment. The Supreme Court has only recently recognized sexual harassment as a form of sexual discrimination, but according to the EEOC it is now the fastest growing employee complaint. The number of sexual harassment charges filed between 1990 and 1996 grew by 150 percent, increasing from 6,127 cases in 1990 to 15,342 in 1996. This surge is attributed to an increased willingness on the part of women to file formal complaints and a Supreme Court ruling, *Harris v. Forklift Systems, Inc.*, that made it easier for plaintiffs to win their cases.[132]

There are two types of sexual harassment. One, the quid pro quo type, occurs when a supervisor or someone in authority demands a sexual favor in exchange for some type of employee benefit, such as a pay raise or promotion. The other type of sexual harassment, the hostile work environment, occurs when an employee is forced to work in an environment where behaviors considered offensive to an employee, such as sexual jokes or teasing, occur. The *Harris v. Forklift Systems, Inc.* decision expanded the concept of the hostile workplace, ruling that an employee does not have to suffer psychological injury to be the victim of sexual harassment. The plaintiff must demonstrate only that the environment created by the offensive conduct was hostile and abusive.

Library employers should take affirmative steps first to educate supervisors about sexual harassment and then to educate staff. Not everyone automatically recognizes the range of conduct that can constitute harassing behavior. Efforts to make all library personnel aware of the problem, to show that such conduct is illegal, and to emphasize that the library will not tolerate such behavior on the part of supervisors or workers are significant parts of any program designed to prevent harassment.[133]

—Laura N. Gasaway,
"Sexual Harassment in the Library"

Sexual harassment is a violation of federal law, and, in most cases, employers are considered liable for the actions of supervisors. In addition, employers can be held liable for the harassment of employees by nonemployees or third parties, defined as customers, clients, or both. If, for example, a public services librarian were continually harassed by a library patron, and the employer knew of the harassment but took no corrective measures, the employer could be held liable.[134] Although most victims of sexual harassment are female, the regulations also apply to female-on-male harassment and same-sex harassment.[135]

The field of equal employment opportunity is rapidly changing. The interpretations of the laws pertaining to EEO are changing as new regulatory agency rulings and court decisions are issued. Library managers dealing with any of the staffing functions should attempt to remain abreast of changes in these regulations and apply them to their organizations. Although federal and state EEO laws have constrained employers in their human resources actions, the laws have worked to make U.S. workplaces more diversified and equitable. The ultimate aim of all EEO regulation is to ensure that every individual, regardless of age, race, gender, religion, or national origin, has an equal right to any job for which he or she is qualified.

Unionization

From the 1970s onward, there was an accelerated movement toward unionization in various white-collar and professional jobs. A substantial number of public-school teachers are unionized, as are a large number of nurses and college professors. Like their colleagues in other professions, a large number of librarians belong to labor unions. Although there are no exact figures available, the most recent estimate is that 25 percent of librarians work in unionized situations.[136]

The history of American workers' attempts to get fair and equitable treatment and to have a voice in the decisions that affect their lives goes back to the earliest days of the colonies. In 1636, a group of Maine fishermen protested the withholding of their wages. The first local craft union was formed in Philadelphia in 1792 by shoemakers. The first national organization of workers that has continued to the present day is the Typographical Union, founded in 1752.[137] Labor continued to strive for better working conditions, shorter hours, and better pay through the 1800s and early 1900s. Some of the conflicts between labor and management were violent, and many people were hurt or killed.

The real foundation of the American labor movement was laid in 1935, when the National Labor Relations Act, popularly known as the Wagner Act, was passed. The act gave employees the right to organize unions and to bargain collectively with employers. The purpose of the act was to encourage the growth of unions and to restrain management from interfering with this growth. To investigate violations and unfair labor practices, the act established the National Labor Relations Board (NLRB). This board has the authority to establish the rules, regulations, and procedures necessary to carry out the provisions of the Wagner Act.

After passage of the Wagner Act, unions began to grow rapidly and continued to grow until the mid-1950s. Although the number of individuals who are members of unions has increased, the proportion of the total labor force that is unionized has shown a decline since then. This decline is attributed primarily to the decreasing number of jobs in manufacturing industries, where the greatest number of unionized workers traditionally were found. But downsizing and cost-cutting efforts in many organizations have led to a new interest in unionization in many organizations where the workers who remain feel overworked and underpaid. In inflation-adjusted dollars, the average weekly wage of most hourly workers has declined, while the gap between the pay of top-level management and workers has increased.

To compensate for this loss of membership in the blue-collar industries, many unions initiated extensive organizing campaigns in the white-collar sector, particularly of public sector employees, such as government workers and public school teachers. Although there is no clear definition of the white-collar worker, the Bureau of Labor Statistics includes professional, technical, managerial, sales, and clerical workers in this category. Until the mid-1950s, white-collar workers constituted a minority of the nation's workforce. Since that time, they have outnumbered blue-collar workers, and the gap continues to widen as automation and foreign competition reduce the demand for factory workers.

In 1995, union members totaled 16.4 percent of all workers.[138] This is a decline in the percentage of unionized workers even from 1983, when slightly over 20 percent of all workers were unionized. The decline in unionization has been concentrated in the private sector. While 1 percent more of public service workers now are unionized (37.7 percent compared to 36.7 percent), the percentage in the private sector dropped from 16.5 percent in 1983 to 10.3 percent in 1995, although the total number of private sector unionized employees still exceeds the number of public sector employees.[139]

White-collar workers, particularly professionals, have been ambivalent about joining unions. Many professionals have felt that membership in a professional organization is the best way to advance their interests and the profession. Other professionals have believed themselves to be more allied with management than with production workers. Other professionals felt that, although unions might be desirable for hourly workers, professionals, with their higher status, did not need them. Nonetheless, as unionization has become more common in the public sector, increasing numbers of librarians, like other professionals, have joined unions. Often librarians are given little choice, when the library is part of a larger bargaining unit, such as a municipal organization or a university. One of the major attractions of unions for most workers is the hope that collective bargaining will improve their salaries and benefits.

> ۞Library employees and other professionals quickly found that their salaries were not growing as rapidly as those of skilled or even unskilled workers. In many municipalities sanitation workers were paid more highly than teachers or librarians, and the fact that this first group was unionized could not be ignored. Professional librarians and teachers found, for perhaps the first time, that they were not immune from layoffs and terminations, and that they no longer had the lifelong job security they had taken for granted. Cuts in government budgets, a decline in school-age populations and a shift to other programs were all taking their toll.[140]

> —Herbert S. White,
> *Library Personnel Management*

Many studies have demonstrated that the primary reason employees turn to unions is because they do not feel that management is responsive to their demands. The two factors influencing employees' interest in unions are (1) a dissatisfaction with their working conditions, and (2) a perception that they cannot change these conditions.[141] Employees usually seek out unions when they think that they cannot get management to address working conditions such as pay, benefits, job security, or chances for promotion. Because many librarians are joining unions or wondering whether such a move might be in their best interest, an understanding of the unionization process is very important to human resources managers regardless of whether their own library is presently unionized.

Forming a Union. The impetus for a union organizing campaign may come from several sources. Union organizers may start talking to employees while they are off the job about the benefits of unionization. If a union represents part of the labor force of a specific organization, members of the unionized group or union organizers may talk to employees of nonunionized units. Employees of a nonunionized organization who are dissatisfied with the policies and practices of the organization may solicit the help of an organizer or may submit a petition signed by at least 30 percent of the employees of the unit to the NLRB.

If the employees initiating the unionization action are successful in obtaining signatures of the required 30 percent of all employees, an election is usually held to determine the desire of all the employees to unionize and to determine the agency that will be designated as the bargaining agent. If the union receives a majority of the votes cast, the union becomes certified as the exclusive bargaining unit of the employees within the organization. The election is carefully supervised by representatives of the NLRB, and procedures are carefully observed by management and union representatives to be sure that no unfair labor practices occur. (Conversely, unions can be decertified if a majority of employees within the organization vote to rescind the union in another election conducted by the NLRB.)

After the local union is established, officers are elected by the dues-paying members. The elected officials usually consist of a president, a vice-president, and a secretary-treasurer. Several committees are formed, such as the bargaining or negotiating committee, which is appointed to negotiate the contract for the union, and the grievance committee, which is appointed to handle the grievances of members. A number of departmental or shop stewards—one from each department—are elected. Their primary responsibility is to listen to worker complaints, handle grievances, and observe that the supervisors live up to the terms of the contract. In all but the largest local unions, union officials work at their regular jobs but are allowed some working time to attend to union business.

Collective Bargaining. After a union has been certified as the exclusive bargaining agent for a group of employees or for a total company, management and the union must bargain. Matters that will be discussed in the bargaining sessions include wages, hours, work rules, and conditions of employment. When agreement on these matters is reached, a contract that both sides are willing to sign and abide by for a stipulated time is prepared.

Although the form such bargaining actually takes varies from situation to situation, it most commonly proceeds as follows: Generally, the organization designates one person as its representative to carry out the bargaining process and to represent management. In a library, that person may be the library human resources officer, an industrial relations specialist, or any other individual delegated to represent management. The union also appoints an individual to act as its chief spokesperson. Its demands almost always involve increased costs and conditions that restrict management's freedom, for instance, requiring a firm to provide job security for employees. The union's initial demands are more than it expects to receive. The spokesperson for management resists the first demands and offers less than the union desires. (It must be remembered, however, that although bargaining is usually thought to involve union demands only, in the recent past, many companies have demanded union concessions or "give-backs," such as reductions in pension plans or medical insurance, and, in many cases, have gotten them.) Many bargaining sessions may be required before both parties agree and a new contract is produced. Although the negotiating process is complex and frequently frustrating, the vast majority of contracts are negotiated without a strike.

Managers of libraries and information centers must recognize that unionization will affect their organizations and their methods of management. As a result of the bargaining process and the signing of a labor contract, the power and authority of management are diminished. Policies and practices affecting employees, which were previously decided by management alone, become subject to joint determination. Wages, hours, conditions of employment, the handling of grievances, and other items relating to employees are determined by the negotiating process.

To date, unionization in libraries has brought mixed results. On the plus side, unions have contributed to the formalization of human resources policies and procedures, improved communications, increased fringe benefits, and improved working conditions. According to one study, university librarians in California who are represented by unions feel great loyalty to them. They feel greater loyalty to their membership in the union than to their membership in professional organizations.[142]

On the negative side, unions have caused substantially more paperwork, contributed to the establishment of more rigid work rules, and created an adversarial relationship between librarians and library managers. A recent study showed that unionized professional librarians in academic research libraries were less satisfied with their jobs than nonunionized librarians, although the relationship between job satisfaction and unionization was also affected by the variables of salary and part-time status of the respondents.[143]

Not enough research has been done yet about the effects of unionization on libraries. Unionization is a complex issue, and, because of its importance and possible impact on the library profession, more facts are needed to document and implement future planning. In libraries, as in all other types of organizations, harmonious working relations are necessary between management and workers. The adversarial relationship that has often resulted from unionization needs to be overcome so that organizations can function more effectively—both for the good of the managers and the workers.

Conclusion

The human resources function is becoming increasingly important in all types of libraries and information agencies. As these organizations become larger and more complex, staffing becomes an even more vital part of library management. In the present era of downsizing and tight budgets, managers need to pay even more attention to staffing processes than ever before. As this chapter has shown, the tasks involved in staffing are many and diverse. For an organization to function efficiently, the staffing function must have a high priority for every manager. All of the component parts of this function must be integrated into a smoothly functioning system that enables employees to fill their work roles in such a way that the organization can operate effectively.

Now is not an easy time to go into human resources management because the field contains many challenges and unanswered questions. According to the ACRL Personnel and Staff Development Officers, the greatest challenges that face personnel administrators in large academic libraries are:

- Budget cuts

- Legal aspects of personnel administration

- Increasing diversity

- Balancing and defining support staff and librarian duties

- Negativity in the workplace

- Recognition and reward systems (noncash)

- Decentralization of personnel responsibilities[144]

These challenges are not exclusive to academic libraries but are found in all types of libraries and information centers and in most other types of organizations. Providing for the best human resources to meet the staffing needs of today presents problems and challenges, but these problems and challenges must be met. Effective organizations are those that are constantly trying to provide the best staffing so that the organization can fulfill its mission, both now and in the future.

Notes

1. Peter R. Young, "Librarianship: A Changing Profession," *Books, Bricks and Bytes: Daedalus* 125, no. 4 (Fall 1996): 124.

2. Charles Handy, *The Age of Unreason* (Boston: Harvard Business School Press, 1989), 24.

3. Sharon Lobel, "In Praise of the 'Soft' Stuff: A Vision for Human Resource Leadership," *Human Resources Management* 36, no. 1 (Spring 1997): 135-39.

4. David R. Bender, "Improving Personnel Management Through Evaluation," *Library Administration and Management* 8, no. 2 (Spring 1994): 109.

5. Maureen Sullivan, "A New Leadership Paradigm: Empowering Library Staff and Improving Performance," *Journal of Library Administration* 14, no. 2 (1991): 73-85.

6. See Shoshana Zuboff's *In the Age of the Smart Machine* (New York: Basic Books, 1988) for a thoughtful discussion of the impact of technology on work.

7. Shoshana Zuboff, "New Worlds of Computer-Mediated Work," *Harvard Business Review* 60 (September-October 1982): 142-52.

8. Michael Armstrong, *Strategies for Human Resource Management* (London: Kogan Page, 1992), 14.

9. Robert W. Goddard, "Work Force 2000," *Personnel Journal* 68 (February 1989): 65.

10. American Library Association, *Library Education and Personnel Utilization* (Chicago: American Library Association, 1976), 3.

11. Michael Gorman, "The Academic Library in the Year 2001: Dream or Nightmare or Something in Between?" *Journal of Academic Librarianship* 17 (March 1991): 4-9.

12. Jerry D. Campbell, "Academic Library Budgets: Changing 'The Sixty-Forty' Split," *Library Administration and Management* 3, no. 2 (Spring 1989): 78.

13. C. Herbert Carson, "Beginner's Luck: A Growing Job Market," *Library Journal* 121 (October 15, 1996): 32.

14. Ann Lawes, "Managing People for Whom One Is Not Directly Responsible," *The Law Librarian* 26, no. 3 (September 1995): 421-23.

15. A recent federal appeals court ruled that Microsoft must provide long-term contractors with benefits. See Beverly Ma, "Independent Contractor Pitfalls: Lessons from Microsoft," *Human Resources Forum* (June 1997): 1.

16. See "Changing the Way We Downsize," *Library and Personnel News* 8 (January-February 1994): 3, for a description of how to downsize in a more humane fashion.

17. U.S. Department of Education, Office of Educational Research and Improvement, National Center for Education Statistics, *Public Libraries in the United States: 1994* (Washington, DC, 1997): 67.

18. U.S. Department of Education, Office of Educational Research and Improvement, National Center for Education Statistics, *Academic Libraries: 1992* (Washington, DC: 1994): 6.

19. Richard A. Lanham, *The Electronic Word: Democracy, Technology, and the Arts* (Chicago: University of Chicago Press, 1993), 134.

20. Allen B. Veaner, "Librarians: The Next Generation," *Library Journal* 109 (April 1984): 623-24.

21. American Library Association, *Library Education and Personnel Utilization* (Chicago: American Library Association, 1976), 3.

22. Allen B. Veaner, "Paradigm Lost, Paradigm Regained? A Persistent Personnel Issue in Academic Librarianship, II," *College & Research Libraries* 55, no. 5 (September 1994): 390.

23. Ibid.

24. Ed Martinez and Raymond Roney, "1996 Library Support Staff Salary Survey," *Library Mosaics* (March-April 1997): 6-10.

25. Special Libraries Association, "Competencies for Special Librarians of the 21st Century" (Washington, DC: SLA, 1996). It can also be seen on the World Wide Web at http://www.sla.org.professional/comp.html.

26. However, in a recent article, it is proposed that library staff could be put into three categories: technicians, librarians, and information managers, with the information manager category roughly comparable to today's professional librarian classification. See Roger C. Greer, John Agada, and Robert Grover, "Staffing: A Model for Libraries and Other Information Agencies," *Library Administration and Management* 8, no. 1 (Winter 1994): 35-42.

27. Handy, *The Age of Unreason*, 90.

28. Ibid., 94.

29. Ann E. Prentice, "Jobs and Changes in the Technological Age," *Journal of Library Administration* 13, nos. 1-2 (1990): 47.

30. Frederick Hertzberg, "One More Time: How Do You Motivate Employees?" *Harvard Business Review* 46 (January-February 1968): 53.

31. Chris Argyris, *Integrating the Individual and the Organization* (New Brunswick, NJ: Transaction Publishers, 1990).

32. Zuboff, "New Worlds of Computer-Mediated Work," 142-52.

33. Prentice, "Jobs and Changes in the Technological Age," 50.

34. Carol P. Johnson, "The Changing Nature of Jobs: A Paraprofessional Time Series," *College & Research Libraries* 57, no. 1 (January 1996): 59-67.

35. Ron Ashkenas et al., *The Boundaryless Organization: Breaking the Chains of Organizational Structure* (San Francisco: Jossey-Bass, 1995), 55.

36. J. R. Hackman and G. R. Oldham, *Work Redesign* (Reading, MA: Addison-Wesley, 1980).

37. Ricky W. Griffin and Gary C. McMahan, "Motivation Through Job Design," in *Organizational Behavior: The State of the Science,* ed. Jerald Greenberg (Hillsdale, NJ: Lawrence Erlbaum Associates, 1994), 33-34.

38. Ibid., 40.

39. Bill Gates, with Nathan Myhrvold and Peter Rinearson, *The Road Ahead* (New York: Viking, 1995), 253.

40. James P. Clifford, "Manage Work Better to Better Manage Human Resources: A Comparative Study of Two Approaches to Job Analysis," *Public Personnel Management* 25, no. 1 (Spring 1996): 99.

41. Marydee Ojala, "Recruiting on the Internet," *Online* 21, no. 2 (March-April 1997): 78-81.

42. Kathleen de la Pena McCook and Kate Lippincott, "Library Schools and Diversity: Who Makes the Grade?" *Library Journal* 122, no. 7 (May 15, 1997): 30-32.

43. Martha Kyrillidau and Kimberly A. Maxwell, *ARL Salary Survey, 1996-97* (Washington, DC: Association of Research Libraries, 1996), 39.

44. David A. Thomas and Robin J. Ely, "Making Differences Matter: A New Paradigm for Managing Diversity," *Harvard Business Review* 74, no. 5 (September-October 1996): 80.

45. Constance H. Corey, "Those Precious Human Resources: Investments That Show You Care Enough to Keep the Very Best," *Library Administration and Management* 2 (June 1988): 128.

46. Peter Hiatt, "Identifying and Encouraging Leadership Potential: Assessment Technology and the Library Profession," *Library Trends* 40 (Winter 1992): 514.

47. Ibid., 515.

48. Adapted from Wayne F. Cascio, *Managing Human Resources: Productivity, Quality of Work Life, Profits* (New York: McGraw-Hill, 1995), 211.

49. Allen B. Veaner, *Academic Librarianship in a Transformational Age* (Boston: G. K. Hall, 1990), 279.

50. Dorothy E. Jones, "I'd Like You to Meet Our New Librarian," *Journal of Academic Librarianship* 14 (September 1988): 221.

51. Shelley L. Rogers, "Orientation for New Library Employees: A Checklist," *Library Administration and Management* 8, no. 4 (Fall 1994): 213-17.

52. Mary M. Nofsinger and Angela S. W. Lee, "Beyond Orientation: The Roles of Senior Librarians in Training Entry-Level Reference Colleagues," *College & Research Libraries* 55, no. 2 (March 1994): 161-70.

53. Peter F. Drucker, *Managing the Non-Profit Organization* (New York: Harper-Business, 1990), 145.

54. Lois Jennings, "Regrowing Staff: Managerial Priority for the Future of University Libraries," *The Public Access Computer Systems Review* 3, no. 3 (1992): 5.

55. Peter M. Senge, *The Fifth Discipline: The Art & Practice of the Learning Organization* (New York: Doubleday, 1990), 3.

56. Ibid., 6-10.

57. For a more in-depth look at staff development, see Sheila D. Creth, *Effective On-the-Job Training: Developing Library Human Resources* (Chicago: American Library Association, 1986).

58. David Marshall Hunt and Carol Mitchell, "Mentorship: A Career Training and Development Tool," *The Academy of Management Review* 8 (July 1983): 475-85.

59. Michael Zey, *The Mentor Connection: Strategic Alliances in Corporate Life* (New Brunswick, NJ: Transaction Publishers, 1990).

60. Joseph Berk and Susan Berk, *Managing Effectively: A Handbook for First-Time Managers* (New York: Sterling, 1991), 93-94.

61. Tinker Massey, "Mentoring: A Means to Learning," *Journal of Education for Library and Information Science* 36, no. 1 (Winter 1995): 52-54.

62. Zey, *The Mentor Connection*, 10.

63. Barbara A. DeLon, "Keeping Plateaued Performers Motivated," *Library Administration and Management* 7, no. 1 (Winter 1993): 13.

64. Judith M. Bardwick, "Plateauing and Productivity," *Sloan Management Review* 24 (Spring 1983): 67.

65. C. Rivers, "Glass Ceilings and Limits on Leadership," *News and Observer* (Raleigh, NC), August 25, 1991.

66. Henry Mintzberg, "Musings on Management," *Harvard Business Review* 74 (July-August 1996): 67.

67. Barbara Conway, "The Plateaued Career," *Library Administration and Management* 9, no. 1 (Winter 1995): 14.

68. Adapted from Deborah E. Ettington, "How Human Resource Managers Can Help Plateaued Managers Succeed," *Human Resource Management* 36, no. 2 (Summer 1997): 228.

69. Bardwick, "Plateauing and Productivity," 69-72.

70. Mary Haack, John W. Jones, and Tina Roose, "Occupational Stress Among Librarians," *Drexel Library Quarterly* 20 (Spring 1984): 67.

71. Julita Nawe, "Work-Related Stress Among the Library and Information Workforce," *Library Review* 44, no. 6 (1995): 30-37.

72. Stanley J. Modic, "Surviving Burnout: The Malady of Our Age," *Industry Week* 238 (February 20, 1989): 28-34.

73. Charles A. Bunge, "Stress in the Library Workplace," *Library Trends* 38, no. 1 (Summer 1989): 93.

74. Marcia Nauratil, "Librarian Burnout and Alienation," *Canadian Library Journal* 44 (December 1987): 385.

75. Haack, Jones, and Roose, "Occupational Stress Among Librarians," 67.

76. Beth Blevins, "Burnout in Special Libraries," *Library Management Quarterly* 11 (Fall 1988): 20.

77. Walt Crawford and Michael Gorman, *Future Libraries: Dreams, Madness, and Reality* (Chicago: American Library Association, 1995): 118-19.

78. Joyce K. Thornton, "Carpal Tunnel Syndrome in ARL Libraries," *College & Research Libraries* 58, no. 1 (January 1997): 9-18.

79. Nancy K. Austin, "Updating the Performance Review," *Working Woman* (November 1992): 35.

80. W. Edwards Deming, *Out of the Crisis* (Cambridge, MA: MIT Center for Advanced Engineering Study, 1982), 101-2.

81. Ibid.

82. However, see Rao Aluri and Mary Reichel, "Performance Evaluation as a Deadly Disease," *The Journal of Academic Librarianship 19* (July 1994): 145-55, for an application of Deming's viewpoint applied to library performance evaluations.

83. Michael Beer, "Making Performance Appraisal Work," in *Managing People and Organizations*, ed. John J. Gabarro (Boston: Harvard Business School Publications, 1992), 196.

84. Brendan McDonagh, "Appraising Appraisals," *The Law Librarian* 26, no. 3 (September 1995): 425.

85. Necia Parker-Gibson and Lutishoor Salisbury, "The Process of Peer Review," *Arkansas Libraries* 53, no. 1 (February 1996): 3-7.

86. Gay Helen Perkins, "The Value of Upward Evaluation in Libraries—Part II," *Library Administration and Management* 9, no. 3 (Summer 1995): 166-75.

87. Richard Rubin, "The Development of a Performance Evaluation Instrument for Upward Evaluation of Supervisors by Subordinates," *Library and Information Science Research* 16 (Fall 1994): 315-28. This article provides considerable detail about the development of a valid and reliable instrument used in one public library.

88. Bodil Jones, "How'm I Doin'?" *Management Review* 86, no. 5 (May 1997): 9-18.

89. George C. Thornton, "The Relationship Between Supervisory and Self-Appraisals of Executive Performance," *Personnel Psychology* (Winter 1968): 441-55.

90. Denver Public Library, Librarian's Committee on Performance Evaluation, *Management Guide to Performance Evaluation* (1971), 1.

91. Joyce P. Vincelette and Fred C. Pfister, "Improving Performance Appraisal in Libraries," *Library and Information Science Research* 6 (April-June 1984): 191-203.

92. Kent E. Romanoff, "The Ten Commandments of Performance Management," *Personnel* 66 (January 1989): 24.

93. Saul W. Gellerman, *Management by Motivation* (Chicago: American Management Association, 1968), 141.

94. "Breaking with Tradition: Changing Employee Relations Through a Positive Employee Philosophy," *Library Personnel News* 8, no. 1 (January-February 1994): 4.

95.   Keith Davis and John W. Newstrom, *Human Behavior at Work: Organizational Behavior*, 8th ed. (New York: McGraw-Hill, 1989), 424.

96.   D. Day, "Training 101: Help for Discipline Dodgers," *Training and Development* 47, no. 5 (May 1993): 19-22.

97.   Richard E. Rubin, *Human Resource Management in Libraries: Theory and Practice* (New York: Neal-Schuman, 1991), 157-58.

98.   Steven A. Jesseph, "Employee Termination, 2: Some Dos and Don'ts," *Personnel* 66 (February 1989): 36.

99.   Karen L. Vinton, "Documentation That Gets Results," *Personnel* 67 (February 1990): 43.

100.   Miriam Rothman, "Employee Termination," *Personnel* 66 (February 1989): 34.

101.   Paul F. Buller, Nancy K. Napier, and Glenn M. McEvoy, "Popular Prescriptions: Implications for HR in the 1990s," *Human Resources Management* 30 (Summer 1991): 265.

102.   Edward E. Lawler III, *Pay and Organizational Effectiveness: A Psychological View* (New York: McGraw-Hill, 1971), 233.

103.   The last survey available, published in 1997, reported the 1996 results. The average salary for a 1996 MLS graduate was $29,480, up 1.7 percent from the previous year's average. C. Herbert Carson, "Counting on Technology," *Library Journal* 122, no. 17 (October 15, 1997): 27-33.

104.   For the latest survey, see Martinez and Roney, "1996 Library Support Staff Salary Survey," 6-10.

105.   Anne Woodsworth and Theresa Maylone, "Reinvesting in the Information Job Family: Context, Changes, New Jobs, and Models for Evaluation and Compensation," CAUSE Professional Paper Series, # 11 (Boulder, CO: CAUSE, 1993), 1-2.

106.   Steve Marquardt and Leslie Foster, "The Groo Award: Participative Recognition of Peer Performance," *Library Administration and Management* 8 (Fall 1994): 209-11.

107.   Philip C. Grant, "How to Make a Program Work," *Personnel Journal* 71 (January 1992): 103f.

108.   Joan M. Bechtel, "Leadership Lessons Learned from Managing and Being Managed," *The Journal of Academic Librarianship* 18, no. 6 (January 1993): 355-56.

109.   Tom Peters and Nancy Austin, *A Passion for Excellence: The Leadership Difference* (New York: Random House, 1985), 259.

110.   William W. Thomas III, ed., *Social Security Manual* (Cincinnati OH: National Underwriter Co., 1997), 219.

111.   Marjorie Watson, "Employee Benefits: Emerging Trends for Librarians," *Bottom Line*, charter issue (June 1986): 29-33.

112.   Charlene Marmer Solomon, "Twenty-Four Hour Employees," *Personnel Journal* 70 (August 1991): 76.

113. U.S. Bureau of the Census, *Statistical Abstract of the United States 1996* (Washington, DC: Government Printing Office, 1996), 430.

114. Ibid., 428.

115. D. J. Treiman and H. I. Hartmann, *Women, Work, and Wages—Equal Pay for Jobs of Equal Value* (Washington, DC: National Academy Press, 1981), 66-67.

116. Janine Kostecki, "Privacy Issues in the Workplace Increasing," *Library Personnel News* 8, no. 2 (March-April 1994): 1-2.

117. Michael Levy, "The Electronic Monitoring of Workers: Privacy in the Age of the Electronic Sweatshop," *Legal References Quarterly* 14, no. 3 (1995): 12-14.

118. Edward D. Bewayo, "Electronic Management and Equity Issues," *Journal of Information Ethics* 4 (Spring 1995): 70.

119. Rosabeth Moss Kanter, "Men and Women of the Corporation Revisited," *Management Review* 76 (March 1987): 16.

120. For a fuller discussion of the laws related to the staffing function in libraries, see Laura N. Gasaway and Barbara B. Moran, "The Legal Environment," in *Personnel Administration in Libraries*, 2d ed., eds. Sheila Creth and Frederick Duda (New York: Neal-Schuman, 1989): 13-39.

121. *Griggs v. Duke Power Company*, 401 U.S. 424 (1971).

122. See, for example, the Association of Research Libraries, Systems and Procedures Exchange Center, *Affirmative Action Programs* (Washington, DC: Association of Research Libraries, 1980).

123. Margaret Myers and Beverly P. Lynch, "Affirmative Action and Academic Libraries," *Directions* 1 (September 1975): 13.

124. Equal Opportunity Employment Commission, *Affirmative Action and Equal Employment for Employers*, vol. 1 (Washington, DC: Government Printing Office, 1974), 3.

125. *Congressional Quarterly Almanac, 104th Congress, 2nd Session, 1996*, vol. 52 (Washington, DC: Congressional Quarterly, 1996), 5-37.

126. Dan Carney, "Effort to Ban Racial Preference at Federal Level Restarted," *Congressional Quarterly Weekly Report* 55, no. 25 (June 21, 1997): 1454.

127. Wayne E. Barlow and Edward Z. Hane, "A Practical Guide to the Americans with Disabilities Act," *Personnel Journal* 71 (June 1992): 53.

128. Teri R. Switzer, "The ADA: Creating Positive Awareness and Attitudes," *Library Administration and Management* 8, no. 4 (Fall 1994): 207.

129. Barlow and Hane, "Practical Guide to the Americans with Disabilities Act," 59.

130. Willie Mae O'Neal, "AIDS: A Perspective on Management Issues," *Emergency Librarian* 21 (January-February 1994): 26-27.

131. Teresa Brady, "The FMLA: No Free Vacation," *Management Review* (June 1997): 43-45.

132.   Larry Reynolds, "Sex Harassment Claims Surge," *Human Resources Forum* (May 1997): 1.

133.   Laura N. Gasaway, "Sexual Harassment in the Library: The Law," *North Carolina Libraries* 49 (Spring 1991): 15.

134.   Teresa Brady, "Added Liability: Third-Party Sexual Harassment," *Management Review* 86, no. 4 (April 1997): 45-47.

135.   Gasaway, "Sexual Harassment in the Library," 14-17.

136.   Stephen G. Brint and Martin H. Dodd, *Professional Workers and Unionization: A Data Handbook* (Washington, DC: Department of Professional Employees, AFL-CIO, 1984), 45 (cited in Frances M. Jones and Patrick L. Jarvis, *Directory of Library Staff Organizations* [Phoenix, AZ: Oryx Press, 1986], 4).

137.   Wendell French, *The Personnel Management Process: Human Resources Administration,* 3d ed. (Boston: Houghton Mifflin, 1974), 725.

138.   U.S. Bureau of the Census, *Statistical Abstract of the United States 1996* (Washington, DC: Government Printing Office, 1996), 436.

139.   Ibid.

140.   Herbert S. White, *Library Personnel Management* (White Plains, NY: Knowledge Industry Publications, 1985), 163.

141.   J. M. Brett, "Why Employees Want Unions," *Organizational Dynamics* 8, no. 4 (Spring 1980): 47-57.

142.   Renee N. Anderson, John D'Amicantonio, and Henry DuBois, "Labor Unions or Professional Organizations: Which Have Our First Loyalty?" *College & Research Libraries* 53 (July 1992): 331-40.

143.   Tina Maragou Hovekamp, "Unionization and Job Satisfaction Among Professional Library Employees in Academic Research Institutions," *College & Research Libraries* 56 (July 1995): 341-50.

144.   "ACRL Personnel and Staff Development Officers Identify the Greatest Challenges," *Library Personnel News* 8, no. 4 (July-August 1994): 4.

Readings

Argyris, Chris. *Integrating the Individual and the Organization.* New Brunswick, NJ: Transaction Publishers, 1990.

Baldwin, David A. *The Academic Librarian's Human Resources Handbook.* Englewood, CO: Libraries Unlimited, 1996.

Belcher, John L. et al. *Alternative Work Schedules.* Newton, MA: Allyn & Bacon, 1989.

Casteleyn, Mary, and Sylvia P. Webb. *Promoting Excellence: Personnel Management and Staff Development in Libraries.* London: Bowker Saur, 1993.

Crawford, Walt, and Michael Gorman. *Future Libraries: Dreams, Madness, and Reality.* Chicago: American Library Association, 1995.

Creth, Sheila D. *Effective On-the-Job Training: Developing Library Human Resources.* Chicago: American Library Association, 1986.

Creth, Sheila, and Frederick Duda, eds. *Personnel Administration in Libraries.* 2d ed. New York: Neal-Schuman, 1989.

Davis, Keith, and John W. Newstrom. *Human Behavior at Work: Organizational Behavior.* 8th ed. New York: McGraw-Hill, 1989.

Handy, Charles. *The Age of Unreason.* Boston: Harvard Business School Press, 1989.

Kanter, Rosabeth Moss. *When Giants Learn to Dance.* New York: Simon & Schuster, 1989.

Limerick, David, and Bert Cunnington. *Managing the New Organization.* San Francisco: Jossey-Bass, 1993.

Matteson, Michael T., and John M. Ivancevich. *Controlling Work Stress.* San Francisco: Jossey-Bass, 1987.

Morrison, Ann M. et al. *Breaking the Glass Ceiling: Can Women Reach the Top of America's Largest Corporations?* Reading, MA: Addison-Wesley, 1987.

Odiorne, George S. *The Human Side of Management: Management by Integration and Self-Control.* Lexington, MA: Lexington Books, 1987.

Pierce Rausch, Erwin, and Michael H. Frisch. *Win-Win Performance Management/Appraisal.* Somerset, NJ: John Wiley, 1985.

Rubin, Richard E. *Human Resource Management in Libraries.* New York: Neal-Schuman, 1991.

Senge, Peter M. *The Fifth Discipline: The Art & Practice of the Learning Organization.* New York: Doubleday, 1990.

White, Herbert S. *Library Personnel Management.* White Plains, NY: Knowledge Industry Publications, 1985.

Woodsworth, Anne, and Theresa Maylone. "Reinvesting in the Information Job Family: Context, Changes, New Jobs, and Models for Evaluation and Compensation." CAUSE Professional Paper Series, # 11. Boulder, CO: CAUSE, 1993.

Zey, Michael G. *The Mentor Connection: Strategic Alliances in Corporate Life.* New Brunswick, NJ: Transaction Publishers, 1990.

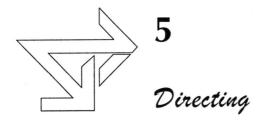

5

Directing

Organizations are indeed social systems and are arenas for inducing cooperative behavior. As such they are quintessentially human and fraught with all the frailties and imperfections associated with the human condition.[1]

—Abraham Zaleznik, "Real Work"

One common definition of management is "getting things done through people." Directing is the managerial function that enables managers to get things done through people—individually and in groups. Directing is related to staffing, because each of these functions is concerned with the organization's employees, but the two functions are different. They each focus on distinct aspects of working with people. Staffing is concerned with providing and maintaining the human resources of an organization; this function provides the human resource base. Directing is focused on leading and motivating these human resources. Directing builds upon staffing in that it takes the human resources of an organization and guides and coordinates them toward achieving the organization's goals. So, although both are concerned with the human side of the organization, they are distinct functions.

Directing is a complex function, because it requires managers to understand the human element in the organization. To be effective at directing, managers must be familiar with what type of rewards are most effective in motivating individuals, and they must know what styles of leadership are most likely to work best in any given situation. They also must understand the importance of communication within the organization. Indeed, if a manager is not careful, the interpersonal aspects of directing can consume huge amounts of energy.

As Abraham Zaleznik has written, the "complexity in human nature . . . leads managers to spend their time smoothing over conflict, greasing the wheels of human interactions and unconsciously avoiding aggression."[2]

Zaleznik warns that managers often spend too much time trying to maintain the human element of the organization. He urges that managers maintain a balance between what are often two competing organizational functions: functions he terms the "interpersonal," the human issues, and the "real work," such as marketing and production. Obviously, managers do a disservice to the organization if they spend a disproportionate amount of time on the interpersonal aspects of management. Balance must be maintained. But the interpersonal functions of directing cannot be neglected, because the human element is essential to the performance of the "real work" of organizations.

For the last century, managers have looked to the behavioral sciences, such as psychology, sociology, anthropology, and political science, for useful insights to help in the directing function, and they have applied many of the findings of behavioral scientists to the workplace. This borrowing has been especially useful, because it has provided managers with many theories to explain human behavior. However, because there has been so much research and because the results of this research have often seemed contradictory, a manager seeking information on the best way to direct often becomes confused and frustrated. It must be remembered that the research was never intended to provide a single, simple prescription for all managers. Indeed, it has become clear that there is no one best way to direct, and no universal theory that is appropriate in all cases.[3] What behavioral science research does provide, however, is a framework for managers to use in assessing their directing methods and a mechanism to suggest possible avenues of improvement. The more managers know about the research relating to motivation, leadership, and communication, the more able they are to draw from this research the elements that will be most useful to them.

Like other managerial functions, directing is done by managers at different levels throughout the organization. In most typical organizations, including libraries, management can be divided into three levels. Top management, which in libraries usually means the director and the assistant and associate directors, is responsible for the overall functioning of the entire organization. Middle management is in charge of specific subunits or functions of the organization. In libraries and information centers, department heads are middle managers. Their management functions are concentrated on the successful functioning of individual areas of the library. The managers in the lowest position of the management hierarchy are supervisors, sometimes called first-line managers. Supervisors direct the activities of individual workers to accomplish the desired organizational objectives. Because supervisors direct the work of all nonmanagement employees, they play a major role in influencing the performance of a work unit and are an important factor in determining the job satisfaction and the morale of the individuals supervised. Although this tripartite division of management is being affected by the organizational changes discussed in chapter 3, and the layers of lower management may be much less distinct in organizations that have adopted team management, even the flattest organizations still have managers who are concerned with directing.

> ‿ Every supervisor and team leader in an organization leads by example, even when it is a bad example. Every one of them has influence on the organization, even if it is a bad influence. We just naturally imitate those in charge. What senior leaders do, what they believe and value, what and whom they reward, are watched, seen, interpreted, and imitated throughout the whole organization.[4]
>
> —Kathleen Huddleston,
> *Back on the Quality Track*

In most organizations, managers on the highest levels have the power to establish organization-wide policy and, by their own style of directing, are influential in setting the tone of directing throughout the organization. Middle managers, in addition to directing their specific subunits or functions, also serve as liaisons between top management and supervisors. Finally, because supervisors are the managers in direct contact with most employees, much of the directing function in an organization is done by these lower level managers; they, like upper level managers, must be skilled in leadership and human relations functions.

Managers at all levels should be familiar with the techniques of good directing so they can create a climate in which people can work together to fulfill the organization's goals. Directing is a difficult undertaking, because its focus is on human behavior. Human behavior is always unpredictable, because it arises from people's deep-seated needs and values systems. As Keith Davis and John Newstrom state, "There are no simple formulas for working with people. There is no idealistic solution to organizational problems. All that can be done is to increase our understanding and skills so that human relations at work can be upgraded."[5]

This chapter presents an overview of the directing function. First, the major research relating to human behavior in the work environment is examined. The three major aspects of directing—motivating, leading, and communication—are considered in turn. The last section of the chapter looks at techniques—especially Total Quality Management—that managers have used as organizations have changed to allow more employee participation in management. When management is no longer the responsibility of just the individual at the top, the three elements of directing must be employed in new ways to make the organization successful. The chapter concludes with a discussion of the contingency approach to management that integrates the many theories of directing into a method that managers can use to match their directing styles to the needs of specific groups of employees in specific work settings.

The Human Element of the Organization

Before managers can direct, they must understand as much as possible about the human element of the organization. For instance, what causes workers to act the way they do? What needs do workers have? How should workers be treated to make them most productive? It was not until the early part of the twentieth century that managers began to realize the importance of the employees and their behavior in organizations. The first management studies were prompted by a desire to improve the productivity of workers. Most of the early management theorists mentioned in chapter 1, including Frederick Taylor and Frank and Lillian Gilbreth, were interested primarily in the efficient performance of employees. The real interest in the human factor in organizations began as a result of the Hawthorne studies in the late 1920s.

The Hawthorne Studies

The Hawthorne studies were discussed in chapter 1 in terms of providing the basis of the human behavior movement in management. Here, they are discussed in terms of the nature of employees working in organizations. Elton Mayo's research at the Western Electric Company in Hawthorne, Illinois, has become a landmark in the modern concept of effective human relations.[6]

As efficiency engineers at the Hawthorne plant were experimenting with various forms of illumination, they noted an unexpected reaction from employees. When illumination was increased, productivity increased. That was not so surprising as the fact that when illumination was decreased, production continued to increase. This same increase in production occurred when the illumination was not changed at all. Mayo was asked to examine this paradox, and the Hawthorne studies resulted.

The studies consisted of two parts. One part involved special six-woman teams of workers. Working conditions for these teams were constantly changed to determine worker fatigue and production. Not only was the illumination changed, but other factors were manipulated, such as rest periods, length of the work day, and coffee breaks. Every change that was made caused production to go up. Baffled by these results, the experimenters decided to return the original conditions. This change was expected to cause production to decrease. Instead, production jumped to a new all-time high. Why? The answer lay not in the changes in the working conditions, but in the changes in the way the workers felt about themselves. By lavishing attention on the workers, the experimenters had made these women feel as though they were an important part of the company. These previously indifferent employees coalesced into congenial, cohesive groups with a great deal of group pride. Employees' needs for affiliation, competency, and achievement were fulfilled, and their productivity increased.

> Each [woman] knew that she was producing more in the test room than she ever had in the regular department, and each said that the increase had come about without any conscious effort on her part. It seemed easier to produce at the faster rate in the test room than at the slower rate in the regular department. When questioned further, each [woman] stated her reasons in slightly different words, but there was uniformity in the answers in two respects. First the [women] liked to work in the test room: "it was fun." Secondly the new supervisory relation, or as they put it, the absence of the old supervisory control, made it possible for them to work freely without anxiety.[7]

The second part of the Hawthorne studies involved interviewing approximately 20,000 workers. Two things became apparent from the interviews. First, work in the factory was dismal and dull at best, and most employees accepted it passively and with a feeling of futility. Second, informal groups of workers emerged, through which the worker acquired a feeling of belonging and being welcome. Management considered these groups to be threats, which was not entirely in error, because one of the primary functions of the groups was to provide a safe retaliation for poor managerial techniques. Slowdowns in production, poor or careless work, and the forcing of all workers to comply with the group's behavior were within the power of the group. But Mayo believed that the group could become a positive force for increasing productivity if management changed its attitude toward the group and used it for positive action.

> ☒ People need to be involved in a meaningful way if they are to be motivated. They need to feel they are part of something bigger than themselves and to understand how their efforts contribute to the big picture. The assumption that workers are content to be treated as outsiders, without access to business information, is one of the major fallacies of the bureaucratic organization.[8]

—Edward Deevy,
Creating the Resilient Organization

The Hawthorne studies are important because they show that:

- employees respond to managerial efforts to improve the working environment;

- employees respond to being allowed to make decisions that affect their work patterns and job behavior;

- the informal group can be a positive force, helping management achieve its goals;

- the informal group needs to develop a sense of dignity and responsibility and needs to be recognized as a constructive force in the organization; and

- the worker must feel needed and welcomed by management.

In short, the Hawthorne studies are a landmark in management research. They were the first to recognize that organizations are social systems and the productivity of workers was a result not only of physical factors but of interpersonal ones also.

McGregor's Theory X and Theory Y

Two influential groups of assumptions about workers were developed by Douglas McGregor in the 1950s.[9] McGregor called these sets of assumptions Theory X and Theory Y. The first set of assumptions, Theory X, reflects what McGregor saw as the traditional, autocratic, managerial perception of workers. McGregor's Theory X assumes:

- Average human beings have an inherent dislike of work and will avoid it if they can.

- Because of this human characteristic of dislike of work, most people must be coerced, controlled, directed, and threatened with punishment to get them to put forth necessary effort toward the achievement of organizational objectives.

- The average human being prefers to be directed, wishes to avoid responsibility, has relatively little ambition, and, above all, wants security.

Theory X is a very pessimistic assessment of human nature. Managers who hold Theory X assumptions about their employees feel the need to tightly structure jobs and supervise workers. This theory assumes that the goals of the employee and the organization are incompatible and places major reliance upon the use of authority to control workers.

After describing Theory X, McGregor questioned whether this perception of workers is adequate in a democratic society in which the workforce enjoys a rising standard of living and has an increasing level of education. McGregor put forth an alternative set of generalizations about human nature and the management of human resources, which he called Theory Y. Theory Y assumes:

- The expenditure of physical and mental effort in work is as natural as play or rest.

- External control and the threat of punishment are not the only means for bringing about effort toward organizational objectives. Individuals will exercise self-direction and self-control in the service of objectives to which they are committed.

- Commitment to objectives is a function of the rewards associated with their achievement. Positive rewards, such as ego satisfaction and self-realization, are the most significant and can be direct products of efforts directed toward organizational objectives.

- The average human learns, under proper conditions, not only to accept but to seek responsibility.

- The capacity to exercise a relatively high degree of imagination, ingenuity, and creativity in the solution of organizational problems is widely, not narrowly, distributed in the population.

- Under the conditions of modern industrial life, the intellectual potential of the average human being is only partly utilized.

Theory Y presents a much more positive picture of people, but the assumptions that constitute this theory are more challenging to managers. These assumptions imply that human nature is dynamic, not static. They indicate that human beings have the capacity to grow and develop. Most important, Theory Y makes management responsible for creating an environment that permits the positive development of individual employees. Managers who accept Theory Y do not try to impose external control and direction over employees but allow them self-direction and control.

> The conditions imposed by conventional organization theory and by the approach of scientific management for the past half century have tied [workers] to limited jobs which do not utilize their capabilities, have discouraged the acceptance of responsibility, have encouraged passivity, have eliminated meaning from work. . . . People today are accustomed

> to being directed, manipulated, controlled in industrial or-
> ganizations and to finding satisfactions for their social, ego-
> istic, and self-fulfillment needs away from the job.[10]

—Douglas M. McGregor,
The Human Side of Enterprise

McGregor's assumptions had a powerful influence in making many managers aware that they had overlooked the potential of individual workers. But,
despite their impact on management practice, these assumptions do not represent a panacea for a manager. In the first place, it must be remembered that
these are assumptions only; assumptions as such have no proof. Theory X and
Theory Y were not based upon research but upon intuitive deduction,
although later researchers have looked at these variables in many settings
and cultures.[11]

It was never McGregor's intention that Theory X be viewed as always
bad and Theory Y as always good. As he states, most people have the potential
to be self-motivated and mature. Some may not realize that potential, however, and the manager may have to create a structured and controlled work
environment for those employees. Even though McGregor was aware of
the difficulties of what he proposed, he nonetheless urged managers to examine their assumptions about workers to see if the managers themselves
are responsible for creating the very conditions they dislike. He presented
a convincing argument that most management actions flow directly from
whatever theory of human behavior managers hold.

Argyris Immaturity-Maturity Theory

Chris Argyris developed a conceptual framework that addresses the
incompatibility between the values of many organizations and those of mature individuals.[12] According to Argyris, as people mature, their personalities change in several ways. First, people move from the passive state of
infancy to the increasingly active state of adulthood. Second, an individual
moves from a state of total dependency as an infant to a state of relative independence as an adult. Third, individuals mature from infants who have
only limited modes of behavior to adults who are capable of behaving in
many ways. Fourth, individuals have only shadowy, erratic interests as infants, but as adults they are capable of deeper and stronger interests. Fifth,
infants and children have only a short time perspective, but adults have a
time perspective that includes not only the present but the past and the future. Sixth, individuals as infants are subordinate to everyone, but as they
mature, they move to equal or superior positions in relation to others.
Finally, as infants or young children, individuals lack an awareness of self,

but, as adults, they have an awareness of self and are able to control this self. According to Argyris's theory, maturation is a continuum. The healthy personality develops along the continuum from immaturity to maturity, although, sometimes, an individual's culture or personality limit maturation. Thus, impediments of various types keep some people from reaching full maturation.

Argyris argued that, not only do most organizations ignore these maturation patterns, but, in fact, many individuals are kept from maturing because of the management practices of the organizations where they work. Many organizations expect workers to behave in an immature way; thus, the work environment is tightly structured, and the individual employee is closely controlled. Employees are encouraged to be dependent and passive—to remain immature. Because workers are treated as immature, they experience frustration, tension, and aggression, and often behave immaturely. For instance, workers may display excessive absenteeism, apathy, or lack of effort.

> An analysis of the basic properties of relatively mature human beings and formal organization leads to the conclusion that there is an inherent incongruency between the self-actualization of the two. This basic incongruity creates a situation of conflict, frustration and failure for the participants.[13]
>
> —Chris Argyris, *Personality and Organization*

Argyris encouraged organizations to take steps to alleviate this situation and give employees a chance to grow and mature as individuals on their jobs. Like McGregor's Theory Y, Argyris's theory contended that people can be self-directed and creative at work, if they are given the opportunity. He recommended that managers make fundamental changes that would allow employees to increase their individual responsibility and encourage employee participation in decision making. If organizations were more participative, flexible, and responsive to the contributions that employees can make, and if conditions in these organizations were compatible with the needs of mature individuals, it would be beneficial to both the workers and to the organization. As will be seen later in this chapter, many modern methods of management, such as Total Quality Management, have adopted these perspectives on workers. Advocates of this type of management view workers as motivated, mature participants who will work to ensure the success of the organization.

Structuring the Human Element in Organizations

Research concerning people in organizations provides managers with some insight into how to structure the human relations aspect of any organization. As Davis and Newstrom point out, there are four basic assumptions about people that every manager should keep in mind:

1. Individual differences. People have much in common, but each person is an individual. From the day of birth, each person is unique, and individual experiences make people even more different. Because of these individual differences, no single, standard, across-the-board way of dealing with employees can be adopted.

2. A whole person. Although some organizations wish they could employ only a person's skill or brain, they must employ the whole person. Various human traits may be separately studied, but, in the final analysis, they are part of one system making up a whole person. People function as total beings. Good management practice dictates trying to develop a better employee, but it also should be concerned with developing a better person overall in terms of growth and fulfillment.

3. Motivated behavior. Psychology has shown that normal behavior has certain causes. These may relate to an individual's needs or the consequences that result from acts. In the case of needs, people are motivated not by what we think they ought to have but by what they want themselves. To an outside observer, an individual's needs may be illusory or unrealistic, but, still they are controlling.

4. Value of the person. This is more an ethical philosophy than a scientific conclusion. It confirms that people are to be treated differently from other factors of production because they are of a higher order in the universe. It recognizes that, because people are of a higher order, they want and deserve to be treated with respect and dignity. Any job, regardless of how simple, entitles the people who do it to proper respect and recognition of their unique aspirations and abilities. This concept of human dignity rejects the old idea of using employees as economic tools.[14]

To a large extent, the human factor in any organization is shaped by managerial actions. Managers have a tremendous impact on the growth and development of individual employees. J. Sterling Livingston used the George Bernard Shaw play, *Pygmalion* (the basis of the later musical *My Fair Lady*), as an analogy for the role he thinks managers play in developing able subordinates and stimulating their success.[15] Just as in *Pygmalion*

Henry Higgins transformed the flower girl into the society lady, managers have the potential to transform their employees. According to Livingston, a manager's expectations are the key to the subordinate's performance and development. If a manager thinks the employee is going to succeed, that employee usually will succeed.

> &Some managers always treat their subordinates in a way that leads to superior performance. But most managers . . . unintentionally treat their subordinates in a way that leads to lower performance than they are capable of achieving. The way managers treat their subordinates is subtly influenced by what they expect of them. If managers' expectations are high, productivity is likely to be excellent. If their expectations are low, productivity is likely to be poor. It is as though there were a law that caused subordinates' performance to rise or fall to meet managers' expectations.[16]
>
> —J. Sterling Livingston,
> "Pygmalion in Management"

Whatever assumption is adopted may serve as a self-fulfilling prophecy, because if managers believe that something is true, they will behave in a way that helps that belief come true. If a manager believes that employees are irresponsible, immature, and lazy, he or she will treat them as if they were. Employees will respond by being frustrated, aggressive, and apathetic, and, thus, the manager's beliefs will be fulfilled. On the other hand, if employees are treated as responsible, capable, and interested in the organization's goals, they usually will respond in like fashion and, thus, fulfill that prophecy.

Motivating

Managers are interested in motivation because it affects both employee performance and organizational effectiveness. Managers motivate by providing an environment that induces workers to contribute to the goals of the organization. Many questions about employees' behavior can best be under- stood by understanding motivation. In every organization, there are some employees who work very hard, and others who do as little as possible; some employees who show up on time for work every day and work after hours when necessary, and others who are frequently late and sometimes fail to come to work at all. It is often said that the first group of employees is motivated and the second is not. But what causes some workers and not others to be motivated? This is a question that has puzzled managers for a long time.

&Most people in this world, psychologically, can be divided into two broad groups. There is that minority which is challenged by opportunity and willing to work hard to achieve something, and the majority which really does not care all that much. . . . [P]sychologists have tried to penetrate the mystery of this curious dichotomy. Is the need to achieve (or the absence of it) an accident, is it hereditary, or is it the result of environment? Is it a single, isolatable human motive or a combination of motives—the desire to accumulate wealth, power, fame? Most important of all, is there some technique that could give this will to achieve to people, even whole societies, who do not now have it?[17]

—David C. McClelland,
"That Urge to Achieve"

Motivation is defined as a willingness to expend energy to achieve a goal or a reward.[18] Thus, motivation is a process governing choices made by individuals among alternate voluntary activities. Evidence has shown that most people do not work to the fullest extent of their capabilities and that most jobs do not require that they do so. In some of the earliest research on motivation, William James of Harvard University discovered that hourly workers working at 20 to 30 percent of their ability were performing well enough not to lose their jobs.[19] He also found that highly motivated workers performed at 80 to 90 percent of their ability. That gap between 20 to 30 percent and 80 to 90 percent is the area that can be affected by motivation.

What motivates individuals varies from individual to individual, and even in the same person changes over time. Motivation is influenced by a number of internal and external forces. Because human beings have a complex psychological makeup, motivation is a complex, multifaceted characteristic related to various desires, drives, needs, and wishes. Many theories have been developed to explain human motivation. Four of the most important for managers are Maslow's hierarchy of needs, Herzberg's two-factor theory, Vroom's expectancy theory, and Skinner's behavior modification.

Maslow's Hierarchy of Needs

One of the most widely known theories of motivation was proposed by psychologist Abraham Maslow. Maslow postulated that all individuals have needs that can be ranked in one predetermined hierarchy. One level of need must be satisfied before an individual pursues the satisfaction of a higher level need. As needs are satisfied, they lose their motivational properties, until they are again aroused. Only unsatisfied needs serve as motivators. Maslow identified five levels of needs:

1. Physiological. The basic needs of a human are food, water, shelter, sleep, and other bodily needs. All are essential to human survival, and until they are satisfied to the degree necessary to sustain life, the other needs will provide little motivation.

2. Safety and security. These are the needs to be free of the fear of physical danger and the deprivation of the basic physiological needs.

3. Social or affiliation. After the first two needs are met, an individual develops a need to belong, to love and be loved, and to participate in activities that create a feeling of togetherness.

4. Esteem. After the social needs have been fulfilled, people need to be more than just a member of a group. Individuals want to be held in esteem, both by themselves and by others. The satisfaction of these needs produces feelings of power, self-confidence, and prestige.

5. Self-actualization. At the highest level, the individual achieves self-actualization, which means maximizing one's potential, to become everything that one is capable of becoming.[20]

Figure 5.1 is a graphic presentation of Maslow's hierarchy of needs.

Fig. 5.1. Maslow's pyramid of human needs.

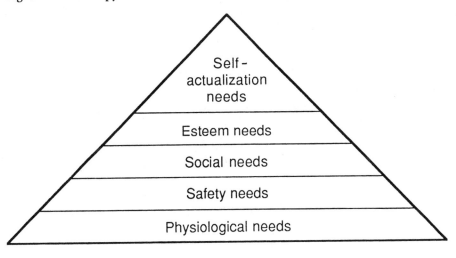

&Thus [the human] is a perpetually wanting animal. Ordinarily the satisfaction of these wants is not altogether mutually exclusive, but only tends to be. The average member of our society is most often partially satisfied and partially unsatisfied in all of his [or her] wants. The hierarchy principle is usually empirically observed in terms of increasing percentages of non-satisfaction as we go up the hierarchy.[21]

—Abraham H. Maslow,
"A Theory of Human Motivation"

The implications of the hierarchy of needs can be useful in understanding what motivates workers. If a person's basic physiological needs are not met—if he or she does not have sufficient food, water, clothing, and shelter—none of the higher level needs will be of sufficient strength to be a motivator. In most cases, physiological needs can be satisfied as long as an individual has enough money. Thus, money, not in itself but because of what it will purchase, is a powerful motivator. In an affluent society like ours, the physiological needs of most individuals are filled and, thus, do not serve as effective motivators.[22]

After a worker's physiological needs are met, filling the security or safety needs becomes paramount. Some security needs are clear: for example, the need to avoid physical harm, accidents, or attacks. Most organizations provide physically safe places to work. But the need for security extends beyond the present into the future. Organizations are able to allay some concerns about the future by providing benefits, such as life and accident insurance and pensions. Job security is very important to most workers; the desire for job security is often a strong motivator, especially when jobs are scarce and unemployment is high.

After the physiological and safety needs have been fulfilled, the worker's social needs become predominant. Humans are social animals; they want to interact with others and be affiliated with a group. The informal organization described by Mayo arises to fulfill workers' needs to socialize and belong to a group.

The esteem needs include both self-esteem and the esteem of others. Workers desire not only to have their work valued by their superiors and their peers but by themselves; they need to derive self-satisfaction from their work. Some employees stay on a job that does not pay well because of the self-satisfaction they get from it. The desire for prestige and power is also a part of esteem needs, as is the competitive desire to outdo other workers. These esteem needs are rarely completely filled. The desire for recognition is never-ending for most workers, and esteem needs can be a potent and reliable source of motivation.

&ℇ Our society during good times almost has a built-in guarantee of physiological and safety needs for large segments of the population. Since many physiological and safety needs are provided for during those times, it is understandable why people would become more concerned with social, recognition, and self-actualization motives. Managers must become aware of this fact and strive to create organizations that can provide the kind of environment to motivate and satisfy people at all need levels.[23]

—Paul Hersey and Ken Blanchard,
Management of Organizational Behavior

The final level of need described by Maslow is self-actualization, or the need to maximize one's potential. This need is rarely completely satisfied, although some individuals, such as Mahatma Gandhi, are credited with having reached full self-actualization.

Maslow's hierarchy has been criticized for being simplistic and artificial. Because every individual is different, many individuals do not pursue needs in the order postulated by Maslow, especially at the higher levels. In addition, it appears that, in most people the needs overlap and combine to some extent.

Although Maslow's theory does have flaws, it has been popular with managers because it provides a conceptual means of understanding the motivation of employees. By identifying an employee's current position in the hierarchy, the manager has an indication of what motivator would be most effective to use in guiding, counseling, and advising the employee to achieve better performance. The hierarchy tells managers that unfilled needs are more motivating than fulfilled needs, and it points out that all needs can never be satisfied, because an individual who satisfies one need immediately begins to try to satisfy another. Managers must realize that need satisfaction is a continuous problem for organizations. Employees will never have all their needs fulfilled, regardless of how hard an organization tries.

Herzberg's Two-Factor Theory of Motivation

In the late 1950s, Frederick Herzberg and his research associates built upon and modified Maslow's hierarchy of needs. Herzberg formulated a theory of motivation that focused specifically upon the motivation of employees in a work environment.[24] Figure 5.2 compares the two theories.

Fig. 5.2. Comparison of Maslow's and Herzberg's motivation theories.

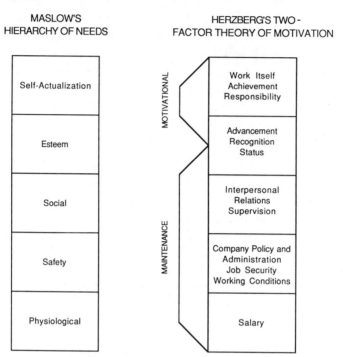

To gather information about what leads to high morale in employees, Herzberg and his associates interviewed approximately 200 engineers and accountants in middle-management positions in the Pittsburgh area. The individuals interviewed were asked to tell what kinds of things about their jobs made them feel happy and satisfied and what kinds of things made them feel dissatisfied.

After the data were analyzed, the researchers discovered that one group of factors contributed to employees feeling good about their jobs. Herzberg called these factors motivators. The motivators, which are closely related to the actual content of the job itself, include achievement; recognition by supervisors, peers, customers, or subordinates of the work accomplished; the work itself—the aspects of the job that give the worker personal satisfaction; responsibility—being able to work without supervision and being responsible for one's own efforts; and advancement. These factors lead to job satisfaction and are effective in motivating individuals to superior performance.

    If I kick my dog (from the front or the back), he will move. And when I want him to move again, what must I do? I must kick him again. Similarly, I can charge a person's battery, and then recharge it, and recharge it again. But it is only when one has a generator of one's own that we can talk about motivation. One then needs no outside stimulation. One *wants* to do it.[25]

—Frederick Herzberg,
"One More Time"

Another group of factors, which Herzberg labeled hygiene or maintenance factors, pertain not to the content of the job itself but primarily to the conditions under which a job is performed. These hygiene or maintenance factors include salary, job security, status, working conditions, quality of supervision, company policy and administration, and interpersonal relationships. These factors did not lead to satisfaction on the job, nor did they serve as motivators. If these factors were inadequate, however, they led to dissatisfaction.

The two sets of factors are relatively independent of each other, and each set affects behavior in different ways. When people are satisfied with their jobs, the satisfaction is connected to the work itself. When they are dissatisfied with their jobs, they are usually unhappy with the environment in which they work. The factors that motivate are intrinsic to the job itself; the factors that cause dissatisfaction are extrinsic.

Later research both supported and rejected Herzberg's model. It appears that his model may be most appropriate for managerial and professional workers. Nevertheless, the two-factor motivational theory has relevance to managers. It implies that the hygiene or maintenance factors must be satisfactory because they provide a base on which to build. If employees are unhappy about their salary, status, or working conditions, they will be discontented in their jobs. But, merely providing these maintenance factors is not enough. If managers want employees to be motivated, they must provide what Herzberg called the motivators, that is, managers must ensure that jobs are interesting and challenging to employees. They must emphasize achievement, recognition, the work itself, and growth, all of which are factors that workers find intrinsically motivating.

Herzberg argued that job enrichment is one of the most effective methods of motivating employees.[26] However, he cautioned against horizontal job loading—merely adding more meaningless tasks to be performed by the worker. In a library, allowing a shelver to shelve both books *and* periodicals is not likely to improve motivation. True job enrichment involves vertical job loading, which consists of making jobs more responsible and challenging. An enriched job uses more of the employee's talents and provides more freedom in decision making. Herzberg's research shows that job enrichment leads to better-motivated and more productive employees.

> ₰ If libraries want to recruit people who value stimulating and challenging jobs they need to emphasize the rewards of working in the library. Fortunately, many self-motivated, committed workers place a high value on psychological reward and are not primarily motivated by money. This is not an excuse to underpay library staff; it simply means that even a library that can't pay top dollar should be able to attract workers who seek responsibility and growth.[27]

> —Kathlin L. Ray, "Toppling Hire-archies"

As a result of interest in job enrichment and its motivational force for workers, many organizations have established "quality of working life" (QWL) programs. QWL is a broad approach to job enrichment that attempts to satisfy the personal needs of employees through their work experience. The QWL focus on individual needs contrasts sharply with traditional personnel programs, with their emphasis on the productive capability of the worker. Proponents of QWL claim that work can be redesigned to meet workers' psychological needs, such as feelings of competency and self-esteem, while at the same time improving productivity. The six major characteristics usually included in QWL programs are autonomy, challenge, expression of creativity, opportunity for learning, participation in decision making, and use of a variety of valued skills and abilities.[28]

QWL has spread quickly among businesses, with business giants like General Motors, Proctor & Gamble, and AT&T adopting such programs. Although QWL is not yet prevalent in libraries and information centers, some are instituting such programs in an attempt to improve working conditions and make jobs more satisfying, both for professional librarians and the support staff.

Vroom's Expectancy Theory

Victor Vroom formulated a model of expectancy that is useful in understanding the motivation of individuals in organizational settings.[29] This theory is more complex than those of Maslow and Herzberg because it does not assume that there is one best way to motivate all workers. Instead, it emphasizes how motivation takes place given an individual's needs and objectives. The theory focuses on individual decision making, on the process that an individual goes through in deciding whether or not to exert the effort to attempt to achieve a particular goal.

Vroom's theory states that people will be motivated to perform to reach a goal if they believe in the worth of the goal and if they perceive that what they do will contribute to the achievement of that goal. The expectancy model is composed of four elements. *Force* is the motivational drive to achieve a goal. *Valence* is the extent to which an individual desires a certain outcome or goal. *Expectancy* is the perceived probability that a particular outcome will lead to a desired result, a result which is called the first-level outcome. *Instrumentality* is the degree to which an individual believes that a first-level outcome is related to a second-level outcome, which is defined as some human need, such as companionship, esteem, or accomplishment. Vroom's model can be stated in the following formula:

Force = Valence x Expectancy x Instrumentality (Motivation)

To illustrate the theory, consider a worker who wants to be promoted. This individual thinks that the best way to achieve the promotion would be to increase job performance. The motivation (force) to improve job performance would be a product of how high is the desire for promotion multiplied by the worker's perception of how likely it is that working harder can improve job performance (expectancy) multiplied by the worker's perception of how likely it is that improved job performance will lead to a promotion. In this example, improved job performance is the first-level outcome and promotion is the second-level outcome.

Vroom's formula is a multiplicative one—as soon as the value of any element drops to zero, so does the motivational force. In the example, if the worker felt that despite improved job performance there was no chance for promotion, the motivation to improve job performance would be zero. Likewise, if the worker felt that, despite any effort, there was no way to improve job performance, again the motivation would be nonexistent.

Vroom's theory is important because it highlights how people's goals influence their efforts; the behavior of an individual is a function of (1) his or her belief in the efficacy of that behavior in achieving a goal and (2) his or her desire to achieve a goal. Because the theory recognizes the importance of various individual needs and motivations, it demonstrates to managers that motivation is highly individualized. A manager must try to learn the special concerns of each employee and what each individual values. The manager must also make clear to employees the connections between performance and reward. Vroom's theory, because it emphasizes the individual, is more difficult to apply than those of Maslow and Herzberg, which are general theories of motivation. But, Vroom's theory avoids some of the simplistic features of Maslow's and Herzberg's work and also seems to more adequately account for the diversity in motivational needs seen in employees.

Behavior Modification

B. F. Skinner, one of the leading proponents of the behavioristic school of psychology, provides managers with still another perspective on motivation. Behavior modification, unlike the other motivational theories discussed, is based on observed behavior, not on individual attitudes, desires, and emotions. Skinner's emphasis is on operant behavior, behavior that has been shaped and modified—that is, controlled—by its consequences. Individuals act as they do because of reinforcements received in the past for similar behavior. Reinforcement is defined as a consequence that follows a response and makes a similar response more likely in the future. Reinforcements can be tangible, for instance, money or food, or intangible, for instance, praise or attention. According to Skinner, there are four methods for modifying behavior: positive reinforcement, negative reinforcement, no reinforcement, and punishment.[30]

> Many things in the environment, such as food and water, sexual contact, and escape from harm, are crucial for the survival of the individual and the species, and any behavior which produces them therefore has survival value. Through the process of operant conditioning, behavior having this kind of consequence becomes more likely to occur. The behavior is said to be strengthened by its consequences, and for that reason the consequences themselves are called "reinforcers."[31]
>
> —B. F. Skinner, *About Behaviorism*

Positive reinforcement, according to Skinner, is the most effective long-range strategy for motivating individual behavior. Positive reinforcement is a reward given after a behavior that the motivator wishes to see continued. Positive reinforcement tends to strengthen the act that it follows and makes that behavior more likely to occur again. Managers can offer a wide range of positive reinforcements, including pay increases, promotions, praise, and approval. When a behavior or act is followed by the termination or withdrawal of something unpleasant, it is called negative reinforcement. For instance, if a supervisor criticizes a worker for coming to work late, the worker's desire to eliminate this criticism may cause the worker to come to work on time. No reinforcement leads to the extinction of a behavior. Because the behavior is not reinforced in one way or another, it decreases in frequency and then stops. If the manager neither praises or criticizes the worker who talks loudly to attract the manager's attention, the unwanted behavior is not being reinforced, and it should stop. Punishment is an unpleasant event that follows unwanted behavior; punishment is intended to decrease the frequency of that behavior. Punishments that managers can inflict include demotion and firing.

Skinner's work has been criticized by those who say it treats humans as passive objects and denies the existence of individual free will. In terms of practicality, it is more difficult to apply behavior modification principles in the workplace than in the controlled setting of a laboratory. Scientists working with rats are able to deprive the animals of food so that they are hungry, then provide food immediately after the desired behavior occurs and be certain that no uncontrolled variable influenced the rats' behavior. Although the work environment provides managers many opportunities to practice behavior modification, managers who try to modify the behavior of employees must do it in an environment where uncontrolled variables are always intruding. Nevertheless, some organizations have used Skinner's principles of behavior modification to motivate employees. One of the most frequently cited success stories of the use of behavior modification in business occurred at Emery Air Freight, where, over a three-year period, the company saved $2 million by identifying performance-related behaviors and strengthening them with behavior modification.[32]

Behavior modification, although difficult to institute, provides managers with several principles that can be applied in any type of organization: Be sure that employees who are performing as desired receive positive reinforcement, and remember that positive reinforcement is more effective in modifying behavior than either negative reinforcement or punishment. Although, traditionally, negative reinforcement and punishment have been popular means of control among managers, they have serious drawbacks and side effects. Among the drawbacks are temporary suspension of behavior rather than permanent change, dysfunctional emotional behavior, behavioral inflexibility, permanent damage to desirable behavior, and conditioned fear of the punishing agent.[33] For example, employees who are punished for talking on the job learn not to talk when supervisors are around but probably still talk in their absence. Also, they are likely to feel resentful about being punished and will find unproductive ways of acting out such feelings by thwarting the supervisors' goals.

Behavior modification works best when a job has specific variables that can be identified and reinforced. Some of the clerical jobs performed by library support staff fall into this category. For instance, error rate is subject to behavior modification techniques. When jobs are more complex, it is more difficult to use behavior modification. Much of the work done by librarians is largely intellectual, and it would be difficult to identify, measure, and reinforce many of the behaviors that constitute such work.

How Should Managers Motivate?

> ℞ The subject of employee motivation is extremely complex. Furthermore, despite all the research that has been conducted and the thousands of articles that have been written, the various theories fail to complement one another. Rather, they seem to confound one another. This makes it very difficult to synthesize findings from the literature and from practice so as to have something of solid, pragmatic value.[34]
>
> —Charles Martell,
> "Achieving High Performance in Library Work"

Motivation is a complex factor, and the manager faces a wide array of approaches for promoting commitment to jobs within an organization. As Harold Koontz, Cyril O'Donnell, and Heinz Weihrich state, "given the complexity of motivating people with varying personalities and in different situations, risks of failure exist when any single motivator or group of motivators is applied without taking into account these variables."[35]

Katzell and Thompson have endeavored to summarize the vast body of research on motivation into a series of seven imperatives: "(a) Ensure that workers' motives and values are appropriate for the jobs on which they are placed; (b) make jobs attractive to and consistent with workers' motives and values; (c) define work goals that are clear, challenging, attractive and attainable; (d) provide workers with the personal and material resources that facilitate their effectiveness; (e) create supportive social environments; (f) reinforce performance; and (g) harmonize all of these elements into a consistent sociotechnical system."[36]

To carry out all of the seven imperatives is a daunting task, but one that managers need to attempt. There is no one simple formula that can tell managers how to motivate employees. A manager must adopt a managerial style that motivates workers to perform tasks efficiently, but, unfortunately, no one prescribed style assures success. Rather, managers must develop individual approaches based on their personality, managerial philosophy, and knowledge of their workers. The effective manager takes advantage of the worker's reasons for working and offers inducements related to those reasons. Thus, a system of inducements, rather than a single inducement for all workers, emerges. Some inducements may have to be negative, but the majority should be positive. A system of inducements is not designed for across-the-board application, but is designed to provide workers with those inducements that best motivate them.

A sound motivational system is based on principles derived from motivation research, on the policies of the organization, and on the manager's philosophy of human needs. Essential to any motivational system is the organization's ability to satisfy employee needs. This is difficult to accomplish, because the needs of humans vary greatly and are subject to change. Maslow's hierarchy of needs gives the manager a guide to the range of needs, from basic life requirements to the social, ego, and creative needs. Herzberg's studies provide information about the need for recognition, achievement, advancement, and responsibility. Vroom's research shows the importance of considering each individual's aspirations and in coupling performance to reward. Skinner's work demonstrates the importance of positive reinforcement to ensure continued desirable behavior.

The policies of the organization should be structured so that the capacity to do good work is not stifled. Good productivity reflects the quality of employee motivation. Frequently, an organization's goals and objectives motivate an employee who wants to be part of and contribute to their achievement. A high degree of success in achieving the goals and objectives creates a positive image of the organization; the worker is proud to be part of the organization and is motivated to promote its success through efficient work.

Any system of motivation depends on managers. The manner in which they apply their knowledge of employee needs and desires, the organizational environment that releases the capacity for work, the quality of training received by capable employees, and the pride the employee has in the organization establish the basic climate of the motivational system. It is the manager's responsibility to exercise sound judgment to make the system work.

Leadership

&Of all the hazy and confounding areas in social psychology, leadership theory undoubtedly contends for top nomination. And, ironically probably more has been written and less known about leadership than about any other topic in the behavioral sciences. Always it seems, the concept of leadership eludes us or turns up in another form to taunt us again with its slipperiness and complexity.[37]

—Warren Bennis,
"Leadership Theory and Administrative Behavior"

Leadership is an elusive quality. One of our most insightful scholars of leadership, James McGregor Burns, has stated that "Leadership is one of the most observed and least understood phenomena on earth."[38] Our failure to understand leadership is not the result of any lack of literature on the topic. Writers in a number of fields have churned out hundreds of books and thousand of articles. A recent review listed over 7,000 books, articles, or presentations on leadership.[39] In another recent review of the literature on the subject, Rost found 331 different definitions of leadership in works written since the turn of the century.[40]

Regardless of how leadership is defined, there are certain elements that are usually present in the definition. The words *influence, vision, mission,* and *goals* are usually found in the definitions. It is commonly accepted that an effective leader has the ability to influence others in a desired direction and thus is able to determine the extent to which both individual employees and the organization as a whole reach their goals. Leadership transforms organizational potential into reality.

Because leaders often function in an organizational or institutional setting, the terms *manager* and *leader* are closely related, but they are not the same. Bennis and Nanus have delineated the difference between leaders and managers as follows:

> "To manage means: to bring about, to accomplish, to have charge of or responsibility for to conduct," "Leading is: influencing, guiding in direction, course, action, opinion." The distinction is crucial. Managers are people who do things right and leaders are people who do the right thing. The differences may be summarized as activities of vision and judgment—effectiveness, versus activities of mastering routines—efficiency.[41]

Although some authors still fail to differentiate between the terms *manager* and *leader*, more commonly a distinction is made. Leaders are needed to "light the way to the future and to inspire people to achieve excellence."[42] Managers are needed to ensure that the organization operates well on a day-to-day basis. Individuals can be good managers without being leaders, and all organizations need them. Effective managers are highly valued by those who work for them because good managers facilitate employees getting their jobs done. Of course, some managers may also be leaders, but it is a mistake to denigrate what managers do by assuming that they are failures if they are not also leaders.[43] Leadership may not be as important to an organization that is enjoying a favorable, nonturbulent environment. But, when an organization needs innovation more than standardization, it needs a leader rather than a manager as CEO. An organization may be managed well but led poorly.[44]

&Leadership has to take place every day. It cannot be the responsibility of the few, a rare event, or a once-in-a-lifetime opportunity.[45]

—Ronald A. Heifetz and Donald L. Laurie,
"The Work of Leadership"

If managers and leaders are not synonymous, are there qualities that every leader possesses? It must always be remembered that there is no one model of a successful leader, and leaders differ in different cultures and historical periods. But despite this variability, according to most experts, each leader must fulfill two major roles. First, a leader must exercise power wisely and efficiently, and second, each leader must, through actions, appearance, and articulated values, present a model that others will want to emulate.[46] The following discussion looks at these two roles a little more closely.

The first role, that of exercising power wisely and efficiently, obviously has close connections to what a good manager does. A leader must be temperate and fair, must set objectives and see that they are carried out, and must make good decisions. The characteristics usually associated with a good manager are also found in a good leader.

The second role, that of presenting a model that others will want to emulate, is the aspect of leadership that is often called *vision*. A leader must provide a vision, a difficult undertaking; a lack of vision is one of the major problems of leaders today. As Henry Steele Commanger wrote a few years ago:

> One of the most obvious explanations of the failure of leadership in our time is that so few of our leaders—and our potential leaders—seem to have any road map. It is hard to lead when you yourself are in a labyrinth.[47]

Although a leader must present a vision to keep an organization from drifting aimlessly, presenting a vision is not enough. A leader must have his or her vision accepted by the followers; the followers must buy into the vision and adopt that vision as their own. They must be energized so that the vision can become reality.[48] With an effective leader at the helm, the goals of the leader and the followers are meshed and congruent.

Getting individuals to buy into a vision is perhaps the hardest task confronted by a leader. As the Chinese philosopher Lao-tzu said long ago, leaders are best when people barely know they exist. When their work is done, their aims fulfilled, the people will say, We did this ourselves. The leader's vision has been so thoroughly ingrained in the followers that they think it was their idea from the beginning.

When leaders fail, it is often because they have not been able to create a vision that is shared. Sometimes people are hired in an organization, and they bring with them a predetermined vision that they want to see fulfilled. They begin to move too quickly, before their vision is accepted by the individuals who are going to have to carry it out. These leaders inevitably fail, because they did not sell the vision to those who had to accomplish it.

In discussing leadership, sometimes the importance of followers is forgotten. A leader is not a leader without followers. Garry Wills has stated that leaders, followers, and goals make up three equally necessary supports for leadership. He defines a leader as "one who mobilizes others towards a goal shared by leaders and followers," and he goes on to state that all three elements are an indispensable part of leadership.[49]

> ☒ Leadership is persuasion, not domination; persons who can require others to do their bidding because of their power are not leaders. Leadership only occurs when others willing adopt, for a period of time, the goals of the group as their own.[50]
>
> —Robert Hogan et al.,
> "What We Know About Leadership"

One of the things we do know about leadership is that the successful organization is almost always set apart from less successful ones by the fact that it is headed by a dynamic and effective leader. This leader has the ability to influence others in a desired direction and, thus, is able to determine the extent to which both individual employees and the organization reach their goals. Leadership transforms organizational potential into reality. Too often, leadership has seemed in short supply. For these reasons, both managers and organization theorists have long been interested in how leadership can be encouraged and developed.

Trait Approach to the Study of Leadership

Early studies on the subject of leadership were concerned with identifying the traits or personal characteristics associated with leadership. The studies were based on the premise that leadership was primarily exercised by great men and that leaders were born, not made. Because all individuals did not have leadership traits, only those who possessed them could be leaders. The assumption was that once the traits were identified, leadership selection could be reduced to finding people with the appropriate physical, intellectual, and personality traits. Leadership training would then consist of developing those traits in potential leaders.

&To argue over whether leaders are born or made is an indulgent diversion from the urgent matter of how best to develop the leadership ability that so many have and that we so desperately need. A Nobel Prize awaits the person who resolves the question of whether leaders are born or made. But until some unanticipated break-through occurs or compelling new data emerge, the argument leads nowhere. The need for leadership in every area of public life has become so acute that we don't have the luxury of dwelling on the unresolvable.[51]

—Warren Bennis, "The Leader as Storyteller"

Many trait studies were conducted, and traits that were said to be associated with leadership, such as energy, aggressiveness, persistence, initiative, appearance, and height, were identified.[52] However, summaries of this research demonstrate its shortcomings: Each study tended to identify a different set of traits. In one summary of more than 100 studies only 5 percent of the traits were found in four or more studies.[53] Eugene Jennings concluded, "Fifty years of study have failed to produce one personality trait or set of qualities that can be used to discriminate between leaders and non-leaders."[54] Although some traits have been found to be weakly associated with leadership, these studies show that there is no such thing as a single leader type. Instead, there is much variation in the skills, abilities, and personalities of successful leaders.

Ohio State and University of Michigan Studies

After the trait studies fell out of favor, interest grew in the actual behavior of leaders. Researchers turned from looking for a single configuration of leadership characteristics to investigating leadership style. This research examined the behavior of leaders: what they do, what they emphasize, and how they relate to subordinates. Paving the way were studies conducted at Ohio State University in the late 1940s and early 1950s. These studies identified two relatively independent dimensions on which leaders differ. One of these dimensions, consideration, refers to the extent to which a leader establishes mutual trust, friendship, respect, and warmth in his or her relationship with subordinates. Initiating structure refers to the leader's behavior in organizing, defining goals, emphasizing deadlines, and setting direction. Consideration and initiating structure are independent of each other; they are not separate ends of a continuum. A high score on one does not necessitate a low score on the other. A leader could be high in both consideration and initiating structure.[55]

Other early studies in this area were conducted by a group of researchers at the University of Michigan's Institute for Social Research. One of the companies this group studied was the Newark office of the Prudential Insurance Company of America.[56] The study, which involved several large clerical departments, tried to identify managers' supervisory styles and their effects on employee productivity. It was recognized that most managers had a fairly clear and constant concept of their jobs. Because of this, the researchers could have the managers describe their jobs, identify objectives and obstacles to achieving those objectives, and discuss their personal methods of reaching those objectives. Based on analysis of the interview data, the researchers identified three types of managers: predominantly production-centered managers, predominantly employee-centered managers, and those with mixed patterns. Because no person is always the same, the word *predominantly* is important. A production-centered manager was one who felt full responsibility for getting the work done; departmental employees were to do only what the manager told them to do. An employee-centered manager recognized that the subordinates did the work and, therefore, should have a major voice in determining how it was done. Employee-centered managers thought that coordinating and maintaining a harmonious environment was the supervisor's main responsibility.

> To be an effective leader, you don't have to be a hero with all of the answers, and you don't have to be a cop overseeing clones. Instead, imagine that your job is to create an environment where your people take on the responsibility to work productively in self-managed, self-starting teams that identify and solve complex problems on their own. If you concentrate on doing this, you'll find your people will need you only for periodic guidance and inspiration, which frees you to spend your time confronting big-picture, common-fate sorts of strategic and organizational issues.[57]
>
> —Oren Harari,
> "Stop Empowering Your People"

The research results were surprising. Contrary to traditional management thinking, which emphasized that permissive management led to employee laxity and carelessness, the departments that had employee-centered managers produced more than those with production-centered managers. The Michigan researchers had to make an assumption that was radical at the time and is still surrounded by controversy: Many workers like their jobs, want to be productive, and would be productive, if given a share of control over their jobs.

Much research since the Prudential study supports this assumption, and the theory applies to many activities other than clerical activities. While it does not solve all supervisory problems, "the theory that workers feel responsible for productivity and that employee-centered supervision is the best way to stimulate this feeling, has plenty of . . . evidence to support it."[58]

Likert Theory of Management

Rensis Likert, in *New Patterns of Management*, summarizes much of the research done at the University of Michigan Institute for Social Research.[59] Likert strongly rejected the theory that concern for good human relations distracts from the primary function of management. He also rejected the theory that concern for good human relations reduces the efficient and profitable operation of an organization. Likert recognized that management's primary responsibility is to assure the best use of the organization's resources, including its human resources. His research shows that strong centralized control of employees is not the best way to achieve operational efficiency or sustained productivity. Indeed, a production-centered managerial style may be detrimental to the organization's interest. Likert describes four prevailing management styles. These styles on a continuum ranging from System 1, exploitative-authoritative, to System 4, participative.

- System 1 management is exploitative-authoritative. In this system, management has no trust or confidence in subordinates. Managers are autocratic, and almost all decisions are made at the top of the organization. Subordinates are motivated by fear and punishment and are subservient to management. Almost all communication in the organization comes from the top of the hierarchy.

- System 2 management is benevolent-authoritative. Management is condescending to employees, who are expected to be loyal, compliant, and subservient. In return, management treats the employees in a paternalistic manner. This system permits more upward communication than System 1, but control is still tightly maintained by top management.

- System 3 is consultative. In this system, management has substantial but not total trust in subordinates. Top management still makes most of the major decisions, but often solicits ideas from subordinates. Control is still primarily retained by top management, but aspects of the control process are delegated downward. Communication flows both up and down in the hierarchy.

- System 4 is participative. Managers have complete trust in subordinates, and much of the decision making is accomplished by group participation. Decision making is found on all levels of the organization. Communication flows up, down, and horizontally among peers. Because of their participation in decision making, employees are strongly motivated to achieve the organization's goals and objectives.[60]

In short, System 1 is a highly structured and authoritarian system of management. The assumptions made about employees under this system closely approximate McGregor's Theory X. System 4 is a participative system based on trust and teamwork. Here, the assumptions made about employees are similar to McGregor's Theory Y. Systems 2 and 3 fall between the two extremes.

Likert concludes that the most effective organizations use the System 4 style of management. Although System 1 may yield favorable results in terms of productivity in the short run, over a period of time, production in System 1 organizations will taper off. In addition, the negative effects of System 1 upon people more than offset any short-term gains in productivity.

Organizations can be found at all points on the continuum. Those that have adopted Total Quality Management or self-directed work teams are moving toward System 4. Undoubtedly, there are more organizations using System 4 now than in the past, but the true System 4 organization is still rare. Most libraries and information centers are at the System 2 or System 3 level.

The Leadership Grid®

In 1964, Robert R. Blake and Jane S. Mouton published *The Managerial Grid*.[61] Since then, they have used the concept of a managerial or leadership grid from their books in management and organization development programs. The theory of the Leadership Grid involves two primary concerns of the organization: concern for production and concern for people. Organizations employ people to produce some item or service that is the reason the organization exists. *Production*, as used here, "covers whatever it is that organizations engage people to accomplish."[62] Managers who are most concerned about productivity focus almost exclusively on the tasks that have to be accomplished; managers who are concerned about people are more interested in the human relations part of the organization.

These two concerns and the range of interactions between them are illustrated in figure 5.3, page 294. Concern for production is represented on the horizontal axis, and concern for people is represented on the vertical axis. Each rating is expressed in terms of a nine-point scale of concern, with 1 in each case indicating minimum concern and 9, maximum concern. A manager with a rating of 9 on the horizontal axis has maximum concern for production; a manager with a rating of 9 on the vertical axis has a maximum concern for people.

Based on the grid, Blake and Mouton describe five leadership styles. A rating of 1,1 would be considered impoverished leadership. Minimum effort is exerted to get the required work done, and minimum concern is paid to employees. A manager with this rating is essentially doing nothing at all for either people or production; he or she has abdicated managerial responsibility. A rating of 1,9 is considered country club leadership. Thoughtful attention to people's need for satisfying relationships leads to a comfortable, friendly atmosphere and work tempo. There is no concern for production. A rating of 9,1 is considered task leadership. Here, operational efficiency results from arranging work conditions in such a way that human elements interfere to a minimum degree. Managers with this rating are autocratic taskmasters. A rating of 5,5 is considered middle-of-the-road leadership. Adequate organization performance is achieved by balancing production with maintaining a satisfactory level of morale. Managers with this rating are adequate in dealing with both people and production but are not outstanding in either capacity. Finally, a rating of 9,9 is team leadership. Work is accomplished by committed people; interdependence, resulting from a common stake in the organization's purpose, leads to relationships of trust and respect. Managers with a 9,9 rating are outstanding in their concern for both people and production.[63]

> Some think that learning how to lead effectively is next to impossible; some believe leadership is a natural ability and either you have it or you don't; and still others think that you can learn it but you can't teach an old dog new tricks. Accepting any of these propositions precludes the possibility of becoming more effective. Though they are value-based beliefs, they rest on false assumptions about human learning. It is as practical to learn to lead effectively as it is to learn arithmetic or to referee a game or to perfect any other applied skill.[64]
>
> —Robert R. Blake and Jane S. Mouton,
> *The Managerial Grid III*

The Leadership Grid is most helpful for identifying and classifying managerial styles. It is useful as a theoretical framework for understanding human behavior in organizations. Using this grid, managers at any level should be able to identify their level of concern for people and for productivity.

Fig. 5.3. The Leadership Grid® figure. From *Leadership Dilemmas—Grid Solutions*, by Robert R. Blake and Anne Adams McCanse. (Formerly the Managerial Grid figure by Robert R. Blake and Jane S. Mouton.) Houston: Gulf Publishing Company, page 29. Copyright © 1991 by Scientific Methods, Inc. Reproduced by permission of the owners.

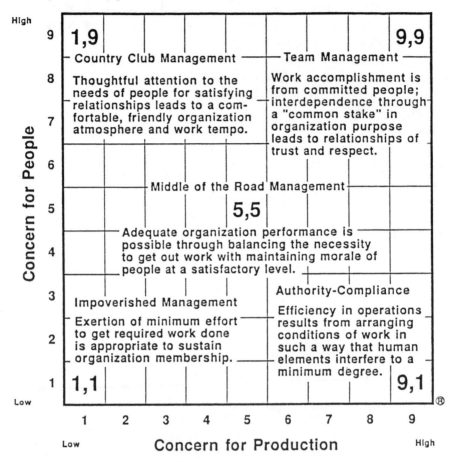

Transformational Leadership

James McGregor Burns described two types of leadership styles: the transactional and the transformational.[65] Transactional leaders see job performance as a series of transactions with subordinates. The transactions consist of exchanging rewards for services rendered or punishments for inadequate performance. On the other hand, transformational leaders are skilled at getting subordinates to transform their own self-interest into the interest of the larger group. Transformational leaders bring out the best in their subordinates. Another researcher described transformation leaders as working to make their interactions with subordinates positive for everyone involved. More specifically, [they] encourage participation, share power and information, enhance other people's self-worth, and get others excited about their work. All these things reflect their belief that allowing employees to contribute and feel powerful and important is a win-win situation—good for the employees and the organization.[66]

This win-win situation is also advocated by Bennis, who states that an organization with an effective leader, one whose vision is accepted by the followers, will, according to Bennis, empower the employees and make them:

1. Feel significant. Each will feel they make a significant contribution to the success of the organization.

2. Engage in learning and feel competent. Good leaders make it clear that there is no failure, only mistakes that provide feedback on what to do next.

3. Feel part of a team. According to Bennis, where there is good leadership there is a feeling of family and unity.

4. Feel work is exciting, challenging, fascinating, and fun. A vital ingredient in organizational leadership is pulling rather than pushing people to a goal. According to Bennis, a "pull" style of influence attracts and energizes people to adopt an exciting vision of the future. This style motivates through identification rather than through rewards and punishments.[67]

> ℺ People jockey for position in a transactional group, whereas they share common goals in a transformation group. Rules and regulation dominate the transactional organization; adaptability is a characteristic or the transformation organization.[68]
>
> —Bernard M. Bass,
> "Does the Transactional-Transformational
> Leadership Paradigm Transcend
> Organizational and National Boundaries?"

Fiedler's Leadership Contingency Model

Likert's systems, the Leadership Grid, and Burns's transformational/transactional categories imply that there is a preferred leadership style. More recent theorists have turned away from the idea that there is one best leadership style. They feel that earlier theorists had little success in identifying consistent relationships between patterns of leadership behavior and group performance. The contingency, or situational, theorists argue that there is no single ideal type of leader but, instead, a number of leadership styles may be appropriate, depending on the situation. Employee-centered leadership may be best under some circumstances, and production-centered leadership may be best under others. According to advocates of contingency theories, the task of a leader is to use the style that is most appropriate in a given situation.

Fred Fiedler developed one of the best-known contingency theories. According to Fiedler's model, three situational variables determine how favorable any particular situation is for the leader. These three situational variables are:

1. leader-member relations: the degree to which group members like and trust a leader and are willing to follow him or her;

2. task structure: the clarity and structure of the elements of the tasks to be accomplished; and

3. power position: the power and authority that are associated with the leader's position.

Fiedler produced and studied eight combinations of these three variables. The combinations range from the situation that is most favorable to a leader (good relations with followers, highly structured task, and strong power position) to the situation that is most unfavorable to a leader (poor relations with followers, unstructured tasks, and weak power position). Figure 5.4 lists each of the combinations. Fiedler then attempted to assess what would be the most effective leadership style in any of these situations. His theory predicts that the task-oriented leader is most effective in situations at either end of the continuum. When situations are most favorable or least favorable for a leader, the production-oriented style is most effective. The human relations, or employee-oriented, style works best when conditions are either moderately favorable or moderately unfavorable for the leader.

Fiedler concludes, "In very favorable conditions, where the leader has power, informal backing, and a relatively well-structured task, the group is ready to be directed on how to go about its task. Under a very unfavorable condition, however, the group will fall apart unless the leader's active intervention and control can keep the members on the job. In moderately favorable conditions . . . a relationship-oriented, nondirective, permissive attitude may reduce member anxiety or intra-group conflict, and this enables the group to operate more effectively."[69]

Fiedler's research is helpful to managers because it improves their understanding of the relationship of the various situational variables involved in leadership. Leadership effectiveness depends on the variables found in each situation. In Fiedler's view, leadership depends as much on the organizational variables as it does on the leader's own attributes.

Fig. 5.4. Fiedler's contingency model relating style of leadership to situational variables. From Fred Fiedler, "Correlations Between Leadership Styles and Group Performance," reprinted from *Psychology Today Magazine* (March 1969), 42. Copyright © 1969 American Psychological Association.

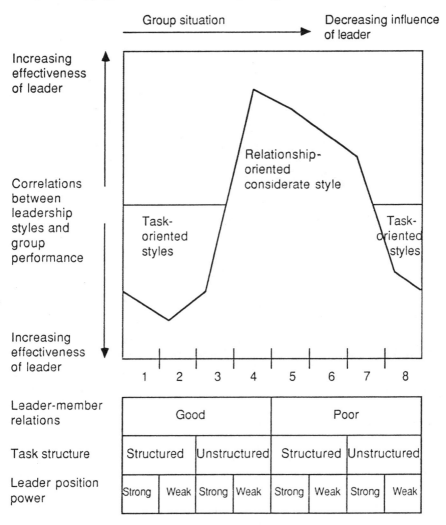

The Leadership Challenge

It is commonly believed that society is suffering from a leadership crisis. People are dissatisfied with their leaders and confused about the type of leadership they want. In sectors as diverse as the federal government, higher education, and librarianship, the questions are the same. Where are the leaders needed, and why do so many promising individuals fail to live up to expectations once they assume leadership positions?

As Bennis writes: "It is both an irony and a paradox that precisely at the time when trust in and credibility of leaders are lowest, when people are both angry and cynical, the nation most needs leaders, people who can transcend the vacuum."[70]

> ℞ The old models of leadership no longer work. In an age of individual rights, paternal protectors appear patronizing. In an age of limits, seductive promises fall flat. In an age of self-expression, even rational authority may seem oppressive. Searching for direction, but critical of anyone who controls us, we look for new leaders, as much in fear that we will find them as that we will not.[71]
>
> —Michael Maccoby, *The Leader*

Although many of the complaints about the lack of leadership are focused on national leaders, the same type of gap between expectations and reality is found in many other arenas, including libraries and information centers. The challenges facing these types of organizations over the next decades will be immense, but the leaders for the transition, those individuals who will guide the organizations through the uncharted waters of tomorrow, have not yet emerged. There are many competent managers, but few seem to possess a clear vision of the future and the knowledge of how to get from here to there. And, in librarianship as in other areas, the same troubling pattern exists. Too often, after individuals have been chosen for leadership positions, they quickly lose their luster.

It is more difficult for individuals to assume leadership roles now for a number of reasons. In the past, people were far less likely to question the authority of a leader. Today's leader must try to inspire confidence and trust in followers who are likely to be at least partially distrustful of authority of all types. Michael Maccoby, for one, is concerned that the traditional forms of leadership do not work any longer. He writes:

> I believe that there is a crisis of authority, a questioning of its legitimacy, because neither the functions of leadership nor the image of the leader fit the needs of large organizations, especially

business and government in an age of rights, limits, new values, and a changing concept of productivity, which have not yet crystallized into a new ideal character.[72]

Many individuals hold the paradoxical view of leadership described by Bennis. They constantly lament the lack of leadership in our society. From all sides come calls for better, more effective leadership. Strong leadership is touted as the cure for much of what ails our society's institutions and organizations. At the same time, many people deeply mistrust leaders. As Herbert White has stated, "We believe in leaders and in leadership, but . . . on a personal basis few of us want to be led."[73]

Because the present is basically an antiauthoritarian age, it is not surprising that it is easier to diagnose the need for more effective leadership than to effect the cure. It is no wonder that so many contemporary leaders fail, when the often turbulent, complex, and crisis-ridden environment in which leadership must now be provided is combined with the modern dislike of accepting authority of any type. Whatever type of leader is chosen, whether authoritarian or laissez-faire, whether outsider or insider, whether older or younger, something always is less than perfect, something always fails to live up to the expectations. It is then a common pattern to discard that leader and begin to look for another.

> In the knowledge era, we will finally have to surrender the myth of leaders as isolated heroes commanding their organizations from on high. Top-down directives, even when they are implemented, reinforce an environment of fear, distrust, and internal competitiveness that reduces collaboration and cooperation. They foster compliance instead of commitment. . . . For those reasons, leadership in the future will be distributed among diverse individuals and teams who share responsibility for creating the organization's future.[74]
>
> —Peter M. Senge,
> "Communities of Leaders and Learners"

Bestsellers in the management literature postulate that there has been a new style of leadership emerging since the early 1980s that can provide guidance in new types of organizations. John Naisbitt and Patricia Aburdene, in *Reinventing the Corporation*, and Thomas Peters and Robert Waterman, in *In Search of Excellence*, sing the praises of people-centered executives who provide leadership in revolutionized workplaces—workplaces that are humane and feature management-worker unity. Naisbitt and Aburdene state that the first ingredient of reinventing the corporation is a powerful vision and "the source of the vision is a leader, a person who possesses a unique combination of skills: the mental power to create a vision and the practical ability to bring it about."[75] Peters and Waterman examine the corporations that they consider the most successful and argue that the best type of leader is a people-oriented leader who can be tender and tough at the same time.[76] Thomas Peters and Nancy Austin, in *A Passion for Excellence*, argue that a manager should no longer be "a cop, referee, devil's advocate, dispassionate analyst, professional, decision-maker, naysayer, pronouncer [but a leader who acts] as cheerleader, enthusiast, nurturer of champions, hero finder, wanderer, dramatist, coach, facilitator, builder."[77] James Belasco, in *Teaching the Elephant to Dance*, argues that leaders at any level of an organization must develop a new strategic approach by empowering employees.[78]

Other experts have pointed out the need for a change in the style of leadership as our nation shifts from an industrial to a postindustrial age. The changes that are occurring in the workplace are, according to Riane Eisler, reflections of a larger societal transformation. Eisler describes two types of social organization models: the dominator and the partnership models. Dominator societies are marked by rigid male dominance, a generally hierarchic and authoritarian social structure, and a high degree of institutionalized violence. The partnership model is marked by more equal partnership between women and men, less institutionalized violence, and a more democratic or egalitarian social structure. She says that the modern workplace was patterned to conform to the requirements of the dominator model—hence its hierarchic and authoritarian characteristics and its top-down chain of command. The author asserts that the workplace is evolving into a more humane, people-centered place that will demand a different type of leadership model.[79]

Rost, too, distinguishes the values of the industrial paradigm from a set of newer, emerging values. He lists the traditional values as (1) the structural-functionalist view of organizations, (2) a view of management as the preeminent profession, (3) a personalistic focus on the leader, (4) a dominant objective of goal achievement, (5) a self-interested and individualistic outlook, (6) a male model of life, (7) a utilitarian and materialistic ethical perspective, and (8) a rational, technocratic, linear, quantitative, and scientific language and methodology. In contrast, the values of this new postindustrial paradigm are collaboration; common good; global concern; diversity and pluralism in structures and participation; client orientation; freedom of expression in all organizations; qualitative language and methodologies; substantive justice; and consensus-oriented policy-making process. Rost asserts that although it is clear that our old notion of the leader is not functioning well, the new model of the postindustrial leader has yet to be formed.[80]

Critics of these works question whether a revolution in leadership style is—or should be—underway. In their view, effective leadership is too complex an issue to be treated in a simplistic, one-approach manner. Leadership cannot be implemented by buzzwords and managerial fads. They feel it is senseless to strictly adhere to either a hard-line or soft-line approach to leadership.[81]

Managers who are concerned with leadership should keep in mind that, despite all the theories about leadership style, research still has not shown whether one style of leadership is superior to the others. The analysis of leadership style is a complex topic, and much of the research that has been done to date has been short-term and scattered. The situational theories, such as Fiedler's contingency model, seem to be the most helpful in dealing with real-life situations. However, such theories, with their emphasis on matching a leadership style to a particular environment or work situation, complicate the manager's task. Many managers would like to be told how to lead; the situational theories say there is no one right way. Instead, effective leaders adapt their style of leadership behavior to the needs of the followers and the situation. Because these factors are not constant, discerning the appropriate style is always a challenge.

Managers should also remember that in most modern organizations, leaders may be found at all levels. To envision the only leader as the person at the top of the organizational hierarchy is to accept an artificially constrained view of leadership.

Communication

&The most important *do* is to build the organization around information and communication instead of around hierarchy. Everybody in the non-profit organization—all the way up and down—should be expected to take information seriously. Everyone needs to ask two questions: What information do I need to do my job—from whom, when, how? And: What information do I owe others so that they can do their job, in what form, and when?[82]

—Peter F. Drucker,
Managing the Non-Profit Organization

Communication plays an important role in directing. Most managers spend a large part of their time communicating with other people; some estimates of the percentage of time a manager spends in communication range as high as 95 percent. In his study of managerial behavior, Henry Mintzberg found that most managerial time was spent in verbal communication, on the telephone, and in meetings.[83]

Since 1938, when Chester Barnard identified the main task of an executive as that of communication, it has been commonly accepted that communication is a critical skill for any manager. Barnard viewed communication as the means by which people are linked together in an organization in order to achieve a central purpose.[84] Communication is the process that makes it possible to unify organizational activity.

Communication in organizations is more varied today than ever before because so many new and varied communication options are available. Electronic mail, voice mail, teleconferencing, and fax provide additional channels of communication for organizations to use both internally and externally. These new methods have helped to eliminate the barriers of time and distance that used to slow down the communication process. In knowledge organizations, such as libraries and information centers, communication is the lifeblood of the organization. Employees in these organizations are constantly involved in the absorption and dissemination of information and ideas. In fact, sometimes people working in information agencies feel that there is so much communication available through so many channels that it leads to confusion. Many employees suffer from information overload. They receive more information than they can assimilate. It is important for all managers to learn how to communicate clearly and concisely.

Many communication models have been developed within the past few decades. Although these models vary, they typically include:

- A *source*. This is the sender of the message. The source has some thought, need, or information to communicate.

- A *message*. The source has to encode the message in some form that can be understood by both sender and receiver.

- The *channel*. The channel is the link between the source and the receiver. The message is transmitted over the channel. A channel can take many forms. For instance, the five senses, especially seeing and hearing, are communication channels. A telephone is another example of a channel that can be used to link the source and the receiver.

- The *receiver*. The receiver is the recipient of the message. The receiver has to decode the message for it to be understood.

- *Noise*. Noise is anything that hinders communication. Noise may occur in the source, the message, the channel, or the receiver. For instance, if the receiver cannot understand the message, noise has occurred. This could be because the message contained ambiguous phrases, because there was static on the channel, or because the message was in a language not understood by the receiver. Even the simplest communication is filled with opportunities for noise to occur.

- *Feedback*. After the receiver receives and decodes the message, the receiver can become a source and provide feedback by encoding and sending a message through some channel back to the original source. Feedback is a response to the original message. It is essential because it allows the original source to know if the message was properly encoded, transmitted, decoded, and understood. Feedback may cause changes in the way a source sends a message, because it allows the source to gain information about how well the message was communicated to the receiver. Feedback is the difference between one-way and two-way communication. One-way communication is never as effective as two-way communication, because the sender has no way of knowing if the message was received and understood.

To illustrate this model, suppose a library director wanted to let a department head know about an important meeting. The library director would be the source of the communication. When the library director provided information about the meeting in the form of a written memo, the written memo would be the message. The channel employed for the communication would be the interorganizational mail system. The receiver is the department head who receives the message and reads it. If the interorganizational mail carrier lost the memo, or if the memo had been mutilated in transit, that would have been noise. The feedback would be the response the department head sends the library director about the meeting. The elements in this simple communication model are illustrated in figure 5.5.

Communication exists in many forms and in many settings. Often, we think of communication primarily in terms of personal communication. However, every organization must have some way to bind its disparate parts if it is to achieve its goals and purposes. Communication provides cohesiveness and direction. As Alex Bavels and Dermot Barrett state, "It is entirely possible to view an organization as an elaborate system for gathering, evaluating, recombining, and disseminating information. . . . Communication is not a secondary or derived aspect of an organization—a 'helper' of the other and presumably more basic functions. Rather, it is the essence of organized activity and the basic process out of which all other functions derive."[85]

> Merely providing an opportunity for communication does not necessarily ensure it will take place.[86]
>
> —John Wright,
> "Look at Management—2"

Fig. 5.5. A model of the communication process.

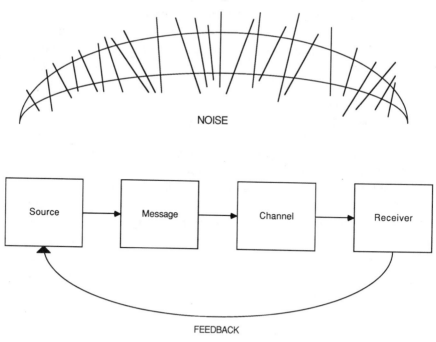

Gerald Goldhaber defines organizational communication as "the process of creating and exchanging messages within a network of interdependent relationships to cope with environmental uncertainty."[87] In Goldhaber's view, all organizational communication shares certain characteristics. It occurs within a complex, open system that is influenced by and influences its environment; it involves messages and their flow, purpose, direction, and media; and it involves people and their attitudes, feelings, relationships, and skills.

Managers should never assume that their style of communication will be understood by all workers. This is especially important to remember as the workforce becomes more diversified. Studies have shown that various ethnic groups and that men and women have different styles of communication, which can lead to misunderstandings. Deborah Tannen has studied gender differences in communication and finds that men's and women's styles vary greatly. She attributes this to different values assimilated by young girls and boys. Males are taught to prize status, independence, and individual power, but females are taught to value connection, interdependence, and the power of community. These differing values lead men and women to communicate in different ways. The resulting differences in the communication styles of men and women can cause misunderstanding in the workplace.[88]

In a similar way, different ethnic groups may have different styles of communication. For example, in some cultures, it is considered rude to maintain eye contact with someone while they are speaking. Some cultures encourage interruption. Every communication practice is based on certain cultural rules, and as our workplaces become more diversified, managers need to understand the cultural differences that may affect communication flows. Just because two people share a common language does not mean that they can easily communicate.

> The difficulty of getting heard can be experienced by any individuals who are not as tenacious as others about standing their ground, do not speak as forcefully at meetings, or do not begin with a high level of credibility, as a result of rank, regional or ethnic style differences, or just personality, regardless of whether they are female or male. Whoever is more committed to compromise and achieving consensus, and less comfortable with contention, is more likely to give way.[89]
>
> —Deborah Tannen, *Talking from 9 to 5*

Types of Communication

Communication can be classified in three general categories: written, oral, and nonverbal. Each of these types of communication plays a specific role in organizational communication and each has certain associated advantages and disadvantages.

Written communication is often required by formal channels of command. Managers write memos, letters, reports, directives, and policies. Written communication provides a lasting record and ensures uniformity in matters like policy. But written communication has many problems. Some of these communications may be poorly written and may not fully explain the action desired or completely define the scope of the problem. Employees may be left with ambiguous instructions. Words used in written communications are frequently unclear and ill defined, and written communication allows no opportunity for immediate feedback and clarification. Hence, it may take a long time to know if the message has been received and understood.

Many companies that have adopted TQM practices have tried to improve their written communication, especially their communication with customers. Organizations are urged to scrutinize their written communication to "see if they have value-added components and eliminated fillers and gobbledygook that dilute our purpose and waste the recipient's time."[90] More and more organizations are attempting to improve their written communications and give them a customer focus.

Electronic mail is a new type of written communication that is becoming prevalent in organizations. Companies of every sort are connecting people to networks that permit the sending of e-mail both internally and externally. E-mail in organizations presents a special set of opportunities and problems. Although considered "written" communication, it is generally not viewed as being as formal as a paper copy of a letter or a memorandum. It is very convenient for the sender, it speeds the delivery of information, and it can be relatively inexpensive in providing wide distribution of messages for little cost. E-mail presents its own set of communication difficulties, however. It has grown as a method of communication faster than rules governing its use. Users are often surprised to learn that e-mail is not necessarily private or deleted when the user thinks it is. Just as organizations usually have policies relating to the use of telephones, fax machines, and mail, there should be policies in place relating to appropriate use of e-mail.[91]

> ❧ Furthermore, because people can communicate so freely on the Internet, how you deal with your employees will be just as visible as how you deal with customers. Theoretically, you could enforce a policy of reading every electronic message your employees send out over their corporate PCs; it is perfectly legitimate to do so, provided you disclose the practice to your employees. But how could you hope to attract and retain talented people with such policies? And besides, whom would you trust to read all those messages?[92]
>
> —Esther Dyson, "Mirror, Mirror on the Wall"

Oral communication, conducted through individuals or groups, also has problems. Not all oral messages are clearly stated. There remains the problem of the ambiguous or misunderstood word. But in oral communication there is opportunity for feedback, through which clarification can be accomplished. Oral communication often is the best way to resolve conflict situations. On the other hand, oral communication can be time-consuming, especially if a large number of people are individually told about a topic.

Nonverbal communication is any type of communication that is not spoken or written. Body language is a specific type of nonverbal communication. Nonverbal communication can provide many clues to an observer; as the old saying goes, actions speak louder than words. Nonverbal communication can contradict, supplement, substitute for, or complement verbal communication. A manager must be especially careful that nonverbal signals do not contradict verbal ones. For instance, a supervisor who claims to have an open-door policy and encourages employees to discuss problems, but who continues to work and fails to establish eye contact with the employee who has set up an appointment to do so, sends that employee a powerful non-verbal message. Nonverbal behavior, although sometimes overlooked, is vital to the process of communication.

Communication Flows

Within an organization, communication flows in three directions: down, up, and horizontally. *Downward communication*, or communication that flows from superiors to subordinates, is the most common type of communication within the organization. Daniel Katz and Robert Kahn identify five types of downward communication: specific job directives, or job instruction; information designed to produce understanding of the task and the relationship to other organizational tasks, or job rationale; information about organizational procedures and practices; feedback to the subordinate about performance; and information of an ideological character to inculcate a sense of mission, or indoctrination of goals.[93]

> ꙮ Central to the evolution of flatter, customer-focused, dynamic organizations is the availability of information within the organization. The traditional movement of information within an organization was based on models derived from a strong hierarchical orientation and from cost constraints that made it very expensive to move information throughout the organization. The availability of information technology and information "highways" now makes it feasible to move information relatively cheaply in multiple directions throughout an organization.[94]
>
> —Jay R. Galbraith et al.,
> *Organizing for the Future*

Although employees expect to receive communication from managers, problems are often associated with downward communication in an organization. The first is that organizations rely too heavily on written or mechanical methods, such as manuals, booklets, memoranda, and newsletters, to diffuse downward communication, even when personal contact and face-to-face communication might be more effective. Second, many organizations suffer from message overload. Because of the ease of sending messages via e-mail and by photocopied documents, some employees are overburdened with memos, bulletins, letters, announcements, and policy statements. Many employees who are inundated with too many messages respond by not reading any of the communications at all. Communication can also be hampered by poor timing. Managers should consider the timing of any communication to be sure it is advantageous for both management and employees. Finally, there is always the problem of filtering of information. Because downward communication usually goes through several layers in an organization, messages may be changed, shortened, or lengthened, and some employees may not receive a message at all. For these reasons, downward communication in many organizations is relatively inefficient.[95]

Upward communication consists of messages that flow from subordinates to superiors. Most of these messages ask questions, provide feedback, or make suggestions. An organization that is inhospitable to upward communication inhibits such communication, despite the fact that upward communication is essential to an organization's effectiveness. Even in organizations that pride themselves on their open-door policy, it is not uncommon to find employees who are afraid to take information to their superiors, especially when that information concerns problems or bad news. Employees are more likely to send upward messages that enhance their own status or credibility and are much less likely to send up messages that make them look bad.

> In the vast majority of companies, if workers know that what they say will be passed along to management with their names attached, they won't speak (or write) their minds. It is the rare organization that is so attuned to its people and so trusted by them that employees feel comfortable telling the whole truth. Besides, compensation for many managers today is partly based on group performance; there can be pressures on team members to be positive. Herein lies the challenge for companies: How can organizations get the kind of unfiltered and vital information critical to their operations—even, perhaps to their survival?[96]
>
> —Barbara Ettorre, "The Unvarnished Truth"

Keith Davis points out that it takes a certain amount of courage for workers, especially lower level workers, to approach their supervisors. He calls the barrier to communication between subordinate and superior the scalar curtain.

> A manager often does not realize how great the upward communication barrier can be especially for blue-collar workers. His status and prestige at the plant are different from the workers'. He probably talks differently and dresses differently. He can freely call a worker to his desk or walk to his work station, but the worker is not equally free to call in his manager. The worker usually lacks ability to express himself as clearly as the manager, who is better

trained and has more practice in communication skills. The worker is further impeded because he is talking to a man with whose work and responsibilities he is not familiar. The result is that very little upward communication occurs unless management positively encourages it.[97]

Managers who want to benefit from the flow of upward communication should be sensitive to the barriers that can be placed in the way of such communications. If managers want to remove some of the barriers, they must be sympathetic listeners and make a practice of encouraging informal contacts with workers. Some methods commonly used to achieve upward communication include grievance procedures, suggestion systems, focus groups, hotlines, group meetings, and opinion surveys. In addition, managers should remember that the same sort of filtering and misinterpreting that is found in downward communication is also prevalent in upward communication.

Horizontal communication, or the lateral exchange of information within an organization, typically fulfills the following purposes: task coordination, problem solving, information sharing, and conflict resolution. Several factors tend to limit horizontal communication within organizations. Information is not always shared in competitive organizations because the employee who possesses the information wants to retain a competitive advantage over others. Specialization also impedes horizontal communication. Most organizations are subdivided into specialized subunits, and members of these subunits may want to further their own subunit's goals rather than communicate with other managers on the same level in order to advance company goals. In addition, excessive specialization may make it difficult for members of one subunit to speak the language of another; even if they were willing to exchange information, they might find it difficult to bridge the horizontal communications gap. Finally, horizontal communication often does not take place because managers have not encouraged frequent horizontal communication nor have they rewarded those who engage in such practices.[98]

Because horizontal communication does not follow the chain of command, precautions must be taken to prevent potential problems. This type of communication should rest on the understanding that these relationships will be encouraged when they are appropriate, subordinates will refrain from making commitments beyond their authority, and subordinates will keep superiors informed of important interdepartmental activities. Although horizontal communication may create some difficulties, it is essential in most organizations to respond to the needs of a complex and dynamic environment. As organizations grow more dependent on a team approach to work, the importance of lateral communication increases.

Much horizontal flow of information takes place in meetings. Some employees spend a great deal of their time in meetings; often these meetings are frustrating and ineffective because they are poorly planned and conceived. Managers at all levels should try to develop the skills and understanding necessary to make meetings successful.[99]

There is some indication that new channels of communication, such as electronic mail, may change the flow of communication within the organization. Because it is more informal than a letter and less threatening than face-to-face conversation, some workers send electronic mail not only to workers on their own level but upward in the organization, to immediate supervisors and to managers even higher up in the organizational structure. As Robert Zmud has stated, "Traditionally, an organization member's zone of influence has been limited by a number of constraints, most of which reflect task designs, authority relationships, and physical, geographic, and temporal boundaries. New information technologies are relaxing many, if not most, of these constraints.[100] Just as the telephone revolutionized organizational communication, the new communication media will bring vast changes to how employees within organizations communicate with each other and the outside world. More research needs to be done to see how these new communication media affect organizational communication.

Informal Organizational Communication

Most of what has been discussed so far concerns the formal communication channels within an organization. These are the message channels that follow the official path directed by the organizational hierarchy. But every organization also has an informal communication system, commonly known as the "grapevine." Although informal channels are neither as predictable nor as neatly designed as those of the formal communication structure, they are remarkably efficient at moving information. Studies of the grapevine have shown that this means of communication is fairly accurate, with over 75 percent of the messages being transmitted correctly.[101] In addition, the grapevine is much faster at moving information than are formal channels.

> The grapevine grows most vigorously in organizations where secrecy, poor communication by management, and autocratic leadership behaviors are found.[102]
>
> —Paul Hersey, Kenneth Blanchard,
> and Dewey E. Johnson,
> *Management of Organizational Behavior*

Although the grapevine can sometimes cause trouble, this informal communication channel is endemic in all organizations. Managers are not able to destroy the grapevine because it serves an essential human need for information. Given the existence of the grapevine, a manager's task is to make it contribute to the accomplishment of the organization's objectives. Managers can do this by using the grapevine, either personally or through trusted staff members. A manager who wants to relay information can feed the grapevine accurate information, which will be transmitted quickly throughout the organization. In addition, the manager should be aware of the messages that circulate on the grapevine. If managers are able to find out what employees are talking about via the grapevine, they may be able to intercept and correct misleading rumors that could damage morale. Thus, intelligent managers admit the existence of the grapevine and use it to their advantage.

The grapevine can be curtailed somewhat by clear, concise, and complete communication through formal communication channels. Rumors often arise because workers are anxious about some situation about which they received little or no information. If management provides information about issues that workers consider important and that they are worried about, fewer rumors would circulate on the grapevine.

In summary, both formal and informal communication is critical to organizations. Managers should pay close attention to the communication within an organization in an attempt to make it as open and free from distortion as possible.

Conflict

One of the common results of poor communication is conflict. Some managers spend a great deal of time trying to avoid conflicts within in the units they manage. Some even feel that the mere existence of conflict is a poor reflection on their ability to manage. This is not necessarily so. Conflict is not bad in itself, and may result in either positive or negative outcomes. Although uncontrolled conflict can be detrimental to an organization and its employees, properly managed conflict can often be helpful.

Managers who feel that they spend a great deal of time trying to resolve conflict situations are probably correct. One study showed that managers reported spending 20 percent of their time dealing with conflict and its impact.[103]

&Top managers are often stymied by the difficulties of managing conflict. They know that conflict over issues is natural and even necessary. Reasonable people, making decision under conditions of uncertainty, are likely to have honest disagreements over the best path for their company's future. Management teams whose members challenge one another's thinking develop a more complete understanding of the choices, create a richer range of options, and ultimately make the kinds of effective decisions necessary in today's competitive environments.[104]

—Kathleen M. Eisenhardt et al.,
"How Management Teams Can Have a Good Fight"

Conflict is usually characterized as being either interpersonal or intergroup. Interpersonal conflict, conflict between two people, is often the result of incompatible personalities or different values or points of view. Intergroup conflict, conflict between groups of employees, can be caused by a number of factors within organizations, but it often arises as a result of competition over scarce resources. Both interpersonal and intergroup conflicts are frequently heightened by poor communication.

People react to conflict in different ways. Research has identified five styles of handling conflict: avoiding, compromising, competing, accommodating, and collaborating. Avoiders try to prevent conflict, compromisers try to split differences down the middle, competitors enjoy conflict, accommodators almost always give in to opposition, and collaborators try to work to find a satisfactory outcome for all parties.[105] The best result of conflict is usually described as a "win-win" outcome, when both parties to the conflict perceive that they have emerged from the conflict in a better position than before. Managers who are skilled as negotiators are able to deal effectively with conflict by helping participants arrive at solutions in which all parties feel that they have come out ahead.

&Negotiators can be categorized as to the kind of outcomes they seek. Basically there are four [types]:

Win-Lose Negotiators want to take home all the bacon. In order to do so they must dominate the other person. . . . Their minds are totally fixed on victory.

Lose-Win Negotiators gain what they want by losing. They are passive negotiators, and the last thing they want is to dominate.

Lose-Lose Negotiators can't stand the thought of the other person's winning, but they don't want to win, either. So, after making certain that the other person loses, they sabotage their own victory.

Win-Win Negotiators want both parties to the negotiation to walk away with enough to show for his efforts for them to still be friends or partners.[106]

—Tessa Albert Warschaw,
Winning by Negotiation

Organizational conflict can have both negative and positive effects. The more negative effects are the ones that are usually thought of first. Working in an environment with a great deal of conflict can lead to stress and divert employees' attention from the work that has to be done. The morale of employees often suffers, as does their motivation to perform well. In cases of extreme conflict, workers have been known to disparage or even sabotage the work of others. Conflict between departments can cause groups to close ranks and hamper cooperation.

On the other hand, sometimes conflict plays a useful role. Conflict can bring previously hidden problems to light so that solutions may be sought. Conflict is considered essential to innovation. If everyone thinks the same thing, changes will not occur. Innovation "takes place when different ideas, perceptions, and ways of processing and judging information collide."[107] At Microsoft, one of the most innovative U.S. corporations, chairman Bill Gates advocates a management style called "armed truce," because employees are encouraged to challenge everyone, including the chairman. Conflict is said to be at the heart of every decision in a company "constantly at war with not only outsiders but also with itself."[108] Properly managed conflict can be energizing.

It is important for managers to realize that a certain amount of conflict is inevitable within any organization. The worst thing managers at any level can do is to try to suppress conflict. It is much better to bring it out, open the lines of communication, and try to come to a mutually beneficial solution. Even if a win-win solution cannot be achieved, employees will be better satisfied if conflicts are recognized and solutions are sought for in a supportive manner.

New Methods of Directing
in Modern Organizations

Modern managers have taken the three major elements of directing—motivating, leading, and communicating—and have used them as the foundations to help reshape modern organizations. Throughout the previous chapters in this book, there has been an emphasis on how the role of employees has grown larger in the past few decades. In the United States and in most other developed countries, there has been a shift from authoritarian-type organizations, in which one person makes almost all of the decisions, to one in which the management is shared by a greater number of employees. The next sections in this chapter will examine these more participative organizations.

Participative Management

> ॐ Participative management is both a philosophy and a
> method for managing human resources in an environment
> in which employees are respected and their contributions
> valued and utilized. From a philosophical standpoint, par-
> ticipative management centers on the belief that people at all
> levels of an organization can develop a genuine interest in its
> success and can do more than merely perform their assigned
> duties.[109]
>
> —Daryl R. Conner,
> *Managing at the Speed of Change*

One decision every manager must make is how much employee participation to allow in management. Over the few past decades, there has been a change in the outlook of both managers and employees in libraries and information centers, as in other types of organizations. As has been discussed, historically most libraries and information centers were organized in a traditional hierarchical structure, and the normal management style was authoritarian, with the director making all decisions. Today's directors find authoritarian leadership styles to be less effective as librarians demand an increased input into decision making.

Many writers have explored the issue of participative management in libraries and information centers. Participative management involves employees in sharing information, making decisions, solving problems, planning projects, and evaluating results. [110] Those who favor greater participation base their opinions on their beliefs that the rank-and-file library staff benefit by having a chance to participate in the governance of the library, that better decisions are made with staff involvement, and that librarians' increased job satisfaction leads to better library service. Writers who take the other view usually support their stand by concentrating on the inexperience of most librarians in management, the amount of time that is consumed by participation, and the inappropriateness of the participative model as a means of operating a complex service organization.

> &A strong trend towards more participative management in libraries would be expected since involvement and participation are said to be crucial to meeting the needs of organizations for changed structures and styles in response to the IT revolution, to developing flexibility, to encouraging staff to generate ideas and to tapping their creative talents, to satisfying the increased expectation of individuals for self-realization, and to increasing productivity. There has undoubtedly been such a trend, but it is very difficult to quantify how widespread it is and how far it has gone. As in industry, much of what library directors say about their participative management may be self-deception or lip-service.[111]
>
> —Maurice B. Line and Margaret Kinnell,
> "Human Resource Management in
> Library and Information Services"

Participative management has the virtue of forcing decision making down to the level where the most relevant information can be found and where the effect of the decision will have the greatest impact. Although few libraries could be considered to operate on Likert's System 4 level, most libraries permit some employee input into decision making, and there is almost always some consultation before decisions are made. In particular, the committee system is used as a method of providing employee input. Participative management does not mean that the management relinquishes its responsibility for the final decisions that are made—participative management should not be confused with management by consensus. As Nicholas Burckel has written, "librarians will have to accept that participatory management is no substitute for individual responsibility and leadership. There will likely always be library directors and just as likely they will be paid considerably more than the rest of the non-administrative staff . . . because they are accountable for the operation of the library."[112] Neither does participative management mean that managers involve all their employees in every decision every time nor do all employees have the same amount of involvement in decision making. The involvement is usually based on familiarity with the decision that needs to be made.[113]

Rosabeth Moss Kanter states that participation works best when it is well managed. In her viewpoint "well managed" systems have the following elements:

> A clearly assigned management structure and involvement of the appropriate line people; assignment of meaningful and manageable tasks with clear boundaries and parameters; a time frame, a set of accountability and reporting relationships, and standards that groups must meet; information and training for participation to help them make participation work effectively; a mechanism for involving all of those with a stake in the issue, to avoid the problems of power and to ensure that those who have input or interest a chance to get involved; a mechanism for providing visibility, recognition, and rewards for teams' efforts; and clearly understood processes for the formation of participative groups, their ending and the transfer of the learning from them.[114]

Although management theory advocates the use of participation by employees, it is sometimes difficult to implement with employees who have not had experience with it before. At the same time, it is usually not easy for managers to give up some of their control and let others contribute to decision making and problem solving. Switching to a more participative system of management requires changes on the part of both managers and employees.

> ✎ Not only are many lower-level employees comfortable being told what to do, but many managers are accustomed to treating subordinates like machinery requiring control. Letting people take the initiative in defining and solving problems means that management needs to learn to support rather than control. Workers, for their part, need to learn to take responsibility.[115]
>
> —Ronald A. Heifetz and Donald L. Laurie,
> "The Work of Leadership"

Managers who use participative management are able to use the perspectives and knowledge of others in their decision making, and thus the decisions made should be better. The amount of participation permitted varies from library to library, but the issues facing libraries and information centers are so complex and the need for specialized expertise so great that the trend toward shared decision making will likely continue.

Japanese Management

In the 1980s managers from all over the world began to study Japanese management techniques because of the phenomenal worldwide success enjoyed by Japanese industry in the 1970s and 1980s. The high quality and reasonable prices of Japanese merchandise made it very competitive on the world market. Productivity in Japan rose 8 percent per year during the 1970s, while productivity in the United States increased less than 2 percent per year.[116] The great success of Japanese manufacturing drew the attention of the entire world. Hundreds of books were written about Japanese management, and Japanese techniques such as Just-in-Time and Quality Circles were introduced to increase quality and productivity in sites throughout the world. Then in the 1990s the economic boom in Japan came to an end, and Japan is now in the midst of its longest recession since the end of World War II. This downturn is the result of the increased competition, the high value of the yen, and the high cost of doing business in Japan.[117]

Many of the managerial practices that had been used in Japan were quite different from those found in the industrialized countries of the West. For instance, traditionally, Japanese workers enjoyed long-term job security. This was especially true in large companies. Typically, employees spent their entire working lives in a single organization. Layoffs in Japanese industry were rare or nonexistent. Great emphasis was placed on seniority, the major factor governing promotions and pay increases. Japanese employers tended to treat their employees in a paternalistic manner, showing concern for the employees both off and on the job. There was a heavy emphasis on imbuing employees with values, including the importance of teamwork, loyalty, and a sense of family. Finally, the type of decision making used was considerably different from that found in most American firms. Japanese management made decisions by consensus. Decision making was based on the concept that change and new ideas should come primarily from below. Japanese industry used quality circles to make many decisions. In these circles, teamwork was stressed as a method to find solutions to work problems. This system stressed group over individual performance. In fact, individual performance was actively discouraged.

Now, Japan's managers are trying to reform some of the practices that seem to be causing problems for their industries: They are looking at the idea of using merit instead of seniority as a basis of promotion, ending the policy of lifetime employment, loosening the strict hierarchical structures, and creating freer working conditions for their workers. Japanese organizations are paying more attention to marketing, and many are implementing Management by Objectives programs to motive workers to "take the plunge into personal initiative and specific goals."[118] The success of Japanese management techniques in the past makes most experts think that the present economic slump in Japanese industry will only be temporary.

> Japan's strength has always been the ability to adjust well in a changing environment. In the eighth century, the country learned from China: in the 16th Spain and Portugal. In the 19th from Germany, France, and Great Britain. In the 20th from the United States. Japanese industrial leaders are, therefore, well-aware of the major management challenges facing them, including: An expensive seniority system, rising unemployment, lack of individual initiative, hierarchical, inflexible structures, and lack of creativity.[119]
>
> —Wolfgang Lux, "Japanese Management"

Quality Circles

When Japan's economy was flourishing, many non-Japanese organizations adapted management techniques used in Japan. Because of the vast differences between the Japanese and other cultures, it was impossible to adopt these approaches without some modification. For instance, William Ouchi proposed that American managers should institute some Japanese practices, especially the practice of creating a family-like quality or "industrial clan" within the organization. Ouchi calls his set of ideas Theory Z, implying that his theory builds on and goes beyond McGregor's Theory Y. The Theory Z model includes (1) job security and opportunity for advancement within the organization to produce strong employee commitment to organizational goals and purposes; (2) the use of group dynamics, particularly the quality circle approach to high-quality products; (3) shrewd world market penetration; and (4) the adaptation of management principles and techniques to the national culture.[120]

The Japanese quality circle concept was adopted by many profit-making firms and to a lesser extent in not-for-profit organizations, including libraries and information centers. Quality circles were originally designed to deal with problems of product quality. A quality circle is a group of employees (usually 7 to 15 people) from the same work area who meet regularly and voluntarily to identify, solve, and implement solutions to work-related problems. The QC members are trained in two techniques: problem-solving methods and group processes. The QC leader usually is a supervisor who is trained by someone experienced in the QC process. This leader trains the circle members. The circle works on one problem at a time, and proposed solutions are presented to management for approval. Quality circles not only identify many worthwhile solutions to problems, but, because of the worker participation, they also enhance morale.

> ✑ The basic philosophy underlying quality circles is that quality awareness through participative management can not only identify the problem situations but can also assist management in solving them. As a Theory Y discipline, the quality circle concept recognizes that people know their jobs best and want to contribute to the success of their company, if given the chance to do so.[121]

—Harry Katzan, *Quality Circle Management*

Quality circles have been used successfully in many American businesses, beginning with Lockheed in 1973. The use of QCs spread widely in this country. To date, QCs have been successful in industries where work outputs and profits can be measured. In general, libraries and information centers do not operate at a profit nor can their success be quantitatively defined. However, in all libraries and information centers, "quality is a concern and can be extended to quality of service, quality of information rendered, quality of individual performance, and to many other areas."[122]

Although a few libraries, including the Duluth and the Chicago Public libraries,[123] did institute QCs, they were never so widely adopted in libraries as in private industry. Recent studies verify that QCs can have a positive impact on organizations and employees, but these studies do not support the larger claims of some proponents that QCs routinely improve employee productivity, morale, and growth, as well as overall organizational effectiveness.[124] Instead of quality circles, more libraries have turned to the broader concept of Total Quality Management to increase overall quality of their products and services.

Total Quality Management

> ✑ No matter how a library's management fabric is cut, it becomes abundantly clear that nearly every aspect of a library can still be improved. The installation of TQM in libraries should not imply that the staff has not been engaged in a continuous improvement process. Quite the contrary. TQM provides a systematic, formalized process for focusing on improvements. It is a process that manages by facts, uses tools for analyzing and measuring work, and evaluates progress on a regular basis.[125]

—Donald E. Riggs,
"Managing Quality: TQM in Libraries"

Many organizations have gone beyond the use of quality circles and have instituted Total Quality Management (TQM). Quality circles are one part of TQM, but the use of QCs alone put the burden of quality primarily on workers. The TQM approach requires a company to be restructured with an emphasis on quality from the top to the bottom of the organization. Although TQM is considered by some to be just the latest management fad, its use is well established in a number of organizations throughout the world, and it continues to gain in popularity. American corporations have spent hundreds of millions of dollars in the past two decades on TQM. This management approach is now being considered and adopted by a growing number of not-for-profit organizations, including libraries and information centers. Countless articles and books have been written about TQM, and it is impossible to give more than an overview here. For readers who wish to learn more about the movement and its application in libraries and information centers, two good sources to consult are *Total Quality Management in Libraries: A Sourcebook* by Rosanna M. O'Neil, and *Quality Management for Information and Library Managers* by Peter Brophy and Kate Coulling.[126] Although one of these books is written largely from the U.S. perspective and the other from the British, they both provide a thorough introduction to the topic and demonstrate the universality of the TQM approach.

The total quality management movement began as a result of the work of American management consultants, such as W. Edwards Deming and Joseph Duran, whom the Japanese imported to help them rebuild their economy after World War II. The consultants' ideas about quality were embraced by the Japanese and were credited with the phenomenal growth of the Japanese economy.

The major impetus for the interest in TQM in the United States was the decline in the relative quality of many American products as the United States faced increasing global competition. In the 1980s it became apparent that Japanese products such as automobiles, televisions, and videocassette recorders were outselling those same products from the United States, not because of their lower prices, but because their quality was almost always better. By producing products of higher quality, American firms hoped to become more competitive. As foreign competition grew, American corporations refocused on quality in an attempt to win back market share.

An investment in quality is seen to be cost-effective because it leads to fewer manufacturing defects, better use of time and money, and fewer delays. Neglecting quality can be expensive. In the United States, 21 to 25 percent of production costs is spent in finding and correcting mistakes; after the additional costs of repairing or replacing defective products is factored in, the total cost of poor quality may approach 30 percent. In Japan, it is 3 percent.[127]

American firms did not become interested in TQM until the 1980s; since then, it has been adopted by a number of the largest U.S. corporations, including Xerox, Motorola, and Federal Express. Interest in TQM is international, and worldwide interest in quality of both goods and services has become more important than ever before. In fact, it has been said that the word *quality* has probably been used more in the last 10 years than in the 10 preceding centuries.[128]

Although there is some variation in the approach to TQM from organization to organization, there are common characteristics. A TQM approach requires an organization to study its procedures with an eye to improving quality. Emphasis is on customer satisfaction and service. In TQM, emphasis is paid to both internal customers and to external customers. Whether internal or external, a customer is defined as "anyone who receives a product, information, or service from another individual or department."[129] TQM focuses on the process rather than the finished product, and the process is always being studied for improvements. "Nothing is ever good enough, the job is never over, and the day you decide you can't make it any better, someone else somewhere else will and drive you out of business."[130] Employee teams monitor the processes, and problem areas are studied and corrected. All employees, from management to line workers, are enlisted in a team effort to improve quality.

> ☙ An old American adage says, "If it ain't broke don't fix it." TQM responds, "Wrong!" Customers, markets, technologies change every day; what's good enough now will be suicide tomorrow.[131]
>
> —Ted Marchese,
> "TQM Reaches the Academy"

One of central concepts of TQM, the Plan, Do, Check, Act (PDCA) cycle, was first described by Deming; this cycle is illustrated in figure 5.6. The PDCA cycle shows the continuous nature of TQM. To produce quality, managers have to plan, have to put in place appropriate methods and processes, have to check the products and processes, and when problems are found, have to take action to correct them, which leads them back into the planning process. All four elements of the cycle are critical to ensure quality in processes and products. TQM involves a continuous process to adapt and improve. The process involves realizing that achieving excellence is not a one-time intervention, but the beginning of a journey that will last forever, because excellence is the journey rather than the destination.[132]

Fig. 5.6. The PDCA cycle.

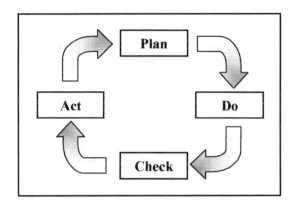

Deming believed that the primary responsibility of quality lay with managers. He urged attention to the processes because he thought that 85 percent of all problems are due to faulty processes and only 15 percent to people.[133] Deming's advice was to stop blaming workers and to look to the system for ways to improve quality.

Deming's 14 points summarizing his beliefs about what organizations need to do to carry out a total quality management program are listed in table 5.1.

Table 5.1—Deming's Fourteen Points

1. Create consistency of purpose toward improvement of product and service, with the objective of becoming competitive and providing jobs.

2. Adopt a new philosophy. We are in a new economic age. Managers need to accept responsibility and take on leadership. We no longer need to live with commonly accepted delays, mistakes, defective materials, and defective workmanship.

3. Cease dependence on mass inspection to achieve quality. Eliminate the need for inspection by building quality in the product in the first place.

4. End the practice of awarding business on the basis of price tag. Move toward a single supplier for any one item, on a long-term relationship of loyalty and trust, to minimize total cost.

5. Constantly improve the system of production and service to improve quality and productivity and thus decrease costs.

6. Begin training and education on the job.

7. Institute leadership. The aim of supervision should be to help people and machines and gadgets to do a better job.

8. Drive out fear so that everyone may work effectively for the organization.

9. Break down barriers between departments. People in research, design, sales, and production must work as a team, to foresee problems of production and use that may be encountered with the product or service.

10. Eliminate slogans, exhortations, and targets when asking for zero defect and new levels of productivity. Such exhortations only create adversarial relationships because most of the cases of low quality and low productivity belong to the system and thus lie beyond the power of the workforce.

11. Eliminate work standards (quotas) on the factory floor and substitute leadership; eliminate management by objective, eliminate management by numbers. Substitute leadership for all of these.

12. Remove barriers that rob the hourly worker of their right to pride of workmanship. The responsibility must be changed from sheer number to quality. Remove barriers that rob people in management and in engineering of pride of workmanship. Eliminate annual or merit rating and management by objective.

13. Institute a vigorous program of education and self-development.

14. Put everybody in the organization to work to accomplish the quality transformation because it is everyone's job.[134]

Organizations practicing TQM use statistical measures and benchmarks to assess how well the process is proceeding. Data is gathered about processes and techniques, and tools such as Pareto charts and fishbone diagrams are used to identify problems and suggest solutions.[135]

Benchmarking is a TQM tool that compares an organization's processes to those of other organizations in an attempt to identify "best practices." Benchmarking is the "systematic sharing of good practices—and good ideas—with the ultimate aim of becoming the department, team or organization against which everyone else wants to benchmark."[136] An organization must first collect quantitative and qualitative data about its own work processes, and then that data can be compared with data collected in other organizations to establish the "best practices," which can then be adopted by all of the organizations. Although in the profit-making sector it is sometimes difficult to get information on a competitor's "best practices," in the public service setting such information is more freely shared.

    Quality is no longer viewed in terms of what managers can afford, it is seen as an area in which they can't afford to make compromises. Quality is not so much a competitive tool as a ticket just to board the train.[137]

—Kathleen Huddleston,
Back on the Quality Track

    Business and engineering rganizations are obvious candidates for TQM. They have well-defined products and clearly delineated processing segments. They are able to identify critical processes and measure results. These types of organizations strive for a decrease in production variations, an increase in reliability, a decrease in lead time, and an increase in profitability. All of these factors lend themselves to the TQM approach.[138]

    Interest in TQM has spread more slowly to the not-for-profit and service sector. The fit between TQM and the needs of these organizations was initially less apparent. The statistical quality controls and reliability engineering that are part of TQM do not fit not-for-profit organizations as well as they do manufacturing concerns.

    Perhaps not-for-profits were also slower to adopt TQM because it is costly. One estimate of the cost of implementing TQM in a university was that "[it] requires a long-term commitment (five years), takes a lot of time (up to 20 percent of the normal workload), and costs lots of money."[139] Unlike for-profit corporations, which can save large amounts of money in production costs by doing things right the first time, not-for-profits, initially at least, often increase their costs by adding TQM. However, more recently, many not-for-profit organizations have concluded that the benefits derived from the continuous quality approach more than makes up for costs.

    TQM was developed for industry. Industry has visible products; the requirements of most products are not usually too hard to define, and the performance of neither the products nor the processes involved in them is hard to measure. All industries that are not monopolies have competitors, and they have to fight to acquire and keep markets. . . . Libraries, on the other hand, have few visible products, and the performance of most of their output is very hard to measure. . . . Their market is largely captive . . . and they have few competitors. What incentive do they have to improve quality except pride?[140]

—Maurice B. Line,
"Relating Quality Management
to Strategic Planning"

Maurice Line explains that libraries do have a reason for applying TQM principles. As he notes, these organizations face an increasing amount of competition as alternative sources of information grow. Libraries will be bypassed if they have imprecise objectives, provide services that are little needed, fail to provide services that are necessary, offer services of poor quality, or continue with inefficient procedures. Perhaps, there may be "little danger of libraries experiencing sudden death, but there is a real danger of marginalization and erosion."[141]

The central focus of TQM is quality, and in service organizations this means quality of service. In fact, serving customers well is of equal status with producing a flawless, useful product. A number of companies have set a course for improving customer satisfaction, among them Nordstrom, Federal Express, Lands' End, Disney World, Southwest Airlines, and Wal-Mart Stores.[142]

A number of academic researchers have looked at the topic of how to improve customer satisfaction. Berry, Parasuraman, and Zeithaml recently summarized their 10 most important findings from a 10-year study of customer quality. None of their results is really unexpected, but they provide a useful checklist of core principles for TQM advocates in service organizations.

- Listening precedes action. Conformance to company specifications is not quality; conformance to customers' specification is.

- Reliability is the core of quality service. If customer service is not reliable, customers lose confidence in the organization's ability to do what it promises. Friendliness from the staff and apologies never compensate for unreliable service.

- Service customers just want the basics. Most customers do not have any extravagant expectations.

- Poor quality is a design, not a people problem. Reliable customer service depends on how well various elements function together as a service system, and design flaws in any part of the system can reduce quality.

- Good recovery can save poor delivery. If a customer is not satisfied with the original service, a satisfactory response to that customer's complaint can produce a satisfied customer. If an organization does not respond effectively to a customer complaint, it compounds the service failure resulting in the most dissatisfied customers of all.

- Surprising customers (positively) pays off. Seek excellence in both outcome and process to develop truly outstanding performance.

- Customers expect fair play. Customers expect to be treated fairly and are mistrustful and resentful when they think this expectation is not being met.

- Teamwork promotes excellence. Service "teammates" are an important dynamic in sustaining a server's motivation to serve. Coworkers who support each other and achieve together can be an antidote to service burnout.

- Employee research is important to improvements. Employees are customers of internal service and the only people who can accurately assess internal service quality. These employees can offer insights into conditions that reduce quality and thus serve as early-warning systems for the organization.

- Leadership is servitude. Leaders should serve the servers, inspiring and enabling them to achieve. These leaders see their role as setting a direction and a standard of excellence and giving people the tools and freedom to perform.[143]

> Some characteristics of quality of service are as easy to quantify and measure as the characteristics of quality of manufactured product. Accuracy of paperwork, speed, dependability of time of delivery, care in handling, care in transit, are important characteristics of service and are easy to measure. . . . The customer's reaction to what he calls good service or poor service is usually immediate, whereas reaction to the quality of a manufactured product may be retarded.[144]
>
> —W. Edwards Deming, *Out of the Crisis*

TQM is definitely enjoying widespread success as organizations enter the twenty-first century. But not everyone is an advocate. Although many companies have reported great success in using TQM, others have tried it and abandoned it. Some, such as Douglas Aircraft, invested a great deal of money in TQM, only to find it unworkable because of business setbacks that required large layoffs. Florida Power and Light, which had won Japan's Deming Prize for quality management, curtailed its program when employees complained about excessive paperwork. The Wallace Company, a Houston oil supply company, implemented TQM but subsequently filed for Chapter 11 bankruptcy protection.[145] Proponents of TQM argue that these setbacks are temporary, and that TQM will eventually produce results. They point out that the Japanese began using quality improvement efforts in the 1950s and did not begin to see significant rewards until the 1970s.[146]

In a recent article, Oren Harari argues that TQM does not work, not because its focus on quality is misguided, but because the TQM operations often become so cumbersome that they overshadow the reason the company is in business.[147] It is true that TQM can result in the formation of more bureaucracy to implement quality, and, especially when it is first being implemented, it can seem to add to the workload of everyone. If quality does not become "the religion, organizing logic, and culture of the firm, but instead gets stalled as internal programs run by technocrats,"[148] it will fail. If TQM is put in as a quick fix (forgetting that quality is a never-ending journey), or if the managers of the organization only pay lip service to the technique, it will not succeed. However, despite some failures, interest in TQM is still strong in corporate America as companies try to find ways to excel in the global economy.

> ஐ Libraries must build into their organizational structures and their approaches to work, the ability to identify, anticipate, and quickly respond to constantly changing customer needs. They must be capable of leaps forward and breakthrough performance. They must reduce cycle times for implementing new services. They must be able to anticipate those needs rather than wait for customer needs to be articulated fully. And they must be ready to abandon formerly successful approaches to work, strategies, processing systems, services and products that do not continually prove their value to customers.[149]
>
> —Carla J. Stoffle et al.,
> "Choosing Our Futures"

Libraries and information centers, like other organizations, need to pay more attention to quality, and TQM is a system that allows them to do so. All libraries and information agencies have certain processes, for example, copy cataloging or overdue billings, which could be greatly improved by TQM methods. In addition, the TQM emphasis on improving quality in service could help libraries and other service organizations maintain the support of their "customer" base in an era of increasing competition. Even if TQM is not adopted by all not-for-profit organizations, its emphases on quality and customer service should be championed by managers and workers in these organizations if they wish to continue to play an effective role in society. Because, as Susan Jurow writes:

Even if TQM fades as a management tool at some point in the future, it will have left behind its own important legacy in two key concepts. The first is the need to focus on the customer in the development of products and the delivery of services. The second is the need to be constantly aware of process both in development and delivery, and vigilant for opportunities for improvement.[150]

It is easy to dismiss TQM as just the latest management fad, but often fads have something valuable to teach us. If TQM provides a way to make libraries and information centers more interested in quality, customers, teamwork, and getting things done right the first time, it is a fad worth adopting.

The Contingency Approach to Management

The varying approaches to management can be seen on the shelves on any large bookstore or library. The number of management titles is vast—and whether the subject being covered is reengineering, TQM, or MBO, its advocates will claim that it is the way to transform modern organizations, while its critics will say it is inherently flawed. Is it any wonder that some managers become cynical? They view every new approach as just a passing fad. Every few years there is a new theory that sweeps the management world, and the skeptical managers assume if they wait awhile, the enthusiasm for that approach will soon fade, and a new fad will take its place.

Many of the varying and often contradictory perspectives on directing have been covered in this chapter. What is clear is that neither behavioral scientists nor experts from any other discipline have been able to provide managers with a specific prescription or universal theory about the most effective way to direct. Unlike early theorists in management who relied on principles to provide the one best way, most modern management theorists are convinced that there are few across-the-board concepts that apply in all instances. The situations with which managers deal are much more complex than originally realized, and different variables require managers to adopt different approaches. Instead of advocating a universal best theory, most contemporary management experts urge managers to be flexible and to adapt to the situation at hand. These experts, if asked how a manager should act, would say, "It all depends."

&No quick introduction of uncoordinated parts will address the whole problem. Quality control circles, "Theory X" reorganizations, team building, two-week organizational development programs, etc., etc.,—each has its uses, but unless there is an overall *fit* of all the managerial parts over time, there will be little sustained leverage and few results.[151]

—Richard Tanner Pascale
and Anthony G. Athos,
The Art of Japanese Management

Managers should not become skeptical about the diversified approaches to management being offered to them. Instead, they should realize that in the case of directing, as in most other instances, "one size does not fit all." There is no quick fix or magic solution. But this does not mean that managers should not become familiar with as many of the approaches or "tools" as possible. All of these new methods are useful, but none of them is guaranteed to be effective in every situation. Instead, managers have to look at the organization and its goals and then adopt a management strategy that will match the overall needs of the organization, its employees, and its customers.

Contingency, or situational, theory, discussed briefly in chapter 1, allows managers to maintain the flexibility necessary to manage modern organizations. Contingency theory recognizes that every organization is unique, existing in a unique environment with unique workers and a unique purpose. This theory is used to analyze individual situations and understand the interrelationships among the variables to help managers determine what specific managerial actions are necessary in any particular situation. What is appropriate in one situation may be inappropriate in another. According to contingency theory, effective management differs depending on the variables associated with various individual situations. The best techniques can be selected only after one is aware of the particular circumstances of each case.

The contingency approach to management has been advocated by many managerial experts. For instance, on pages 295-97, the contingency leadership theory of Fred Fiedler was described. But, despite the current popularity of this approach, Jay Lorsch, one of the earliest proponents of contingency management, reminds us that contingency theory is "a relatively new development [and] it has many of the problems of any young body of knowledge. It is not well integrated. There are still disputes about the relevant variables and the meaning of certain terminology. It is also a relatively complex set of ideas."[152]

Howard Carlisle identified nine variables, five internal and four external, that are significant in almost every management situation and that must
be considered when using the contingency management approach.[153] The
internal variables are the purpose of the organization, the tasks involved in
performing the operations required to attain the purpose of the organization, the technical content or technology of the tasks and operations, the
nature of the people who perform the tasks, and the structure of the operation. Because an organization's existence and effectiveness depend on its
ability to adjust to external conditions or forces, a contingency manager
must take into account the external variables, which include political and
legal forces and institutions, technological forces and institutions, sociocul-
tural forces and institutions, and economic forces and institutions. All of
these variables are interdependent, and the manager cannot focus on any
one of them in isolation. Because of the varying status of the nine contingency variables, each situation a manager faces involves different conditions
and calls for different management concepts.

Another framework that can be used for analysis in contingency management is the 7-S framework, which was developed by McKinsey and Company,
the largest management consulting company in the world. The 7-S framework
is very popular, in part because it served as the basis of research for two best-
selling management books: *The Art of Japanese Management* and *In Search
of Excellence.* The McKinsey 7-S framework includes the following variables:
strategy, structure, systems, staff, style, skills, and shared values (sometimes
called superordinate goals). The seven variables are interconnected, and
the key to effective management involves not only making correct choices
within the area of each variable but also establishing an effective pattern
among them, a fitting together that helps the whole organization function.
The 7-S framework, like the Carlisle variables, helps a manager to focus
upon the interrelated factors that have an impact upon an organization
and to choose the most appropriate way to apply contingency approaches
to management decisions.

In short, contingency management suggests there be a fit between the
task, the people, the organization, and the external environment. In each
organization, managers must be sure that each unit develops structures,
measurement schemes, and reward practices that encourage its members
to focus on the appropriate set of activities and issues.

> One of the most difficult things for most of us to under-
> stand is that organizations are dynamic. Particularly as one
> moves up the organizational ladder, matters become less
> tangible and less predictable. A primary characteristic of
> managing, particularly at higher levels, is the confrontation
> of change, ambiguity, and contradiction. Managers spend

much of their time living in fields of perceived tensions. They are constantly forced to make trade-offs, and often find that there are no right answers. The higher one goes in an organization, the more exaggerated this phenomenon becomes.[154]

—Robert E. Quinn,
Beyond Rational Management

Managers who wish to use the contingency approach must understand the complex and interrelated causes of behavior in an organization and then use their intelligence and creative ability to invent a new solution or to judge which existing solutions might best be used.[155] Library managers using this approach might decide that different sections of the library would benefit from different styles of directing. For example, a part of a technical services department that performs highly standardized, repetitive work might benefit from a more task-oriented style of management. In the same library, a more people-oriented style of management might be appropriate for the reference department.

The contingency theory can be used in functions of management other than directing. For instance, there is no one best way for an institution to be organized. There are also no surefire approaches to planning, controlling, or managing human resources. Many variables, such as size, type of organization, and type of tasks being performed, play a role in the choice to be made. In the broadest sense, contingency theory applies to all of the managerial functions.

Although the contingency theory requires a fundamental shift from the traditional concept that there is one best way of doing things, it provides managers with a comprehensive model that can be used to achieve maximum effectiveness in all managerial functions. With the contingency approach, the performance of managerial functions is closely tied to analysis of the total system—the organization, its subsystems, and its environment. Contingency theory offers a flexible approach that is better suited to the complexity of management than are other approaches. "The basic deficiency with earlier approaches is that they did not recognize the variability in tasks and people which produces this complexity. The strength of the contingency approach . . . is that it begins to provide a way of thinking about this complexity, rather than ignoring it."[156] Although the contingency approach to management certainly does not provide all of the answers, it points to a new direction in which management theory and practice appear to be evolving.

Conclusion

Directing deals with the human element within the organization, specifically with how to motivate, lead, and communicate. It is the most interpersonal aspect of management. The ultimate aim of directing is to allow the organization to achieve its objectives through the activities of the people employed within it. Directing means getting employees to work efficiently and to produce results that are beneficial to the organization. In short, directing is getting things done through other people for the good of the organization. James L. Hayes, former dean of the School of Business Administration at Duquesne University once observed:

> The [person] who is new to management hears [the definition] this way: "Management is getting things done *through other people.*" Now at last I have a kingdom and someone to work for me. . . . Then [the manager] can sweep down to [the] subordinate all the nasty jobs. . . . However, [the manager] later reaches the point of maturity [and] hears the definition with a different emphasis: "Management is *getting things done* through other people." It is when [the manager] gets the sense of responsibility for accomplishment that he [or she] is a manager.[157]

Because directing is complex and multifaceted, managers often find it one of their most challenging and important tasks. The need for managers to excel at directing becomes more pressing as organizations grow larger, as the rate of change in the environment increases, and as demands by employees for a more rewarding work life proliferate.

Notes

1.   Abraham Zaleznik, "Real Work," *Harvard Business Review* 75, no. 6 (November-December 1997): 56.

2.   Ibid.

3.   John J. Morse and Jay W. Lorsch, "Beyond Theory Y," *Harvard Business Review* 48 (May-June 1970): 61-68.

4.   Kathleen Huddleston, *Back on the Quality Track: How Organizations Derailed and Recovered* (New York: American Management Association: 1995), 57.

5.   Keith Davis and John W. Newstrom, *Human Behavior at Work: Organizational Behavior*, 8th ed. (New York: McGraw-Hill, 1989), 4.

6.   Saul W. Gellerman, *The Management of Human Relations* (New York: Holt, Rinehart & Winston, 1966), 27.

7. George C. Homans, "The Western Electric Researches" (1941; reprinted in *Management Classics*, 3d ed., ed. Michael T. Matteson and John M. Ivancevich [Plano, TX: Business Publications, 1986], 41).

8. Edward Deevy, *Creating the Resilient Organization: A Rapid Response Management Program* (Englewood Cliffs, NJ: Prentice-Hall, 1995), 48.

9. Douglas M. McGregor, *The Human Side of Enterprise* (New York: McGraw-Hill, 1960), chaps. 3, 4.

10. McGregor, *The Human Side of Enterprise*, 322.

11. For a description of an application of McGregor's principles in an information center in another culture, see C. S. Champawat, "Douglas McGregor Visits Jaipur Information Centre," *Herald of Library Science* 20, nos. 1-2 (January-April 1981): 28-37.

12. Chris Argyris, *Integrating the Individual and the Organization* (New York: John Wiley, 1964).

13. Chris Argyris, *Personality and Organization: The Conflict Between the System and the Individual* (New York: Harper & Row, 1957), 175.

14. Davis and Newstrom, *Human Behavior at Work*, 9-12.

15. J. Sterling Livingston, "Pygmalion in Management," *Harvard Business Review* 47 (July-August 1969): 81-89.

16. Livingston, "Pygmalion in Management," 81.

17. David C. McClelland, "That Urge to Achieve," *THINK Magazine* 32 (November-December 1966): 19.

18. Dale S. Beach, *Personnel: The Management of People at Work* (New York: Macmillan, 1985), 295.

19. Cited in Paul Hersey and Kenneth H. Blanchard, *Management of Organizational Behavior: Utilizing Human Resources* (Englewood Cliffs, NJ: Prentice-Hall, 1982), 4.

20. Abraham H. Maslow, *Motivation and Personality*, 2d ed. (New York: Harper & Row, 1970), 35f.

21. Abraham H. Maslow, "A Theory of Human Motivation," *Psychological Review* 50 (July 1943): 395.

22. It is important to remember that workers' basic needs are not fulfilled in all cultures. See, for example, Kalu U. Harrison and P. Havard-Williams, "Motivation in a Third World Library System," *International Library Review* 19, no. 3 (July 1987): 249-60.

23. Hersey and Blanchard, *Management of Organizational Behavior*, 43.

24. Frederick Herzberg, Bernard Mausner, and Barbara Bloch Snyderman, *The Motivation to Work*, 2d ed. (New York: John Wiley, 1959).

25. Frederick Herzberg, "One More Time: How Do You Motivate Employees?" *Harvard Business Review* 46 (January-February 1968): 55.

26. Ibid., 53-62.

27. Kathlin L. Ray, "Toppling Hire-archies: Support Staff and the Restructured Library," *Continuity and Transformation: Proceedings of the ACRL 7th National Conference* (Chicago, IL: ACRL, 1995), 85.

28. Charles Martell, "Achieving High Performance in Library Work," *Library Trends* 38, no. 1 (Summer 1989): 82.

29. Victor H. Vroom, *Work and Motivation* (New York: John Wiley, 1964).

30. B. F. Skinner, *Science and Human Behavior* (New York: Macmillan, 1953).

31. B. F. Skinner, *About Behaviorism* (New York: Vintage Books, 1976), 44.

32. E. J. Feeney, "At Emery Air Freight: Positive Reinforcement Boosts Performance," *Organizational Dynamics* 1 (Winter 1973): 41-50.

33. F. Luthans and R. Kreitner, *Organization Behavior Modification* (New York: Scott, Foresman, 1975), 118.

34. Martell, "Achieving High Performance in Library Work," 78.

35. Harold Koontz, Cyril O'Donnell, and Heinz Weihrich, *Essentials of Management*, 3d ed. (New York: McGraw-Hill, 1982), 416.

36. Raymond A. Katzell and Donna E. Thompson, "Work Motivation: Theory and Practice," *American Psychologist* 45 (February 1990): 151.

37. Warren Bennis, "Leadership Theory and Administrative Behavior: The Problem with Authority," *Administrative Science Quarterly* 4 (1959): 259.

38. James McGregor Burns, *Leadership* (New York: Harper & Row, 1978), 2.

39. Bernard M. Bass, *Bass and Stogdill's Handbook of Leadership*, 3d ed. (New York: Free Press, 1990).

40. Joseph C. Rost, *Leadership for the Twenty-First Century* (Westport, CT: Praeger, 1991), 44, 70.

41. Warren G. Bennis and B. Nanus, *Leaders: The Strategies for Taking Charge* (New York: Harper & Row, 1985), 21.

42. Fred A. Manske Jr. *Secrets of Effective Leadership*, 2d ed. (Columbia, TN: Leadership Education and Development, 1990), 7.

43. For an illuminating discussion of the differences between management and leadership, see Rost, *Leadership for the Twenty-First Century*, 140-52.

44. Warren Bennis, *Why Leaders Can't Lead* (San Francisco: Jossey-Bass, 1989), 17.

45. Ronald A. Heifetz and Donald L. Laurie, "The Work of Leadership," *Harvard Business Review* 75, no. 1 (January-February 1997): 124-34.

46. Michael Maccoby, *The Leader* (New York: Simon & Schuster, 1981), 14.

47. Henry Steele Commanger, "Our Leadership Crisis: America's Real Malaise," *Los Angeles Times*, part V (November 11, 1979): 1.

48. Manske, *Secrets of Effective Leadership*, 5.

49. Garry Wills, "What Makes a Good Leader?" *The Atlantic Monthly* 273 (April 1994): 70.

50. Robert Hogan, Gordon J. Curphy, and Joyce Hogan, "What We Know About Leadership: Effectiveness and Personality," *American Psychologist* 49, no. 6 (June 1994): 493.

51. Warren Bennis, "The Leader as Storyteller," *Harvard Business Review* 74, no. 1 (January-February 1996): 156.

52. Ralph M. Stodgill, *Handbook of Leadership* (New York: Free Press, 1974).

53. Howard M. Carlisle, *Situational Management: A Contingency Approach to Leadership* (New York: AMACOM, 1973), 124.

54. Eugene E. Jennings, "The Anatomy of Leadership," *Management of Personnel Quarterly* 1 (Autumn 1961): 2.

55. Ralph M. Stodgill and Alvin E. Coons, eds., *Leader Behavior: Its Description and Measurement*, Research Monograph no. 887 (Columbus, OH: Bureau of Business Research, 1957).

56. Gellerman, *The Management of Human Relations,* 32.

57. Oren Harari, "Stop Empowering Your People," *Management Review* 86, no. 2 (February 1997): 49.

58. Gellerman, *The Management of Human Relations*, 34.

59. Rensis Likert, *New Patterns of Management* (New York: McGraw-Hill, 1961).

60. Rensis Likert, *The Human Organization* (New York: McGraw-Hill, 1967), 4-10.

61. Robert R. Blake and Jane S. Mouton, *The Managerial Grid* (Houston, TX: Gulf, 1964).

62. Ibid., 9.

63. Ibid., 9-11.

64. Robert R. Blake and Jane S. Mouton, *The Managerial Grid III* (Houston, TX: Gulf, 1985), 18.

65. Burns, *Leadership.*

66. J. B. Rosener, "Ways Women Lead," *Harvard Business Review* 68, no. 6 (November-December 1990): 120.

67. Bennis, *Why Leaders Can't Lead,* 144.

68. Bernard M. Bass, "Does the Transactional-Transformational Leadership Paradigm Transcend Organizational and National Boundaries?" *American Psychologist* 52, no. 2 (February 1997): 130-39.

69. Fred E. Fiedler, "A Contingency Model of Leadership Effectiveness," in *Advances in Experimental Social Psychology*, vol. 1, ed. L. Berkowitz (New York: Academic Press, 1964), 165.

70. Bennis, *Why Leaders Can't Lead,* 144.

71.   Maccoby, *The Leader*, 23.

72.   Michael Maccoby, "Leadership Needs of the 1980's," *Perspectives on Leadership: Current Issues in Higher Education* 1(Washington, DC: American Association for Higher Education, 1979): 17.

73.   Herbert S. White, "Oh, Where Have All the Leaders Gone?" *Library Journal* 112, no. 16 (October 1987): 68-69.

74.   Peter M. Senge, "Communities of Leaders and Learners," *Harvard Business Review* 75, no. 5 (September-October 1997): 32.

75.   John Naisbitt and Patricia Aburdene, *Reinventing the Corporation* (New York: Warner Books, 1985), 20.

76.   Thomas J. Peters and Robert H. Waterman Jr., *In Search of Excellence: Lessons from America's Best-Run Companies* (New York: Harper & Row, 1982), 43.

77.   Tom Peters and Nancy Austin, *A Passion for Excellence: The Leadership Difference* (New York: Random House, 1985), 265.

78.   James A. Belasco, *Teaching the Elephant to Dance: Empowering Change in Your Organization* (New York: Crown, 1990).

79.   Riane Eisler, "Women, Men, and Management: Redesigning Our Future," *Futures* 23, no.1 (January 1991): 1-18.

80.   Rost, *Leadership for the Twenty-First Century*, 180-81.

81.   See, for example, D. Quinn Mills, *The New Competitors* (New York: John Wiley, 1985).

82.   Peter F. Drucker, *Managing the Non-Profit Organization* (New York: HarperBusiness, 1990), 115.

83.   Henry Mintzberg, "The Manager's Job: Folklore and Fact," *Harvard Business Review* 53 (July-August 1975): 52.

84.   Chester I. Barnard, *The Functions of the Executive* (Cambridge, MA: Harvard University Press, 1938).

85.   Alex Bavels and Dermot Barrett, "An Experimental Approach to Organization Communication," *Personnel* (March 1951): 368.

86.   John Wright, "Look at Management—2: Communication," *Management Accounting* 65 (October 1983): 33.

87.   Gerald M. Goldhaber, *Organizational Communication*, 2d ed. (Dubuque, IA: William C. Brown, 1979), 13-14.

88.   Deborah Tannen, *You Just Don't Understand: Women and Men in Conversation* (New York: William Morrow, 1990).

89.   Deborah Tannen, *Talking from 9 to 5: How Women's and Men's Conversational Styles Affect Who Gets Heard, Who Gets Credit, and What Gets Done at Work* (New York: William Morrow, 1994), 291.

90.   Huddleston, *Back on the Quality Track*, 113.

91. Jenny C. McCune, "Get the Message," *Management Review* 38 (January 1997): 10-11.

92. Esther Dyson, "Mirror, Mirror on the Wall," *Harvard Business Review* 75, no. 5 (September-October 1997): 26.

93. Daniel Katz and Robert L. Kahn, *The Social Psychology of Organizations* (New York: John Wiley, 1966), 239.

94. Jay R. Galbraith and Edward E. Lawler III and Associates, *Organizing for the Future: The New Logic for Managing Complex Organizations* (San Francisco: Jossey-Bass, 1993), 296-97.

95. Goldhaber, *Organizational Communication*, 141-42.

96. Barbara Ettorre, "The Unvarnished Truth," *Management Review* 49 (June 1997): 54.

97. Keith Davis, cited in Goldhaber, *Organizational Communication*, 138-39.

98. Goldhaber, *Organizational Communication*, 141-42.

99. A helpful guide to effective meetings is Barbara I. Dewey and Sheila D. Creth, *Team Power: Making Library Meetings Work* (Chicago: American Library Association, 1993).

100. Robert W. Zmud, "Opportunities for Strategic Information Manipulation Through New Information Technology," in *Organizations and Communication Technology*, ed. Janet Fulk and Charles Steinfield (Newbury Park, CA: Sage Publications, 1990), 115.

101. Davis and Newstrom, *Human Behavior at Work*, 371.

102. Paul Hersey, Kenneth Blanchard, and Dewey E. Johnson, *Management of Organizational Behavior: Utilizing Human Resources*, 7th ed. (Upper Saddle, NJ: Prentice-Hall, 1996), 355.

103. Kenneth W. Thomas and Warren H. Schmidt, "A Survey of Managerial Interests with Respect to Conflict," *Academy of Management Journal* 10 (June 1976): 315-18.

104. Kathleen M. Eisenhardt, Jean L. Kahwajy, and L. J. Bourgeois III, "How Management Teams Can Have a Good Fight," *Harvard Business Review* 75, no. 4 (July-August 1997): 77.

105. Thomas and Schmidt, "A Survey of Managerial Interests with Respect to Conflict," 317.

106. Tessa Albert Warschaw, *Winning by Negotiation* (New York: McGraw-Hill, 1980), 4-5.

107. Dorothy Leonard and Susan Straus, "Putting Your Company's Whole Brain to Work," *Harvard Business Review* 75, no. 4 (July-August 1997): 111.

108. Herbert S. White, "Never Mind Being Innovative and Effective—Just Be Nice," *Library Journal* 120 (September 15, 1995): 47.

109. Daryl R. Conner, *Managing at the Speed of Change: How Resilient Managers Succeed and Prosper Where Others Fail* (New York: Villard Books, 1993), 198.

110.　Ibid.

111.　Maurice B. Line and Margaret Kinnell, "Human Resource Management in Library and Information Services," in *Annual Review of Information Science and Technology*, vol. 28, ed. Martha E. Williams (Medford, NJ: Learned Information, 1993), 333.

112.　Nicholas C. Burckel, "Participatory Management in Academic Libraries: A Review," *College & Research Libraries* 45 (January 1984): 32.

113.　Conner, *Managing at the Speed of Change*, 198.

114.　Rosabeth Moss Kanter, *The Change Masters: Innovations for Productivity in the American Corporation* (New York: Simon & Schuster, 1983), 275.

115.　Heifetz and Laurie, "The Work of Leadership," 129.

116.　Richard Tanner Pascale and Anthony G. Athos, *The Art of Japanese Management: Applications for American Executives* (New York: Simon & Schuster, 1981), 20.

117.　Wolfgang Lux, "Japanese Management: The Rise and Fall and Rise of the Topmost Revered Nation for Management Expertise," *Management Review* 49 (June 1997): 36-39.

118.　Ibid., 39.

119.　Ibid., 38.

120.　William Ouchi, *Theory Z* (Reading, MA: Addison-Wesley, 1981).

121.　Harry Katzan, *Quality Circle Management* (Blue Ridge Summit, PA: TAB Books, 1989), xii.

122.　Deborah A. Mourey and Jerry W. Mansfield, "Quality Circles for Management Decisions: What's in It for Libraries?" *Special Libraries* 75 (April 1984): 89.

123.　Ibid., 92; Joan S. Segal and Tamiye Trejo-Meehan, "Quality Circles: Some Theory and Two Experiences," *Library Administration and Management* 4 (Winter 1989): 16-19.

124.　Mitchell Lee Marks, "The Question of Quality Circles," *Psychology Today* (March 1986): 46.

125.　Donald E. Riggs, "Managing Quality: TQM in Libraries," *Library Administration and Management* 7, no. 2 (Spring 1993): 73.

126.　Rosanna M. O'Neil, *Total Quality Management in Libraries: A Sourcebook* (Englewood, CO: Libraries Unlimited, 1994). Peter Brophy and Kate Coulling, *Quality Management for Information and Library Managers* (Aldershot, UK: Aslib/Gower, 1996).

127.　V. Daniel Hunt, *Quality in America: How to Implement a Competitive Quality Program* (Homewood, IL: Business One-Irwin, 1992), 9.

128.　D. Price, "The Quality Concept and Objectives," in *Gower Handbook of Quality Management*, ed. D. Lock (Aldershot, UK: Gower, 1990): 3-11.

129.　O'Neil, *Total Quality Management in Libraries*, 171.

130. Lloyd Dobyns and Clare Crawford-Mason, *Quality or Else: The Revolution in World Business* (Boston: Houghton Mifflin, 1991), 59.

131. Ted Marchese, "TQM Reaches the Academy," *AAHE Bulletin* 44, no. 3 (November 1991): 5.

132. Riggs, "Managing Quality," 77.

133. W. Edwards Deming, *Out of the Crisis* (Cambridge, MA: MIT Center for Advanced Engineering Study, 1986), 21.

134. Deming, *Out of the Crisis*, 23-24.

135. For more information on these techniques and others, see any standard text on the topic of TQM, including the O'Neil and the Brophy and Coulling texts cited above.

136. Brophy and Coulling, "Quality Management for Information and Library Mangers," 98.

137. Huddleston, *Back on the Quality Track*, 301.

138. Rosanna M. O'Neil, Richard L. Harwood, and Bonnie A. Osif, "A Total Look at Total Quality Management: A TQM Perspective from the Literature of Business, Industry, Higher Education and Librarianship," *Library Administration and Management* 7, no. 4 (Fall 1993): 246.

139. Ibid.

140. Maurice B. Line, "Relating Quality Management to Strategic Planning," *Inspel* 28, no. 2 (1994): 221.

141. Ibid.

142. Ron Zemke, "The Service Revolution: Who Won?" *Management Review* 86, no. 3 (March 1997): 11.

143. Len Berry, A. Parasuraman, and Valarie Zeithaml, "Improving Service Quality in America: Lessons Learned," *Academy of Management Executive* 8, no. 2 (Fall 1994).

144. Deming, *Out of the Crisis*, 186.

145. Jay Mathews with Peter Katel, "The Cost of Quality," *Newsweek* 120 (September 7, 1992): 48-49.

146. Ibid.

147. Oren Harari, "Ten Reasons TQM Doesn't Work," *Management Review* 38 (January 1997): 38-44.

148. Tom Peters, quoted in "Strategic Planning," *Total Quality* 5, no. 10 (October 10, 1994): 1.

149. Carla Stoffle et al., "Choosing Our Futures," *College & Research Libraries* 57 (May 1996): 213-33.

150. Susan Jurow, "Tools for Measuring and Improving Performance," in *Integrating Total Quality Management in a Library Setting*, ed. Susan Jurow and Susan B. Barnard (Binghamton, NY: Haworth Press, 1993), 125.

151. Pascale and Athos, *The Art of Japanese Management,* 201.

152. Jay W. Lorsch, "Organization Design: A Situational Perspective," *Organizational Dynamics* 6 (Autumn 1977): 4-5.

153. Howard M. Carlisle, *Management: Concepts and Situations* (Chicago: Science Research Associates, 1976), 58-59.

154. Robert E. Quinn, *Beyond Rational Management* (San Francisco: Jossey-Bass, 1988), 3.

155. Jay W. Lorsch, "Making Behavioral Science More Useful," *Harvard Business Review* 57 (March-April 1979): 174.

156. Morse and Lorsch, "Beyond Theory Y," 68.

157. James L. Hayes, cited in Ernest Dale, *Management: Theory and Practice*, 2d ed. (New York: McGraw-Hill, 1969), 5.

Readings

Belasco, James A. *Teaching the Elephant to Dance: Empowering Change in Your Organization.* New York: Crown, 1990.

Bennis, Warren, and Nanus Burt. *Leaders: Strategies for Taking Charge.* New York: Harper & Row, 1985.

Berk, Joseph, and Susan Berk. *Managing Effectively: A Handbook for First-Time Managers.* New York: Sterling, 1991.

Brophy, Peter, and Kate Coulling. *Quality Management for Information and Library Managers.* Aldershot, UK: Aslib/Gower, 1996.

Burns, James McGregor. *Leadership.* New York: Harper & Row, 1978.

Cleveland, Harlan. *The Knowledge Executive: Leadership in an Information Society.* New York: E. P. Dutton, 1985.

Conner, Daryl R. *Managing at the Speed of Change: How Resilient Managers Succeed and Prosper Where Others Fail.* New York: Villard Books, 1993.

Deevy, Edward. *Creating the Resilient Organization: A Rapid Response Management Program.* Englewood Cliffs, NJ: Prentice-Hall, 1995.

Deming, W. Edwards *Out of the Crisis.* Cambridge: MA; MIT Center for Advanced Engineering Study, 1986.

Dewey, Barbara I., and Sheila D. Creth. *Team Power: Making Library Meetings Work.* Chicago: American Library Association, 1993.

Dobyns, Lloyd, and Clare Crawford-Mason. *Quality or Else: The Revolution in World Business.* Boston: Houghton Mifflin, 1991.

Fulk, Janet, and Charles Steinfield, eds. *Organizations and Communication Technology.* Newbury Park, CA: Sage Publications, 1990.

Gardner, Howard. *Leading Minds: An Anatomy of Leadership.* New York: Basic Books, 1995.

Helgesen, Sally. *The Female Advantage: Women's Ways of Leadership*. New York: Doubleday, 1990.

Hersey, Paul, Kenneth H. Blanchard, and Dewey E. Johnson. *Management of Organizational Behavior: Utilizing Human Resources*. 7th ed. Upper Saddle, NJ: Prentice-Hall, 1996.

Hunt, V. Daniel. *Quality in America: How to Implement a Competitive Quality Program*. Homewood, IL: Business One-Irwin, 1992.

Jurow, Susan, and Susan B. Barnard, eds. *Integrating Total Quality Management in a Library Setting*. New York: Haworth Press, 1993.

Kanter, Rosabeth Moss. *The Change Masters: Innovation and Entrepreneurship in the American Corporation*. New York: Simon & Schuster, 1983.

Kotter, John. *The Leadership Factor*. New York: Free Press, 1988.

Lawler, Edward E. *High Involvement Management: Participative Strategies for Improving Organizational Performance*. San Francisco: Jossey-Bass, 1986.

O'Neil, Rosanna M. *Total Quality Management in Libraries: A Sourcebook*. Englewood, CO: Libraries Unlimited, 1994.

Peters, Tom, and Nancy Austin. *A Passion for Excellence: The Leadership Difference*. New York: Random House, 1985.

Quinn, Robert E. *Beyond Rational Management*. San Francisco: Jossey-Bass, 1988.

Tannen, Deborah. *You Just Don't Understand: Women and Men in Conversation*. New York: William Morrow, 1990.

Vroom, Victor H., and Arthur G. Jago. *The New Leadership: Managing Participation in Organizations*. Englewood Cliffs, NJ: Prentice-Hall, 1988.

Weick, Karl E. *Sensemaking in Organizations*. Thousand Oaks, CA: Sage Publications, 1995.

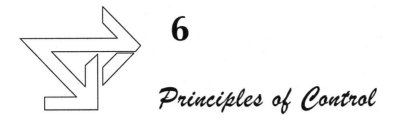

6

Principles of Control

A Vice-President of a major company, which specializes in strategic planning, wrote that perhaps planning has become a fetish. "Fetish" in this context means a task providing an illusion of control in an environment that is clearly out of control; at least one can forecast, gather statistics, write reports and hold meetings to provide the illusion of activity and control.[1]

—Rosabeth Moss Kanter, *The Change Masters*

Control, and the planning activity it accompanies, has received a great deal of discussion, debate, and some amount of dissension in recent management literature. By most authorities it is viewed as a progressive element, with techniques being applied toward achieving success, rather than a more negative view of stifling initiative. With this positive approach, the issue of control permeates most aspects of this text—from the discussion of setting goals and evaluating the organization's progress toward achieving them, to organizing libraries and information centers toward providing the services needed by users, to staffing and leadership and the motivational factors desirable in integrating the individual employee's goals with those of the organization. Evaluation, accountability, and cost, all necessary components, are intertwined in those aspects.

A gradual shift in the orientation from a preoccupation with input measures, mostly internal in nature, to a user orientation, with primary emphasis on output measures and accountability, has tended to balance quantitative and qualitative factors in the controlling process, with as much emphasis being placed on the output factors of service and performance as was formerly placed on statistics and paper pushing. This reorientation has removed control from the mundane, stationary category and placed it on a fluid, innovation-seeking plateau, with less a view of "looking over the shoulder" than one of working together in identifying weaknesses that need to be corrected, correcting those weaknesses, and then evaluating the results.

343

Initially, in any discussion of controls, some distinction must be made between the act of controlling and the mechanisms for that control. The two are obviously interrelated—effective "controlling" within an organization depends on the types of controls that are in place. Controlling is the act, and controls are the means, the tools or measurements that, when applied efficiently and effectively, provide information for decision making. The former, according to Drucker, pertains to an end, while the latter is the means; the first is concerned with events and the other with facts; one is analytical and operational, concerned with what was and is, while the other deals with expectations.[2] The management of resources requires determination of what resources the organization has at its disposal, or should make available, and how those resources can be employed to achieve the mission of the organization. It requires strong financial planning and feedback mechanisms to ensure success.

An all-encompassing definition of control would take into account any action or process that alters results. In that regard, it is a global term, not narrowly defined. Controlling involves setting standards, establishing criteria, developing policies and budgets, conducting personnel performance evaluation, and scheduling actions to achieve objectives, then monitoring the outcome on a periodic basis, and, finally, providing some type of feedback mechanism to ensure efficiency and effectiveness in the achievement, suggesting adjustments or alternatives to the situation in place. In a library or information center setting, just as in most other types of organizations, control relates to human resources, physical resources, and information resources. Although the primary controlling aspect is usually a financial one, because no other element can be effectively developed without money, controlling must also take into consideration costs that cannot be easily measured in monetary terms. These include both effective performance and customer satisfaction. The function of controlling, because it requires accurate and timely information for the control, coordination, and monitoring of data, has become heavily dependent upon technology (data processing, communications technology, and office automation) to provide efficient information. Elements that can be controlled in such an organizational context include time, money, quality, and quantity. Factors can be put into place to control and measure each of them.

Ultimate control in the library and information services setting is usually to some degree external. Most information centers are accountable to higher public or private sector funding authorities that provide primary impetus and funding for the operations of that organization. In libraries and information centers this control is exercised by regulatory groups, such as trustees or committees—through the superintendent or school committee, town administrator or citizen-elected committee, chancellor, president, or both—or the board of directors of a corporation or a higher education institution. In an academic setting, the library or information center is legally bound by constitutional provisions, charters, articles of incorporation, and general or special laws applicable to the educational institution as a whole. In special or corporate libraries, the controlling function is exercised through one of the divisions of the organization—usually the research division, the sales division, or the manufacturing division—on behalf of the ultimate controlling body, which is the corporate or company board of directors. The city manager, mayor, or superintendent, who acts on behalf of the ultimate controlling body, which is the city council, school committee, or other governing authority, controls public libraries and school libraries. These external authorities are controlling agents for the information center because of their overall institutional charge and because of their funding and fiduciary responsibilities.

Besides those bodies directly related to the controlling function of an information services organization, numerous outside groups are involved in such aspects as standards, certification, and accreditation of libraries, librarians, and other information specialists. For example, higher education accrediting bodies, such as the North Central Association of College and Secondary Schools in the United States, influence through their observations of and recommendations about the libraries and information centers within institutions they accredit; the American Library Association influences libraries through the establishment of standards for various types of libraries and library services and through its Committee on Accreditation, which is responsible for setting standards for library and information science education; state departments of education establish guidelines for the certification of school librarians or media specialists and establish standard formulae for the allocation of funds; and special-interest groups, such as the Medical Library Association, set certification standards and continuing education requirements for their members.

Some groups and agencies exist primarily to regulate the activities of the information centers and to measure, to one extent or another, the actions and output of those organizations. Laws, including local, state, national, and even international ones, regulate activities. For example, planning, constructing, and maintaining library buildings may be controlled through municipal ordinances and regulations, building codes, zoning, and fire regulations; and international copyright agreements or international standards promulgated by the International Standards Organization may direct the services of an information center. Broader legislation, for instance, state and federal funding legislation, places certain other controls on the operation of libraries and information centers. Such regulatory agencies and their authority vary from one part of the world to another, but their intent remains the same. Examples can be found from Austria to Zimbabwe and from Auckland to Zurich.

Other bodies that exert some external control on libraries include unions, special interests groups, and political bodies. Through collective bargaining, unions can influence hiring, salaries, working conditions, fringe benefits, and so forth, and political bodies can influence the appointments of individuals, the allocation of monies, and even the disbursal of funds within libraries and information centers. Often, pressures are placed on information services by outside bodies, in areas of hiring new staff and in issues relating to collection development, censorship and intellectual freedom, and use of library services and facilities. Friends of the Library is a good example of a group of well-meaning supporters that may expect to have some say in the directions libraries will take, sometimes in return for charitable contributions.

Requirements for Adequate Control

Controls are concerned with keeping things on track, successful progress toward meeting specified objectives, and, therefore, locating any operational weakness so that corrective action can be taken. While plans determine what should be done, controls assure that it is done, acting as the tools and techniques for implementing the planning process. In order to avoid failure, controls are both desirable and, if applied consistently and fairly, necessary. At the operational level, controlling techniques relate to such things as policies, procedures, task analysis, and job audits. Control implies the existence of goals and plans and the regulation of the organization's activities toward those goals. The most effective controls prevent deviations from plans by anticipating that such deviations will occur unless immediate action is taken. However, other types of control are also necessary for feedback, and they naturally emanate from the planning process.

Controls are necessary in all types of organizations, but, in a large organization, they are particularly important to provide managers with facts in a comprehensible form when they are required. In a strictly theoretical sense, controls are guides for the organization; they indicate how effectively the organization is progressing toward meeting its established goals. At the heart of control is the concept of accountability, the obligation of reporting to a higher authority on the exercise of responsibility and authority. As not-for-profit organizations, most libraries and information centers do not have the monetary profit incentive of for-profit organizations and, therefore, establish different controls and measurements, or at least take a different approach in using them. All types of information centers must demonstrate the "value of service" or "value-added" aspect to the larger organization of which they are a part. Through accountability, the library and information service manager is, more than ever before, expected to evaluate the institution's performance to make sure that the human and material resources are effectively and efficiently employed toward achieving the goals of the larger institution. In the past, some libraries relied on the "public good" view of library services. This is no longer adequate in the current competitive environment.

> ॐ The control of an undertaking consists of seeing that everything is being carried out in accordance with the plan which has been adopted, the orders which have been given, and the principles which have been laid down. Its object is to point out mistakes in order that they may be rectified and prevented from occurring again.[3]
>
> —Henri Fayol,
> *Industrial and General Administration*

To be effective, controls must be objective and must reflect the job they are to perform. In addition, they should be established and agreed upon before they are needed, to minimize conflict. At the least, the controls should point up exceptions at critical points. In addition, any control system that does not pose corrective actions after deviations occur is little more than an interesting exercise. In other words, there must be an action plan accompanying the evaluation process. After activities have been initiated, some sort of control mechanism must be established to monitor progress and to correct performance to achieve goals. Given those guidelines, individuals at all levels are responsible for making sure the organization is on course. Controls, wherever they are found and whatever they control, involve three steps: establishing standards, measuring performance against standards, and correcting deviations.

Establishing Standards

Standards are established criteria against which subsequent performance can be compared and evaluations can be made. Most often they are developed, or at least devised, from the organizational goals.[4] Standards fall into two basic classes: those relating to material and performance—including quality, quantity, cost, and time—and those relating to moral aspects—including the organization's value system and ethical criteria that may be used to establish some sort of code of ethics. Standards may be physical, representing quantities of products, units of service, work-hours, and similar things that can be evidenced and measured through time-and-motion studies; they may be stated in monetary terms, such as costs, revenues, or investments, which are evidenced through record keeping, cost analysis, and budget presentation; or they may be expressed in other terms that measure performance, such as performance rating and appraisal systems. Of course, there are some other factors that are difficult to evaluate and measure, and they require a different approach to measurement. For instance, how does one measure commitment of individuals to organizational goals?

General standards, such as those proposed by the American Library Association, are important as guides, but they do not necessarily provide meaningful evaluation for the individual library or information center for a number of reasons. Morris Hamburg points out these weaknesses:

1. Most of the standards are descriptive in nature.

2. Most of the standards that prescribe quantitative objectives are arbitrarily formulated.

3. The emphasis of the standards is directed toward evaluating the input resources of the library.

4. The standards discourage experimentation with different programs and different allocations of input resources.[5]

Some standards are nebulous and almost impossible to measure, some are simply guidelines for proceeding,[6] and others combine qualitative evaluation with quantitative formulae.[7] If a scientific control method is to be used, then the standards should be measurable, to the extent possible. In any case, to be effective, standards should be acceptable to those whose performance is regulated by them. The process of applying performance standards should be explained and agreed upon rather than forced. By human nature, if standards are forced, some resistance will surely occur.

> ✂ The first step is to measure whatever can be easily measured. This is OK as far as it goes. The second step is to disregard that which can't be easily measured or to give it an arbitrary quantitative value. This is artificial and misleading. The third step is to presume that what can't be measured easily really isn't important. This is blindness. The fourth step is to say that what can't be easily measured really doesn't exist. This is suicide.[8]
>
> —McNamara Fallacy, in *The Age of Paradox*

Measuring Performance Against Standards

In any organization, measuring performance is a continuous process, whether it is related to systems measurement or personnel performance. There are many activities for which it is extremely difficult to develop sound standards, and there are many activities that are hard to measure. Others—for instance, the number of titles cataloged in a month, or the number of volumes circulated—are easier to measure. What is important is to keep accurate records of what is done. If records are not kept, if the output cannot be measured objectively, then it is difficult to assess how much actual performance deviates from the planned performance, to determine a measure of success. This feedback, or measuring performance, is an important factor in the controlling process. Efforts have been made to identify and define elements in libraries that can facilitate intra- and interlibrary communication in the control process.[9] Reporting elements used in libraries and information centers that have attempted to measure performance include personal observation, statistical data, oral reports, and written reports.

Besides feedback, the other type of basic control is prevention, which attempts to predict what will happen by setting parameters. Goal setting in the planning process is a good example of this type of control. Goal setting takes information about past performance and introduces it into decisions about adjustments that are needed for future actions. Such a process is just as important to an ordinary control process as it is to a more complex, automated one.

> ℒPreventative control processes, as the name implies, attempt to prevent deviations from developing in the conduct of organizational behavior. Feedback control processes rely on information from actual performance and are designed to correct deviations after they have developed.[10]
>
> —Walter Jack Duncan,
> *Essentials of Management*

A simplified example of detecting deviations in libraries, which combines elements of goal setting and feedback, is a monthly budget balance sheet that might show, for instance, that by the month of July, three-fourths of the amount budgeted for telephone calls for the year has already been expended and that, unless corrective action is taken, the organization will overrun the budgeted amount in that category well before the end of the calendar year. A decision must be made on how to keep this from happening.

Cybernetics, which has become increasingly important in the control feedback process, studies the interaction of communication and control as fundamental factors in all human activity and now is being applied to many large organizations, including libraries and information centers. Basically, cybernetics is a self-regulating method by which messages that the system sends to itself indicate deviations from the desired course. This may be expressed in a very simplified diagram that shows how the information flow makes possible the self-regulation of the system (see fig. 6.1).

Fig. 6.1. With cybernetics, an organization can provide feedback to itself.

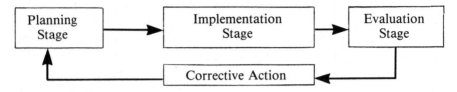

Communication is the most important aspect of a feedback control system because it involves transmitting and receiving messages or information—in this case, data used to make the decisions that control the system's behavior. Again, a simplified diagram illustrates the process (see fig. 6.2).

Fig. 6.2. Communication is key to a feedback control system.

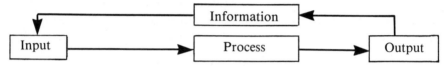

Correcting the Deviation

The third aspect of control is the comparison or evaluation of standards in relation to performance. After standards have been agreed upon, some sort of analysis must be performed to measure the activity against the standard. Techniques such as cost-benefit analysis and time-and-motion studies are commonly employed to measure the standards of performance for operations. Performance appraisal assures the organization that an individual is meeting the standard and also reassures the individual that his or her contribution is significant. There has been some criticism of introducing techniques that impose strong control on personnel, because it is maintained that, although such techniques may have short-term benefits for the organization, such as higher output and economies, they may, in fact, be detrimental to the health of the organization because of deterioration of attitudes, motivation, and communication. In addition, not everything can be quantified; judgment and flexibility are necessary. Subjective judgment, in areas like perceived loyalty to the organization, may overshadow performance. Personnel performance is even more difficult to measure, because actions and responsibilities are more complex, less regulated, and require greater initiative, thus, are less quantifiable. In other words, not all quantitative measures accurately reflect the quality of an activity. For example, a rare-books cataloger may perform original cataloging on two items during an eight-hour period. The quality of that activity must be measured delicately, objectively, and with full understanding of all nuances involved.

The next step is to correct any deviations from the norm. This correction can be achieved by exercising organizational prerogative, for instance, in the case of personnel, by reassignment or clarification of duties, by additional staffing, by better selection and training of staff, or by some other method of restaffing. Corrections can also be made by adjusting goals or developing new or alternative plans.

Techniques of Control

Evaluation

The evaluation process identifies areas needing improvement with an aim toward taking corrective action. It is a process and should not be considered a one-time thing or even a sometime thing, but, rather, an ongoing review of operations. This aspect of controlling is inextricably tied to the planning process, because it is impossible to evaluate unless it is known what is to be evaluated. How effectively and efficiently a library or information center is meeting the goals and objectives identified in the planning process can be measured through this evaluation. If the whole process is viewed as a circle, the evaluation step brings one back to decision making.

> ℚ If an evaluation involves online bibliographic searching one can establish service performance in such terms as cost, quantities produced, quality, timeliness, availability, cost per search, and so on. However, one can also determine the effectiveness of searching in terms of user satisfaction, amount of use, purpose of use and consequences of use on the user's work.[11]
>
> —Jose-Marie Griffiths and Donald W. King,
> *A Manual on the Evaluation of*
> *Information Centers and Services*

Evaluation can come from a variety of sources. Cost-benefit analysis, budget analysis, performance evaluation, and collection evaluation are examples of techniques used in the evaluation process. Accountability in libraries has fostered the development of many prescriptive techniques to measure the efficiency of library operations and the effectiveness of library services.

 captionℒ The most important contribution the manager will make is a commitment to evaluation; a headset that demands systematic information and that builds in procedures to generate the required information flow on a continuing basis.[12]

—Rekha Agarwala-Rogers and
Janet K. Alexander,
"Evaluation of Organizational Attitudes"

When one thinks of internal controls, mechanical controls come to mind first, including circulation control, automated serials, and the like. These technological controls are only one example of tools that are used to measure library operations. The computer has become an invaluable aid to decision making, particularly for larger library organizations. It has been used effectively, although in a limited number of situations, in establishing models for library operations through decision theory, game theory, graph theory, queuing theory, and simulation exercises, among other applications. Many more basic techniques and tools are employed in the control process in the library, particularly as libraries become more accountable for their operations. These include varying operations, such as management information systems and operations research. Because they are sophisticated techniques, often applicable only to large library systems, they are only briefly mentioned here.

Cost-Benefit Analysis

"Cost-benefit analysis can be defined as a systematic approach which seeks to (1) determine whether or not a particular program or proposal is justified, (2) rank various alternatives appropriate to a given set of objectives, and (3) ascertain the optimal course of action to attain these objectives."[13] It is a form of analysis that considers both direct and indirect costs in the allocation of resources. The technique is used to examine both the current budget allocation process and to ascertain the level of financial support required, establishing some specified benefits of both new and existing programs. It requires a statement of the problem, accompanied by estimation of costs and benefits associated with each alternative identified, in order to compare them with each other and with the benefits that are sought. The objective is to identify that one alternative offering the greatest benefits at the lowest costs.

Several factors must be identified in the process, including any external constraints that need to be built into the mathematical models as parameters. It also requires identification of input costs and output benefits. Time factor consideration requires delineation of costs involving research and development, investment, and operations. There must be recognition that there will likely be a time lag between initiation and achievement of the initial benefits. Because the topic is a detailed one, requiring extensive description, it is only mentioned here to give the reader some idea of its approach. The process has been lauded but also lambasted as "an infallible means of reaching the new Utopia to a waste of resources in attempting to measure the unmeasurable."[14]

The technique of cost-benefit analysis, simply stated, involves choosing from alternatives when measurement in dollars or other specific measures may not be enough or even possible. Wherever possible, however, some specific measures should be established. For instance, if the objective is the improvement of referral service at the information desk, the number of in- person, telephone, or online inquiries answered or unanswered as well as patrons' judgment of staff, and satisfaction with the service can all measure effectiveness. As the term suggests, the method is used to identify not only the cost of a program but also the benefits of the various alternatives that must be considered. The emphasis of cost effectiveness is on output; each alternative is weighed in terms of effectiveness or costs against the objective that has been set. In some cases, cost models can be developed to show cost estimates for each alternative, or effectiveness models can be developed to show relationships between the alternatives and their effectiveness. Cost-benefit analysis is often confused with cost effectiveness, but, as F. W. Lancaster points out, there is a subtle difference.[15] Cost-benefit analysis is concerned with the cost, cost effectiveness with the value. Cost-benefit analysis says, "Which is the best (least expensive, or efficient) way to perform an operation?" and is an analysis of value; while cost effectiveness asks, "This is what the service costs. Is it worth it?" (that is, "Is it effective?"), which is a measure of quality. The process of cost-benefit analysis has been greatly enhanced by the development of software packages.

> ‽At different times . . . different management systems are in vogue. Some of these systems represent real innovation; more often someone 'reinvents the wheel.' "[16]
>
> —Bruce H. DeWoolfson Jr.,
> "Public Sector MBO and PPBS"

Management Information Systems

There are several basic tools useful to measure the output of services. These include a number of techniques relating to operations control, among them Management Information Systems (MIS), which is another technological tool to gather data, summarize it, and present it as information to be used in the control process. A precursor to the Decision Support Systems (DSS), MIS is a process established to organize information for decision making. MIS is not in itself the electronic data-processing and software systems, but rather a process that employs data processing and other online analysis to provide required information. It is "an organized method of providing past, present, and projection information related to internal operations and external intelligence. It supports the planning, control and operational functions of an organization by furnishing information in the proper time frame to assist in the decision-making process."[17]

Well-ordered Management Information Systems can be enhanced through control and evaluation techniques, including Management by Objectives (MBO), the Gantt Chart, and Program Evaluation and Review Technique (PERT) or the Critical Path Method (CPM). These and others have received some recent criticism from those who believe that Management Information Systems represent simply a process, sometimes with adequate reference to strategic planning, operations planning, or budgets, and that their objectives have no relationship to other developments. There is no doubt that, to be effective, Management Information Systems must be reviewed and, if adopted, have a direct relationship to what is desired as far as information retrieval for library operations is concerned. Technology has made it easier to standardize procedures and to apply mechanical methods to measure them. Management Information Systems are viewed as ways of collecting data to improve efficiency and effectiveness. Typically, they involve financial information, personnel information, performance information, and user information, all related to the feedback aspect of control. Because the MIS involves developing complicated systems that integrate hardware, databases, and software; educating and training staff; and so forth, the process is too lengthy to discuss here. It is sufficient to say that these systems are important parts of organizations today. Newer techniques, such as expert systems, which are offshoots of MIS, also are beginning to affect management of libraries. Some techniques, which have been around for some time, are useful tools in the management information systems approach. These are cost-benefit analysis and time-and-motion study.

Decision Support Systems (DSS)

Decision Support Systems (DSS), as an extension of MIS, takes advantage of the continuous development in the database management and modeling arena to offer software that supports computerized decision making. It is more interactive in that it can respond to messages and present alternative approaches upon which decisions can be made. It can simulate situations and project outcomes. This computer-assisted analysis is an effective tool for financial planning, among other activities. It allows for testing assumptions, factoring risks, and exploring alternatives. It is particularly useful when managers are presented with problems that have more than one solution, thereby enhancing their decision-making options.

Motion studies enable a library system to record in flowchart form the present method of doing things, to analyze the method's effectiveness, and, from this analysis, to improve the method. The new method of doing things can then be timed to report the performance standard. Time studies complement motion studies in determining performance standards. A third element in this quantifying process is cost—that is, attaching a dollar figure to the activities of an individual. Both time and cost vary with the level of expertise of the individual performing the task and the institution in which the work is taking place. Many time-and-motion studies have been and are being done in libraries, particularly relating to routine tasks, such as pasting pockets in books, typing subject headings on preprinted cards, or preparing items for the bindery.

Operations Research

> Making objectives explicit, deriving suitable measures of the extent of meeting them, developing simple quantitative relations between input and output, and identifying constraints that one should strive to remove have proved considerably more valuable than the mere manipulation of complicated mathematical models.[18]
>
> —M. Elton and Brian Vicker,
> "The Scope of Operational Research in the
> Library and Information Field"

Two terms that are closely related and often used interchangeably are *operations research* and *systems analysis*. Actually, the latter emerges from the former. Operations research (OR) today is largely identified with specific techniques, such as linear programming, queuing theory analysis, dynamic programming, statistical models, Monte Carlo (randomizing) methods, gaming and game theory, and other computer simulation models. It grew out of the military's needs during World War II and occupies the interest of a number of different groups, particularly statisticians and mathematicians.

Operations research is an "experimental and applied science devoted to observing, understanding and predicting the behavior of purposeful [worker-machine] systems, and operations researchers are actively engaged in applying this knowledge to practical problems."[19] This definition can be further refined to: "the use of scientific methods to study the functions of an organization so as to develop better methods of planning and controlling changes in the organization. It can be viewed as a branch of management, engineering or science. As part of the field of management, its purpose is to assist decision makers in choosing preferred future courses of action by systematically identifying and examining the alternatives which are available to the manager, and by predicting the possible outcomes for such actions."[20]

> The operations researchers soon joined forces with the mathematical economists who had come into the same area—to the mutual benefit of both groups. . . . No meaningful line can be drawn any more to demarcate operations research from scientific management or scientific management from management science.[21]

—Herbert A. Simon,
The New Science of Management Decision, rev. ed.

From the late 1960s to the 1990s, applied operations research has come into its own in the library decision-making process. This is primarily because in recent years decision making in general has emphasized the mathematical and statistical approach rather than a judgment-based approach. The emphasis of the mathematical approach was facilitated primarily by the application of scientific methods and technological development, the major impact coming with the development of the computer, which is necessary for the manipulation of complex data. One use to which computers have been put is modeling of organizations or systems. Conceptual models, used for decision making, are simply computer-based attempts at simulating reality. They are powerful means of testing various alternatives without changing the commitments involved in a typical decision. The primary approach of operations research consists of a broad view of the problem by the whole organization. This is succeeded by a team initiative, using personnel with different backgrounds from different departments, with the team addressing the economic-technical aspects of the total system. The key components to the process, then, are application of the scientific method; using a systems approach to problem solving; and employing mathematical, probability, and statistical techniques and computer modeling. Statistical analysis is made easier with the software systems for modeling technologies available today. Still, some types of statistical analysis require a different approach to gathering data that can then be analyzed electronically.

In terms of control, the major contribution of operations research has been in constructing models that can be used in the decision-making process. To accomplish this, a basic knowledge of systems analysis is necessary. Again, the important first step, as in most techniques, is to identify objectives and then to look at variables that might influence the objectives.

These are expressed mathematically to determine the best alternative in terms of the objectives set. The system currently in use is described. Based upon this analysis, a series of mathematical models is developed to describe the interrelationships within the organization. Data are then collected to measure the system, or, if data are not available, assumptions or speculations are made. This information provides the basis for a working model for a new system. With this information in hand, the librarian is able to make decisions based on the alternatives presented. The analytical statistical technique and the techniques of probability theory are employed.

It has been pointed out that the use of operations research in libraries is based on the application of the scientific approach to practical problems: "It normally operates in four distinctive stages: (1) Description of the system being considered, especially by means of mathematical models and computer simulations; (2) Measurement, using objective data wherever these can be obtained; (3) Evaluation, the presentation of relevant information to the system manager (here the librarian) to aid in making decisions between different courses of action; (4) Operational control, assisting the development of ways and means of achieving the objectives aimed for over a period of time."[22] The greatest potential of operations research lies in predicting the future by employing the mathematical models rather than in knowing the present by analyzing past experimental data.[23] Because of the technique's complexity and its use of mathematics and computers, as well as the costs of modeling, most librarians have not yet applied operations research to improve managerial control.

Also, there are limits to this approach. The quantitative method can be no better than the assumptions and estimates used in it. Its greatest limitation to use in libraries is that quantitative analysis is not adaptable to all situations. Some variables in libraries are very difficult to quantify; yet, to achieve a proper quantitative analysis, all variables must be assigned quantitative weights either through amassed data or through estimates. Therefore, a great deal of judgment is required, first to know when to use the quantitative method and then to know how to estimate costs of activities. In addition, quantitative analysis can become very elaborate and costly. One criticism of the technique is that it does not emphasize human factors enough, because such factors are difficult to model mathematically. Also, this method demands some knowledge of mathematics and statistical concepts, and these are areas where librarians are thought to be at their weakest; we have relied heavily on nonlibrarians to provide this expertise. Finally, it should be remembered that use of quantitative tools concerns only one phase of the decision-making process. It is a kind of management information that is infrequently used to identify the problem or develop alternatives.

One specific technique used by operations researchers is linear programming. Certain conditions must exist to make its use effective: "(1) Goals must be stated in mathematical terms; (2) Alternatives must be available and stated; (3) Resources (are required which) are usually limited; (4) Variables must be interrelated."[24] Sometimes the cost of linear programming outweighs its benefits, because it is difficult, if not impossible, to quantify the required data. "Linear programming is concerned with optimizing a decision problem by analyzing interrelationships of system components and contributions of these components to the objective function."[25]

PERT

A technique of control in the planning process that is highly applicable to library operations is PERT (Program Evaluation and Review Technique), developed a number of years ago by the U.S. Navy's Special Projects Office to plan the Polaris weapon system. A method of planning and scheduling work, PERT is sometimes called the Critical Path Method (CPM). It involves identifying all of the key activities in a particular project; devising the sequence of activities and arranging them in a flow diagram; and, finally, assigning duration of time for the performance of each phase of the work to be done. This technique consists of enumerating events whose completion can be measured. "Most likely" times are then calculated for the accomplishment of each event, so that one can see how long it would take for the progression of events to be completed. This model-building network approach is most effectively used for major projects that are one-time events. An example would be the opening of a new library. Activities can be plotted to allow the librarian to determine the most expeditious route—or critical path—that can be taken to carry out the event. As with other techniques discussed, in PERT, one must be able to state objectives, then activities must be enumerated and estimates must be given for the time required for each of these activities. The abbreviated, two-path diagram in figure 6.3 illustrates the concept.

Fig. 6.3. The PERT diagram shows the planned schedule of a task, in graphic format, of a two-path approach.

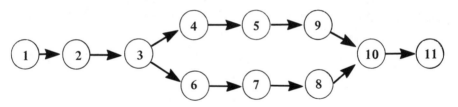

Figure 6.3 suggests that there are two paths to be taken—say, from the time the idea of a new library is formulated until the building is ready for occupancy (O represents events and → represents activities). Times would be assigned for each activity (say, three weeks between events 4 and 5, one week between 6 and 7). As illustrated, either path 1-2-3-4-5-9-10-11 or path 1-2-3-6-7-8-10-11 can be taken. If time is of the essence, the shorter route might be more desirable. Time is the key element in the critical path schedule. Perhaps a bit more detail, illustrating the CPM concept, can demonstrate the critical issue of time. (See fig. 6.4.) The time required to complete the series is the greatest sum of the combined time requirements. Of the four paths illustrated (1-2-5-8; 1-3-5-8; 1-4-6-8; and 1-2-7-8), the longest path, with work going forth on all four paths simultaneously, is 1-2-7-8. This path takes 15 weeks to complete and is the critical path that controls the schedule, more or less, for the whole project.

Fig. 6.4. A four-path PERT diagram can be used to illustrate the critical paths of complex, multipart projects.

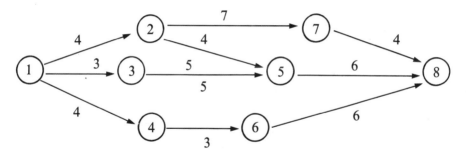

The PERT/CPM technique allows one to analyze a project in depth before it is initiated. This not only gives the decision-maker an idea of the time frame involved but also aids in identifying potential weaknesses. The biggest disadvantage of PERT is its overemphasis on time at the expense of more detailed attention to cost. This disadvantage has led to the development of PERT/COST, which introduces the cost factor into the process. When the system to be studied is complex and when a number of events are involved, it becomes very expensive to establish a cost for each event. PERT is used mainly in industry, but some library systems have explored its value in the planning process, particularly when the process is a complex and lengthy one.

This brief discussion in no way conveys the importance or potential of mathematical or statistical controls, and does not even begin to present all of their variations. Volumes have been written on each of the topics; interested readers should consult the appropriate headings in the library literature for a fuller discussion.

As was mentioned earlier in this chapter, the computer is having great influence on the management of library operations. The effects of electronic data processing on circulation control, acquisitions of library materials, serials control, and other functions are significant. In addition, computerized services, such as online cataloging through OCLC, RLIN, and other networks, and access to bibliographic databases enable libraries to measure more adequately service output and costs. The possibility of using mathematical or statistical control techniques, therefore, becomes greater. Expert systems have been developed to monitor performance and are being widely applied in problem-solving activities of information services.

Budgetary Control

> ℘As a planning document, the budget is a presentation of the library's objectives in terms of specific programs to be carried out within a specified period of time. In that regard, it can be considered a plan set forth in financial terms. As a political document, the budget, when stated and approved in terms of full funding for "visible" programs, is a statement of the importance of library services relative to other . . . services.[26]
>
> —Ann E. Prentice, *Public Library Finances*

"Which comes first, planning or budgeting?" is a question often asked. "Neither," must be the answer, because each depends upon the other and cannot stand alone. Cost predictions must be based upon a realistic picture of what is available to accomplish service objectives, both those in existence and those being planned, which have to be based upon what monies are likely available. It is this concept that pulls together the various aspects of the financial or operational plan and relates it to the services plan. It is a process that must be viewed as a whole, with equally important parts being linked together through the goals and objectives of the organization.

Budgeting relies on predicting what will be needed to function financially in the future. A close relationship does exist between budgeting as a planning technique and as a control technique. Indeed, the budget is perhaps the best and most important control device to measure library programs and their effectiveness. In its simplest form, the budget can be stated in terms of income and expenses. One good definition of budgetary control is that stated by the International Management Institute, which defines it as a method of rationalization whereby estimates covering different periods of time are, by the study of statistical records and analytical research of all kinds, established for all and everything that affects the life of a business concern and that can be expressed in figures. "A budget is not only a financial plan that sets forth cost and . . . goals . . . but also a device for control, coordination, communication, performance evaluation and motivation."[27]

Budgets, when viewed as evaluation tools, as commitments or contracts with funding authorities for services and programs to be rendered, can indicate how successfully the goals and objectives are being addressed. Budgeting is that part of the total planning equation that "assures that resources are obtained" and then "used effectively and efficiently" in accomplishing objectives.[28] Budgeting for libraries and information centers is usually on a yearly cycle, although it is sometimes required to construct operational plans that project two or three years into the future. The budget for any current cycle, or even for future ones, will inevitably be affected by past commitments, established standards of service, existing organizational structure, and current methods of operations. If changes are proposed to those factors, consideration must be given to preparing the organization for change, a topic that is discussed elsewhere in this volume.

There are several different types of budgets. For libraries and information centers, operations budgets are the most important, with a focus on revenue and expenses. However, a second type of budget, capital budget, involved with capital investments such as a new building, should be mentioned. This type of budget is developed to reflect expenditures over the estimated period of a project's development. Other types of budgets, which primarily relate to for-profit organizations, are not included here. Some components, which are typically taught in accounting courses, such as the financial budget, with subsets of cash flow, capital expenditures, and balance sheets, are only mentioned in this discussion.

The budgeting process is not just an inside controlling mechanism. As discussed elsewhere in this volume, libraries and information centers do not operate within a vacuum. External forces, which are called PEST (political, economic, social, and technological factors), must be considered as constant environmental factors that affect the budget and the process of budgeting. In the section of chapter 7 on the *change process*, other factors such as value, organizational culture, commitment, and vision are discussed. They also influence priorities within the monetary allocation arena.

The operating budget is a stated program that reflects the goals and objectives of information service and defines the manager's authority to act. Funds for the organization's operation, depending on the type of library or information system, come from local, state, regional, or national government sources; foundation support or endowments; nongovernmental organization allocations; tuition; fees; gifts; or from a number of other funding sources. Funds may come to the library directly or to the parent organization, with designation for library use. Noninstitutional funding is likely to fluctuate more widely than institutional support, and institutional support can depend on the parent organization's commitment to seeking the various types of funds that are then funneled to the library. It also can depend on the projected fiscal year's budget outlook. Therefore, budgets are not a sure thing. In recent years, all types of libraries and information centers have engaged in fund-raising activities, tapping nontraditional areas of budgetary support for special projects or capital expenditures. Still, the greatest amount of budgetary support comes from the parent institution. Determination of that amount is usually based on expressed needs, which are justified by services offered or projected or, to a lesser extent, on standards that have been established for particular types of libraries or information centers, such as ALA standards for public, school, junior college, college, and university libraries. These needs are often defined on budget forms like that reproduced in appendix E.

The capital budget has less relevance in this discussion. Capital costs are large-expense items to be planned for in projected future budgets. After capital costs are funded, yearly expenses are calculated and transferred to the operations budget as deposits and are then charged against that budget. For instance, approval and installation of a mainframe computer system would be considered a capital expense, requested separately, and budgeted in the capital budget. Expenditure of funds to pay for the mainframe would be reflected, most probably, in a separate account. The two types of budgets discussed here are presented as distinct; however, a combination of budgeting systems is often used.

As a total process, the budgeting concept involves several discrete steps, from the guidelines that are issued by upper management in the larger organization or unit of which the library is a part; to the execution of the budget through the fiscal year's appropriation and expenditures; to the point when an audit is conducted to determine, in retrospect, how the allocated funds were actually spent. In between are the most important parts of the process: preparation of the budget, with justification for amounts and categories being requested, and review and approval by funding authorities. The latter step provides the best opportunity for the library to present its case, to enlighten authorities about not only what is being requested but also, more importantly, why it is being requested. However, this excellent public relations opportunity is a delicate session in which a balance must be achieved between just the right amount of information and information overload. To strike that balance, librarians have used all sorts of public relations gambits.

One great danger in budgeting is the problem of disguised needs. Librarians are often accused of asking for much more than they actually need; indeed, they tend to base current budget justifications on past budgets. In other words, if a library spent a certain amount last year for equipment, that amount becomes this year's floor, even though the same kind and extent of equipment may not be needed this year. In all fairness, this approach is sometimes encouraged by the budgeting technique being employed by institutions. However, this kind of incremental thinking can prompt automatic reductions in library budgets by those who hold the purse strings, whether they are city managers, college or company presidents, or school superintendents.

The budgeting process is a time-delay process. A budget is usually prepared one year—or, in some cases, two or three years—in advance. In the latter instances, it is extremely difficult to project what the needs will be even with strategic planning. In most cases, a library must follow the budget system and budgeting cycle used by the larger system, whether that is the university, college, city government, school district, or corporation. Usually, guidelines for the preparation of the budget come from the school committee, the state or local funding agency, the college or university administration, or the corporation's fiscal officer.

Although many libraries have a separate staff concerned primarily with budgets and the accounting process, most involve a number of employees in the budget-planning process. The supervisors most familiar with a particular unit or aspect of the operation frequently estimate budget requests for programs or units. A coordinating agent—either the director, his or her representative, or a committee—is responsible for pulling the budget requests together and presenting the total budget to the funding authority. Timetables for budget preparation and presentation are essential so that wide support can be gained.

Shrinking monetary allocations have changed the economic picture for not-for-profit organizations in recent years. This has focused greater attention on library budgets and the determination and justification of budget allocations has taken on new meaning and urgency. More and more, as there is greater financial constraint, librarians find themselves spending greater amounts of time in budgeting review, analysis, and presentation.

The budgetary aspect of control becomes even more important as costs rise. With rising costs, librarians are forced to prepare comprehensive reports on the library's financial status so that effective allocation, as well as accurate projections for future funding, can be made. This is the beginning of the formal process that is later magnified to the level of the whole town, district, university, or company. Most often, the librarian is required to make a formal budget presentation, which is substantiated by back-up documentation, such as an index of inflation for library materials or trends in higher education that affect libraries.

Financial problems are steadily compounded by the reality of inflation, reduced budgets, and the information explosion, and libraries are finding themselves forced to seek alternative routes for funding. These include federal and state funding, as well as private foundation and individual citizen funding. A new political role, with extensive public relations requirements, is being forced on libraries. Libraries depend on governmental support as well as private-sector support to extend their budget dollars. Fund-raising, through lobbying and direct solicitation, has become a way of life for enhancing budgets. Libraries have become innovative and assertive in seeking funds outside normal budgeting sources and channels. Special projects and capital budgets are often supported by outside funding sources.

Budgeting Techniques for Libraries and Information Centers

> ❧Adequate financial resources must be available to ensure payment of obligations arising from current operations. Materials must be purchased, wages paid, and interest charges and due dates met. The principal means of controlling the availability and costs of financial resources is budgeting.[29]
>
> —James H. Donnelly et al.,
> *Fundamentals of Management*

Library budgeting techniques include traditional approaches used by many organizations and more innovative techniques that have only recently found their way into libraries. The shift, just as in the planning process, has taken place from viewing budgets in terms of input to looking at output. The more traditional types of budgeting, to be discussed below, include: (1) line-item, in which expenses are divided into categories such as salaries, benefits, materials, equipment, etc.; (2) lump-sum, or a total amount for the whole unit under consideration; and (3) incremental budgets, in which percentage increases are related to the previous year's budget. An interim view of budgets might represent such techniques as performance budgeting, in which the attitude is that performance measures could be instituted to support justifying input costs as a factor of output measures. Planning Programming Budgeting System (PPBS, see page 372), MBO (discussed in chapter 2), and zero-based budgeting (ZBB, see page 374) are budgeting approaches that look at programs, objectives, and benchmark costs respectively. As newer techniques or approaches are considered, costs of converting to them must be considered. The advantages of a different approach must be clear before one decides to switch from one to another.

Line-Item Budgets

Probably the most common type of budget divides objects of expenditure into broad input classes or categories, such as salaries and wages, materials and supplies, equipment, capital expenditures, and miscellaneous, with further subdivisions within these categories. Its primary disadvantage is that items within these categories can be designated to such a degree that it becomes difficult, if not impossible, to shift them; thus, this system can be inflexible. For example, within the broad category of materials and supplies, it may become desirable to add subscription money for new periodicals after the budget has been set. One might wish to accomplish this by transferring money from equipment, because it has been determined that the library can do without an additional personal computer. However, budgeting authorities usually frown upon this kind of transfer. If it is not completely discouraged, it is often made very difficult to accomplish because of the paperwork and red tape involved. Line-item budgeting is sometimes called incremental budgeting, because the object is usually to add on to existing figures, assuming that all currently existing programs are good and necessary. It usually requires no evaluation of services and no projection of future accomplishments.

There are several advantages to the line-item approach. For one thing, line item budgets are easy to prepare. Most are done by projecting current expenditures to the next year, taking cost increases into account. This type of budget is easy to understand and to justify because it can be shown that the allocated funds were spent in the areas for which they were budgeted. The funding authority can easily understand a request to add a new position or to increase the supplies budget by 10 percent because that is the average amount that postage, telephone charges, and other supplies rose last year. The greatest disadvantage to the line-item approach is that there is almost no relationship at all between the budget request and the objectives of the organization. Using the line-item approach simply projects the past and present into the future. An example of a line-item budget is given in table 6.1 on page 367. In recent years, there has been a sharp rise in what is categorized as other (that is, equipment, contracts, supplies, and the like) because of the costs of implementing technological innovations, from the purchase of computer equipment to telecommunications and online database searching charges.

A more primitive variation on the traditional line-item approach is the lump-sum approach. In this form of budgeting, a certain dollar amount is allocated to the library, and it becomes the responsibility of the library to decide how that sum is broken into categories that can be identified. These categories are usually the same ones mentioned under line-item budgeting: sala- ries and wages, materials and supplies, equipment, capital expenditures, and miscellaneous, or overhead. This might seem more flexible than line-item budgeting, but it still does not relate the objectives to services. Libraries using this technique are forced to develop programs within the dollar figure allocated, instead of the other way around.

However, it was concern for the relevance of this sort of approach that led to the development of some of the following budgeting principles, which focus instead on output.

Formula Budgets

Formula budgeting uses predetermined standards for allocation of monetary resources. This approach has been adopted by several large library systems, particularly academic libraries, by state library agencies for appropriating state funds. The reason is that, after the criteria for budget requests have been established, they can be applied across the board to all units within the library system. The popularity of a formula budget over a program-based budget is:

1. A formula budget is mechanical and easy to prepare.

2. Because of the formula budget's application to all institutions in the political jurisdiction, there appears to be justification for monies requested.

3. Governing bodies have a sense of equity, because each institution in the system is measured against the same criteria.

4. Fewer budgeting and planning skills are required to prepare and administer a formal budget.[30]

Additional advantages of formula budgets, which have received acceptance in more than half of all statewide systems of higher education, are that they:

1. facilitate inter-institutional comparison,

2. facilitate comparisons from year to year,

3. reduce paperwork in the budgeting process,

Table 6.1—The Line-Item Budget
(*Note*: This budget, with expenditures assigned to broad categories, is easy to prepare.)

BUDGET REQUEST FORM I

SUMMARY

Department or Program: LIBRARY

Department No.: 02876

For Fiscal Year: 1996-1997

Control Number	Expenditures	Actual Prior Year 1994-95	Budget Current Year 1995-96	Budget Request 1996-97
	SALARIES			
100	Full-time emp.	730,000	784,750	809,500
101	Part-time emp.	27,050	27,860	29,200
102	Hourly wages	34,000	35,360	40,000
	STAFF BENEFITS			
103	Social Security	54,750	58,855	60,700
104	Retirement Acct.	65,700	70,625	72,850
105	Unemployment Comp.	4,675	5,025	5,200
106	Worker's Comp.	4,160	4,475	4,600
107	Life Insurance	3,505	3,765	3,900
108	Health Insurance	39,600	42,250	49,175
109	Accident Ins.	400	470	485
110	Disability Ins.	5,250	5,600	6,300
	MATERIALS			
120	Books	120,000	127,200	137,375
121	Serials	180,000	165,500	180,400
122	Binding	36,000	37,800	40,450
123	Media	86,500	92,300	97,650
124	Inst. materials	17,000	17,850	18,750
	OTHER			
150	Utilities	39,000	40,150	42,150
151	Supplies	25,500	26,500	27,825
152	Telephone	22,000	22,880	23,950
153	Travel	19,200	19,975	20,975
154	Postage	9,500	9,975	10,475
155	Insurance	8,000	8,450	8,900
156	Equipment	23,700	36,500	38,300
157	Vehicle cost	17,600	18,850	19,800
158	Service contracts	15,800	16,600	17,450
159	Consultants	3,700	3,850	3,850
	TOTAL	1,592,590	1,683,415	1,770,210

4. eliminate extraneous details,

5. provide a systematic, objective allocation technique, and

6. connote mathematical infallibility.[31]

The formulae, which are usually expressed in terms of a percentage of the total institutional cost, focus on input, rather than activities, and are, therefore, more applicable to specific aspects of library operations, for instance, collection development. They determine what the library will get, not how the library will spend it. In that sense, formula budget allocations may be thought of as a combination lump sum and formula approach. For instance, the budget-related standard of the "Standards for College Libraries" states,

> The degree to which the college is able to fund the library in accord with institutional objectives is reflected in the relationship of the library appropriation to the total educational and general budget of the college. It is recommended that library budgets, exclusive of capital costs and the cost of physical maintenance, not fall below six percent of the college's total educational and general expenditures if it is to sustain the range of library programs required by the institution and meet appropriate institutional objectives. This percentage should be greater if the library is attempting to overcome past deficiencies, or to meet the needs of new academic programs.[32]

Other formulae have applied a fixed dollar figure per full-time equivalent student and faculty or have attached collection and staff figures to programs offered.

Formula budgeting in libraries probably got its impetus from the Clapp-Jordan formula, which provided a theoretical model for measuring the adequacy of library resources.[33] Other formulae have been developed since then—most notably the Michigan system formula, the California University formula, and the Washington State formula.[34] The one that continues to have wide appeal for academic libraries is the "Standards for College Libraries," budget standards, which relates three formulae: holdings (formula A), staff (formula B), and facilities (formula C).[35] Formula A serves as a good illustration of the criteria used (see table 6.2).

Budget formulae vary in degree of sophistication. One disadvantage to formula budgeting is that some functions cannot be related to those formulae and must receive separate justification. Perhaps the biggest fallacy in such an approach is that it assumes a relationship between the quantity being expressed and the quality of service.

Table 6.2—"Standards for College Libraries," Formula A—Holdings
Reprinted with permission of the American Library Association, excerpt taken
from "Standards for College Libraries 1986" prepared by the College Library
Standards Committee, which appeared in *College & Research Libraries News*,
March 1986, vol. 47, no. 3, copyright © 1986 by ALA.

FORMULA A—

1.	Basic collection	85,000 vols.
2.	Allowance per FTE faculty member	100 vols.
3.	Allowance per FTE student	15 vols.
4.	Allowance per undergraduate major or minor field	350 vols.
5.	Allowance per master's field, when no higher degree is offered in the field	6,000 vols.
6.	Allowance per master's field, when a higher degree is offered in the field	3,000 vols.
7.	Allowance per 6th-year specialist degree field	6,000 vols.
8.	Allowance per doctoral field	25,000 vols.

A "volume" is defined as a physical unit of a work which has
been printed or otherwise reproduced, typewritten, or handwritten,
contained in one binding or portfolio, hardbound or paperbound,
which has been catalogued, classified, and/or otherwise prepared
for use. Microform holdings should be converted to volume-
equivalents, whether by actual count or by an averaging formula
which considers each reel of microfilm, or five pieces of any other
microform, as one volume-equivalent.

Program Budgeting

Program budgeting is not new; it was introduced by U.S. President
Lyndon Johnson over thirty years ago and since then, has been used around
the world. It is, however, a relatively new concept in budgeting for libraries
and information services programs. The process is concerned with the organization's activities, as opposed to individual items or expenditures, which were
the concern of the line-item and formula-based approaches. In that regard it
is similar to PPBS but is more flexible. Its approach maintains that it is possible to relate the programs to accomplishment of time/action objectives or
activities that are stated in output terms in the strategic planning process.
In a way, it can be said that program budgeting developed along with strategic planning, because that planning process is based upon establishing

costs of individual programs, which requires accounting as well as budgeting. A program budget emphasizes the library's activities, so that dollars can be assigned to programs or services provided. For example, if a public library system provides bookmobile service for the community, the cost of that service (staffing, materials, and overhead) is calculated. In this way, one can see exactly what the bookmobile service costs. Based on the total program, one can decide whether to continue, modify, or delete the service. "Program budget is the most effective . . . method of explaining needs to funding bodies," but it is relatively little used in libraries at this point.[36] Focus is on alternatives. For instance, other than simply withholding funds from the next lower-ranked services in a priority list, other alternatives can be explored, including trying to reduce the cost of providing a certain level of services for those already chosen, thereby allowing the next listed priority to be funded. Another alternative might be to increase charges, say for value-added services to individuals and organizations, thereby adding to the pool of nondirect sources of funds, which might in turn support the next level on the priority list. An example of a program budget is given in table 6.3.

A technique similar to program budgeting is performance budgeting, which bases expenditures on the performance of activities and emphasizes efficiency of operations. This approach requires the careful accumulation of quantitative data over a period of time. Techniques of cost-benefit analysis are required to measure the performance and establish norms. Performance budgeting has been criticized, because the economy aspect overshadows the service aspect. This approach is sometimes called function budgeting, because costs are presented in terms of work to be accomplished. A good example of this is processing materials—from submission of an order until the time that the volume is on the shelf and the cards are in the catalog. All activities involved (verifying the author, title, and so forth; ordering, receiving, cataloging, and classifying; providing book pockets, call number, and catalog cards; and filing cards in the catalog and placing the volume on the shelf) can be analyzed as to average time for the activity and average cost per item. Therefore, careful cost and work measurements can be applied to each activity. Fixed costs of building maintenance, heating, lights, equipment, and other items that are variable but are directly related to the work being done must also be added to the final cost. Performance budgeting measures quantity rather than quality of service. As with any detailed budgeting activity of this sort, the costly time and efforts may overshadow benefits of awareness and participation involved. Two techniques, PPBS and ZBB, are spin-offs of program budgeting.

Table 6.3—Program Budget Sheet

Organization: COUNTY LIBRARY
Program: BOOKMOBILE SERVICE
Objective: This service is offered to county residents who reside more than three miles from a public library. Specific services offered include providing basic reference collection of encyclopedias, handbooks, and dictionaries and a rotating collection of circulating materials on a variety of subjects for all levels of readers. Makes two stops per day, covers seven miles, five days per week.

Costs:

Personnel Service

Librarian	$28,500
Driver	20,000
Stocker (to load, unload truck, 4 hrs. per week @ $6.00 x 52 weeks)	1, 248
Benefits	9,700
SUBTOTAL	$59,448 (1)

Materials

Books (2,000 volume collection x $36 average + $10.20 processing costs	$72,000
Periodicals (15 subscriptions @ $40 each)	600
Repairs, binding, etc.	175
SUBTOTAL	$72,775 (2)

Other

Vehicle depreciation	$1,600
Maintenance, gasoline (30 mi. per week x 52 weeks x 26¢ per mile)	405
Insurance	600
SUBTOTAL	$2,605 (3)

TOTAL (Subtotals 1 + 2 + 3)	$134,828

Planning Programming Budgeting System (PPBS)

Planning Programming Budgeting System (PPBS) was developed by Rand Corporation and introduced to the Department of Defense by Robert McNamara in 1961. President Lyndon Johnson directed all principal government agencies to implement it, and, by 1965 it was being used by all of these agencies. Many complex organizations, of which libraries are a part, are now using PPBS or some form of it. These include state and local governments, college and university systems, and industry. Like management by objectives (MBO), which has lost its popularity in recent years, PPBS is no longer as widely used as it once was.

The PPBS approach combines the best of both program budgeting and performance budgeting. The emphasis is on planning. Like MBO and program budgeting, it begins with the establishment of goals and objectives, but the controlling aspect of measurement, which is paramount in performance budgeting, is also part of PPBS. It emphasizes the cost of accomplishing goals (programs) set by the library, instead of stressing objects, which the more traditional budgets highlight. This approach forces one to think of the budget as a tool to allocate resources rather than to control operations. The steps important in PPBS are:

1. Identifying the objectives of the library.

2. Presenting alternative ways to achieve those objectives—with cost-benefit ratios presented for each.

3. Identifying the activities that are necessary for each program.

4. Evaluating the result so that corrective actions can be taken.

This approach reemphasizes the desired steps in the control process. Figure 6.5 is an example of the preliminary development of a PPBS approach for a particular library.

In essence, PPBS is a scientific approach to budgeting that improves the decision-making process, which calls for systematic analysis of alternative ways of meeting objectives. The crux of PPBS is the selection of appropriate criteria for evaluating each alternative against relevant objectives; it combines the functions of planning (identifying objectives), translating that to a program (staff and materials), and, finally, stating those requirements in budgetary terms (financing). Headings for a PPBS summary sheet are shown in figure 6.6.

Fig. 6.5. Library service measurement framework (LSMF). Model developed by Dr. Robert DeNoble on the basis of work done at Peat, Marwick, Mitchell & Co., Boston. Reproduced with permission.

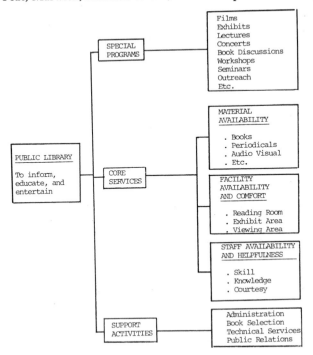

Fig. 6.6. Headings for a PPBS summary sheet are self-explanatory.

County of:	Program Summary
Operating Budget: (Year)	
Program: (Title of program)	
Goal: (Brief operational goal)	
Description: (Brief description of program)	

The PPBS approach allows one to enumerate programs and assign costs to those programs. The figures that are the outcome of PPBS are "extremely useful in determining future priorities and direction, in requesting funds, and in justifying the value of libraries and their services."[37] It also allows funding agencies to place programs into perspective and to evaluate the effects of cutting monies from or adding monies to the budget. As one can imagine, the required detailed examination of every aspect of the operation is not only time-consuming but cumbersome as well. It requires goals, objectives, and activities to be stated in measurable terms and then mandates the follow-up activity of measuring the results. Despite these drawbacks, some modification of the intent of this approach is being used in some libraries today.

A good example of a modified PPBS approach is the Vigo County (Indiana) Public Library summary of activities, which indicates eight program categories (see table 6.4).

Zero-Based Budgeting

> &ZBB focuses its activities on answering two basic questions: a) are the current activities efficient and effective? and b) should current activities be eliminated or reduced to fund higher-priority new programs or to reduce the current budget?[38]
>
> —P. A. Phyrr,
> "The Zero-Base Approach to
> Government Budgeting"

One newer technique of budgeting, which has been used primarily in industry and government but also in different types of libraries and information centers, although in a very limited number of cases, is zero-based budgeting (ZBB). The current international interest began to develop in the late 1960s and early 1970s, starting with the Texas Instruments Company. The method was further popularized by U.S. President Jimmy Carter when he was governor of Georgia. However, the U.S. Department of Agriculture used a form of it as early as 1962.

Under conventional budgeting systems, last year's budget is used as a baseline and is adjusted to reflect current situations. Justification is given for increases (i.e., the telecommunications charges will be higher). With ZBB, each unit of the budget must be justified and placed in a hierarchy. Activities are broken into packages and funds are allocated in their package hierarchy until funds are no longer available, the cutoff point.

Table 6.4—Community Use of a Public Library
Reprinted with permission of the American Library Association from "Toward PPBS in the Public Library," Edward N. Howard, *American Libraries,* April 1971, p. 391, copyright © 1971 by the American Library Association.

Community Use of the Vigo County Public Library for the Six Months' Period January to June 1969				
Input Cost	Service Category	Program Objective	Output Totals	Cost per Output
$92,866	SELF SERVICE	Provide facilities, library materials and equipment.	203,587 persons	$ .45
$77,524	LENDING SERVICE	Lend library materials for home and office use.	324,481 items	$ .24
$42,398	INDIVIDUAL SERVICE	Furnish information, reader advisory, and reference assistance.	40,301 persons	$ 1.05
$ 7,878	ALERTING SERVICE	Promote awareness of the library and use of its resources.	908 productions	$ 8.67
$ 5,202	OUTREACH SERVICE	Provide library materials for the physically or environmentally handicapped.	10 stations	$520.20
$14,288	CONTROL SERVICE	Maintain control of materials through registration of patrons and overdue reminders to borrowers.	12,173 persons	$ 1.17
$20,106	GROUP SERVICE	Provide specialized services to groups, agencies, and organizations.	459 groups	$ 43.80
$ 3,720	RESEARCH SERVICE	Perform research service for public officials, ministers, business and industry managers, labor and other civic leaders.	150 researchers	$ 24.80

The ZBB approach is not a procedure, but rather an approach that requires organizations to review and evaluate each of their service programs and activities on the basis of both output measures as well as costs. Important steps can be cited in ZBB as identifying decision packages or units, ranking of those packages, and preparing operating budgets that reflect those units. In identification of decision packages, the package identified should be the lowest unit for which budget can be prepared. It requires a description of each activity within that management unit. This process of description requires the identification of goals and objectives, a statement of alternatives, the reason for the activity, consequences of not introducing the package, detailed measurement of performance, and the costs of the activity. Of course, the size and complexity of the organization will determine the number of units identified.

A unit may be described along functional lines (i.e., circulation), by smaller units in larger organizations (i.e., reserve function of circulation), or as a special program of the organization (i.e., outreach services to underserved populations). Care must be exercised so that decision units are large enough to reflect major portions of a person's time; smaller distribution would probably be meaningless because it might eliminate only a small fraction of a full-time salary, for instance. After a decision unit is identified, a series of decision packages is identified, each including goals and objectives, and so forth. The process of specifically identifying decision packages focuses on the "best way" of doing things, either through cost savings or efficiency of service. Of course, after alternatives have been suggested, quantitative measures must be established to monitor output, which are usually expressed in financial terms. With all the decision packages developed, using the objectives as guides, they are ranked in priority order and are presented for approval or rejection, the decision being based on position in the hierarchy and affordability.

Ranking "decision packages," or setting priorities within each unit of the organization, forces decisions about the most important activities within that unit of the organization. The technique allocates limited resources by forcing decision-makers to concentrate on identifying the most important programs and projects to be funded. Each unit of the organization conducts the same process. After each unit identifies its priorities, the priorities of all units are amalgamated into one pool, and the process is repeated in light of the decision packages' importance to the total organization. Each decision package relates, to some extent, to others, and this interrelationship must be considered in ranking them, because related decision packages share costs of personnel and resources. For example, ready reference is dependent upon an up-to-date, fully processed reference collection, which depends upon the selection, acquisition, and processing of materials— involving staff and materials budgets in those units. At some level in the hierarchy of priorities is a cutoff level and decision packages that fall below it are not funded. Because setting priorities at the organization level involves every unit within the organization, clear guidelines for ranking must be established. The process of priority formulation helps the manager to rank and, in some cases, delete activities because of obsolescence, inefficiency, or change of policy or objectives.[39]

Basically, ZBB is not concerned with what happened previously but with what is required in the future. In this approach and in its development, ZBB is very similar to PPBS; it requires careful analysis of activities that should take place in the library and requires justification for each unit of work identified. By forcing an organization to identify areas of greater and lesser importance, ZBB emphasizes planning and fosters an understanding, by all units, of the total organization. It helps maintain vitality in the organization by constantly assessing and questioning programs.[40] It forces each unit manager and the unit workers to identify priorities within their unit of the organization. Identifying priorities and stating them in terms of cost forces the unit to answer: "Is it really worth it?" and "Are there alternatives to achieving this objective?" The ZBB approach requires that justification for each program start at point "zero," and it requires that this be done each year. Of course, after a decision unit has been identified, that particular unit does not need to be reidentified each year; it needs to be further described only if changes occur, although it still must be considered in the list of priorities and costs must be recalculated.

The ZBB process should provide an indication of the real cost of various library activities, an estimate of the minimum cost level necessary to provide each service, a ranking of library functions to facilitate support, a discovery of unnecessary duplication of effort, and a framework for the establishment of criteria for continuous evaluation of performance.

It is assumed in the ZBB model that the sum of those units receiving top priority status is less than the current budgeted amount and that a cutoff will occur at some point. This attitude allows for a reduced level at which activities can be carried out to meet the essential objectives of the organization. Table 6.5, page 381, and table 6.6, page 382, illustrate, in an abbreviated way, the process involved in establishing a decision-package statement and how that package might fit into the priorities of the organization. This approach requires effective communication and efficient training of personnel involved in the approach.

Developing Techniques for Allocating Resources

Entrepreneurial Budgeting

Like several other approaches to budgeting in times of change, this is a recently developed attitude toward budgeting that is being experimented with in both the public and private sectors. It differs from traditional techniques in that the ultimate controlling authority decides, beforehand, what the budget base will be, for example, not more than last year's budget, plus 5 percent. This may appear, initially, to be similar to an incremental budget, but in fact it is quite different. Simply stated, it allocates a pool of money to the unit or organization that is then responsible for managing it within the program priorities identified. If there are funds remaining at the end of the year, they are rolled forward, thus avoiding the usual rush at the end of a fiscal year when the "use it or lose it" mentality takes over. This "profit sharing" approach improves morale and supposedly management.[41] It decentralizes decision making with incentives to be more innovative.

Allocation Decision Accountability Performance (ADAP)

This experimental and innovative technique is mentioned only briefly here, because there is little experience with its use in libraries and information service agencies. A budgetary hybrid, it combines aspects of both PPBS and ZBB. It has received awards worldwide and is being adapted by a number of local government agencies. The key aspect is that three budgets must be submitted: the first requesting an increase, the second recognizing a modest decrease, and the third presenting a budget below which the organization cannot function. Administrators are asked to identify whole programs that could be eliminated if necessary. Budgeting authorities can compare the current year's budget with preceding years, and, if the same programs are identified as expendable with some frequency, they become candidates for elimination. Despite this pitfall, it is a better way to budget, because it allows the administrator to eliminate programs that have relatively poor performance.[42]

Integrated Planning and Control System (IPCS)

Recently, there have been attempts to bring together the planning and control phases of operations into one system, called Integrated Planning and Control System (IPCS). However, this approach is more useful in for-profit institutions and is only mentioned here because it is so new. The IPCS does suggest that budgetary control cannot be thought of in isolation.

Best, Optimistic, and Pessimistic (BOP)

Rolling budgets, variable budgets, contingency budgets, and flexible budgets are based on varying revenue projections, again applying primarily to for-profit organizations. Sometimes the set of assumptions in this approach are called Best, Optimistic, and Pessimistic (BOP) of assumptions: *Best* assumes normal operating conditions; *optimistic* assumes there will be problems, but the problems can be surmounted; and *pessimistic* assumes "if everything goes wrong."[43] By participating in such exercises management becomes aware of the broad range of possibilities, in both possibilities and coping strategies, and in these economic times, that is not a useless exercise.

Responsibility Center Budgeting

Rising costs and tightening budgets have forced greater accountability among institutions of higher education. This system of budgeting is the approach of "each tub on its own bottom" and is being implemented in several large universities, having found its way into higher education through the corporate sector. It forces institutions to identify their units that are capable of self-support, including all academic units with tuition- and fee-paying students, faculty capable of bringing in contracts and grants, and other central administrative units as well as academic support units, including libraries and information centers. Direct institutional support is augmented by other sources of funding—appropriations from governments, contracts, endowments, and contributions. Basically, this approach forces decision making down into all of those units where costs are directly related to academic priorities. Heated debates revolve around how the central administration allocates funds to units. For example, "how charges for space, libraries, and other services [will] be allocated; and how the hardware and software needed to run the new information systems [will] be configured."[44] It requires that the administration recognize and support units that exist for the "Public good—such as the physical plant, technology, and the library [and that they] must receive funding that is adequate, but at taxation levels that the academic units can support financially and intellectually without seriously attenuating RCM's [Responsibility Center Management] underlying incentives."[45]

Bracket Budgeting

Finally, bracket budgeting is an analytical procedure that complements conventional budgeting techniques. It is a combination of modeling and simulation in which the computer performs an integral role. The computer must be programmed to perform various calculations, which requires considerable computer expertise and probably is much too complex to be beneficial in most library situations. It is most useful in for-profit organizations, where uncertainty can wreak havoc on the profit.

Software Applications

> ⚘Information technology turns the budget into a meaningful set of instructions that optimize . . . performance under changing conditions.[46]
>
> —W. J. Burns Jr. and F. W. McFarlan,
> "Information Technology Puts Power
> in Control Systems"

Many libraries use computers in preparing budgets. Indeed, budgetary control was one of the first functions to make use of the computer in libraries. Several financial modeling, budget, financial planning, and data manipulation software packages are applicable to library budgeting. These have been developed both commercially and in-house for specific organizations.

They are available for purchase or license or, sometimes, are in the public domain. Budgeting makes use of software called an electronic spreadsheet, and popular spreadsheets, including Lotus 1-2-3, SuperCalc, MultiPlan, VisiCalc, Perfect-Calc, Context MBA, Symphony, Excel, .dbf, SAS, ORacle, ClarisWorks, SQL Server, SPSS for Windows, and Framework, have become powerful decision tools in the controlling process for libraries. As the name implies, a spreadsheet is an electronic version of the columnar worksheet used for years.[47] Because spreadsheets make number crunching easy, libraries can adjust or revise budgets and projections without expending great amounts in terms of personnel and time. Some libraries even use computer modeling and forecasting to prepare financial plans. However, software tools are only one part of the budgeting process—the mechanical part. Thought and imagination are also needed to successfully prepare and defend a budget.

Accounting and Reporting

The final aspect of budgeting to be mentioned here is keeping accurate records of what has been disbursed, what has been encumbered, and what remains. Before the budget has been approved by the proper authority, a mechanism for keeping track of both expenditures and encumbrances must be in place. This must record not only what has been spent but also must set aside funds for items ordered but not yet received, so that funds will be reserved and available for their payment when they do arrive. Established account categories and numbers play a vital role in this process to identify such items as salaries, materials acquired or ordered, equipment installed, etc. Periodic statements of expenditures and an audit of the expenses at the end of the year provide important feedback to the budgetary process. An accounting process allows for efficient and effective adjustments to the process, when and where they are needed. The process has been greatly enhanced by the use of electronic spreadsheets and other software packages available for financial planning on microcomputers and other equipment. These systems have helped the auditing process, reduced the need for double bookkeeping records, and facilitated reporting by allowing projections of cost activities. Reporting is usually accomplished through monthly records prepared by the accounting office, either as a part of the library or as a part of the larger organization, such as the city government. Monthly statements can act as benchmarks to inform the library staff of how they are progressing, financially, toward the library's objectives and, at the same time, alert them to potential problem areas (i.e., overexpenditures). This monthly summary statement, or balance sheet, is typical in most organizations. Cost accounting was probably the first application of computer databases for operations of library and information services.

Table 6.5—Form for Decision Package Statement

DECISION PACKAGE STATEMENT	Prepared by: Ralph Lorenzo Date: 11 / 22 / 1986
Program Name: Children's Division	**Priority Rank:** 1
Department: Public Services Department Hilsdale Public Library	**Level:** 1 of 3

Statement of Purpose (Goals and Objectives—what is to be accomplished):
Provide library services to children (preschool to teen-aged years).
Work in conjunction with town's school department to offer comprehensive services to children of the town.

Description of Activity: 1) Direct summer reading program for children of the town; 2) Offer story hour and puppet shows for preschool through second grade; 3) Select children's materials for the public library collection; 4) Interpret questions of informational, educational, and recreational nature; 5) Coordinate library services for children in the community.

Benefits Desired Results: Enable children to explore, with guidance, good literature; aid in providing informational services to school children both in their school work and in their quest for knowledge, encourage children to explore areas of interest on their own.

Related Activities: School library service in the town's elementary schools.

Alternatives, Other Options (to achieve same or partial results):
1) Let schools assume full responsibility
2) Public Services (general) assume responsibility for limited services

Consequences (If activity is not approved/is eliminated):
Service to children would be seriously curtailed, thereby abrogating one of the original charges from the town to the library.

Costs/Resources Required:	**Prior Period**	**Budgeting Period**
Personnel:		
Professional (3/4)	13,200	14,900
Paraprofessional (1/2)	6,650	7,100
Hourly wages (10 per week @ $3.65)	1,898	1,898
Secretarial (1/4)	3,750	4,010
Operations:		
Supplies	800	880
Equipment	300	450
Materials	8,200	9,600
Travel	—	350
Other	150	190
TOTAL	$34,948	$39,378

Approved by: Myrna Avrey	Title: Library Director	Date: 12/3/86

Table 6.6—A Ranking System Form That Indicates the Cutoff Point for Funding

FISCAL YEAR: 1987-88

Level of Effort	Rank within System	Package Name	Current Year Commitment	Planned Addition/Deletion to Current Commitment	Projected Addition to Commitments	Cumulative Expenses
1	1	Administrative Services	$ 43,040	$ 3,300		$ 46,340
1	2	Public Services (general)	67,042	4,800		71,842
1	3	Technical Services	95,972	12,350		108,322
1	4	Children's Division	34,948	4,430		39,378
2	5	Branch Library (North)		103,500		103,500*
2	6	Young Adult Division			$ 25,370	25,370
2	7	Bookmobile Service			29,100	29,100
2	8	Branch Library (East)			92,600	92,600
2	9	Music & Art Division			15,600	15,600
TOTAL			$241,002	$128,380	$162,670	$532,052

Organization: Town of Hilsdale
Department: Hilsdale Public Library
Prepared by: Myrna Avrey
Date: 12/19/86

*Note: Example indicates that, in addition to current unit commitments with increases, the town has agreed to fund second priority level unit which is ranked number 5 in the priorities of the library. This means that the budget for the fiscal year 1987-88 will be $369,382, an increase of $128,380. (It should be remembered that this example is given to show a priority system and not to indicate "next year" potential funding of all priorities. One can see that the extent of priorities listed in this example and the costs involved are certainly long-range. For this reason individual managers would be discouraged from preparing such "ideal" priority lists using the ZBB model because the time involved in establishing such an extensive list would be great.)

Because accounting is an independent function, many large libraries employ accountants in staff positions; their primary responsibility is to report facts as they exist or have existed. Such accountants are not normally responsible for making decisions that affect the operations of the library. However, they are most helpful in collecting relevant cost data for anticipated decisions and in making cost studies that might be keys to decision making.

> ℚ The role of the accounting system in any organization is to assist management in performing its duties and achieving the organization's goals. In this capacity accounting systems and accounting reports are not ends in themselves. Rather, they are tools to assist managers in performing their function.[48]
>
> —Jacob Birnberg,
> "Accounting Information for Operating Decisions"

Along with accounting goes the important element of reporting— reporting to the funding authority, reporting to the staff, and reporting to the public, however that might be defined. Reporting procedures can take a variety of forms: formal written reports, with detailed statistical documentation, or informal reports, such as memos, staff meetings, board meetings, or newspaper articles. In reporting, the librarian's public-relations responsibility becomes most evident. Only by conscientiously selling the library and its services can the librarian hope to maintain a level of activity and funding. The purpose is to be so convincing that support for library activities will increase or, at minimum, remain the same. Public relations for librarians is an art through which information and persuasion solicit public support for the causes that are set forth in the goals of the library. Public relations is an integral part of the goals and objectives and the budgeting procedure in a library. This is the library's primary means of gaining and holding the support necessary to develop programs. It is also a way of expanding that support through new financial initiatives.

Conclusion

Controlling means establishing mechanisms to ensure accountability in relation to an organization's mission. Although the monetary aspect is the most obvious example of control, it is only one part of the overall pattern to remain reliable and realistic in a fluid environment of fiscal and technological change.

Notes

1.   Rosabeth Moss Kanter, *The Change Masters: Innovation for Productivity in the American Corporation* (New York: Simon & Schuster, 1983), 50.

2.   Peter F. Drucker, "Controls, Control and Management," in *Managerial Controls: New Directions in Basic Research*, ed. C. P. Bonini, R. K. Jaedicke, and H. M. Wanger (New York: McGraw-Hill, 1964), 286.

3.   Henri Fayol, *Industrial and General Administration* (Geneva: International Management Institute, 1929), 77.

4.   George Schreyogg and Horst Steinman, "Strategic Control: A New Perspective," *Academy of Management Review* 12 (January 1987): 91.

5.   Morris Hamburg et al., *Library Planning and Decision-Making Systems* (Cambridge, MA: MIT Press, 1974), 38-39.

6.   For example, "Guidelines for Two-Year College Learning Resources Programs," *College & Research Libraries News* 33, no. 7 (December 1972): 305-15.

7.   For example, "Standards for College Libraries, 1985," *College & Research Libraries News* 46, no. 5 (May 1985): 241-52.

8.   McNamara Fallacy quoted in *The Age of Paradox* by Charles Handy (Boston, MA: Harvard Business School Press, 1994), 221.

9.   Mary Jo Lynch, ed., *Library Data Collection Handbook* (Chicago: American Library Association, 1981).

10.   Walter Jack Duncan, *Essentials of Management*, 2d ed. (Hinsdale, IL: Dryden Press, 1978), 408.

11.   Jose-Marie Griffiths and Donald W. King, *A Manual on the Evaluation of Information Centers and Services* (New York: American Institute of Aeronautics and Astronautics, 1991), 7.

12.   Rekha Agarwala-Rogers and Janet K. Alexander, "Evaluation of Organizational Attitudes," in *Management Principles for Nonprofit Agencies and Organizations*, ed. Gerald Zaltman (New York: AMACOM, 1979), 539.

13.   Alan Walter Steiss, *Strategic Management and Organizational Decision-Making* (Lexington, MA: Lexington Books, 1985), 117.

14.   A. R. Prest and R. Turvey, "Cost Benefit Analysis: A Survey," *The Economic Journal* 85 (March 1965): 583.

15.   F. Wilfred Lancaster, "The Evaluation of Library and Information Services," in *Evaluation and Scientific Management of Libraries and Information Centers*, ed. F. W. Lancaster and C. W. Cleverdon (Leyden, The Netherlands: Noordhoff, 1977), 4.

16.   Bruce H. DeWoolfson Jr., "Public Sector MBO and PPBS: Cross-Fertilization in Management Styles," *Public Administration Review* 36 (July-August 1975): 387.

17.   Walter J. Kennevan, "Management Information Systems," in *Management of Information Handling Systems*, ed. P. W. Howerton (Rosell Park, NJ: Hayden, 1974), 78.

18. M. Elton and Brian Vicker, "The Scope of Operational Research in the Library and Information Field," *ASLIB Proceedings* 25, no. 8 (1973): 319.

19. "Guidelines for the Practice of Operations Research," *Operations Research* 19 (September 1971): 1138.

20. Ferdinand F. Leimkuhler, "Operations Research and Systems Analysis," in *Evaluation and Scientific Management of Libraries and Information Centers*, ed. F. W. Lancaster and C. W. Cleverdon, 131.

21. Herbert A. Simon, *The New Science of Management Decision*, rev. ed. (Englewood Cliffs, NJ: Prentice-Hall, 1977), 17.

22. A. Graham Mackenzie and Michael K. Buckland, "Operations Research," in *British Librarianship and Information Science*, 1966-70 ed. H. A. Whatley (London: Library Association, 1972), 24.

23. Ching-chih Chen, *Applications of Operations Research Models to Libraries* (Cambridge, MA: MIT Press, 1976), 3.

24. Richard I. Levin and Charles A. Kirkpatrick, *Quantitative Approaches to Management*, 2d ed. (New York: McGraw-Hill, 1971), 161.

25. Sang M. Lee and L. J. Moore, *Introduction to Decision Science* (New York: Petrocelli-Charter, 1975), 90.

26. Ann E. Prentice, *Public Library Finances* (Chicago: American Library Association, 1977), 1.

27. Izzettin Kennis, "Effects of Budgetary Goal Characteristics on Managerial Attitudes and Performance," *The Accounting Review* 54, no. 4 (October 1979): 707.

28. Robert N. Anthony and Regina E. Herzlinger, *Management Control in Non-Profit Organizations* (Homewood, IL: Business One-Irwin, 1975), 17.

29. James H. Donnelly et al., *Fundamentals of Management* (Homewood, IL: Business One-Irwin, 1992), 272.

30. Kenneth R. Allen, *Current and Emerging Budgeting Techniques in Academic Libraries*, ED 071 726 (Washington, DC: Office of Education, Department of Health, Education and Welfare, 1972), 18.

31. Gary M. Shirk, "Allocation Formulas for Budgeting Library Materials: Science or Procedure?" *Collection Management* 6, no. 3-4 (Fall-Winter 1984): 37-38.

32. "Standards for College Libraries, 1985," 251.

33. Verner W. Clapp and Robert J. Jordan, "Quantitative Criteria for Adequacy of Academic Library Collections," *College & Research Libraries* 26 (September 1965): 371-80.

34. Robert E. Burton, "Formula Budgeting: An Example," *Special Libraries* 66 (February 1975): 61-67. University of California, Office of the Vice President for Finance, "Library Workload Measures" (University of California, Berkeley, 1963, Mimeographed), 1-20. University of Washington, Office of Interinstitutional Business Studies, *Model Budget Analysis System for Program 05 Libraries* (University of Washington, Olympia, 1970, Mimeographed), 1-16.

35. "Standards for College Libraries, 1985," 244, 247, 249.

36.   Michael E. D. Koenig and Diedre C. Stam, "Budgeting and Financial Planning for Libraries," in *Advances in Library Administration*, vol. 4 (Greenwich, CT: JAI Press, 1985), 92.

37.   Marilyn J. Sharrow, "Budgeting Experience—at the University of Toronto Library," *Canadian Library Journal* 40 (August 1983): 207.

38.   P. A. Phyrr, "The Zero-Base Approach to Government Budgeting," *Public Administration Review* 37 (January-February 1977): 1.

39.   Ching-chih Chen, *Zero Based Budgeting in Library Management* (New York: Gaylord Professional Books, 1980), 36.

40.   Ricky W. Griffin, *Management*, 3d ed. (Boston: Houghton Mifflin, 1990), 697.

41.   Dan A. Cothran, "Entrepreneurial Budgeting: An Emerging Reform?" *Budgeting and the Management of Public Spending* (Cheltenham, UK: An Elgar Reference Collection, 1996), 446.

42.   Sarah Ann Long and Donald J. Sager, "Management for Tough Times," *American Libraries* 20, no. 6 (June 1989): 546.

43.   Jay H. Loevy, "Microcomputer Applications in Budgeting," in *Handbook of Budgeting*, 2d ed., ed. H. W. A. Sweeney and R. Rachlin (New York: John Wiley, 1987), 770.

44.   W. W. Wilms, C. Teruya and M. Walpole, "Fiscal Reform at UCLA: The Clash of Accountability and Academic Freedom," *Change* 29, no. 5 (September-October 1997): 43.

45.   D. L. Slocum and P. M. Rooney, "Responding to Resource Constraints," *Change* 29, no. 5 (September-October 1997): 56.

46.   W. J. Burns Jr. and F. W. McFarlan, "Information Technology Puts Power in Control Systems," in *Revolution in Real Time* (Cambridge, MA: Harvard Business Review Book, 1991), 206.

47.   Robert M. Donnelly, "Organizing and Administering the Budgeting Process," in *Handbook of Budgeting*, 2d ed., ed. H. W. A. Sweeney and R. Rachlin (New York: John Wiley, 1987), 119.

48.   Jacob Birnberg, "Accounting Information for Operating Decisions," *Management Principles for Nonprofit Agencies and Organizations*, ed. Gerlad Zaltman (New York: AMACOM, 1979), 478.

Readings

Accounting Standards. Norwalk, CT: Financial Accounting Standards Board, 1991.

Aragon, George A. *Financial Management*. Boston: Allyn & Bacon, 1989.

Auld, Lawrence W. S. *Electronic Spreadsheets for Libraries*. Phoenix, AZ: Oryx Press, 1986.

Brigham, Eugene F. *Financial Management: Theory and Practice*. Chicago: Dryden Press, 1988.

Brophy, Peter. *Management Information and Decision Support Systems in Libraries*. Brookfield, VT: Gower, 1986.

Carroll, T. Owen. *Decision Power with Spreadsheets*. Homewood, IL: Dow Jones-Irwin, 1985.

Chambers, Raymond J., and G. W. Dean, eds. *Accounting, Management and Finance*. New York: Garland, 1986.

Clark, Philip M. *Microcomputer Spreadsheet Models for Libraries*. Chicago: American Library Association, 1985.

Connors, Tracy D., and Christopher T. Callaghan. *Financial Management for Nonprofit Organizations*. New York: AMACOM, 1982.

Cronin, Mary J. *Performance Measurement for Public Services in Academic and Research Libraries*. Washington, DC: Association of Research Libraries, 1985.

Developing Indicators for Academic Library Performance. Washington, DC: Association of Research Libraries, 1995.

Estabrook, L. S., ed. *Applying Research to Practice*. Urbana-Champaign, IL: University of Illinois Press, 1992.

Expert Systems in ARL Libraries (ARL SPEC Kit no. 174). Washington, DC: Association of Research Libraries, 1991.

Farley, Ruth A., and Bill Katz. *Finance, Budget and Management for Reference Services*. New York: Haworth Press, 1988.

Flowerdew, A. D. J., and C. M. E. Whitehead. *Cost-Effectiveness and Cost/Benefit Analysis in Information Science*. London: London School of Economics and Political Science (QSTI Report no. 5206), 1974.

Hernon, Peter, and John V. Richardson, eds. *Microcomputer Software for Performing Statistical Analyses: A Handbook Supporting Library Decision-Making*. Norwood, NJ: Ablex, 1988.

Koenig, Michael E. D. *Budgeting Techniques for Libraries and Information Centers*. New York: Special Libraries Association, 1980.

Kraft, D., and B. Boyce, eds. *Operations Research for Libraries and Information Agencies*. San Diego, CA: Academic Press, 1991.

Lancaster, F. W. *If You Want to Evaluate Your Library*. Champaign, IL: University of Illinois Graduate School of Library and Information Science, 1988.

Lee, Sul H., ed. *Acquisitions, Budgets and Material Costs: Issues and Approaches*. New York: Haworth Press, 1988.

Lynch, Beverly P., ed. *Standards for University Libraries*. The Hague: IFLA Section of University Libraries and Other General Research Libraries, 1986.

Martin, Murray S. *Budgetary Control in Academic Libraries*. Greenwich, CT: JAI Press, 1978.

Martin, Murray S., ed. *Financial Planning for Libraries*. New York: Haworth Press, 1982.

Milling, Bryan E. *The Basics of Finance: Financial Tools for Non-Financial Managers*. Naperville, IL: Sourcebooks Trade, 1991.

Prentice, Ann E. *Financial Planning for Libraries*. Metuchen, NJ: Scarecrow Press, 1983.

Roberts, Stephen A. *Cost Management for Library and Information Services*. London: Butterworths, 1985.

Rosenberg, Philip. *Funding for Public Libraries: A Manager's Handbook*. Chicago: American Library Association, 1985.

Savoie, Donald J., ed. *Budgeting and the Management of Public Spending*. Cheltenham, UK: An Elgar Reference Collection, 1996.

Sellen, Betty-Carol, and Betty J. Turock, eds. *The Bottom Line Reader: A Financial Handbook for Librarians*. New York: Neal-Schuman, 1991.

Smith, G. Stevenson. *Managerial Accounting for Libraries and Other Non-Profit Organizations*. Chicago: American Library Association, 1991.

Spurga, Ronald C. *Balance Sheet Basics: Financial Management for Nonfinancial Managers*. New York: Franklin Watts, 1986.

Sweeny, H. W. Allen, and Robert Rachlin. *Handbook of Budgeting*. 2d ed. New York: John Wiley, 1987.

Trumpeter, Margo, and Richard Rounds. *Basic Budgeting for Librarians*. Chicago: American Library Association, 1985.

Turock, Betty J., and Andrea Pedolsky. *Creating a Financial Plan*. New York: Neal-Schuman, 1992.

Umapathy, Srinivasan. *Current Budgeting Practice in U.S. Industry*. New York: Quorum Books, 1987.

Van House, Nancy A. et al. *Output Measures for Public Libraries: A Manual of Standardized Procedures*. 2d ed. Chicago, IL: American Library Association, 1987.

Wacht, Richard F. *Financial Management in Nonprofit Organizations*. 2d ed. Atlanta: Georgia State University Business Press, 1991.

Ward, Patricia L., ed. *Performance Measures: A Bibliography*. BLRDD Report no. 5705. Loughborough, UK: Loughborough University, CLAIM and Public Libraries Research Group, 1982.

Whalen, Edward L. *Responsibility Center Budgeting: An Approach to Decentralization Management for Institutions of Higher Education*. Bloomington, IN: Indiana University Press, 1991.

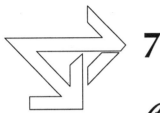

7

Changing Library and Information Systems

Impetus for Change

Doctors and executives alike complain that they cannot keep up with the latest developments in their fields. Hardly a meeting or conference takes place today without some ritualistic oratory about "the challenge of change." Among many there is an uneasy mood—a suspicion that change is out of control.[1]

—Alvin Toffler, *Future Shock*

Change is rampant in organizations. Some advocate reengineering the organization[2] and are busy restructuring, while others maintain that we are in an "age of unreason."[3] From both of those perspectives it is obvious that the future is no longer what it used to be. It is a time of discontinuity, ferment, some would even maintain chaos,[4] which demands renewal and new approaches for stable organizations and dissolution or revamping of others. Organizations, particularly knowledge based not-for-profit ones such as libraries and information centers where change is very apparent, have seen dramatic changes brought on by several factors, but primarily by new technologies. Forces external to the organization, as well as those within the organization, have precipitated this change process—sometimes planned and other times unplanned—in both values and attitudes toward work life and organizational structures, and in management theory and practice.

It is obvious in today's information world that an increasing intense pressure for change is inevitable. Forces that are directly driving strategic initiatives for change in library and information services include costs of services, speed of delivery, entrepreneurial activities, and quality of the value-added service, all enhanced by the development of a technological climate that promotes a reconfiguration of organizations and those services. In such an environment, the significance of what is done and how something is done is balanced by questioning why "it" is done or, in some cases, why "it" is not done. Resources—people, materials, and methods; knowledge, skills, and techniques—components to which long-established management principles have been applied, are the core of this changing information organization's life.

Each one of those components is affected by this phenomenon of change. In most cases, implementation of change requires a reorientation of the people working in the organization. This sometimes places the organization on a confrontation course, as it is a threatening process, either because individuals don't understand why it is necessary, or they don't want to understand—they are perhaps satisfied with the current status because they have a vested interest in it and believe they know what is best. Resistance to change is the greatest barrier to the metamorphosis that is expected and, indeed, required. Most of the time, this resistance stems from improper information. From the top and through every level of the organization, this reorientation requires accepting new ideas, learning new skills, breaking old habits, and adapting new behavioral patterns. Change can be just as threatening to managers as to other staff members, because decision making of a more mundane nature now can be made by machines, rather than the managers. In this setting, managers feel a loss of authority, unable to control certain outcomes. When this happens, they sometimes attempt to control the systems design itself. The threatening process of change must be approached deliberately and with much gentle preparation and persuasion. In such a scenario every member of the organization is expected to become a risk-taker.

> ☟Mediocrity can permeate an entire organization, producing acceptance of missed deadlines and quality deficits, aimless meetings that begin late, reports and presentations long on flash but short on substance. In a culture of mediocrity, complaining, blaming, and making excuses replaces accountability.[5]
>
> —Nicholas Imparato and Oren Harari,
> *Jumping the Curve*

Libraries and other information service centers are exciting, innovative, changing—even turbulent—organizations today. They offer vital services and added value to an information society by selecting a vast array of resources and access points that provide the right bit of information, at the right time, for the right seeker of information, in the right format, and at the right cost. Measuring the value of that information through acquisition, organization, access, and delivery is vital in the life of information-oriented libraries and other information organizations, and it is the responsibility of librarians and other information professionals. This greatly enhanced goal requires human interaction and technological interplay for its success. The acceleration of change—in technology, in mobility, in urbanization, in internationalization, in economics—has affected libraries and other information centers as much as any other organization.

Drucker asserts that "the present is a time of great entrepreneurial ferment, where old and staid institutions suddenly have to become very limber."[6] He maintains that major changes that have affected many organizations are those relating to (1) the introduction of new technologies, which creates new industries and render existing industries obsolete; (2) the emergence of a world economy that involves a world market or global shopping center; (3) the development of a changing political and social matrix, involving much disenchantment with current major institutions; and (4) the creation of a "knowledge economy" in which about half of the funds available are spent on procuring ideas and information and in which knowledge has become the central factor of production.

The effects of change are not limited to any one country, developed or emerging, or one type of setting, whether it is a public, academic, school, or special library or information center. Libraries and other information centers in every part of the world are experiencing the challenging phenomenon that enables a paradigm shift in information-oriented organizations: from an ownership mentality, obsessed with in-house activities, to a universal information-access attitude, collaborating and sharing resources and services.

However, many workers and managers in those information organizations discount change as a force in the organization's life, while they might embrace it in their personal lives. For example, almost a third of all American workers are "discounters," who routinely reject the significance of potential future change; another 40 percent are "extrapolators," who believe that the trends of the recent past will continue into the foreseeable future. However, 40 percent of the discounters and extrapolators indicate that they are currently going through a major, self-initiated change in their own lives or careers, and another 40 percent are actively planning to undertake such a change.[7] How can this dichotomy of attitudes be explained, this initiation of change in personal lives but resistance to change in the organizational life? Perhaps the answer lies in the organizational culture and value system as barriers to change.

Educating, informing, and involving knowledge workers is the first step in any planned change process. Information about needed change helps individuals and organizations adjust to the inevitable. The "looking around" aspect of the planning process, the performance evaluation and motivational aspects of the staffing function, the leadership effectiveness training of the directing functions, and the feedback options and budgeting applications of the controlling endeavor provide important information about both external and internal forces promoting and facilitating change, and they offer options for making tough choices, decisions about future directions of the information organization. Of course, risk is the primary factor in this equation. But what is the alternative?

> ✏The global information network creates a complex and intense dimension for librarians unknown to their predecessors. The amount, diversity, and speed of information available through state-of-the-art technology have surrounded library managers with a continual flow of new directions and opportunities.[8]
>
> —Susan C. Curzon, *Managing Change*

Economic constraints coupled with technological developments have precipitated inter-type, intra-type, and international cooperative efforts in technical production (creating, acquiring, and organizing) and public services (accessing, evaluating, and distributing) areas of libraries and information centers, from cooperative acquisitions and cataloging to computerized interlibrary loan, from resource sharing (networking, online access, CD-ROM purchasing and use, etc.) to other online information services offered in conjunction with publishers, vendors, other information centers, and, indeed, other units of the parent organization. International organizations, including the International Federation of Library Associations and Institutions (IFLA), are important partners in addressing issues of international significance. The environment is one of inter-activity, both online and on paper.

Staff participation in the decision-making process; unionization and collective bargaining efforts; decentralization of information services; flattening of organizational hierarchies; and collaborative employer-employee workplace arrangements, including programs like maternity and parental leave, flex-time and flex-place, part-time and job-sharing, and an end of mandatory retirement age—all of which are designed to meet growing needs and interests—are having an impact on organizational culture and character.

🔖An organization that actively responds to pressures for change can prompt its members to introduce innovations on their own more readily than an organization that is stagnant and inflexible.[9]

—Robert A. Cooke,
"Managing Change in Organizations"

Only a few short years ago, managers of libraries and other information centers spent little time on external matters, but today a major portion of their time is spent on external matters, such as civic organizations, trustees or corporation board meetings, fund-raising efforts with philanthropic foundations and individuals, collective bargaining sessions, Friends of Libraries group meetings, and meetings with higher administration and funding agencies or authorities in defense of the budget or other public relations matters.

🔖Managers spend their time reacting to crisis, seizing special opportunities, attending meetings, negotiating, talking on the telephone, cultivating interpersonal and political relationships, gathering and disseminating information, and fulfilling a variety of ceremonial functions.[10]

—Richard DeGennaro,
"Library Administration and
New Management Systems"

The need and desire to constantly be in touch with an organization's primary customers, to gauge their information-seeking patterns, and assess their information needs in order to develop plans, policies, practices, and procedures that satisfy those needs brings new challenges of changing patterns and attitudes. "The whole world is by now a richly interactive system"[11] that requires managers to be proactive in their relations with external bodies and workers to be committed to the priorities of the organizations that they serve. This interactive system finds organizations tentatively moving away from what might be called the authoritarian hierarchy to smaller work groups in which people manage themselves.

The information services center is a complex organization, relying upon a trusting relationship among its various units. Workers' role in adopting a changed environment is further enhanced as they are allowed, as far as capabilities permit, to grow beyond a traditional hierarchical job to the point of being involved in team problem-solving activities.[12] Work

design is becoming more flexible and self-organized, and human networking is replacing the pyramid, in many cases, as the organizational form. In
order for libraries and other information centers to achieve their common
mission of becoming knowledge-based organizations, as well as organizations that facilitate knowledge acquisition, professional information intermediaries working in those no-longer institution-bound organizations are
becoming coordinators and directors. There is a flattening of the organization so that communication and decisions are more immediate and apparent. This flattening of the organization requires greater collaboration as
new approaches to management planning, systems development, and control develop. Seeking a balance between delegation and control is a meaningful challenge for those who are ultimately responsible for action.

The introduction of highly specialized staff also affects approaches to library and information management and challenges organizations to offer new
incentives to workers. Employees are more sophisticated and articulate and
are less willing to settle for the lower-level needs so well described by Maslow
(see pp. 274-77). John Naisbitt and Patricia Aburdene have written that managers should be encouraged to become more like teachers and coaches—"We
have to think increasingly about the manager as teacher, as mentor, as devel-
oper of human potential,"—rather than as a whip-wielding autocrat trying to
force change.[13]

> Traditional departments will serve as guardians of stan-
> dards, as centers for training and the assignment of special-
> ties; they won't be where the work gets done. That will
> happen largely in task-focused teams.[14]
>
> —Peter F. Drucker,
> "The Coming of the New Organization"

This change cannot occur by edict alone; it is not possible for top
management to decree change and then expect others to make it happen.
Such an approach, without proper preparation, would only create an atmosphere of uneasiness and mistrust, which is sure to have an adverse effect. To implement new ideas and services requires participation by those
who will be affected by such change. Managers are learning to manage
transition and to cope with the continuous barrage of new ideas, technologies, information, as well as interpersonal, interorganizational, and intraorganizational relations. However, "managing participation is a balancing
act: between management control and team opportunity; between getting
the work done quickly and giving people a chance to learn; between seeking volunteers and pushing people into it; between too little team spirit
and too much."[15] Therefore, first understanding what the change process

means, and then becoming committed to it, is a continuing process from the time that an organization first officially recognizes, and therefore encounters, the need to change to the point when it is internalized and institutionalized, as illustrated in figure 7.1.

At every point along that continuum the process can be, and sometimes is, aborted for a variety of reasons. For instance, with the understanding point, a person can have a "positive perception," in which the process continues, or a "negative perception." If it is negative, steps must be taken to bring that person along to the point of understanding and being positive. This does not mean coercion, rather it means education and therefore gentle persuasion.

Fig. 7.1. The continuum of change ranges from preparing for change to the point where there is total commitment to change.

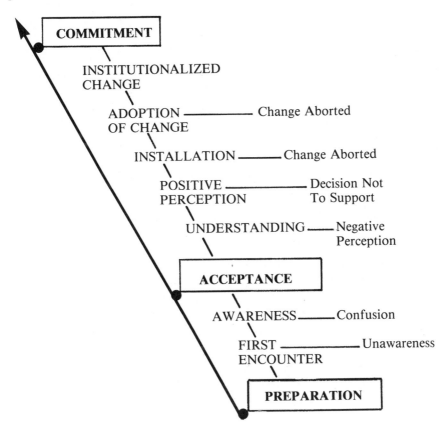

Types of Change

Two types of change are prevalent in information organizations. One is unplanned change, likely to be disastrous, which presents a situation that forces the organization to react. Such change is usually out of control or mismanaged and can prove destructive to any organization. The other type is planned change, which brings about renewal or recommitment on the part of the organization and people working in it. Although change is sometimes forced upon an organization by outside influences, it most often comes from within as a calculated effort on the part of people working in the organization. A knowledgeable approach to managing change enables library and information services administrators to retain the strategic vision of the organization and at the same time make choices about costly technological and facility investments.[16] It involves a deliberate progression toward renewing the organization by creating conditions and soliciting resources to accomplish that transition. Reordering of priorities, retraining staff, reorganizing space, renewing equipment, restructuring the hierarchy, and redirecting the financial resources—all requirements in a change process—are expensive to implement, yet inevitable in the life of libraries and other information-intensive organizations. This process is a delicate one. For instance, redefinition of work roles among levels of staff working in libraries is often demanded and sometimes welcomed, but the process can bring with it tension and conflict.

Negative forces, such as poor management, which can cause organizational decay, have forced change just as much as positive forces, such as expansion and growth, have facilitated change. One technique to bring about positive change in libraries and information centers is through employment of change agents—either individuals within the organization (self-appointed or management-appointed) or brought in from outside the organization—who are responsible for adapting the organization's structure to a changing environment, directing the speed and focus of organizational change, and controlling conflict. The cycle of change is illustrated in figure 7.2.

The internal environment that fosters change includes the organizational structure itself, the decision-making process, and the process of communications, all of which are management controlled. In addition, modification of attitudes and behavior of individuals, a much more delicate process—one that is not management controlled—is just as important a factor in the internal environment.

Fig. 7.2. Change is an evolutionary, cyclical process. From *Innovations and Organizations* by G. Zaltman, Duncan and Holbek, copyright © 1973. Reprinted by permission of John Wiley & Sons, Inc.

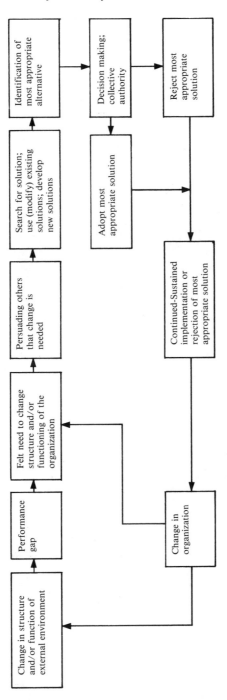

> ໕ Change the culture, and the majority of current organiza-
> tional problems will be solved.[17]

> —David C. Wilson, *A Strategy of Change*

In addition to inside pressures, change in organizations that provide information services comes from a variety of other sources: pressures of the external environment (customers and government authorities), changes in directions (goals and objectives), reconfiguration of technology (systems development and access to international communications sources such as the Internet), and modification of the overall physical plant (buildings— branches often spread throughout the world). All of these have had an effect on libraries and other information centers and are causing changes in the structure, the individuals' attitudes, and the individuals themselves, both as managers and as workers.

For the first time in history, technological developments and innovations are outpacing the human endeavor to cope and to develop programs that technology is capable of supporting. This simple fact, combined with the social, political, and economic pressures of the day, necessitates organizations with a vastly different profile than it was possible to envision only a few short years ago.

> ໕ Libraries could be substantially changed by the adoption
> of technological innovation in information service or made
> obsolete by competition.[18]

> —Miriam A. Drake,
> "Managing Innovation in Academic Libraries"

Environmental pressures and relationships dictate tasks, technologies, and even the structure of organizations. Those influence the attitudes, habits, and values of persons working in the organization, as well as the overall organization itself, on the social, technical, and political levels. For instance, in the United States, library legislation enacted during the New Frontier and Great Society days of the 1960s had a tremendous impact on the resources and organization of many libraries, on their physical buildings, technological development, and access to resources. Likewise, change in attitude among some elected officials as to the government's role and responsibilities has had an impact on the change process in libraries and information centers. The question of fee-based services versus free services in public libraries, with the concomitant issues of the data rich but information poor, is another social question that influences both individuals working in libraries and information centers and their guiding principle and operation. These are but two examples of library and information services being forced to change internally to respond to external pressures. Figure 7.3 represents some of internal and external pressures.

Fig. 7.3. The internal/external environment of libraries and information centers.

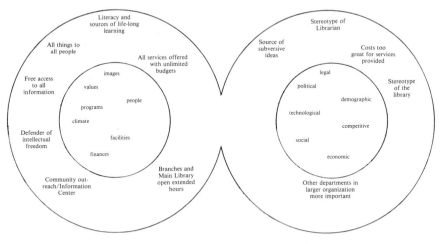

Information-Oriented Organizations as Open Systems

Several variables can change libraries and other information centers, including direction, or their purpose—and their responsibility—to a larger community; users and potential users, the most important resource, including their attitudes and motivation; the organizational structure of the whole operation; and technology, with its influence on output. Those various components must be considered as a whole, because each one affects and interacts with all of the others.

Stated another way, the library or information center is, basically, an open system that receives input from the outside, absorbs it, transforms that information, and then transmits it to the environment. The organization has a number of subsystems that respond to this change cycle. First, goals and objectives are determined, to an extent, by that larger environment or system, and, if the organization is to be successful, it depends on that outside input to be able to produce usable output. Second, the psychosocial subsystem is formed by individuals and groups interacting in the system and with those outside the system. Third, the structure of the organization determines the way assignments are divided and work is carried out; those are reflected in documents like organization charts, performance evaluation processes, policies, and procedures manuals. Finally, the specialized knowledge, skills, and techniques required, and the types of machinery and equipment involved, shape the technical subsystem. Each of these subsystems interacts in informal and formal ways within the system. This interaction is reflected in the total managerial subsystem that encompasses parts of the entire organization and is subject to greatest change. Figure 7.4 illustrates the interrelationships.

Fig. 7.4. Organizational system. From *Organization and Management* by F. E. Kast and J. E. Rosenzweig, copyright © 1985. Used with the permission of McGraw-Hill Book Company.

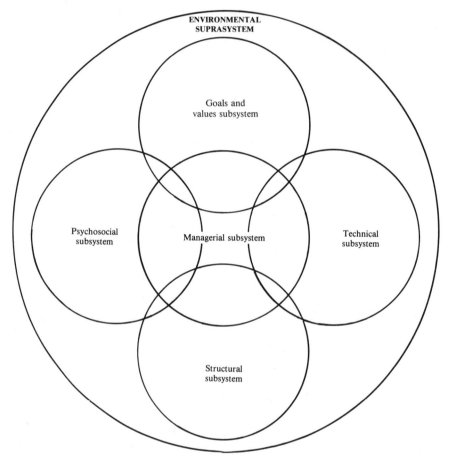

&Literature on organizational change indicates the relative weakness of efforts to change only structure (e.g., job design), only people (e.g., sensitivity training), or only technology (e.g., introducing new equipment or a new computer).[19]

—-Clayton P. Alderfor,
"Change Processes in Organizations"

Writers describe the environment of organizational structure as either placid or turbulent.[20] Either state can reflect organizational change, although, when it does occur, whether the occurrence is planned or unpredicted, it is almost always with tension, anxiety, resistance, and conflict. It should be pointed out that change is often effected unilaterally by the hierarchy where the "definition and solution to the problem at hand tends to be specified by the upper echelons and directed downward through formal and impersonal control mechanisms."[21] This attitude and approach is one of the major causes of resistance to change. It is important to try to analyze and minimize that resistance. Resistance can occur because:

1. People do not understand or do not want to understand. Certain categories of people resist change more than others. It has been said that people who have been in an organization longer are more resistant to change because they have more time and money vested in the status quo. People who have less time invested have no strong commitment to the old way and are more adaptable to new situations.

2. People have not been fully informed. Communication is the key in any change process, and it is management's responsibility to see that everyone is kept fully informed. Unfortunately, information about change is sometimes restricted, thereby causing resistance. Several experts have pointed out that not only will "providing opportunities for individuals to have influence over and participate in the change process" lessen resistance to change, but also providing continuing involvement after the initial change effort "will produce significant increases in motivation, satisfaction, and performance."[22]

3. People's habits and securities are threatened. Sometimes, people may feel their basic assumptions, personal values, sources of security, or friendships are being threatened.

4. People are happy with the status quo, with the way things are now and with current priorities. When groups of individuals are comfortable together, group norms and pressures influence attitudes toward change.

5. People have vested interests and definite perceptions of what is needed or wanted, even if they agree that change is necessary. They may want change to occur, but on their terms. With the increase in size of organizations, there comes a greater disparity of backgrounds, attitudes, and values, thereby allowing greater likelihood of individual or group resistance.

6. Rapid change, or, the speed with which change occurs, causes greater strain on the organization. The organization itself may not be able

to cope. Such strain forces pseudo-consensus on groups and places greater reliance on the managers as coordinators, negotiators, and arbitrators, as well as motivators.

7. Finally, rapidly changing technology and societal conditions render some individuals obsolete. It is impossible to remain in the same job for life; even if a person did remain in one position, the job itself would change. Obsolescence is one of the most serious problems facing professionals in today's society. Obsolescence means the degree to which professionals lack the up-to-date knowledge or skills necessary to maintain effective performance. In addition, many things, including the information explosion and dynamic change stimulated by the knowledge revolution; personal characteristics, particularly psychological; and work environment and climate influence obsolescence. The acceleration of change has resulted in a progressive decline in the useful lifetime of formal professional education and makes continuing education vital.

Changes that affect libraries and information centers and resistance to those changes, either on the part of library managers or other librarians, follow the same pattern as changes in society in general. A glance at the history of library and information service management development reveals changes that have taken place in management attitudes and actions over the last century.

> ⊠In today's environment, nothing is constant or predictable. . . . Three forces, separately and in combination, are driving today's (organizations). . . . Customers, Competition, and Change.[23]
>
> —Michael Hammer and James Champy,
> *Reengineering the Corporation*

Management Change in Information Services Organizations— A Historical Perspective

From its very inception, library management, as might be expected, showed no identifiable characteristic that would set it apart from other organizational management. Trends, theories, and techniques introduced in organizations and in the management literature found their way into library practice and over the years have been adapted with varying degrees of success. The integration of those theories and techniques into library operations is reported in the library literature.

In 1887, F. M. Cruden, then librarian of the St. Louis Public Library, stated that "the duties of a chief executive of a library differ in no essential way from those of a manager of a stock company. . . . The librarian may profit by the methods of the businessman."[24] Arthur E. Bostwick, addressing the New Zealand Library Association in 1891, advocated adoption of the methods of business efficiency in the operation of the library.[25] A number of other librarians, including Charles C. Williamson, emphasized the value to libraries of industrial methods, pointing out that "no one has attempted yet to treat comprehensively the principles and philosophy of library service or library management."[26] This was stated at the time of the development of the scientific management school, whose theories had already been applied to a number of industrial situations but not yet to libraries. It was not until the 1930s that particular attention was paid to the application of scientific management to libraries. Donald Coney emphasized the "new" approach by stating that "scientific management furnishes library administrators with a useful instrument for orientating their activities."[27] Twenty years later, in 1954, Laurence J. Kipp published an article that discussed the application of scientific management to library operations for the period of 1920 to 1950.[28] Arthur T. Kittle, in his dissertation, pointed out that scientific management did not receive serious attention in libraries until after World War II.[29]

Ralph R. Shaw began his landmark studies of the scientific management of library operations in the late 1940s and early 1950s. In one study he analyzed two trends in library management—specialization and integration of specialties into a functional organization.[30] These two conflicting trends, which he termed micromanagement and macromanagement, are evident in library organization today. In 1954, Shaw, writing as editor of an issue of *Library Trends*, noted "a trend toward the application of scientific management to libraries."[31]

> ℚ Data processing methods stimulated interest in scientific management, as is evident in the first detailed presentation of principles and techniques of scientific management as they apply specifically to library oriented problems.[32]
>
> —Richard M. Dougherty
> and Fred J. Heinritz,
> *Scientific Management of Library Operations*

Some librarians have always been reluctant to use scientific management tools because they do not believe that library work lends itself to systematic analysis. "They overlook, however, the high percentage of library tasks that consist of repetitive, mechanical routines that do lend themselves to such analysis."[33]

The influence of the human relation's school on libraries also became particularly evident in the early 1930s; the issues relating to people working in libraries began to receive attention, and preparation for library administrators emphasized the personnel relations approach. An article by J. Periam Danton emphasized the trend toward analyzing the human side, where personnel administration became paramount to the democratization of the library organization.[34] This was further expounded in Clara W. Herbert's 1939 volume on personnel administration.[35] Among Herbert's recommendations were greater attention to personnel administration, greater consideration of basic organization directed toward the simplification and coordination of activities, greater staff development, and better working conditions.[36]

E. W. McDiarmid and John M. McDiarmid, in the late 1930s recognized two paramount problems applicable to libraries: the need to delegate authority to the level of responsibility and the need to define library objectives and their influence on the administration.[37] This issue received attention in the library press. Amy Winslow, in her 1953 paper, emphasized staff participation in "democratic organization."[38] Ernest J. Reese's 1959 article on library administration noted, among other things, an increase in staff participation in management of libraries.[39]

With respect to the social systems school, several works cited the development of library management in relation to the larger institution and the community the library serves. C. B. Joeckel, a pioneer in the field of library management, suggested that "library administrators will do well to seek models from comparative study in the fields of public administration, in business, in industry, and in education."[40] The library institute at which Joeckel's paper was presented was, perhaps, the landmark event in the analysis of library administration. Twenty years later, Paul Wasserman supported Joeckel's contention that "in a very real sense library administration is only an extension of public administration."[41]

Elizabeth W. Stone's survey showed a tendency toward "emphasis upon theory and principles and basic functions, bringing with it corresponding deemphasis upon specific technical skills."[42] This is substantiated when one examines the volumes that have been published in the last decade on organization and administration of specific types of libraries—academic, public, school, and special.

It is also important to look at the quantitative, or mathematical, school and the influence it has had on library operations. From the late

1960s into the current decade managers of libraries have used applied operations research in decision making.[43] In the 1960s, an original group of researchers, led by Philip Morse at MIT, and a later group, headed by Ferdinand Leimkuhler at Purdue, studied library problems using operations research. Two reports from other sources illustrate this trend. In 1972, the Wharton School at the University of Pennsylvania finished a study that had been supported by a federal grant to design and develop a model for management information systems for universities and large public libraries.[44] That report classified library functions into 17 categories, and it proposed that those categories be used as a basis for program budgeting systems in libraries. Ching-chih Chen, in her dissertation, demonstrated how library administrators in their everyday decision making could use operations research techniques.[45]

Issues of major research journals, chapters in management collection treatises, and monographs on librarianship make it clear that management topics are receiving increasing attention. The proceedings of several national conferences of the Association of College and Research Libraries and the Public Library Association present the thoughts and concerns of academic and research librarians in several major areas, including administration and management.[46] An issue of *Library Trends* addressed the dilemma of "How we can optimally integrate the technical and human resources that we manage toward achieving the library's service mission and, at the same time, manage working arrangements and role relationships so that people's needs for self-worth, growth, and development are significantly met in our libraries."[47] On the same topic, Elizabeth W. Stone researched a commissioned study for the National Commission on Libraries and Information Science (NCLIS). In addition, the issue of participative management has been addressed in research studies.[48] An example, drawn from a number of volumes on the subject of personnel in libraries, is a report done for the Illinois State Library, which identifies the kinds of activities that are typical of the training and background of individuals working in libraries.[49] A King Research study attempted to identify competencies needed by professionals working in libraries.[50] Other important and timely views have been presented by Sheila Creth and Frank Duda as well as Barbara Conroy in their examinations of staff training and development.[51] Buckland proposes a redesign of library services[52] and Dougherty and Hughes look at future steps,[53] while Crawford and Gorman identify factors influencing future developments.[54] Drabenstott provides a useful bibliography on the "Library of the Future."[55]

Other special issues of *Library Trends* have focused on "Effective Resource Allocation in Library Management," which examined "evaluative techniques and procedures used by librarians to determine the effectiveness of their programs (e.g., surveys, cost accounting, systems analysis, operations research,

PPBS, MBO, PERT)," and "Systems Design and Analysis for Libraries," which viewed systems analysis as a management tool to be used in "seeking out the fundamentals of a situation and applying to this study rigorous scientific methods, with the aim of finding an optimal solution to the problems facing managers."[56] Those topics, and their subtopics, are constantly revisited.[57] In addition, Charles McClure's thorough review and writings on the topic of planning, including issues of the *Journal of Library Administration* and the feature article in the *1986 ALA Yearbook*,[58] as well as Donald Riggs's treatise on a particular aspect of planning, keep that important topic foremost in the minds of some.[59] The importance of measurement and evaluation of library services continues to receive attention, as is evidenced by major works on the topic.[60]

Reports on networking present the state of the art. *Resources and Bibliographic Support for a Nationwide Library Program* was commissioned by NCLIS. A second report, cosponsored by NCLIS, addressed the structure and governance of networks. "Library Networks: Promise and Performance" emphasized the need for developing networks that include all types of libraries. *Networks for Networkers* took what is probably the most comprehensive view on problems and potentials of library networking. Susan K. Martin's periodical state-of-the-art reviews are tools of awareness of the ferment in networking.[61]

Perhaps the unit that is contributing the most, on a continuing basis, to the study of library management is the Association of Research Libraries, with a sister organization in Australia. Through funding from the Council on Library Resources, the association developed its Office of Management Studies, recently renamed the Office of Leadership and Management Studies, which is responsible for a number of projects relating to library management. One primary activity has been the issuing of "SPEC kits" on topics of major interest, including goals and objectives, collective bargaining, performance evaluation, job analysis, and planning. The office developed a self-study guide, "Management Review and Analysis Program" (MRAP) for larger academic libraries and an Academic Library Development Program for smaller academic libraries. Through task forces, both guides, aimed at improving productivity and staff morale, examine planning and control processes, organizational development, and personnel needs and relationships in individual libraries. During the late 1980s many university libraries in North America implemented the planning process, using that technique. Since then MRAP has been transformed, no longer using a manual but instead providing a general framework and using the "assisted self-study" approach to engage a steering committee in "just-in-time" planning. Through its University Library Management Studies Office, the Association of Research Libraries publishes occasional papers on relevant topics, and through its Management Studies Office it publishes SPEC (Systems and Procedures Exchange Center) flyers.

Another analytical study of note is the by-now classic one for Columbia University Libraries.[62]

Most important, the issue of women and minorities as managers is receiving due consideration. Although the profession is a female-dominated one, at least in numbers, the majority of top management positions in North America are still held by males, mostly white males. The causes for this have been discussed in the literature, at conferences, and in institutes, such as *Library Management Without Bias*. Organizations, such as the Status of Women in Librarianship Committee of the American Library Association, through writings and research studies have also identified issues and become proactive partners in developing a vital, previously neglected, resource.[63] The outlook has gradually changed as the mentor system, as opposed to the "old-boy network," has begun to function and as individuals are hired and promoted based on their abilities and qualifications rather than gender or race.

Collections of readings on management topics of interest to library management should prove helpful to both the novice and the experienced manager in considering issues of importance to the management process.[64]

Before leaving the topic of change, it is useful to reiterate some of the issues already discussed in other sections of this text, particularly the one relating to the future of libraries and information services. Discussions, reported in the literature, at conferences, and elsewhere, confirm activities in relation to reengineering libraries and information services for the next century. These include individual organization's strategic thinking[65] and group thinking.[66] Most of these reports and discussions identify financial constraints, automation, organizing for efficiency and effectiveness, and vision for the next century as major focal points for consideration of organizational restructuring.

It is evident that the various management theories developed—scientific management, human relations, and quantitative—are being applied to library operations today. The continued use, development, and refinement of those thoughts and techniques will result in more efficient and effective library service.

Conclusion

Change requires constant reexamination of each previously identified role in goal-oriented, information-intense organizations, where teamwork and process are replacing individualism and a task orientation. In the information service sector, customer, client, or user needs have become the focus of service, with each member of the organization recognizing the potential of direct communication with the client or, at the very least, performing support activities that facilitate access. To be future focused then, information services organizations must anticipate and redefine customer needs on a regular basis, expanding and shifting services as needs arise.

Notes

1. Alvin Toffler, *Future Shock* (New York: Bantam Books, 1970), 19.

2. Michael Hammer and James Champy, *Reengineering the Corporation* (New York: HarperBusiness, 1993).

3. Charles Handy, *The Age of Unreason* (Cambridge, MA: Harvard Business School Press, 1990).

4. Dirk van Gulick, *Encounter with Chaos* (New York: McGraw-Hill, 1992).

5. Nicholas Imparato and Oren Harari, *Jumping the Curve: Innovation and Strategic Choice in an Age of Transition* (San Francisco: Jossey-Bass, 1994), 105.

6. Peter F. Drucker, *The Age of Discontinuity: Guidelines to Our Changing Society* (New York: Harper & Row, 1979), 177.

7. Daniel Yankelovich, *New Rules: Searching for Self-Fulfillment in a World Turned Upside Down* (New York: Random House, 1981), 79.

8. Susan C. Curzon, *Managing Change* (New York: Neal-Schuman, 1989), 13.

9. Robert A. Cooke, "Managing Change in Organizations," in *Management Principles for Nonprofit Agencies and Organizations*, ed. Gerald Zaltman (New York: AMACOM, 1979), 205.

10. Richard DeGennaro, "Library Administration and New Management Systems," *Library Journal* 103 (December 15, 1978): 2447.

11. Stafford Beer, "The World We Manage," *Behavioral Science* 18, no. 3 (1973): 198.

12. Victor Turner, *The Ritual Process* (Chicago: Aldine, 1969), 47.

13. John Naisbitt and Patricia Aburdene, *Re-inventing the Corporation* (New York: Warner Books, 1985), 54.

14. Peter F. Drucker, "The Coming of the New Organization," in *Revolution in Real Time* (Cambridge, MA: Harvard Business Review Books, 1991), 6.

15. Rosabeth Moss Kanter, *The Change Masters: Innovation for Productivity in the American Corporation* (New York: Simon & Schuster, 1983), 275-76.

16. Curzon, *Managing Change*, 13.

17. David C. Wilson, *A Strategy of Change* (London: Routledge, 1992), 69.

18. Miriam A. Drake, "Managing Innovation in Academic Libraries," *College & Research Libraries* 40, no. 6 (November 1979): 503.

19. Clayton P. Alderfor, "Change Processes in Organizations," in *Handbook of Industrial and Organizational Psychology*, ed. Marvin D. Dunnett (Skokie, IL: Rand McNally, 1976), 670.

20. F. E. Emery and E. L. Trist, "The Causal Texture of Organizational Environments," *Human Relations* 18 (February 1965): 21.

21. L. E. Greiner, "Patterns of Organization Change," *Harvard Business Review* 45 (1967): 120.

22. Alan C. Filley, R. J. House, and S. Kerr, *Managerial Process and Organizational Behavior* (Glenview, IL: Scott, Foresman, 1976), 491.

23. Hammer and Champy, *Reengineering the Corporation*, 17.

24. Gertrude G. Drury, *The Library and Its Organization* (New York: H. W. Wilson, 1924), 83-84.

25. Arthur E. Bostwick, "Two Tendencies of American Library Work," *Library Journal* 36, no. 6 (January 1911): 275-78.

26. Charles C. Williamson, "Efficiency in Library Management," *Library Journal* 44, no. 2 (February 1919): 76.

27. Donald Coney, "Scientific Management in University Libraries," in *Management Problems*, ed. G. T. Schwennig (Chapel Hill: University of North Carolina Press, 1930), 173.

28. Laurence J. Kipp, "Scientific Management in Research Libraries," *Library Trends* 2 (January 1954): 390-400.

29. Arthur T. Kittle, "Management Theories in Public Administration in the United States" (Ph.D. diss., Columbia University, 1961).

30. Ralph R. Shaw, "Scientific Management in the Library," *Wilson Library Bulletin* 21 (January 1947): 349-52.

31. Ralph R. Shaw, "Scientific Management," *Library Trends* 2 (January 1954): 359-483.

32. Richard M. Dougherty and Fred J. Heinritz, *Scientific Management of Library Operations*, 2d ed. (Metuchen, NJ: Scarecrow Press, 1966, 1982), 8.

33. Ibid.

34. J. Periam Danton, "Our Libraries—-The Trend Toward Democracy," *Library Quarterly* 4 (January 1934): 16-27.

35. Clara W. Herbert, *Personnel Administration in Public Libraries* (Chicago: American Library Association, 1939).

36. Ibid., xiii-xiv.

37. E. W. McDiarmid and John M. McDiarmid, *The Administration of the American Public Library* (Chicago: American Library Association, 1943).

38. Amy Winslow, "Staff Participation in Management," *Wilson Library Bulletin* 27 (April 1953): 624-28.

39. Ernest J. Reese, ed., "Current Trends in Library Administration," *Library Trends* 7 (January 1959): 333-36.

40.   C. B. Joeckel, ed., *Current Issues in Library Administration: Papers Presented Before the Library Institute at the University of Chicago, August 1-12, 1938* (Chicago: University of Chicago Press, 1939), vii-ix.

41.   Paul Wasserman, "Development of Administration in Library Service: Current Status and Future Prospects," *College & Research Libraries* 19 (November 1958): 288.

42.   Elizabeth W. Stone, *Training for the Improvement of Library Administration* (Urbana: Graduate School of Library Science, University of Illinois, 1967), 15.

43.   Don R. Swanson and Abraham Bookstein, eds., *Operations Research: Implications for Libraries* (Chicago: University of Chicago Press, 1972).

44.   Morris Hamburg et al., *Library Planning and Decision Making Systems* (Cambridge, MA: MIT Press, 1974).

45.   Ching-chih Chen, *Applications of Operations Research Models to Libraries* (Cambridge, MA: MIT Press, 1976).

46.   Robert D. Stueart and Richard D. Johnson, eds., *New Horizons for Academic Libraries* (New York: K. G. Saur, 1979). Michael D. Kathman and Virgil F. Massman, eds., *Options for the 80's: Proceedings of the Second National Conference of the Association of College and Research Libraries* (Greenwich, CT: JAI Press, 1983). Suzanne C. Dodson and Gary L. Menges, eds., *Academic Libraries: Myths and Realities: Proceedings of the Third National Conference of the Association of College and Research Libraries* (Chicago: American Library Association, 1984). Danuta A. Nitecki, ed., *Energies for Transition: Proceedings of the Fourth National Conference of the Association of College and Research Libraries* (Chicago: American Library Association, 1986).

47.   Elizabeth W. Stone, ed., "Personnel Development and Continuing Education in Libraries," *Library Trends* 20, no. 1 (July 1971): 3.

48.   U.S. National Commission on Libraries and Information Science, *Continuing Library and Information Science Education*, submitted by E. Stone et al. (Washington, DC: American Society for Information Science, 1974). Maurice P. Marchant, *Participative Management in Academic Libraries* (Westport, CT: Greenwood Press, 1976).

49.   Myrl Ricking and Robert E. Booth, *Personnel Utilization in Libraries: A Systems Approach* (Chicago: American Library Association, 1974).

50.   Jose-Marie Griffiths and Donald W. King, *New Directions in Library and Information Science Education* (Westport, CT: Greenwood Press/ASIS, 1986).

51.   Sheila Creth and Frederick Duda, eds., *Personnel Administration in Libraries* (New York: Neal-Schuman, 1981). Barbara Conroy, *Library Staff Development and Continuing Education* (Littleton, CO: Libraries Unlimited, 1978).

52.   Michael Buckland, *Redesigning Library Services: A Manifesto* (Chicago: American Library Association, 1992).

53.   Richard M. Dougherty and Carol Hughes, *Preferred Futures for Libraries* (Mountain View, CA: Research Libraries Group, 1991).

54.   Walt Crawford and Michael Gorman, *Future Libraries: Dreams, Madness and Reality* (Chicago: American Library Association, 1995).

55. Karen M. Drabenstott, *Analytical Review of the Library of the Future* (Washington, DC: Council on Library Resources, 1994).

56. H. William Axford, "Effective Resource Allocation in Library Management," *Library Trends* 25, no. 4 (April 1975): 547-72. F. Wilfrid Lancaster, "Systems Design and Analysis for Libraries," *Library Trends* 21, no. 4 (April 1973): 463.

57. Donald H. Kraft and Bert R. Boyce, *Operations Research for Libraries and Information Agencies* (New York: Academic Press, 1991).

58. Charles R. McClure, ed., "Planning for Library Services," *Journal of Library Administration* 2, nos. 2-4 (1982); and "Library Planning: A Status Report," in *The ALA Yearbook of Library and Information Services, 1986* (Chicago: American Library Association, 1986), 7-16.

59. Donald E. Riggs, *Strategic Planning for Library Managers* (Phoenix, AZ: Oryx Press, 1984).

60. Ernest R. DeProspo, E. Altman, and K. E. Beasley, *Performance Measures for Public Libraries* (Chicago: American Library Association, 1973). Lowell Martin et al., *Library Response to Urban Change: A Study of the Chicago Public Library* (Chicago: American Library Association, 1969). F. Wilfrid Lancaster, *The Measurement and Evaluation of Library Services* (Washington, DC: Information Resources Press, 1977). Douglas Zweizig, *Output Measures for Public Libraries* (Chicago: American Library Association, 1994). *See also* Charles R. McClure et al., *A Planning and Role Setting Manual for Public Libraries* (Chicago: American Library Association, 1993).

61. U.S. National Commission on Libraries and Information Science, *Resources and Bibliographic Support for a Nationwide Library Program*, submitted by Vernon E. Palmour et al. (Rockville, MD: Westat, 1974). Allen Kent and Thomas J. Galvin, eds., *The Structure and Governance of Library Networks* (New York: Marcel Dekker, 1979). Leon Carnovsky, ed., "Library Networks: Promise and Performance," *Library Quarterly* 39, no. 1 (January 1969): 1-108. Barbara E. Markuson and Blanche Woolls, eds., *Networks for Networkers: Critical Issues in Cooperative Library Development* (New York: Neal-Schuman, 1980). Susan K. Martin, *Library Networks, 1986-87* (White Plains, NY: Knowledge Industry Publications, 1986).

62. Allen Booz and Hamilton, Inc., *Organization and Staffing of the Libraries of Columbia University* (Westport, CT: Redgrave, 1973).

63. Ching-chih Chen, ed., *Library Management Without Bias* (Greenwich, CT: JAI Press, 1980). E. J. Josey and Kenneth E. Peeples, *Opportunities for Minorities in Librarianship* (Metuchen, NJ: Scarecrow Press, 1977). Kathleen M. Heim, *The Status of Women in Librarianship* (New York: Neal-Schuman, 1983). Betty Jo Irvine, *Sex Segregation in Librarianship* (Westport, CT: Greenwood Press, 1985).

64. Ruth J. Pearson, ed., *The Management Process: A Selection of Readings for Librarians* (Chicago: American Library Association, 1983). Beverly P. Lynch, ed., *Management Strategies for Librarians: A Basic Reader* (New York: Neal-Schuman, 1985). Margaret S. Jennings et al., *Library Management in Review*, vol. 2 (Washington, DC: Special Libraries Association, 1987).

65. Joanne Euster et. al., "Reorganizing for a Changing World" (personal correspondence, April 3, 1997). Mary Elizabeth Clack, "Continued Organizational Transformation: The Harvard College Library's Experience," *Library Administration*

and Management 10, no. 2 (April 1996): 98-104. Beth J. Shapiro and Kevin Brook Long, "Just Say Yes: Reengineering Library User Services for the 21st Century," *Journal of Academic Librarianship* (November 1994): 285-90.

66.   "Strategic Visions for Librarianship: Issues," LIBADMIN Listserv (December 15, 1991). "Strategic Visions Discussion Group: Values and Qualities of Librarianship," (discussion draft), LIBADMIN Listserv (January 18, 1992). Richard M. Dougherty and Carol Hughes, *Preferred Library Futures II: Charting the Paths* (Mountain View, CA: Research Libraries Group, 1993).

Readings

Anthony, William P. *Envisionary Management: A Guide for Human Resource Professionals.* New York: Quorum Books, 1988.

Appleyard, Brian. *Understanding the Present.* London: Pan Books, 1992.

Argyris, Chris. *Knowledge for Action.* San Francisco: Jossey-Bass, 1993.

Arms, Caroline, ed. *Campus Strategies for Libraries and Electronic Information.* Bedford, MA: Digital Press, 1990.

Astin, Helen S., and Carole Leland. *Women of Influence, Women of Vision.* San Francisco: Jossey-Bass, 1991.

Beer, Stafford. *Beyond Dispute: The Invention of Team Syntergrity.* New York: John Wiley, 1994.

Belasco, James A. *Teaching the Elephant to Dance: Empowering Change in Your Organization.* New York: Crown, 1990.

Belker, Loren B. *The First-Time Manager.* New York: AMACOM, 1993.

Benedetto, Richard F. *Matrix Management: Theory in Practice.* Dubuque, IA: Kendall/Hunt, 1985.

Beniger, James R. *The Control Revolution: Technological and Economic Origins of the Information Society.* Cambridge, MA: Harvard University Press, 1986.

Block, Peter. *Stewardship: Choosing Service over Self-Interest.* San Francisco: Berrett-Koehler, 1993.

Boss, Richard. *Telecommunications for Library Management.* White Plains, NY: Knowledge Industry Publications, 1985.

Bradford, C., and A. Cohen. *Managing for Excellence: The Guide to Developing High Performance in Contemporary Organizations.* New York: John Wiley, 1984.

Bridges, William. *Managing Transition.* Reading, MA: Addison-Wesley, 1991.

Burton, Terrence T., and John W. Moran. *The Future Focused Organization.* Englewood Cliffs, NJ: Prentice-Hall, 1995.

Cambel, Ali Bulent. *Applied Chaos Theory: A Paradigm for Complexity.* Boston: Academic Press, 1993.

Cargill, Jennifer, and Gisela M. Webb. *Managing Libraries in Transition*. Phoenix, AZ: Oryx Press, 1988.

Change in Libraries and Information Services, ed. By Lewis Foreman. London: HMSO, 1993.

Cummings, Anthony M. et al. *University Libraries and Scholarly Communication*. Washington, DC: Association of Research Libraries, 1992.

Davenport, T. H. *Process Innovation: Reengineering Work Through Information Technology*. Cambridge, MA: Harvard Business School Press, 1993.

Durzon, Susan C. *Managing Change: A How-To-Do-It Manual for Planning, Implementing and Evaluating Change in Libraries*. New York: Simon & Schuster, 1989.

Emerging Virtual Library. ARL SPEC Kit no. 186. Washington, DC: Association of Research Libraries, 1992.

Flynn, Patricia M. *Facilitating Technological Change*. Cambridge, MA: Ballinger, 1988.

Fomburn, Charles J. *Turning Points: Creating Strategic Change in Corporations*. New York: McGraw-Hill, 1992.

Gulick, Dirk van. *Encounter with Chaos*. New York: McGraw-Hill, 1992.

Handy, Charles. *The Age of Paradox*. Boston: Harvard Business School Press, 1994.

Hannan, Michael T., and J. Freeman. *Organizational Ecology*. Cambridge, MA: Harvard University Press, 1989.

Helgeson, Sally. *The Female Advantage: Women's Ways of Leadership*. New York: Doubleday, 1990.

Imparato, Nicholas, and Oren Harari. *Innovation and Strategic Choice in an Age of Transition*. San Francisco: Jossey-Bass, 1994.

Kanter, Rosabeth Moss. *The Change Masters: Innovation for Productivity in the American Corporation*. New York: Simon & Schuster, 1983.

————. *When Giants Learn to Dance*. New York: Simon & Schuster, 1989.

Kennedy, Paul. *Preparing for the Twenty-First Century*. New York: Random House, 1993.

Kilmann, Ralph H. *Managing Beyond the Quick Fix*. San Francisco: Jossey-Bass, 1989.

Kotter, John P. *Leading Change*. Boston: Harvard Business School Press, 1996.

Lawler, Edward E. III. *The Ultimate Advantage: Creating the High-Involvement Organization*. San Francisco: Jossey-Bass, 1992.

Mintzberg, Henry. *Structuring in Fives: Designing Effective Organizations*. Englewood Cliffs, NJ: Prentice-Hall, 1983.

Nadler, David A. et al. *Organizational Architecture: Designs for Changing Organizations*. San Francisco: Jossey-Bass, 1992.

Naisbitt, John. *Megatrends: Ten New Directions Transforming Our Lives*. New York: Winner Books, 1982.

National Research Council. *Human Resource Practices for Implementing Advanced Manufacturing Technology*. Washington, DC: National Academy Press, 1986.

Oakley, Ed, and Doug Krug. *Enlightened Leadership: Getting to the Heart of Change*. New York: Simon & Schuster, 1991.

Pasmore, William A. *Creating Strategic Change*. New York: John Wiley, 1994.

Peters, Tom. *Thriving on Chaos: Handbook for a Management Revolution*. New York: HarperCollins, 1987.

————. *Liberation Management: Necessary Disorganization for the Nanosecond Nineties*. New York: Alfred A. Knopf, 1992.

————. *The Tom Peters Seminar: Crazy Times Call for Crazy Organizations*. London: Pan Books, 1994.

Peters, Tom, and Robert H. Waterman Jr. *In Search of Excellence: Lessons from America's Best Run Companies*. New York: Harper & Row, 1982.

Saunders, Laverna M., ed. *The Virtual Library: Visions and Realities*. Westport, CT: Meckler, 1993.

Senge, Peter M. *The Fifth Discipline: The Art & Practice of the Learning Organization*. New York: Doubleday, 1990.

Sproul, S., and L. Kiesler. *Connections: New Ways of Working in the Networked Organization*. Cambridge, MA: MIT Press, 1992.

Stacey, Ralph D. *Managing the Unknowable: Strategic Boundaries Between Order and Chaos*. San Francisco: Jossey-Bass, 1993.

Trezza, Alsphonse F., ed. *Changing Technology: Opportunity and Challenge*. Boston: G. K. Hall, 1989.

Walton, Richard E. *Innovating to Compete*. San Francisco: Jossey-Bass, 1987.

————. *Up and Running: Integrating Information Technology and the Organization*. Boston: Harvard Business School Press, 1989.

Waterman, Robert H. *The Renewal Factor: How the Best Get and Keep the Competitive Edge*. New York: Bantam Books, 1987.

Wilson, David C. *A Strategy of Change*. London: Routledge, 1992.

Worley, Christopher G. *Integrated Strategic Change*. Reading, MA: Addison-Wesley, 1996.

Zuboff, Shoshana. *In the Age of the Smart Machine: The Future of Work and Power*. New York: Basic Books, 1988.

Appendix A
Mission, Goals, and Objectives

UNIVERSITY OF NORTH CAROLINA
AT CHAPEL HILL
ACADEMIC AFFAIRS LIBRARY
LIBRARY MISSION STATEMENT

The Library of The University of North Carolina at Chapel Hill has been built by the efforts of students, faculty, librarians, staff, and devoted friends of the University for a period of over two centuries. In that time, it has changed greatly and grown beyond what those who gave it birth could have imagined, but its mission remains the same. Its collections and services provide access to cumulated human knowledge for the University's students, faculty, staff, associated researchers, and the citizens of North Carolina in support of their study, research, teaching, scholarship, publishing, community service, and cultural enrichment.

In pursuing this mission, the Library will:

- Select and acquire as much of the recorded human knowledge needed by the Library's users for their current and anticipated University-related activities as available financial resources allow.

- Provide bibliographic control for the materials in its collections, and, insofar as feasible, for information sources not in its collections.

- Interpret the Library collections and services to users, assist them in utilizing those collections and services, and provide them with access to information sources located elsewhere.

- Make the collections available to users within legal limitations while preserving them for future use.

- Cooperate with other organizations for the advancement of scholarship and effective utilization of the records of human experience and knowledge.

- Revise and adapt its services appropriately for the changing needs of its users, the growing volume and complexity of publication in printed and nonprint forms, the changing methodologies in retrieval and delivery of information, and the changing requirement of its collections for organization and preservation.

April 23, 1996

BALTIMORE COUNTY PUBLIC LIBRARY
REPOSITIONING FOR THE FUTURE
Long Range Plan IV 1994-1999

Mission Statement

To provide for Baltimore County residents in a cost-effective manner:

- Library materials and information services
- Leadership in the delivery of electronic services through:
  providing access to these resources;

415

supplying information to the public about these resources; and participating in public policy discussions influencing these resources.

Roles

Experience with using the four roles listed below, from the publication of the *Public Library Association Planning and Role Setting for Public Libraries* (ALA, Chicago, 1987), led the staff of BCPL to modifications included in this plan. The changes were based on their observation that the original groupings did not mirror the way BCPL makes decisions about services and resources. The new groupings facilitate decision making and avoid overlap.

1. Information and Learning Support Center: Negotiate, identify and deliver timely information to individuals of all ages with a variety of needs:

- Focused, factual requests
- Citizen education in community affairs
- Career and job related development
- Format education programs
- Self-directed learning

Special efforts could include the following:

- Provide information in a wide range of subject areas and in a variety of formats
- Deliver information on site, by telephone, fax and remote access
- Provide services such as document delivery, mailing labels, lists and online searching
- Repackage information to ensure value in meeting the customers' needs

2. Young Children's Support Center: Library services to young children, birth through third grade, and their parents, care givers and teachers will encourage children and care givers to develop and maintain a habit of regular library use. As a Young Children's Support Center, the library recognizes its special role as one of the first providers of educational and social opportunities in a young child's life and that children in this age span progress through a broad range of cognitive, emotional and physical abilities.

Special efforts could include the following:

- Provide developmentally appropriate materials and services which promote children's language skills, reading readiness and emergent literacy
- Provide parents, teachers and care givers with resources and services to support their efforts to develop children's interests, experiences and knowledge
- Work with other agencies and organizations in their efforts to promote public library use for school readiness and reading readiness
- Serve as a clearinghouse for information on agencies and organizations serving children, parents, care givers and families, for interagency as well as customer use
- Recognize varying community needs, allowing branches to target services and materials to specific segments of the child and care giver community

3. Popular Interest Support Center: Provide timely delivery of materials which are demanded, wanted and/or anticipated by many individuals of all ages

Special efforts could include the following:

- Materials valued by a wide group of patrons
- Materials valued by a targeted market segment, such as African Americans, Russian immigrants, Hispanic and Asian Americans
- Fiction and nonfiction for browsing customers
- Nonfiction use for self-directed learners
- Materials in various formats, with special sensitivity to emerging nonprint formats, such as the electronic book
- Materials which depict the human experience for readers, viewers, listeners of all ages, especially children. These materials provide opportunities to expand the child through vicarious experiences, hero identification and problem solving
- Reader advisory services

4. Organization Support Center: Provide customized information services to organizations of all types

Special efforts could include the following:

- Provide information and services to businesses, small entrepreneurs as well as large companies, to support local economic development
- Provide information to local, state and federal government officials and staff for policy formulation and program management
- Provide information and varied services to nonprofit organizations
- Assist government agencies and organizations in dissemination of information about their services
- Provide specialized services, such as document delivery, online searching services, packaging and interpreting information, mailing lists, research on issues
- Delivery of information on-site, by telephone, fax and remote access

STRATEGIC DIRECTIONS

New emphases in strategic directions, like almost all changes in this plan, are the result of the three major changes in the library's environment: funding, demographics and technology. Responsiveness to the public is not new at BCPL. In fact, it is a foundation of their famous "Give 'Em What They Want" philosophy recently detailed in the book of the same name. Increased attention to responsiveness is appropriate when changes are coming thick and fast, as they will in the next five years.

FUTURE DIRECTIONS

It should be noted that the activities listed under each strategic direction in this section are for the short term only. It is widely believed that rates of change make the future so uncertain that drawing up a comprehensive set of projects for the next five years would not be useful.

It should also be noted that the project list for each strategic direction ends with "Implement Window On the World." To accomplish all of these strategic directions, Baltimore County Public Library will provide a Window On the World (WOW) for its customers. What is WOW? More information, easier to locate, more convenient to use.

Every computer terminal in the Baltimore County Public Library System will soon be a Window On the World (WOW), a gateway to information and to information about information. Opening the Window On the World the inquirer will find:

- The BCPL catalog and circulation status of all items
- Catalogs from other libraries
- A community information file
- A periodicals index
- A health information index
- A newspaper index
- Full-text encyclopedias and periodicals
- Much, much more

WOW may well be the innovation that shifts the paradigm of the library as a building with books to a publicly supported information service available in multiple sites. WOW will run on the CARL System, BCPL's new Automated Integrated Library System which features:

- A graphical interface (GUI) for children and adults
- The capability to print or download screens to computer disks
- Routines enabling patrons self charge, return and inquiry
- Routines enabling patrons to place their own reserves

Paying for printouts, as well as for other library services such as photocopying, will be easy. Library users can obtain and use a WOW Card, a library card which serves also as a debit card.

Enhance cost effectiveness

- Implement WOW Card use
- Extend voice message system throughout the library system
- Review use of staff resources
- Review existing and proposed fees to ensure that costs do not outweigh benefits
- Reconsider Sunday openings
- Implement Window On the World

Enhance responsiveness

- Continue to work closely with the Board of Library Trustees to ensure that the library's policies and priorities reflect the needs of the residents of Baltimore County
- Develop and implement annual branch service plans which use local demographic information
- Recognize the interdependence of Maryland's library users and resources by working closely with the Division of Library Development and Services, Maryland State Department of Education
- Develop and implement team relationships at the administrative level to support branches
- Implement Window On the World

Enhance access to and delivery of services
- Consider instituting customized services
- Implement role based systemwide teams
- Implement Window On the World

Enhance staff ability to provide services
- Ensure effective staff training for every innovation in service delivery
- Ensure staff training for ongoing services
- Ensure staff participation in decision making as appropriate
- Continue to provide open communication
- Implement Window On the World

HARVARD COLLEGE LIBRARY
COMMITMENT TO RENEWAL
A Strategic Plan
February 3, 1992

Mission Statement

The Harvard College Library supports the teaching and research activities of the Faculty of Arts and Sciences and the University. Beyond this primary responsibility, the library serves, to the extent feasible, the larger scholarly community. The library acquires, organizes, preserves, and makes readily available collections of scholarly materials in all media and formats.

The library fulfills its mission by providing intellectual access to materials and information available at the University and elsewhere, by providing assistance and training in the location and use of these materials by providing facilities and services for research and study.

- **Creating the Future from the Past: A New Vision of the Library**

The fundamental purpose of the library is, as it always has been, to support research and instruction in the college and university and the research of scholars from around the world. It is not enough for the library simply to accommodate inevitable change. Rather, it must be responsive to new conditions, while preserving the distinctive and useful features of the past. Maintaining a browsable, open stack collection and striking a balance between old and new books are examples of the latter, improving library services and providing more congenial spaces for the use of library materials illustrate the former. The library's challenge in this period of transition is to devise a strategy that retains the best of the past while creating an organization that is responsive to change and provides leadership in shaping the future. What are needed are a coherent vision and principles to enable the library to chart this course.

The library, as someone once observed, is not a building, but the collection inside. In truth, the library is not just a collection, either, it is also an association of people who come together to do something that cannot easily be done alone. As an association of people organized by functions—collecting, cataloging, services—the library is dedicated to supporting research and instruction. Its purpose and goals are, in one sense, dependent on the purpose and goals of the larger community, the *universitas*, of which it is a part.

The associative nature of the library suggests four principles that ought to govern the library in the future. These principles are: unity of vision, stewardship, quality, and collective action and cooperation.

The business of the library is communication of information—printed, aural, visual, and electronic—and it is the library's support of scholarly communication that provides the glue that binds and connects the various academic parts of the community to the whole. To be effective in its mission to support the diverse academic programs of the university, the library must create a shared vision. The key to success will be the creation in fact, as well as in name, of a unified Harvard College Library that supports all of the scholarly fields we are committed to serving.

The second principle of the library as association is stewardship. A steward is one who manages on behalf of the community; the steward neither owns the content nor the specific functions for which he or she is responsible. Stewardship involves two ideas: the conservation of existing resources, including collections, staff, and space, through planned change, and the acceleration of conscious change in the areas of technology, services, and intellectual access to maintain and even increase the quality of support for learning. Stewardship represents, therefore, both the husbanding of existing resources that are essential to the academic community and a deliberate effort to introduce new sources of information and services that will become increasingly important in the future. Within the Harvard context, stewardship entails (1) selecting the materials and sources needed for instruction and research; (2) managing the collection, that is, maintaining, preserving, cataloging, and servicing the materials acquired; (3) improving intellectual access by making it easier for the user to discover the full range of research materials, nonprint sources, as well as books held in storage; (4) providing training and instruction in locating needed information and using library resources with the aim of helping users to become self-sufficient; and (5) developing new skills for staff, who ultimately determine the quality of the library.

A community also calls for an unusual commitment to quality and excellence in performing the functions that define it. Devotion to quality is not a function of perfection; instead, it derives from a recognition that the success of the whole is dependent on the quality of contribution of each part and requires, therefore, constant attention to process and procedures. Moreover, a commitment to quality will encourage the participation of staff at all levels and functions in determining the most effective and efficient methods for operating the library. This is the surest antidote to unfettered bureaucracy.

Finally, the new vision of the library calls for collective action and collaboration. The library's mission to support research and instruction can no longer be entirely satisfied locally; future success will depend upon collective action within the Harvard community and active collaboration with national and international research institutions and libraries. Collection development and storage, electronic transmission of information, preservation, intellectual access, and the development of standards for new technologies are a few of the areas in which the Harvard community can benefit from cooperative efforts with others.

STRATEGIC GOALS AND OBJECTIVES

The Library will focus on five strategic goals during the 1990s. These are space and catalog conversion, collections and access, library use and services, reallocation of resources, and new technologies.

- **Space and Catalog Conversion**

The acute shortage of space for books is the most urgent issue confronting the College Library. Failure to resolve this issue will undermine day-to-day operations and jeopardize our ability to achieve the goals and objectives of the Strategic Plan. The solution to the library's space needs is the Harvard Depository. What the Harvard Depository provides, in addition to secure and climate-controlled stacks, is adequate shelf space for the foreseeable future. The transfer of materials to the Harvard Depository also presents an opportunity, indeed, it requires us to reconsider the purpose and uses of Widener and the other College libraries during this period of intellectual and technological change. But solving the space problem depends not only on the availability of the Harvard Depository, it depends as well on the effective use of the Harvard Online Library Information System (HOLLIS). More than just a computerized version of the card catalog, HOLLIS is a powerful and versatile management system that facilitates the transfer of materials between libraries and the Harvard Depository. Unfortunately, only one-third of the library's catalog records are represented in HOLLIS, and this is a serious impediment to its use. Operating a library system that is only partially computerized is inefficient since users and staff must work with two systems. To make HOLLIS a fully effective public catalog and an efficient management system, all the remaining pre-1976 catalog records must be converted to machine-readable form and made available in HOLLIS. Thus, retrospective conversion of the card catalog is a high priority because it will permit the effective use of the Harvard Depository to solve the library's space problem, even as it significantly improves scholarly access to all of Harvard's collections.

STRATEGIC GOAL I:

Provide for growth of collections by converting the card catalog to machine-readable form, enabling the use of most effective use of closed-stack storage at the Harvard Depository and in the Yard.

We will pursue two objectives to achieve this goal:

1. *Define and create the on-site collection. Balance collection growth and existing space in the Yard by moving one million volumes from Widener and develop and implement a plan that will enable the library to maintain a steady-state of growth in the Yard.*

Widener and nearly all of the other 10 libraries in the College Library are filled to or beyond their working capacity. The College Library has a total of nearly 7 million volumes and adds about 150,000 volumes a year. At the current growth rate, it will double in size in 25 years. We have a solution to this problem in the Harvard Depository, a state-of-the-art closed stack facility for books and other research materials, located at Southborough, 35 minutes from Cambridge. Each unit has a capacity of approximately 2 million volumes (more than half the capacity of Widener/Pusey), and there is room for 10 units. Materials are stored in secure, climate-controlled space, and are delivered the next day. In addition, more intensive use must be made of existing stack space in the Yard. By employing compact storage technology, the amount of browsable, open-stack space in the yard can be increased. The success of these efforts will ultimately depend on our ability to develop a comprehensive collection-use plan that identifies which books need to be consulted on-site and which books can be retrieved from closed-stacks. Librarians and faculty will need to achieve consensus on what to send to storage and how best to use valuable library space in the Yard.

2. *Catalog conversion. Convert the library's card catalog to machine-readable form and make them available in HOLLIS.*

The retrospective conversion of pre-1976 catalog records is the single most important measure we can take, not only to improve intellectual access to Harvard's collections, but, equally important, to facilitate the transfer of materials between Widener and the Harvard Depository. To make HOLLIS a fully effective public catalog and library management system, all the remaining pre-1976 catalog records must be converted to machine-readable form and made available on HOLLIS. Preliminary estimates put the number of records to be converted in the College Library's catalogs at 3.5 million (nearly 5 million records for the entire university). Completion of this project will facilitate access to the library's older and most important research collections.

- **Collections and Access**

The dramatic escalation in the cost, quantity, and forms of research material will affect the library's ability to maintain traditional collection practices. Great research collections, it is now recognized, demand the commitment of resources not only to build collections, but also to manage and preserve them. In the past, we were inclined to think of the collection as the material owned by a library. A better definition of collection is one based on the principle of stewardship or collection management, that is, selection, acquisitions, cataloging, preservation, security, maintenance, and services; these are the real costs of acquiring a book and building a collection. Moreover, as the library continues to build and manage the collection, it must also provide resources for new services and technologies, which will be increasingly important for research. Indeed, the electronic transmission of texts and images will transform our understanding of research collections and change, too, library functions that are needed to support them. To meet these new instructional and research needs, informational services will need to be tailored. An unacknowledged problem resulting from these changes is how to find what is needed from information sources that seem to be increasing geometrically. The explosion of information sources and the success of libraries in making it accessible threatens to overwhelm students and scholars; a challenge for the library will be to devise ways to help users navigate this sea of information and find what they need in the form in which they need it. The greatest hope for a solution to this dilemma may be technology, but, in the near term, reference librarians will be severely tested.

STRATEGIC GOAL II:

Strengthen the research collection by sustaining acquisitions and improving intellectual access, preservation, security, and maintenance of the collection.

The following four objectives are designed to achieve this goal.

1. *Ensuring the future of collections. Maintain the strength of the library's traditional book and journal collections and enrich them with new types of materials—including visual, electronic and multimedia formats—by increasing endowment funds.*

The new information technologies will increase greatly the quantity and range of research resources available to library users, but they are no substitute for continuing to build strong traditional collections and services. The library's book, journal and manuscript collections are and will continue to be the mainstay of our library and its services to users through this decade and the next. We cannot build our new computer-based information capabilities at the expense of our traditional collections and services; we must do both. At the same time, the continued growth in the quantity of publications and escalating costs will oblige the library to devise methods to evaluate the quality of acquisitions, reduce inappropriate duplication, and promote cooperative collection development agreements. We must also seek to balance the collecting and processing of research materials and alter the methods for processing and storing collections in order to support acquisitions within existing on-campus space and, through more efficient operations, with fewer staff members.

2. *Improving intellectual access to research materials. Complete the retrospective conversion of the card catalog and strengthen intellectual access by introducing new databases to HOLLIS, devising better cataloging methods, and developing the subject skills of library staff who help students and scholars to locate needed information and sources.*

The retrospective conversion of pre-1976 catalog records is clearly the single most important measure we can take to improve intellectual access to Harvard's collections and to make HOLLIS a fully effective public catalog. The library has an enormous investment in its collections; recording them in HOLLIS will ensure that important materials are not overlooked. An online catalog is simply a more efficient means of finding bibliographic information. Boolean search strategies are more powerful than the traditional card catalog. Adding reference works, abstracts and indexes, text and a variety of other informational databases to the "catalog" will transform the catalog into a cultural database; it will also increase the efficiency of doing research and change the very process by which scholars create and use information. These changes to the traditional structure of the catalog, coupled with changes in the methods and use of research collections, will require librarians to re-examine cataloging principles and traditional methods of providing intellectual access to research materials. The need to improve intellectual access to research materials, as well as the need to contain costs, will fundamentally alter traditional descriptive practices and the work of librarians in the future. Finally, to assist researchers in navigating an increasingly complex universe of information, the library must seek to identify and develop staff with subject expertise and make this expertise more readily available to students and scholars. To do this, more members of the library's staff will have multiple responsibilities that cut across the lines separating traditional library functions. Improved interaction between scholars and librarians will help users to be better informed about the research needs of students and scholars. In the long run, the aim is to relate collections and services to the research agendas of specific disciplines by developing discipline-competent teams within the library to address users' needs.

3. *Preserving collections through climate controls. Install air conditioning, new lighting, and security in Widener Library and renovate and improve the climate control systems for Houghton, Pusey, and Lamont libraries.*

Improving the storage environment for the collections is the single most important preservation action that can be taken by Harvard. Paper degrades 4 times as fast at 80 degrees Fahrenheit and 50 percent relative humidity (typical summer conditions) as it does when stored at 68 degrees Fahrenheit and 40 percent relative humidity, and 8 times as fast as the conditions currently attainable at the Harvard Depository. Moreover, excessive heat and humidity, air pollution, and exposure to the ultraviolet light that is present in natural and fluorescent light all accelerate the deterioration of research materials and cause irreversible damage. The sulfur dioxide, ozone, and nitrogen dioxide present in urban Boston and Cambridge are powerful catalysts to chemical reaction. Installing climate controls and new lighting in Widener and upgrading equipment in Pusey and Lamont are essential elements in preserving the library's collections.

4. *Preserving collections through technology. Strengthen the library's preservation program by raising endowment funds for mass deacidification, a conservation*

> *laboratory, and the preservation of research materials through microfilming and the use of imaging technologies.*

The library must find the means to preserve its collections, which are deteriorating at an alarming rate. Storing lesser-used materials in the climate-controlled Harvard Depository and dramatically improving environmental conditions in Widener will enable the library to concentrate its preservation resources on the most heavily used portions of the collection. The library must, therefore, intensify efforts to review materials for preservation decisions. We have already developed a comprehensive preservation program and are also participating in a national federally funded preservation project. We need to endow this program, create a conservation laboratory under the direction of a professional conservator, and explore promising opportunities for using imaging technologies for preserving materials and making them accessible to users.

- ## Library Use and Services

From its inception, Widener Library and, indeed, all of the libraries that comprise the Harvard College Library, were regarded not just as storehouses for books, but as the places where students and faculty worked. One of the advantages of Harvard's distributed library system is convenient physical access and the ease and efficiency with which scholars can locate and use research materials. The continued growth of the collection, however, has resulted in the dispersion of materials throughout the campus and even off-site. The loss of physical proximity to research materials makes browsing less effective and the use of materials inconvenient. Research efficiency has also been compromised by the absence of a comprehensive reference collection and the lack of a coherent organization of books, based on their predominant use, in the stacks of the central library complex. These deficiencies have prompted academic departments, primarily in the humanities, to request separate, departmental reference collections; the result of such fragmentation is further erosion in basic library services and increasing costs to FAS. In other fields, especially in the physical sciences, proximity to basic reference tools and research literature will be increasingly in electronic form, which may begin to change the informational needs of some of the faculty science libraries for support and services. The pattern of undergraduate use of libraries has also changed since Lamont Library was first conceived of as a separate library for undergraduates. Dramatic changes in publishing at the end of World War II have made instructors less reliant on textbooks. Harvard's adoption of the core curriculum may have also accelerated the increasing use of the research collections by Harvard undergraduates. The need for a high-use undergraduate collection remains, but this collection, by itself, is no longer sufficient for undergraduate learning, a fact demonstrated by the growing undergraduate use of research collections in Widener and elsewhere.

The cumulative impact of these changes in library use and services has diminished the efficiency of research by scholars and the quality of learning by students. Effective research depends not only on the availability of research resources, but also on timely access to them. As academic fields continue to develop diverse patterns of research and communication, the library must provide a growing array of specialized resources and services. The library will respond to this new environment by: (a) improving services and physical access to source materials; (b) expanding the reference collection and providing greater support by subject specialists; (c) developing and implementing plans for gateway libraries in Lamont and Cabot, thereby both improving undergraduate learning and creating better access to research collections for all members of the Harvard community; and (d) providing better coordination of informational services and library support for scientists at Harvard.

STRATEGIC GOAL III:

Help students and faculty to achieve maximum benefit from library services and resources by making use of the library more convenient and efficient.

The library will pursue three objectives to achieve this goal:

1. *Conversion of Lamont and Cabot to "gateway" libraries. Renovate, refurbish, and equip Lamont Library and incorporate programs and technology in Cabot Library to create gateway libraries that will focus on the effective use of information technology by the entire Harvard community. Advanced technology and skilled staff, dedicated to undergraduate education, will provide support for experiments in instruction, database development, and scholarly communication.*

The idea of a gateway library is predicated on the notion that research ought to inform instruction and that interdisciplinary studies and information technologies are transforming the ways of knowing. Learning how to use electronic information effectively in a variety of formats and on networks is an increasingly important part of undergraduate education. The historic role of the library as a place to consult books and journals must be supplemented by one that incorporates emerging information technologies into a program devoted primarily to undergraduate education and that introduces students to information sources at Harvard and beyond. Recent studies suggest the importance of small group study and active class participation as key ingredients in learning. The gateway libraries should, therefore, incorporate group discussion rooms and rooms for working with various audio-visual materials, as well as multi-media workstations and individual carrels and study space as part of the plan. Although information technologies may soon become ubiquitous, a complete renovation of Lamont and full integration of new technologies into Cabot will enhance library services and instruction in the humanities and the sciences for the entire Harvard community. Incorporating state-of-the-art technologies and employing information specialists will provide the College with needed facilities to support: (a) the creative use of technology in teaching; (b) an instructional program at Lamont, Hilles, and Cabot to assist students and faculty in making the most effective use of HOLLIS and other research tools and library resources; and (c) experiments in teaching, creating text databases and multi-media applications, and exploring different modes of publication and scholarly communication.

2. *Library service. Improve the research use of collections in the central library by the following measures: define and enlarge the open-stack research collection, create a more convenient and useful shelving plan within Widener/Pusey, establish a secure reading room for the use of noncirculating materials, design a new space for Government Documents, Microtexts and other nonbook collections, and greatly improve access to and delivery of research materials directly to students and scholars.*

The library is filled beyond capacity and we can no longer view it primarily as a storage facility. In the future, the central library complex (Widener/Pusey/Lamont/-Houghton) must be dedicated to the *use* of books as well as government documents, electronic databases, audio-visual materials, photographs and images, ephemera, manuscripts, and other forms of research materials, regardless of where particular items and collections may be stored. In order for this new mission to work, the library will need to devote greater attention and resources to improving services for the delivery and use of research materials. If faculty and students cannot put their hands on the materials they need, then the library has failed them. Patrons need a fully-functional online reserve system that provides faculty and course list indexing. They also need a system that provides online ordering and renewal capabilities, and other interactive facilities that will be time-saving and offer a fair tradeoff for reduced proximity to every item in the collection. Moreover, faculty members and librarians working together must develop a profile of the books and research materials that need to be browsable and used on-site. We must also improve the arrangement of collections in the stacks based on the relationship of classes to their primary uses. In addition, we must greatly enlarge the central reference collection and provide a separate reading room and seminar rooms for its use. Growing concern for preservation and security demand the creation of a supervised reading room in the central complex in conjunction with a photocopy service center in order to reduce damage to fragile materials and to permit the use of noncirculating materials. Finally, we will move the Government Documents and Microtext Reading Room to the first floor of Lamont to create a facility that is appropriate to its high level of use and the quality of its collections.

3. *Science libraries. Access the informational and research needs of Harvard scientists and, in collaboration with science faculty, develop procedures for improving the coordination of library policies and services for the sciences.*

With the exception of Kummel Library of the Geological Sciences and the research collection for mathematics in Cabot Library, scientists at Harvard are served primarily by libraries administered by departments. Proximity to basic reference tools and research literature has always been extremely important to scientists and the departmental structure has worked well. The growing importance of electronic information, however, is not only changing the informational needs of some science departments, but it raises a number of issues that are also of concern to the College Library. Preservation, duplication, and the storage of older materials, for example, are important to the College Library as well as to the science libraries. The science community ought to be involved in discussions about policies concerning the library information system, including decisions about which databases are mounted in HOLLIS. Similarly, agreements with other institutions for sharing resources and providing document delivery are difficult without the participation of science departments. The libraries serving scientists must not be perceived as balkanized special interests, and the boundary between them and the College Library must not become a barrier to providing service to the scientific community. Instead, the College Library needs to achieve a better understanding of the informational and research needs of scientists in order to provide more effective library services to this part of the Harvard community. As technology begins to change research methods and library use, especially in the sciences, the College Library must encourage the participation of scientists in planned coordinated library policies and services. The Harvard College Library must develop the kind and level of library and informational support for the sciences that its distinguished programs require.

• **New Technologies**

New technologies and telecommunications promise to transform scholarly communication and are already having a significant impact on academic libraries. The rapid development of national networks will make it possible to transmit huge quantities of data, text, and images from coast to coast and around the world. High-speed transmission and new computer and networking technologies will permit scholars to edit text and images; to cross-reference and link documents, independent of location; to browse online digital libraries; and to search large text and image databases and retrieve selected documents. In short, we have entered a period of extraordinary, perhaps even revolutionary, change in the way in which information is stored, packaged, transmitted, and used. Because of the strength of its collections,

Harvard has a special obligation and, indeed, a unique opportunity to participate in these developments.

At present, HOLLIS is the only major information system available across the campus. Although the library is committed to providing access to the expanding universe of information through library systems and technology, it will be limited in its ability to do so by the absence of a ubiquitous campus network. Without an electronic infrastructure, students and scholars at Harvard will be severely hampered in their efforts to participate in the rapidly evolving information and telecommunications environment. Failure to address computing needs systematically and structurally throughout the university will jeopardize the library's efforts to provide access to electronic information.

STRATEGIC GOAL IV:

Build and support computer and communication technologies and implement a comprehensive program for delivering electronic research materials in the College Library.

The library will pursue three strategic objectives:

1. *Support electronic information. Provide the infrastructure to support the use of electronic information in the library and link it to emerging campus networks.*

The library must not only acquire the electronic sources needed for research, but also provide the infrastructure—facilities, equipment, and staff—to support a growing array of texts, databases, and other forms of electronic information. To ensure that students and faculty have maximum access to electronic information and resources, the library must develop strong partnerships with the Office of Information Technology and other campus libraries and information providers within the University. In addition to providing the equipment and network support needed for electronic information, the library must also take the lead in providing assistance and instruction in the using of these systems by students and faculty.

2. *Support information management. Take the lead in supporting information management at Harvard.*

When the card catalog is fully converted to machine-readable form and entered into HOLLIS, one will no longer have to come to the library to examine catalogs, order, recall, and renew books, peruse indexes, and perform a variety of other traditional library research tasks. These achievements will fuel expectations for making primary resources, including texts, images, and multi-media applications, accessible electronically. By linking content and format, text and images, computers enable users to manipulate large quantities of information and provide a tool of enormous potential for improving research and instruction. The library will take primary responsibility for identifying, acquiring, organizing, and making accessible electronic sources in a variety of formats—CD-ROM, optical disks, online information sources made available through Local Area Networks or campus-wide networks. The future of electronic information and resources clearly resides in rapidly evolving networks; it will be the library's responsibility to manage and support the use of information and help to make it directly accessible to our users.

3. *Library role in networking and information technology. Play a leading role in national developments in networking and information technology.*

The dramatic development in new technologies and, in particular, the increasing importance of national information networks for research, point to Harvard's need to participate in these forums. Decisions about the structure and use of national high-speed data networks, for example, the National Research and Education Network, will have a profound impact on scholarly communication and research in the future. Moreover, important decisions made at the national level—copyright and licensing agreements, the development of standards and interface protocols, and promoting the publication of primary sources—will have a significant influence on the way in which the library supports electronic information on campus. The library must, therefore, participate in the development of national information policies as well as interinstitutional collaborative activities regarding information management to ensure that these policies and activities reflect the research and instructional needs of Harvard College. Active participation in the Research Library Group is an important first step in this process.

- **Reallocation of Resources**

The most difficult challenge for the library will be deciding how to reallocate resources in accordance with its mission and new vision. If it is the association of librarians organized around functions that defines the library, then greater attention must be devoted to training and developing staff. Moreover, as both library functions and the needs of students and scholars evolve in response to a changing information environment, the purposes and uses of library buildings and space will be redefined, encountering tradition at every turn. Upgrading services, providing for new technology, and improving intellectual access to research materials will require additional funds and more staff and space for these activities, most of which will have come from the reallocation of existing resources. The historic migration of collections out of Widener into separate libraries, each with its own staff, has clearly come to an end and the policy of maintaining innumerable departmental libraries must be weighed against total library costs, as well as user convenience. Just as the cost of maintaining the collection demands greater coordination among units and less duplication, so, too, the use of space to house it and the deployment of staff to service it will require a clearer definition of the purpose and contribution of each unit toward achieving the most efficient use of existing resources.

Computerization and improvements in electronic access will fundamentally alter the way the library functions. These also provide opportunities to reconsider how space and other resources are allocated in support of the library's mission. Capital funds will be needed for renovating existing buildings and spaces, but the directions outlined in this Strategic Plan will also require the reallocation of existing resources, perhaps most critically, space and staff. In sum, the library must redefine and even shrink some aspects of its current operation in order to expand other activities and carry out its new vision and plans for supporting teaching and research at Harvard.

STRATEGIC GOAL V:

Maintain the excellence of the library in a changing intellectual, technological, and economic environment by reallocating human, fiscal, and space resources.

Pursuing two objectives will enable the library to maintain its traditional excellence:

1. *Unify the Harvard College Library. Create a unified College Library that is responsive to changes in the intellectual environment while supporting research and teaching, primarily with existing space, staff, and financial resources.*

Faced with rising costs and limited resources, the library must reconsider the role of each of the eleven libraries and numerous departments and collections in the Harvard College Library. In the past, the structure of the library reflected the academic structure of the College; decisions to allocate space, staff, and funds were based in part on assumptions about the nature of research that may no longer prevail. The current structure and organization of the College Library continues to reflect these assumptions and decisions. Studies confirm the increase in interdisciplinary research and also indicate that patterns of use are not necessarily reflected in the current organization of the library. We need, therefore, to examine the organization, access policies, staffing, and use of space in the library from the perspective of the relationship of collections and their principal users.

2. *Central library complex. Create a coordinated central library complex (Widener, Lamont, Pusey, and Houghton) with concentrated bibliographic and access services and collections.*

Creating a coordinated central library complex is important not only for making research more convenient and efficient, but also as a way of reducing costs by eliminating redundant operations and improving the efficiency of the library. Planning a coordinated central library complex will also encourage consideration of related collections and activities that are currently dispersed and therefore, inconvenient to use. For example, one of the aims of this Plan is to improve services and physical facilities for Government Documents and Microtexts (currently located in the basement of Lamont). The renovation of this facility provides an opportunity to reconsider this operation's connection to related collections and resources scattered across the campus. Littauer Library houses important collections on labor relations and state documents but also duplicates some materials held in Widener and Government Documents. The Harvard Data Center houses important materials in electronic form, some of it duplicating information in print or microform held by the library. In short, here is an opportunity to think about how these collections and resources can be more effectively arranged to support research.

MIAMI-DADE PUBLIC LIBRARY SYSTEM
VISION TO REALITY
A 5-Year Plan 1995-2000

Mission Statement
To maintain and improve public library services reflecting the diverse informational, educational, and recreational needs of the community.

Vision: AUTOMATION—Residents of Dade County will have easy access to automated resources for information, learning and enjoyment through the Library's new computer system.

Action Plan:

- The Library, in conjunction with the Southeast Florida Information Network (SEFLIN), will install a Freenet to provide free electronic access to community-oriented databases and information resources.
  Date: Completed

- The Library will implement, during 1995-96, a new turnkey computer system with the following features:
  - On-Line Public Access Catalog
  - Circulation Control Module, including self-charge at key locations
  - Electronic Mail/Message System
  - Acquisitions for speedier ordering of library materials
  - Serials Control
  - Inventory Control
  - Telephone Notification System for reserves
  - ADA enhancements at key locations
  - Electronic databases
  Date: December, 1996

- The Library will provide access to and assistance for patrons in using the Freenet
  Date: Ongoing

- The Library will bring up the Internet, including the World Wide Web, at larger libraries
  Date: Ongoing

Vision: COLLECTION DEVELOPMENT—The Library will provide the residents of Dade County with print and electronic resources reflecting the diverse informational, educational, and recreational needs of the community.

Action Plan:

- The Library will seek to place before the voters of Dade County a referendum for a special tax to establish a new Book Trust replacing the current one, which is scheduled to expire in FY 2000
  Date: October, 1997

- The Library will continue to purchase books on a wide variety of subjects reflecting the many needs and interests of Dade County citizens
  Date: Ongoing

- The Library will provide on-line access for walk-in patrons to a wide variety of informational databases
  Date: October, 1996

- The Library will provide dial-in access to the Library's bibliographic and informational databases
  Date: October, 1996

- The Library will offer materials in a variety of media, both hard copy and electronic
  Date: Ongoing

- The Library will improve the location and visibility of the Library's special collections
  Date: October, 1997

- The Library's materials budget will target substantial expenditures for purchase of materials in languages other than English
  Date: October, 1995

- The Library will establish significant collections on African-American history and culture at four additional branch locations: Main Library, South Dade Regional, Culmer/Overtown, and Model City, while continuing to maintain and enhance the North Dade Regional collection
  Date: Ongoing through end of FY 98-99

Vision: **DIVERSITY**—The Library will promote materials and programs reflecting the multi-ethnic community.

- The Library will conduct a needs assessment of underserved areas of the community updating the information annually
  Date: First survey of patrons completed. Next survey due October, 1996, and one each year until 2000

- The Library will pursue funding to support outreach to underserved parts of the community, including recent immigrants
  Date: First attempts completed by October, 1996

- The Library will publish information about its services in languages other than English
  Date: New immigrant bibliographies completed. Applications in Spanish and French by January, 1996. Multi-language flier by 1997

- The Library will promote its programs, materials, and special services via Spanish, Haitian and other media
  Date: Work with African-American and Haitian communities through local media. Ongoing

- The Library will work with agencies serving immigrants, publicizing new and existing materials and services
  Date: Ongoing

- The Library will conduct library card registration drives among new immigrants
  Date: Ongoing

- The Library will continue to support equal employment opportunity to all qualified applicants, including recruitment and retention of minorities
  Date: Ongoing

- Using corporate funds, the Library will continue Hispanic Heritage and Black History programming
  Date: Ongoing

Vision: LIBRARY FACILITIES—The Library will enhance library facilities to meet current standards of excellence.

Action Plan:

- The Library will seek funding, either through Bond Issue 2000, or through a combined Book-Facilities Bond Issue to repair and enhance existing facilities
  Date: 1998

- The Library will seek to bring all facilities into compliance with the Americans with Disabilities Act (ADA) regulations
  Date: Ongoing through FY 95-96

Vision: SERVICE TO POPULATIONS WITH SPECIAL NEEDS—The Library will provide equal access to all aspects of library service for people with disabilities.

Action Plan:

- The Library will pursue funding to make library facilities, collections and programs ADA-accessible
  Date: Ongoing

- The Library will increase public awareness of collections and equipment for people with disabilities
  Date: Ongoing

- The Library will provide special assistance and training for people with disabilities in the use of the new computer system
  Date: December, 1996

- The Library will provide sensitivity training for staff in serving people with disabilities
  Date: December, 1996

Vision: ADULT ILLITERACY—The Library will use its personnel and collections to combat adult illiteracy.

Action Plan:

- The Library will work with other local agencies to certify tutors who will work with adult learners
  Date: Ongoing

- The Library will maintain collections of High/Low and New Reader materials to stimulate an interest in reading
  Date: Ongoing

- The Library will publicize Project L.E.A.D.'s literacy efforts in order to attract more tutors and students
  Date: Ongoing

- The Library will provide computerized literacy services at additional branch sites
  Date: December, 1997

Vision: SERVICES TO POPULATIONS WITH SPECIAL NEEDS—
The Library will provide library access to senior citizens both through improved physical access to buildings and materials, and through continued emphasis on Connections, the Library's book by mail for the Homebound.

Action Plan:

- The Library will publicized the Library's improved access to buildings and special equipment for the visually and hearing-impaired
  Date: September, 1995

- The Library will include information on Connections in local newspapers and other publications geared toward senior citizens
  Date: September, 1995

- The Library will provide promotional materials to increase programming at senior centers, retirement communities, nursing homes and other related facilities
  Date: September, 1995

- The Library will pursue funding sources that will assist senior citizens on fixed incomes needing financial assistance with postage for returning books by mail
  Date: June, 1996

Vision: STAFF DEVELOPMENT—The Library will provide training and career opportunities for employees.

Action Plan:

- The Library will provide training to promote multicultural understanding among all staff
  Date: Ongoing

- The Library will target training in automated services, with special focus on the Internet, the Freenet, and the new automated system
  Date: Ongoing with special training on the new system in 1996

- The Library will expand training in customer relations and will collect materials, videos as well as books, on the subject
  Date: Ongoing

- The Library will offer regular scheduled training opportunities at a variety of library sites, to encourage team-building, to enable accessibility to systemwide staff, and to promote employee development
  Date: Ongoing

- The Library will target staff training for adult and circulation professionals and para-professionals
  Date: Ongoing

Vision: YOUTH SERVICES—The Library will develop programs to support reading readiness among preschoolers.

Action Plan:

- The Library will expand services to licensed day care providers and certified preschools, both public and private
  Date: September, 1996

- The Library will develop a plan to establish working partnerships at the Branch Library level with selected groups serving the preschool population
  Date: September, 1996

- The Library will target parent education by offering a variety of informational, recreational, and developmental programs on early childhood
  Date: September, 1997

- Through Family Literacy, the Library will develop reading readiness programs for the most at-risk children and their families
  Date: September, 1997

- The Library will seek funding to establish Preschool Learning Centers in every library of the service area. A Preschool Learning Center

is a toddler-scale environment containing books, music, video, puppets, educational games, and a computer with reading-readiness software
Date: September, 2000

- The Library will seek funding to establish Early Childhood Resource Centers in the North and South areas of the County, to assist childcare providers and teachers with appropriate materials, resources, educational games, book lists, and software
Date: September, 2000

- The Library will target a portion of the Children's Budget towards purchase of materials for preschool children
Date: September, 1996

Vision: YOUTH SERVICES (continued)—The Library will establish effective and collaborative partnerships with appropriate educational organizations and community agencies serving the 18 and under age group, developing resources and programs that respond to student needs.

Action Plan:

- The Library will continue to promote and expand its Booktalk Program to 7th and 9th grade students
Date: September, 2000

- The Library will identify public and private schools in each library's area
Date: September, 1996

- The Library will develop bibliographies with career information for use by students and their families
Date: September, 1997

- The Library will seek funding to establish Homework Centers in libraries, including both computerized and written information
Date: September, 2000

THE UNIVERSITY OF IOWA LIBRARIES
STRATEGIC PLAN
1995-2000

MISSION
The University Libraries has primary responsibility within the University to support access, develop and deliver information resources in all formats, and ensure the preservation of knowledge. Through building collections and providing access to information sources held elsewhere, and through provision of instructional and

research services, the Libraries support the teaching, learning and research mission of the University while also providing leadership within the state and nationally in addressing information needs for a literate citizenry.

GOALS

Information and instructional services are designed and delivered, using various methodologies to meet current and changing information needs for a diverse university community in support of teaching, learning, research, and service.

Build local collections in all formats to ensure access to the most critical resources for teaching and research. Ensure access to information resources world-wide, both electronic and print, through licensing, enhanced connectivity, and consortia arrangements. Through the combination of on site resources and access to resources held elsewhere, support the full range of university programs and educational activities.

GOALS, OBJECTIVES, STRATEGIES

1—Information and instructional services are designed and delivered using various methodologies to meet current and changing information needs for a diverse university community in support of teaching, learning, research, and service.

OBJECTIVE A: Information services both on-demand and by appointment available in all libraries via existing and emerging information technologies as well as through direct staff assistance.

STRATEGY #1. Through an evaluation and assessment process, including input from the user community, develop and implement new strategies and service models to maximize the use of expert staff in the provision of information services.

STRATEGY #2. Use as appropriate new information technology and interactive instructional programs, including self-instruction and self-paced learning tools, to reach the greatest number of clients in a timely and convenient manner.

STRATEGY #3. Continually evaluate ways to effectively publicize information services throughout the University community to ensure that students, faculty and staff are aware of the availability of information resources and services.

STRATEGY #4. Working with staff of Continuing Education to identify and implement methods for meeting the information needs of the increasing number of UI students enrolled in off-site courses taught via the ICN or by faculty traveling to other locations.

STRATEGY #5. Explore, with librarians at Regents libraries and the CIC libraries, ways in which reference expertise and services can be shared and/or enhanced, particularly through electronic connections.

OBJECTIVE B: Maintain as a top priority the development and delivery of instructional programs and materials to assist students, faculty, and staff in acquiring the skills and knowledge to achieve information literacy in order to secure information needed immediately and throughout their lives.

STRATEGY #1. Explore, define, and adopt appropriate methods, technologies and media (active learning, computer assisted instruction and multimedia) to enhance learning about information resources and the development of critical skills for evaluating information and data.

STRATEGY #2. In collaboration with the College of Liberal Arts faculty explore whether all GER courses should have a segment devoted to information skills and, if so, how this might be delivered to students.

STRATEGY #3. In collaboration with Colleges, as appropriate, explore programs for development of information management skills by graduate and professional students (College of Medicine students, for example).

STRATEGY #4. In collaboration with faculty, develop course-related instruction on information resources focused on the subject content of the course.

STRATEGY #5. As staffing permits, offer additional Research Seminars on specific subjects and topics for faculty and graduate students based on clear needs of users.

STRATEGY #6. Explore opportunities for offering technology-related instruction in conjunction with ITS staff, and subject-related instruction in conjunction with staff in Departmental and Institute libraries.

2—Build local collections in all formats to ensure access to the most critical resources for teaching and research. Ensure access to information resources world-wide, both electronic and print, through licensing, enhanced connectivity, and consortia arrangements. Through the combination of on site resources and access to resources held elsewhere, support the full range of university programs and educational activities.

OBJECTIVE A: Select materials for on-site collections and provide improved access to collections held remotely that support teaching, research, and service in all fields and disciplines at the University of Iowa.

STRATEGY #1. Provide University administration and others with clear data and background information on funding required to acquire information resources to support current programs as well as new teaching and research initiatives, and to support added costs of information in electronic and multimedia formats within an environment of escalating costs for scholarly and research information.

STRATEGY #2. Strengthen resources supporting international and interdisciplinary studies, and studies in support of diversity by increasing librarians' awareness of resource needs and seeking external support for improving collections.

STRATEGY #3. Develop proposals and strategies for an aggressive fund raising effort, working with key University administrators, the Foundation staff and, as appropriate, faculty to substantially enhance financial support for collections through private gifts and foundation giving.

STRATEGY #4. Continue aggressive approach to acquire federal grants in conjunction with the College of Liberal Arts grants officer and faculty as well as faculty from other Colleges.

OBJECTIVE B: Ensure the timely organization of information sources following acceptable standards to provide access to local and remote holdings in all formats for University users and for individuals at other institutions in order to enhance cooperation on a state, regional, national and international scale.

STRATEGY #1. Ensure that accurate, effective, and timely access is provided to library materials and information resources in all formats following acceptable standards.

STRATEGY #2. Participate in local, regional and national efforts as appropriate to contribute to the organization of electronic resources accessed via the Internet or local gopher systems.

STRATEGY #3. Taking into account discipline-specific needs, establish clear priorities for timely processing of new materials based on available resources.

STRATEGY #4. Seek funding to complete conversion of remaining non-electronic catalog records (approximately 500,000) to on-line format to allow for full participation in the CIC/Virtual Electronic Project (requires access to bibliographic records for resource sharing) and to enhance cooperation on a state, regional, national and international basis.

STRATEGY #5. Work with faculty and others to acquire, analyze, organize, and make available in electronic format research data and other information (textual, numeric, bibliographic, and multi-media) for the campus and nationally.

STRATEGY #6. Participate in national library community efforts working with publishers (particularly local and society publishers) to develop and implement standards for presentation of data on title pages (or equivalent) in order to ensure accurate and timely bibliographic access.

OBJECTIVE C: Develop and enhance methods for access and delivery of information in electronic format.

STRATEGY #1. Explore, with partner libraries within the state and beyond, the cost and feasibility of joint site licenses and other means of providing shared access to information resources.

STRATEGY #2. Expand cooperative collection development programs and interlibrary loan service with Iowa State University, the University of Northern Iowa and other Iowa institutions as staff and other resources are available to support this effort.

STRATEGY #3. Develop with colleagues from the CIC institution libraries, an effective plan within the Virtual Electronic Library project to implement cooperative collection development and resource sharing and seek ways to involve faculty in identified subject areas.

STRATEGY #4. Expand access to and delivery of information in electronic format of all types whether accessed through the Internet, a single work station, or a campus network.

STRATEGY #5. Support the development of interinstitutional and commercial document delivery services that serve differing information needs of users for timely access, with a delivery goal of 48 hours or less.

STRATEGY #6. Enhance campus access to information with a fee-based document delivery service for materials from the Main Library and eleven departmental libraries to meet faculty needs for timely access to information no matter the campus location.

STRATEGY #7. Explore issues of copyright related to faculty publications through the Task Force on Copyright.

OBJECTIVE D: Support a comprehensive preservation program, ensure the future availability of the library collections and resources that represent a major intellectual, cultural and financial investment for the University.

STRATEGY #1. Develop priorities and processes to ensure that both circulating collections and special collections receive the proper preservation and/or conservation treatment.

STRATEGY #2. Maintain and update the Libraries' disaster plan and organize an ongoing training program to ensure that staff can respond appropriately and in a timely manner in the event of a fire, flood or other disaster that will endanger the collections.

STRATEGY #3. Identify and pursue opportunities for continued participation in appropriate local, regional and national preservation projects that will enhance the UI collections.

STRATEGY #4. Seek additional University funding as well as external support (from foundations, private donors or federal grants) for preservation and conservation efforts.

STRATEGY #5. Integrate awareness of preservation concerns into collection management activities and involve subject specialists in preservation projects and priorities. Ensure that careful consideration is given before acquiring materials needing extensive preservation attention.

STRATEGY #6. Make appropriate use of digital and other technologies in addressing preservation needs.

3—Recruit, develop and retain a diverse staff representing the range of knowledge, skills and talents required in a rapidly changing university environment.

OBJECTIVE A: Achieve a diverse staff with the necessary range of knowledge and expertise to support University programs.

STRATEGY #1. Work with appropriate campus offices and groups to assist in attracting individuals from under-represented groups for support staff positions.

STRATEGY #2. Diversity Committee work with staff to identify potential ways to attract minorities to the library staff; to advise on recruitment for library professional positions; to develop materials to be used in the recruitment process; and to recommend goals and monitor progress toward creating a more diverse library staff and a welcoming environment for all staff and users.

STRATEGY #3. Explore establishing a permanent Research Library Fellows Program as a postgraduate internship, with an emphasis on recruiting minority librarians.

STRATEGY #4. Improve Professional and Scientific staff salaries to assure a competitive posture nationally in order to recruit and retain highly qualified professionals, and to assure comparable worth with other University of Iowa professional staff.

OBJECTIVE B: Achieve an appropriate balance between professional, support and student staff for provision of library services and programs.

STRATEGY #1. Review openings to determine appropriate staffing level or reallocation potential.

STRATEGY #2. Provide University administration and others with clear data and background information on funding required to increase the number of support staff to adequately support programs and services throughout the library system.

OBJECTIVE C: Provide opportunities for professional development and contributions by the Libraries' professional staff which are necessary to provide leadership locally and nationally.

STRATEGY #1. Enable staff to sustain their own growth and development in a constantly changing environment with release time and financial support, including research leave.

STRATEGY #2. Encourage supervisors and administrators to provide sufficient support and guidance for librarians to successfully contribute as professionals and to advance through the promotion system.

OBJECTIVE D: Ensure the full use of human resources and the provision of an environment where all staff are able to work productively.

STRATEGY #1. Establish and maintain a comprehensive personnel program.

STRATEGY #2. Implement integrated approach to ostentation, training and development opportunities for all staff using appropriate local and external resources as well as varying technologies and formats.

STRATEGY #3. Ensure an effective on-the-job training program.

STRATEGY #4. Make available internal internships and job exchange opportunities.

4—State-of-the-art information technology is integrated into all aspects of library services, collections and operations to provide users the best possible access to information resources and services both on campus and world-wide.

OBJECTIVE A: Continue to enhance and expand the library on-line system to ensure access to the broadest possible array of bibliographic information from local collections as well as from external sources.

STRATEGY #1. Seek funding from University administration adequate to maintain and, as appropriate, enhance library and information technology for public access and staff operations and activities (i.e., Oasis and other public access systems, Information Arcade, office automation and the like).

STRATEGY #2. Assuming adequate funding, continue expansion and enhancement of OASIS providing full functionality in all library units, and providing full access to holdings and status information for University Libraries collections.

STRATEGY #3. Evaluate the existing integrated library system and complete a detailed needs assessment considering available library systems to ensure that a viable, fully functional system (that maintains a competitive position for the UI with other universities) is in place for the year 2000.

OBJECTIVE B: Provide access to the widest possible range of information resources via electronic technology.

STRATEGY #1. Update all intrabuilding telecommunications networks and off-site teaching locations to utilize state-of-the-art transmission technologies compatible with and taking full advantage of the campus and state fiber optic network.

STRATEGY #2. Provide networked access to campus licensed/owned electronic information including full text, numeric, bibliographic, graphical, and multi-media materials regardless of the source.

STRATEGY #3. Work with other academic libraries (primarily through the CIC Virtual Electronic Library and the Iowa Library Information Network projects) to establish workable linkages through Z39.50 and other protocols to external information resources, including on-line catalogs of other libraries, cataloging resource files, reference databases and full text resources.

STRATEGY #4. Replace all ASCII terminals and sub-486-class workstations with updated workstations in all staff and public locations.

STRATEGY #5. Work with faculty through the Task Force on the Networked Electronic Information Environment to examine issues related to electronic publishing and distribution of information via computer networks.

OBJECTIVE C: Continue to use the Information Arcade as a model to encourage advances in the application of new technologies for teaching, learning, and research.

STRATEGY #1. Secure adequate recurring funding for Information Arcade operations.

STRATEGY #2. Support innovative curriculum development by faculty using new technologies.

STRATEGY #3. Expand use of Information Arcade for library instruction.

5—Library staff seek to establish active partnerships with colleges, academic departments and programs in the development of new initiatives and in addressing problems of scholarly communication and publishing.

OBJECTIVE A: Establish relationships to ensure consistent advance communication from academic programs to the University Libraries with regard to curricular and programmatic changes that will affect library collections and services.

STRATEGY #1. Establish liaison relationships with academic departments and programs, and maintain effective communications through such means as attending departmental meetings and electronic mail.

STRATEGY #2. Establish process with Provost, deans and academic department chairs to ensure that an assessment of impact on library collections and services is conducted with the appropriate subject librarian when new degree programs and/or a major shift in the curriculum and research within an academic program is being considered.

STRATEGY #3. Continue to work with various University committees and groups to facilitate communication between students, faculty, staff and the Libraries.

STRATEGY #4. As a result of the Hardin Library for the Health Sciences strategic planning process implement alternative models of collaboration and service for faculty in the health sciences Colleges and clinical care providers in the Health Sciences Center.

OBJECTIVE B: Support new research and teaching initiatives through the timely acquisition of needed library and information resources.

STRATEGY #1. Secure "start-up" funds for library and information resources for new faculty appointments in cooperation with the Provost's office and Colleges.

STRATEGY #2. Work with Vice President for Research, and staff of Sponsored Programs to establish a process to review major grant requests to determine potential impact on library collections and services.

OBJECTIVE C: Increase the understanding of faculty and graduate students about the processes and problems of scholarly communication, and provide campus-wide leadership in identifying and implementing alternatives.

STRATEGY #1. Library staff keep faculty and administrators informed about current issues related to scholarly communication and its transformation through dissemination of information electronically.

STRATEGY #2. Library staff work in partnership with faculty and others on campus to experiment with alternative means of creating, preserving, organizing and disseminating scholarly information through electronic means.

6—Continue focus on public outreach programs to increase the visibility of university libraries to numerous constituencies, and to expand access to its resources for Iowa citizens.

OBJECTIVE A: As a University intellectual and cultural center, and to promote the value of the University Libraries initiate programs on diverse topics for a variety of audiences.

STRATEGY #1. Sustain and strengthen the exhibition/speaker series program, Chautauqua event, and other offerings working with the Friends Advisory Board and Friends volunteers.

STRATEGY #2. Initiate cooperative ventures with other University departments/programs to present symposia, lecture series, and related programs on timely topics.

OBJECTIVE B: Increase general awareness of the value of the University Libraries to the State through a comprehensive public relations program and by providing avenues for public access to library resources as appropriate.

STRATEGY #1. Publicize events, collections, services, staff activities of the Libraries through diverse media approaches in cooperation with University Relations.

STRATEGY #2. Coordinate efforts with University Relations to effectively use the mass media on the local, state, regional and national level.

STRATEGY #3. Continue to work with campus programs such as Admissions, Graduate College, etc. to provide orientation and topical programs for prospective and newly enrolled students and parents.

STRATEGY #4. Continue to work with the Alumni Association to provide programs for alumni groups visiting campus, in the state, and nationally.

STRATEGY #5. Work with the State Library and libraries and information centers throughout the State to provide access and linkages to resources within the State and over the Internet through the Iowa Library Information Network (ILIN), the Iowa Research and Education Network (IREN), and the Access Plus program.

STRATEGY #6. Improve dissemination of health sciences information by electronically linking community colleges offering health sciences education and community hospitals with the Hardin Library for the Health Sciences.

OBJECTIVE C: Increase number of donors including alumni and other individuals as well as the level of giving to the University Libraries by members of the University and by those outside the University community.

STRATEGY #1. With vigorous support of the UI central administration, the UI Foundation, the Libraries' development officer and appropriate library staff substantially increase the level of private giving.

STRATEGY #2. Fully utilize the Director of Library Development's abilities and skills to develop specific action plans for increasing private giving.

STRATEGY #3. Substantially increase annual giving as well as average amount of individual gifts.

STRATEGY #4. Develop and implement a plan to identify and solicit major prospects to ensure private support at substantial monetary levels.

STRATEGY #5. Create an endowment of at least five million dollars for information resources in electronic form with the aid of UI central administration and UI Foundation.

STRATEGY #6. Continue to strengthen the Friends Advisory Board as an active leadership group for library development and public outreach efforts.

STRATEGY #7. Develop and implement plans for major library campaigns to fund high priority initiatives in the acquisition and delivery of information resources.

STRATEGY #8. Continue to work with Sponsored Programs and other departments to identify and secure federal funding as well as funding from private foundations and other sources.

7—Physical facilities provide efficient space for the housing and preservation of collections, workspace for staff and the provision of services in a technologically sophisticated environment.

NEW YORK STATE LIBRARY
New York State Education Department

A Strategic Plan for the
Division of Library Development

Improving Library Services for All

THE DIVISION OF LIBRARY DEVELOPMENT
The New York State Library is located in the Office of Cultural Education within the State Education Department. The State Library has two divisions, Library Development and the Research Library. Both serve the people and the libraries of the State. The Division of Library Development, working in partnership with the 74 library systems, brings cost-effective modem library services to the millions of people who use New York's 7,000 academic, public, school and special libraries.

Our Vision: The Library Development Team helps librarians, trustees and public officials find new ways of serving people and making library resources available to all the people.

Our Mission: The Library Development Team develops and improves the library services that all New Yorkers need for their lifelong learning and enjoyment.

Who We Are: The Library Development Team is comprised of 22 people, 11 of whom are Library Development Specialists, four Education Program Assistants, an Education Program Aide and six secretarial and support staff.

What We Do: The Library Development Team is a strong voice for local, State and Federal library services. Librarians, trustees, public officials and community leaders depend on the Library Development Team to help find new ways of making library services and resources available to people of all ages.

1.   All New Yorkers will have access to electronic doorway library services provided by libraries transformed by technology.

1. Number of libraries that meet the basic requirements to become Electronic Doorway Libraries.

2. Number of libraries that go beyond basic Electronic Doorway Library services.

3. Number of people who have access to Electronic Doorway Library services.

2.   Libraries and library systems will provide high-quality, cost-effective services that meet the needs of their communities.

1. Percent of systems' plans of service that include provisions for assessing customer needs and satisfaction.

2. Number of public libraries that meet minimum standards #1–5 and 10; and standard #6 by 1997; and standards #7, 8, 9, 11 by 1999.

3. Number of member plans of service reported to their School Library Systems.

3.   Public policy will acknowledge and support the roles of libraries in a learning society.

1. Instances when public policy initiatives of the Regents and other State officials acknowledge and support the role of libraries.

2. Instances when the Governor and/or State Legislature acknowledge the importance of libraries through legislation, state aid and other means.

4.   Libraries and archives will identify, preserve and make available information of enduring significance for the use of present and future generations.

1. Number of bibliographic records converted from paper into a machine readable form.

2. Number of applications received in the Conservation/Preservation (C/P) grant program.

3. Increase in the average score of C/P grant applications. (Note: the score is based on how well applying institutions adhere to professional standards in the preservation/conservation of their collections.)

5. **The Library Development staff will provide high-quality, cost-effective services to their customers.**

    1. Customers who are satisfied with Library Development services.

6. **Library Development will have a supportive work environment for all staff.**

    1. Increase in staff satisfaction with the Library Development work environment.

    2. Increase in staff training.

    3. Increase in cooperative efforts among Library Development and the Research Library, Office of Cultural Education and other State Education Department offices.

LIBRARY DEVELOPMENT KEY STRATEGIES

To address Library Development's Goals 1–4:

A. Make effective use of new technologies in libraries and library systems, including making all the state's libraries electronic doorways to information.

    1. Work with an Action Committee to complete the third statewide automation plan (Electronic Doorway Library Action Plan) by Spring 1997.

    2. Continue Library Development's Electronic Doorway Library Recognition Program.

    3. Work with systems and libraries to develop a Library Services and Technology Act program that encourages library and system initiatives in electronic technology.

    4. Provide staff development opportunities to increase Library Development Specialists' knowledge of major technological issues facing libraries through self-directed learning, field contacts and attendance at meetings and conferences.

B. Improve planning and evaluation of library services in order to help librarians, trustees and other customers advance today's library services and new developments.

    1. Work with library systems, central libraries and others to further develop and test the plan of service process during 1996 and 1997.

    2. Reexamine Free Direct Access issues and develop recommendations for Regents review.

3. Continue to work with PULISDO to help educate libraries and systems on the value of the minimum standards for public libraries and encourage libraries to meet or exceed those standards.

4. Use technology to improve the quality, timeliness and usefulness of the information which Library Development disseminates about libraries and library systems.

5. Provide Library Development Specialists with professional development opportunities on major planning and evaluation issues and tools in order to assist libraries and systems as needed.

C. Integrate advocacy and legislation with technology planning in order to ensure that State and federally supported programs and services meet the most pressing library needs.

1. Coordinate Library Development advocacy related to State and Federal funding for State Operations and Local Assistance in collaboration with the Research Library, the Office of Cultural Education, the New York Library Association and others.

2. Continue to seek passage of legislation important to libraries and library systems including but not limited to:
    The Electronic Doorway Library Services bill
    Funding of library aid in Education Law
    The Regents Omnibus Technology in Education Act

3. Advocate in collaboration with others for the formation and funding of the Commission on Library Services.

4. Work with systems and libraries to identify necessary changes to Commissioner's Regulations as the need arises.

To address Library Development's Goal 5:

D. High-quality, cost-effective services to our customers.

1. Expand use of technology to deliver services.

2. Review current operations and processes to improve services to customers.

3. Improve dissemination of information to customers.

4. Improve discretionary grant program processes.

To address Library Development's Goal 6:

E. Improve communication among Library Development team members.

1. Engage staff in interactive communication skills training once every six months.

F. Advocate for adequate resources for the Library Development team.

  1. Identify and advocate for the personnel resources needed to carry out Library Development's work.

  2. Identify and advocate for the other resources needed by Library Development.

G. Focus on training and staff development.

  1. Assess staff training needs.

  2. Develop and implement a plan.

H. Improve decision making at all levels.

  1. Clarify Library Development team's relationship with the Acting Director.

  2. Engage staff in a process to clarify levels of authority for individual and team decision making.

I. Continuously improve management of time to improve quality and efficiency of work processes.

  1. Streamline existing processes and eliminate secondary activities.

  2. Explore possibilities for working from remote locations.

  3. Explore Alternative Work Schedules.

J. Improve the physical environment of the Library Development offices.

  1. Work within the State Education Department and with others to improve physical environment.

  2. Develop internal processes in Library Development to improve physical environment.

K. Improve communication with others within the State Education Department.

  1. At the Library Management Team, the Research Library Executive Group, and Library Development Specialists meetings, discuss how Library Development and the Research Library can increase cooperation.

  2. Identify specific collaborative initiatives among the Research Library, Office of Cultural Education, other State Education Department offices and Library Development.

October 1996

Appendix B
Organization Charts

MIT Libraries

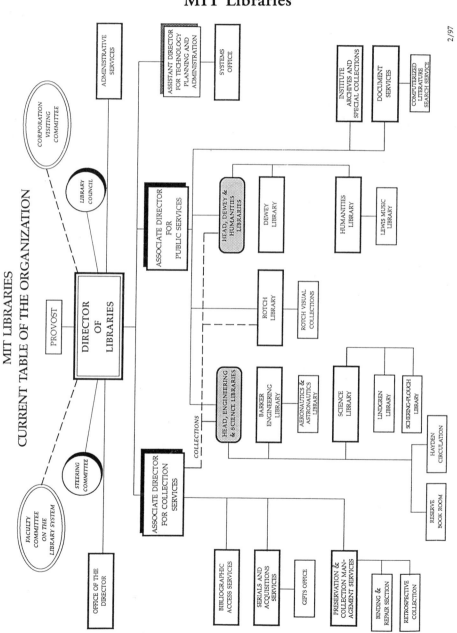

MIT LIBRARIES
CURRENT TABLE OF THE ORGANIZATION

2/97

Boston Public Library

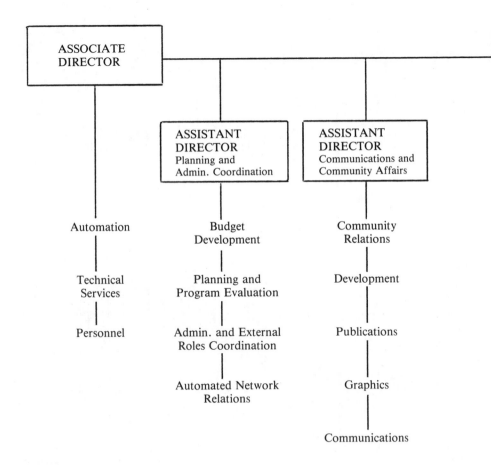

ASSOCIATE
DIRECTOR

ASSISTANT
DIRECTOR
Planning and
Admin. Coordination

ASSISTANT
DIRECTOR
Communications and
Community Affairs

Automation

Technical
Services

Personnel

Budget
Development

Planning and
Program Evaluation

Admin. and External
Roles Coordination

Automated Network
Relations

Community
Relations

Development

Publications

Graphics

Communications

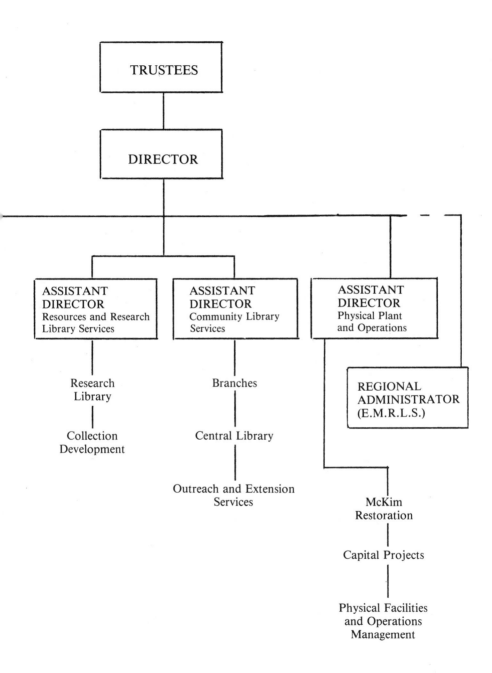

TRUSTEES

DIRECTOR

ASSISTANT
DIRECTOR
Resources and Research
Library Services

ASSISTANT
DIRECTOR
Community Library
Services

ASSISTANT
DIRECTOR
Physical Plant
and Operations

Research
Library

Branches

REGIONAL
ADMINISTRATOR
(E.M.R.L.S.)

Collection
Development

Central Library

Outreach and Extension
Services

McKim
Restoration

Capital Projects

Physical Facilities
and Operations
Management

University of California at Irvine

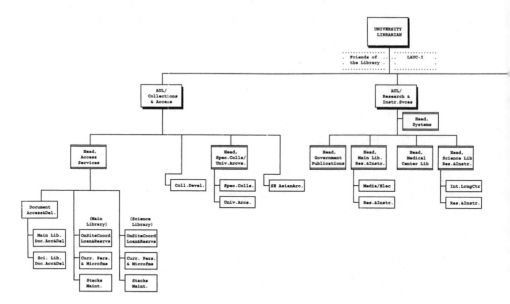

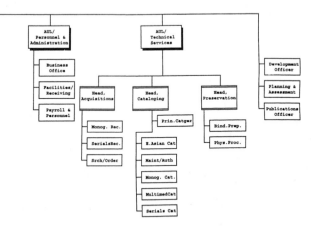

University of Southern California

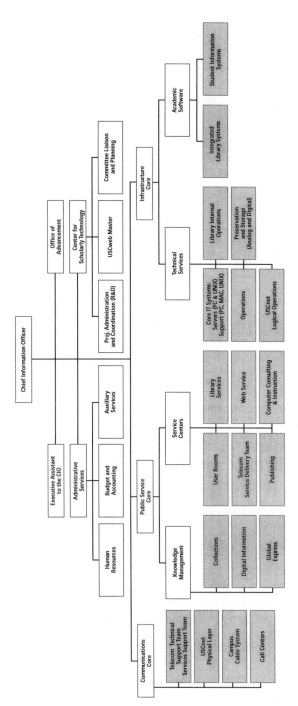

UNIVERSITY OF SOUTHERN CALIFORNIA

Information Services Division

Appendix C
Position Descriptions

Duke University Libraries

POSITION: Women's Studies Archivist and Resource Specialist

UNIT/LIBRARY: Collection Development Team, Special Collections Library

GENERAL DESCRIPTION: Provides leadership for building the Women's Archives in the Special Collections Library and women's studies resources in both the SCL and Perkins Library. Under the general supervision of the Director of Collection Development in the SCL, identifies and acquires materials pertinent to Women's Studies, acts as a liaison with faculty regarding library collections and services in this field, provides reference assistance, and facilitates the processing and cataloging of materials.

DUTIES:

1. Provides leadership for efforts to strengthen the Women's Archives program in the SCL, giving attention to collection development, processing and cataloging, reference and outreach, and public programming and donor relations.

2. Directs and evaluates the work of other Women's Archives staff (i.e., librarians, interns, student assistants hired specially for Women's Archives projects and activities) in areas such as reference, outreach, and web development.

3. In consultation with the SCL Collection Development Team, other resource specialists, and Women's Studies faculty, develops and regularly reviews collection development policies and guidelines for the acquisition of women's studies materials in all formats for Perkins and Special Collections Libraries.

4. Identifies appropriate out-of-print and manuscript/archival materials and acquires them as gifts or purchases, working directly with donors and private sellers of such materials, as well as with book and manuscript dealers.

5. Selects and orders current published materials in women's studies and consults with bibliographers in related fields who also acquire such materials.

6. Initiates and oversees special projects undertaken with income from the Women's Studies Archivist Endowment.

7. Meets regularly with the SCL Collection Development Team for planning of team and library goals and objectives, and with other discipline-based resource specialist teams as appropriate.

8. Consults with the SCL Technical Services Team, facilitating the processing and cataloging of manuscript collections relating to women's studies.

9. Insures growth and development of the SCL Women's Archives web site.

10. Serves as liaison for the libraries with the Women's Studies Program and related academic departments concerning the development and use of the women's collections.

11. Provides and oversees women's studies reference assistance, bibliographic instruction, and outreach for the SCL. Provides general reference assistance and service in the Special Collections Research Room on a back-up basis and rotating Saturday and holiday service.

12. Attends various academic programs and conferences to keep informed about research trends and needs in the area of women's studies, both at Duke and in general.

13. Contributes to other Special Collections and Perkins teams and projects as appropriate.

QUALIFICATIONS:

Position requires an ALA-accredited MLS and/or an advanced degree in an appropriate subject field; demonstrated knowledge of and interest in women's history and women's studies; familiarity with standard archival procedures; a minimum of two years of professional archival/special collections experience; and ability to work in a team environment, and to communicate effectively with users and donors of special collections materials. Experience with building circulating collections in an academic library and with creating and using web resources.

8/4/97

POSITION DESCRIPTION:

Reference Librarian, Reference/Interlibrary Loan Team, Perkins Library. (Team: This position is based in the Reference/Interlibrary Loan Home Team, which is part of the Information Services Quality Circle).

SUMMARY:

The Reference Librarian is responsible for assisting users of the library in their information retrieval activities. The primary focus of this position is reference service. A significant portion of the incumbent's time will be spent at the Reference Desk (including night, weekend and holiday duty), providing a high level of service to people who come into the library, as well as those seeking assistance from remote locations (e.g., e-mail and telephone inquiries). This activity includes the use of electronic (e.g., on-line database services, CD-ROM systems, and networks) and traditional information resources. The incumbent will also provide library user instruction, including classroom sessions, tours, and individual training. This individual will also concentrate on developing print and non-print (e.g., web-based) aids to assist users in an increasingly computerized and networked environment, where user self sufficiency and remote access are increasingly the norm. In producing these materials, and serving as a resource person for others producing their own, the incumbent will interact with other teams throughout the library system. Furthermore, the incumbent will work closely with the team's computer systems technician.

QUALIFICATIONS:

This position requires an advanced degree in information science or librarianship; one to five years professional level experience in public-oriented reference or information access service; expertise in producing print, web-based and other electronic user aids; demonstrated enthusiasm for public service; knowledge of and proficiency with electronic information resources; and a working knowledge of DOS, Windows and Mac computer hardware and software (e.g., communications, CD-ROM and LANs). This person must be flexible, creative, a self-starter, possess excellent oral and written communication skills, and have the ability to thrive in a team-oriented environmemt. A background in the humanities or social sciences is required; foreign language skills and expertise in business or statistical resources are strongly desired.

May 9, 1997

Summary Position Description
President of the Boston Public Library*

The Organization

A leading American historian has called The Public Library of the City of Boston "one of the five great libraries of the world." The first municipally funded library in the United States and among the first free public libraries in the world, it was also the first to establish branches to bring library services to local communities. Today, it is one of very few libraries in the world renowned both for superb capacity to support scholarly research in diverse disciplines and for the quality of its branch facilities and community outreach activities. The Library's collections total more than 27 million items and, true to its heritage as the first to permit citizens to borrow popular materials, its 26 branches make its resources readily available to people of all cultures and circumstances.

The Research Library is the second largest public facility of its kind in the nation. In addition to a formidable general collection, it features more than 200 special collections providing primary source material, much of it unique, in a very wide variety of topic areas. Well over two million people visit the Central

*Reprinted with permission of the Boston Public Library.

Library each year to tap its store of six million books, including more than one million rare volumes, and its huge collections of original prints, musical scores, films, public papers and other materials. More than half of these visitors are from outside Boston, and many come great distances to use resources unavailable elsewhere in such concentration.

The General Library and branch libraries are a vital part of the institution's service and provide literacy, local history, large print and audio-visual collections as well as strong book collections. An innovative program called the Gateway Project offers Internet services to children and links all Boston Public Schools to the library, an example of the library's historic tradition and commitment to children's services. Outreach to the broadest range of community organizations has been a hallmark of the branch system. The system runs thousands of special programs each year, many of them geared to the distinctive cultures and traditions which are among Boston's most precious civic assets.

The Research Library anchors one side of Copley Square in a landmark building designed by Charles Pollen McKim and opened in 1895. Art historian Peter Wick characterizes the McKim Building, a National Historic Register site, as "perhaps the most admired, discussed and influential public building in the American architectural revolution of the nineteenth century." The building is currently undergoing restoration and renovation with the first of three phases completed. The effort to return the building to its original grandeur is funded with a combination of public and private funds. An elegant newer building, designed by Philip Johnson and opened in 1972, is the heart of the General Library featuring the circulating collection and the institution's administrative offices.

Including both its central facilities and its branches, the Library employs about 540 people and has an annual budget of about $32 million. It is a Department of the municipal government of Boston and a statutory charitable organization governed by a Board of nine Trustees appointed by the Mayor. Private funds are raised to help supplement significant City and State resources by the Boston Public Library Foundation, a private organization established in 1992 by business and community leaders.

Responsibilities of the Appointee

The appointee will be the first person to hold the title of President of the Library. He/she will be vested with all of the duties and authorities customarily assigned to the head of a public agency working within the framework of a municipal government. Beyond this, however, the appointee will also be expected to shape the strategic vision which will keep the Library at the forefront in both research capability and service delivery to local communities, and to exert the leadership necessary to realize that vision. This will require a strong leadership presence, extensive external representational and fund raising activity as well as management and oversight of Library operations. The new title recognizes the full scope of these responsibilities and the extraordinarily high level of skill and inspirational qualities required to carry them out.

Assuming that the appointee elects to follow through with the current organizational plan, he/she will be assisted by a Chief Librarian who will devote the bulk of his/her attention to the internal affairs of the institution. The three Assistant Directors who are responsible for the operating units will report directly to this senior management team.

The President is appointed by the Board of Trustees, who set institution policy within the parameters of City ordinances and administrative processes. The Trustees meet bi-monthly and take an active public role in representing the institution and working with the Foundation and a variety of community and user advisory groups including the Citywide Friends, individual Friends' groups and the Associates of the Boston Public Library to refine service delivery and enlarge the resources available to support Library activities. The Library President is an employee of the City of Boston.

Qualifications

The appointee to this position should combine as many as possible of the following characteristics:

- Exceptional leadership qualities, as demonstrated in success as head of an institution or unit engaged either in library activities or in the non-profit, academic, government, or business world.

- Deep personal commitment to the concept of a public library and to achievement of its crucial mission, together with knowledge of a library's principles and practices.

- Recognized personal stature within a relevant discipline or professional community. An advanced degree in library science is much preferred, though candidates with arguably equivalent experience will be considered.

- The energy, creativity, strategic vision, imagination, stamina and proven leadership skill necessary to lead an organization to a new level of excellence and high technological sophistication, and to motivate others to share the new goals and work to achieve them.

- Capacity to deal easily and effectively with a broad diversity of individuals, organizations and communities, including other governments and agencies, and to represent the Library as a peer with the leaders of Boston's other great educational and cultural institutions.

- A balanced perspective which recognizes, values and integrates the goals of the Research Library and those of the branch system.

- Capability to raise private funds effectively, preferably as demonstrated in a previous position.

- Managerial capacity and experience at a senior level, and an open, collaborative management style suited to constructive relations with a Board of Trustees, a highly skilled staff, and a motivated City Administration.

- Familiarity with the pressures of public life and the resilience to deal with the complexities of political and governmental decision making.

- Willingness to relocate to Boston and to reside within the City limits.

Eligibility for Appointment

The City of Boston engages employees without regard to race, creed, gender, age or any other category recognized as discriminatory by law. All who feel they fulfill the qualifications are invited to apply.

Compensation Package

It is anticipated that the appointee's starting salary will be in the range of $105-125,000, as established in the City Budget. The salary is reviewed and may be adjusted annually. The City provides generous pension, health, vacation and other fringe benefits.

Timing of Appointment

The Screening Committee, which includes a majority of members who are deeply involved in Library affairs but are not Trustees, will begin considering candidates in the latter part of July. The Committee will make recommendations to the Trustees after completing its review. The Board of Trustees will then make the appointment. The appointee will then assume the position at the earliest feasible date thereafter.

To nominate candidates, to apply, or for further information, please contact:

Edward K. Hamilton, Chairman
Hamilton, Rabinovitz & Alschuler, Inc.
10 Universal City Plaza, Suite 1960
Universal City Station
Los Angeles, California 91608
(818) 509-7339 (voice); (818) 509-7331 (fax)

Appendix D
Performance Evaluation Forms

Emory University
Performance Evaluation Non-Supervisory

Employee: Social Security Number:
Class Title: Dept Name & No.:Univ. Libraries/2870
Supervisor: Scheduled Review Date:
Period Covered:
From: To: Eval. Date:

Evaluation Scheduled
Unscheduled by request of Employee
Unscheduled by request of Supervisor

1. List Below Primary Job Responsibilities. (Use capsule phrase from Position Questionnaire for each primary area of responsibility.) (For complete and official Position Description see Position Questionnaire Notebook in Library Administrative Office.) Comment on each area of responsibility. Assign one of the five evaluation terms (Unacceptable, Marginal, Satisfactory, Commendable, Superior) to each area of responsibility.

Use of Instructions and Constructive Criticism: Does employee readily accept and use suggestions, instructions and constructive criticism to improve performance?

Comments and evaluation (citing specific observations and facts):

Unacceptable ( ); Marginal ( ); Satisfactory ( ); Commendable ( ); Superior ( )

PERFORMANCE EVALUATION FACTORS

1. Knowledge of Work: Necessary knowledge of the elements of work assignments.

Demonstration: Learns, understands and retains the elements of work assignments and duties.

Remembers instructions of job tasks without repeated orders from supervisor.

Comments and evaluation:

Unacceptable ( ); Marginal ( ); Satisfactory ( ); Commendable ( ); Superior ( )

2. Quantity of Work: The progress made on tasks that results in the expected quantity of work.

Demonstration: Meets the established standards for required quantity of work. Uses time effectively and efficiently.

Comments and evaluation:

Unacceptable ( ); Marginal ( ); Satisfactory ( ); Commendable ( ); Superior( )

3. Quality of Work: The extent to which work meets the required standards for quality.

Demonstration: Organizes and checks work to meet required standards or objectives. Thoroughly and accurately accomplishes job duties. Results are consistently dependable.

Comments and evaluation:

Unacceptable ( ); Marginal ( ); Satisfactory ( ); Commendable ( ); Superior ( )

4. Adaptability: The capacity to adapt to new situations. Demonstration: Readily copes and adapts to changes in routines, work load, work assignments and new situations.

Comments and evaluation:

Unacceptable ( ); Marginal ( ); Satisfactory ( ); Commendable ( ); Superior ( )

5. Initiative: The capacity to undertake and perform job duties independently but with appropriate and responsible usage of supervisory support. Demonstration: is a self-starter but also seeks supervisory assistance and guidance when necessary. Contributes new ideas or improved methods to the work process.

Comments and evaluation:

Unacceptable ( ); Marginal ( ); Satisfactory ( ); Commendable ( ); Superior ( )

6. Dependability: Reliability in following assigned work schedules and attendance standards.

Demonstration: Regularly follows assigned schedules, meets attendance standards and satisfactorily completes assignments in a timely manner. Can be relied upon.

Comments and evaluation:

Unacceptable ( ); Marginal ( ); Satisfactory ( ); Commendable ( ); Superior ( )

7. Personal Conduct: The standards of personal behavior established to maintain effective job performance including contributing to a safe and healthful work environment. Demonstration: Regularly complies with the standards of personal behavior including a satisfactory working relationship with others. Is safety conscious.

Comments and evaluation:

Unacceptable ( ); Marginal ( ); Satisfactory ( ); Commendable ( ); Superior ( )

SUPERVISOR'S SUMMARY: Consider all the factors before summarizing and commenting on employee's performance for this review period.

Significant changes since last evaluation:

Recommendations for accomplishment of development needs and training:

Mutually established performance goals and objectives:

Supervisor's Signature: Date:

Department Head or Designee's Review: Comments:

Signature: Date:

Department Head or Designee

Employee's Summary Comments: Carefully consider all the factors before giving your comments on the performance evaluation received.

Your signature indicates that you have discussed this evaluation with your supervisor. It does not necessarily indicate agreement with the content.

Signature: Date:
Employee

Signature: Date:
Division Director

Signature: Date:
Vice Provost/Director of Libraries

12.1.2 PERFORMANCE REVIEW STATEMENT

Name of Professional   Supervisor's Name

Title, Rank   Title

                                     Six Month Review
                                     Annual Review
Dates   Covered by Review:
From:
To:

Professional: (non-probationary only)

   wishes to receive comments on his/her progress towards achieving promotion

   does not wish to receive comments on his/her progress towards achieving promotion

Date Performance Review conference scheduled:

Date Performance Review Statement must be filed in Administrative Office:

NOTE: See Procedures for Completion of Six Month and Annual Performance Review

PART I. PROFESSIONAL'S STATEMENT
ON JOB ACCOMPLISHMENTS
AND ANNUAL ACTIVITIES

Using the outline below as a guide, compile a list of job accomplishments and activities covering the period June 1st of last year through the present. This statement will serve as Part I of the Performance Review Statement and will be reviewed by the supervisor in the preparation of Part II Supervisor's Statement. The due date for Part I will be set by the supervisor to allow time for completion of the review process according to the Calendar for All Review Cycles.

1. Job Accomplishments (use job description as outline to summarize significant job accomplishments)

2. Annual Activities

    a. University and Library activities (committee memberships, assignments and offices held)

    b. Workshops, institutes, meetings and conferences (attended, directed, or participated in as an instructor or panelist)

    c. Professional association memberships (committee memberships, assignments and offices held)

    d. Publications and papers presented

    e. Honors and awards

    f. Research and/or studies being pursued

    g. Significant miscellaneous activities

PART II. SUPERVISOR'S STATEMENT

In preparing this statement, please refer to: Part I (Professional's Statement of Job Accomplishments and Annual Activities), the professional's job description, and the criteria for the professional's rank as stated in the *Appointment, Promotion, and Separation Policies Concerning Permanent Professional Library Staff in the General Libraries of Emory University*. The written review should cover all of the areas below and include specific examples of strengths and weaknesses in job performance:

- Job responsibilities (include only those responsibilities you supervise)
- Interpersonal skills as they relate to job responsibilities (examples may include the ability to: establish and maintain good working relationships, communicate effectively orally and in writing with library users and staff, offer and accept constructive criticism, clearly explain use of library resources and technical rules and procedures, instruct groups effectively)
- Service and professional development activities
- Overall evaluation of performance (include significant changes since last evaluation if appropriate)
- Preparation and progress toward achieving reappointment
- Preparation and progress toward achieving promotion (only upon request of the professional)

PART III. CONFERENCE SUMMARY AND CONCLUSION

The following statement summarizes the facts and goals/plans mutually established at the performance review conference.

My signature does not indicate that I agree or disagree with this evaluation, simply that it was discussed with me and opportunity was provided for my comments.

Professional's signature   Date
and optional comments (may attach a separate page):

1 have prepared this evaluation and reviewed the professional's comments:

Supervisor's signature   Date

PART IV. ADDITIONAL SIGNATURES

The following individuals have read this performance review:

Department Head's signature   Date
and optional comments:

Division Director's signature   Date
and optional comments:

Vice Provost, Director of Libraries' signature   Date
and optional comments:

Library Human Resource Officer's signature   Date

A copy of the completed and signed Performance Review Statement is sent to the professional and the original is placed in the professional's evaluation file.

Duke University Libraries
Annual Professional Update and Evaluation

(Detach this sheet and use it as the beginning page of the completed evaluation form.)

The librarian fills in the following blanks:

Name of librarian _____ Date _____

Department _____ Position _____ Rank _____

Date of professional appointment at Duke _____

    to present position _____ to present rank_____

Period covered by update and evaluation_____
    (indicate leaves of absence or part-time work)

    I have been notified of upcoming review for _____ reappointment; _____ promotion; _____ continuing appointment.

For librarians not being reviewed by CAP, the annual evaluation process begins July 1. It includes an update of the librarian's job description, an update and self-evaluation of job-related and other professional activities, an evaluative essay by the supervisor, and the librarian's response to this evaluation. In some cases, as for multiple-role librarians and librarians in large departments, more than one supervisor may serve as evaluator. When librarians are being reviewed by CAP for promotion and continuing appointment, the process begins no later than July 1 and should be completed by August 1, at which time all documents must be deposited with the Personnel Librarian. For remaining librarians, the process should be completed and the documents deposited within 90 days after their initiation, or October 1.

This form is designed to provide information to aid the librarian to grow professionally. In addition, it will serve as the basis for promotion and continuing appointment decisions, salary determinations, and other personnel actions. The criteria for promotion in the paper "Ranking Structure for Duke University Librarians" and the criteria for continuing appointment in the paper "Continuing Appointment" provide basic guidelines for the evaluation.

This form or a comparable form will be used in the Law Library and the Medical Center Library by deleting phrases or sections containing references to positions and to CAP which are not applicable to those libraries.

PROCEDURES

The librarian and evaluator complete STEPS I–V below on separate sheets. The first and last of these sheets are attached to this instruction sheet. STEPS VI–VIII are on the final page. In providing information on separate sheets, use the corresponding STEP numbering and lettering of the procedures.

STEPS I–III are to be completed by September 1.

STEP I. Job description. The librarian and evaluator decide whether the current job description is fully adequate. If no change is needed, a copy of the current description is attached to the evaluation form. If changes are required, the current description is revised or a new job description is prepared. In either of the latter cases, a copy of the current description and of the revised description is attached to the evaluation form, one copy retained by the librarian, and one copy retained by the department head.

STEP II. Professional achievement and growth. The librarian completes STEPS II and III and gives them, along with this form, to the evaluator.

A. Job-related activities. Describe activities of the preceding year in your area of work responsibility. Highlight special projects, innovations, work that received recognition outside the department, etc.

B. Other professional activities.

1. List library-related activities outside regular duties, such as committee work, special projects, liaison with other departments (if not included in A above), etc.

2. List university service outside the library.

3. List professional affiliations, indicating memberships, offices, committee work, etc. Indicate level of participation.

4. List conventions, conferences, workshops, etc. attended. Indicate level of participation.

5. List courses or degrees completed. Indicate whether audited or taken for credit, name of institution, and date. Provide any appropriate description of course content.

6. List research and publications. Include books, articles, reviews, and oral or written presentations of a professional nature.

7. List classes taught. Indicate institution, course, and date.

8. List any other relevant activities or recognition not covered in the above categories, such as honors, consultant work, etc.

C. If you are being reviewed for promotion to Library Assistant Senior, list the names of three to five persons who are qualified to evaluate your work and/or professional contributions and who may be consulted by CAP for additional information. If you are being reviewed for promotion to the upper two ranks or for continuing appointment, list the names of at least six persons according to the above directive. CAP may consult additional persons as it deems appropriate. Include the address for any person not connected with the Duke University libraries. Your supervisor is automatically included in the evaluation procedure and therefore is not listed here.

STEP III. Self-evaluation. Based on information supplied in STEPS I and II, assess and evaluate your own professional growth and achievement during the preceding year. Indicate progress toward achieving last year's goals and include goals for next year's work.

STEP IV. Supervisory evaluation. The evaluator completes this STEP and returns it to the librarian within ten days. The evaluator may wish to discuss a draft copy with the librarian before completing the final evaluation. Sections A through C may be combined in a single essay.

In an analytical essay:

A. Discuss the librarian's work performance, based on job description attached and information supplied in STEPS II and III. Include an evaluation of the appropriateness of the goals set.

B. Discuss the overall development of the librarian, using as a starting point information presented in STEPS II and III.

C. State whether the librarian's performance 1) fails to meet professional standards for his rank and position; 2) meets these professional standards; or 3) more than meets professional standards for his rank and position and to what extent.

   If the librarian does not have continuing appointment, indicate whether progress toward continuing appointment is satisfactory and, if not, why not.

D. State whether you recommend this librarian for: renewal of appointment; non-renewal of appointment; continuing appointment; and/or promotion in rank. Fully justify the recommendation in the essay which precedes it.

STEP V. Librarian's response. The evaluator returns the form, completed through STEP IV, to the librarian, who comments, if he wishes, on the evaluation and returns the form, completed through STEP V, to the evaluator within five days.

UPDATE AND EVALUATION
(Detach this sheet and add to end of completed evaluation form)

STEP VI. Conference. Within one week of the completion of STEPS I–V, the librarian and evaluator meet and discuss the document fully and attach their signatures. These signatures indicate that both parties have fully discussed the evaluation (STEP IV) and the librarian's response (STEP V).

Evaluator's signature_____ Date_____

Librarian's signature_____ Date_____

STEP VII. The evaluator forwards the form (completed through STEP VI) to his immediate supervisor for review. Signature indicates that the reviewing librarian has read the librarian's evaluation and response.

Signature of reviewing librarian_____ Date_____

Comments:

If the reviewing librarian holds a position below that of Assistant University Librarian, he forwards this form to the appropriate librarian at that level or above for signature and for comments if appropriate.

Signature of Assistant or Associate _____ Date_____
University Librarian

Comments:

STEP VIII. By July 1 librarians being reviewed by CAP must submit a job description and the names of suggested references to the Personnel Office. By August 1 (for librarians being reviewed by CAP) or October 1 (for all other librarians) the highest level reviewing librarian must deposit the entire annual update and evaluation form in the office of the Personnel Librarian, who then contacts the librarian being reviewed for final comments and signature. The completed update is thereafter available to the library administrators, the librarian's supervisors, the reviewed librarian, and CAP when required for its deliberations.

It shall be the responsibility of the Personnel Librarian to provide a copy of the update to the individual librarian.

Librarian's signature _____ Date _____

Comments:

Academic Affairs Library
University of North Carolina at Chapel Hill
PERSONNEL EVALUATION CHECKLIST

Employee Name————————————————————————

Department————————————————————————

Evaluation Period Beginning: July 1, 1996   Ending: June 30, 1997

Forms Sent to Department Head on   March 15, 1997

Please return completed personnel evaluation document to personnel
office, CB#3932 by ___June 30, 1997___

1. Employee is given Job Duties Outline (Form A) and Employee Self-Assessment Form (Form B), and supervisor is given Personnel Evaluation Form (Form C) **at least four weeks before the Due Date.**

2. Employee returns Form B to Supervisor **at least two weeks before the Due Date.**

3. Supervisor gives Employee completed Personnel Evaluation Form (Form C).

4. Performance Appraisal Interview is held **within one week of the Due Date.**

5. The final copy of the Personnel Evaluation Form (Form C) is signed by both parties **within one week of the interview.**

6. All appropriate documents are forwarded to Reviewer upon completion.

7. All documents returned to Personnel Office **by the date indicated above.**

PERSONNEL EVALUATION PROCEDURES*

Performance appraisal is the process of identifying the major responsibilities of a position and measuring the performance of an individual in that position. It also supports an employee's on-the-job growth and development. The program of performance appraisal in the Academic Affairs Library at the University of North Carolina at Chapel Hill is designed to make a positive contribution toward the following goals:

1. Providing staff with an assessment of their performance;
2. Strengthening communication between supervisors and staff;
3. Encouraging staff to grow and improve in their current positions and to set appropriate goals and objectives; and
4. Matching needs of library staff with existing educational and training opportunities and identifying new areas in which training should be provided.

The Jobs Duties Outline (Form A) is an essential document in the performance appraisal process as it describes the primary and secondary responsibilities of a position. *This document is kept on file in the employee's department where it can be readily accessible to both the supervisor and the employee.*

[NOTE: In the case of a new position being created, this document is prepared for the first time by the supervisor; however, it is the responsibility of the employee to revise this document as duties change and to review such revisions with the supervisor.]

Prior to undertaking written evaluations, both the employee and the supervisor should examine the Job Duties Outline. The purpose of this review is to ensure that the supervisor and the employee share a clear and accurate understanding of the duties performed by the employee and the areas of responsibility assigned to the employee. It also ensures that any changes in the content and emphasis of duties performed since the hiring of the incumbent or since the last revision of the job outline are agreed upon and recorded. This outline is distinct from the position description maintained by the Library Personnel Office, which is used for the purpose of recruitment.

*Reprinted with the permission of the University of North Carolina Libraries.

STAGE ONE

At least four weeks before the due date, the employee is given an Employee Self-Assessment Form (Form B), which is designed to provide an opportunity for the employee to comment upon his or her job performance and to consider goals for the coming year. Although the completion of this form is optional, it must be signed and returned to the supervisor at least two weeks before the due date. The employee must decide if the self-assessment form will become part of his or her permanent record.

At the same time, the supervisor is given the Personnel Evaluation Form (Form C). After receiving the Employee Self-Assessment Form, the supervisor will complete the Personnel Evaluation Form, taking into account the categories on Form C as appropriate. The supervisor should recognize that the completion of the Self-Assessment Form is at the option of the employee, and that a decision not to complete this form should not be viewed negatively. The supervisor gives the completed Personnel Evaluation Form to the employee for review prior to the Performance Appraisal Interview.

STAGE TWO

Stage Two is a private review session in which the supervisor and the employee discuss the job outline, the past year's performance, goals for the coming year, and opportunities for individual development. This discussion is based on the contents of Forms A, B, and C.

This session will also be the supervisor's opportunity to offer suggestions for development in job-related areas. These suggestions should include responses to any areas in which the employee has expressed interest. The Staff Development Committee has prepared a directory which can be of help in locating assistance in addition to that provided by the Academic Affairs Library. A copy of this directory is available in each library department.

The employee and the supervisor then review the Job Outline (Form A). Changes are made as necessary to ensure that it is still an accurate description of the employee's job.

Stage Two of the performance appraisal procedure should be completed within one week of the due date.

STAGE THREE

After the discussion between the employee and the supervisor, the supervisor may revise Form C and should then return it to the employee, who may attach comments. Within one week of the interview, the final appraisal document is sent to the supervisor's supervisor for signature. It is then returned to the Library Personnel Office.

It is important that all participants in the process remember that performance appraisal is an educational opportunity, that it should be a positive tool for staff development, and that to be an effective process for all concerned it should be done on time.

Summary Timetable of Performance Appraisal Procedures

1. Employee is given Employee Self-Assessment Form (Form B), and supervisor is given Personnel Evaluation Form (Form C) **at least four weeks before the due date.** The employee should review the Job Duties Outline (Form A) as revised and updated during the preceding year.

2. Employee returns Form B to the Supervisor **at least two weeks before the due date.**

3. Supervisor gives Employee completed Personnel Evaluation Form (Form C).

4. Performance Appraisal Interview, including a review of the Job Duties Outline for the upcoming year, is held **within one week of the due date.**

5. The final copy of the Personnel Evaluation Form (Form C) is signed by both parties **within one week of the interview**, and copies of all documents are given to the employee.

6. All appropriate documents are forwarded to Reviewer **upon completion.**

7. All documents except the Job Duties Outline are returned to Personnel Office **by the date indicated** on the Personnel Evaluation Checklist. The Job Duties Outline is retained on file in the employee's department.

FORM A

JOB DUTIES OUTLINE

Employee Name_____

Working Title_____

Supervisor _____

Date _____

In outline form, list your primary and secondary responsibilities. Use the back of this sheet if necessary.

PRIMARY RESPONSIBILITIES:

SECONDARY RESPONSIBILITIES:

FORM B

EMPLOYEE SELF-ASSESSMENT

Name _____

   Self-assessment, as part of the appraisal process, can help you to review the previous year's achievements, to gain insight into the nature of your responsibilities, and to gain perspective on personal development and growth in your position. Many supervisors and employees have found regular attention to job and career goals useful and important to an accurate and helpful performance appraisal. Although this form is an optional part of the performance appraisal process, you should be aware of its value for staff development. You may complete all, part, or none of it, and go into as much detail as you choose. Whether or not you fill out this form, please sign it and be prepared to return it to your supervisor at least two weeks before the due date. Your supervisor will give you the Personnel Evaluation Form (Form C) for your review prior to the appraisal interview.

1. **Your Performance Over the Past Year.** Comment briefly on your performance. You may wish to do so in terms of any or all of the following criteria: job knowledge; working relationships; quality of work; quantity of work; dependability; organization and planning; communication skills; initiative; leadership; and an optional category or categories on which you and your supervisor have agreed. You might also want to refer to last year's goals.

2. **Your Performance in the Year to Come.**

    a. What performance goals would you like to set for the next year?

    b. What changes or activities will you undertake to meet these goals?

    c. What can your supervisor, your fellow workers, and/or the Library do to assist you in meeting these goals?

3. **Your Career Goals.**

a. What are they? (Long and/or short term.)

b. What will you do in the next year to move toward them?

☐ I would like this assessment to become part of my permanent record.
☐ I would like this assessment returned to me.
☐ I choose not to complete this form.

Signed _____ Date _____

FORM C

PERSONNEL EVALUATION FORM

NAME _____ Date _____

Comments on the following categories as appropriate should be provided on a separate sheet of paper. You are free to organize your comments as you wish. Any optional categories should be agreed upon before the beginning of the appraisal year.

A. PERFORMANCE (Comments should be based on performance of responsibilities listed in the Job Duties Outline and on last year's goals.)

1. Job knowledge (Degree of technical knowledge, understanding of procedures and methods)
2. Quality of work (Competence, accuracy, neatness, thoroughness)
3. Quantity of work (Use of time, volume of work accomplished)
4. Working relationships (Ability to work co-operatively with supervisor, co-workers, other staff, and patrons)
5. Dependability (Reliability, punctuality, and ability to adhere to schedules)
6. Oral and writing skills (Ability to communicate effectively)
7. Organization/Planning (Ability to organize your own work and the work of others and, where appropriate, to do short- and long-term planning)
8. Initiative (When appropriate, ability to accept responsibility, work without supervision, develop new and better procedures)
9. Leadership (When appropriate, ability to lead; this may include supervisory skills such as training and directing subordinates, delegation, evaluation of employees, and decision-making)
10. Optional categories_____. Please specify category name(s).

B. SPECIAL ACCOMPLISHMENTS/CONTRIBUTIONS

C. STRENGTHS

D. AREAS NEEDING DEVELOPMENT

E. GOALS FOR THE NEXT 12 MONTHS—Indicate how they are to be accomplished and how they will be evaluated. (To be completed during discussion with employee.)

Signature of Supervisor _____ Date_____

Signature of Employee_____ Date_____

My signature indicates that I have read and discussed this evaluation with my supervisor. It does not necessarily indicate that I agree with this evaluation.

Employee Self-Evaluation (Form B) attached   _____ Yes
     _____ No

Other employee comments attached   _____ Yes
     _____ No

Signature of Reviewer_____ Date_____

February 9, 1994

University of Iowa
Performance Appraisal Form

University of Iowa Libraries Performance Evaluation
System for Professional Staff*

I. INTRODUCTION

Performance evaluation is one component of a program that seeks to develop a staff capable of providing library services and resources of the highest quality possible.

The primary objectives of performance evaluation are to enhance the quality of library services at the University of Iowa and to promote the professional development of library staff through a regular and systematic assessment of individual performance.

Planning, communication, and evaluation are not independent. This document concentrates on the evaluative process but it does so in the context of individual plans (annual goals and objectives) and of the communication (formal and informal) used to develop these plans and to measure progress. Though the document focuses on two markers in the annual cycle (the planning conference to set individual goals and objectives and the performance review), it is important to remember that it is the continuing dialogue throughout the cycle that will ensure that goals and objectives are refined to meet changing circumstances and that progress toward attaining the goals is being made.

The performance evaluation procedures outlined below will be reviewed and revised periodically to ensure that they continue to contribute constructively to fulfilling the Libraries' responsibilities to the University of Iowa and the state university system.

II. TIMETABLE

The timing of the planning and review steps reflects University requirements and the practicalities of institutional planning. Because the planning and review cycles are not identical, the annual review will cover the final achievements of one year's plan as well as progress made on the next year's.

What follows is a general timetable. Specific dates for each year will be issued by the administration on or before the first of March.

---

*Reprinted with permission of the University of Iowa Libraries.

Planning Process (Current year): Setting of Goals and Objectives

April: Preliminary work begins on the individual's goals and objectives for the coming year. Goals and objectives should be revised as needed throughout the year.

July: Department/unit goals and objectives set. At this time staff members revise their individual goals and objectives in consultation with their primary supervisors where appropriate. This is the planning conference referred to below.

Evaluation Process (Following year)

March: Staff members prepare annual activity reports on the basis of their job description and the goals and objectives agreed upon previously. Reports will be given to the primary supervisors only. Further distribution is in accordance with procedures described below.

April: Evaluation conferences with primary supervisors held.

May: Equity review by Executive Council.

III. CONTRIBUTORS TO PLANNING AND REVIEW

This document assumes that, for the purpose of planning and of performance evaluation, each staff member has one primary supervisor. (In the case of those staff members whose responsibilities are split 50/50, the staff members should be fully evaluated by each supervisor and planning should involve both.) Other key people may be asked to contribute to planning and/or performance evaluation, and the primary supervisor will be responsible for identifying them in advance in consultation with staff.

IV. JULY PLANNING CONFERENCE

1. After departmental and unit goals and objectives for the year have been set, the staff member prepares and/or revises a set of individual goals and objectives based on the following concepts. Consult the University of Michigan's guide, "Performance Goals: What They Are and How They're Written" (December 1986) for a useful compilation of examples in the following categories. (The language below is quoted from the guide. Modifications are shown in square brackets.)

   Continuing Goals: "[Continuing] goals are the major substance of [an individual's] work and are the goals by which performance is most heavily judged. They should cover all primary ongoing job responsibilities and should, therefore, be related to [the individual's] job description.... Whenever possible, [continuing] goals should be stated in terms of desired results, not as activities."

Problem-solving Goals: "Problem-solving goals often relate to continuing responsibilities. They may solve a specific problem or address a need to bring productivity or quality of service up to an established standard."

Innovative Goals: "Innovative goals are new plans, innovations, one-time efforts that require special planning."

Developmental Goals: "Developmental goals apply to an individual learning a new job or developing a new skill that will improve job performance."

Additional/Other Professional Contributions: Professional contributions would include "goal statements covering major committee or other University Libraries assignments that require a significant commitment of time." Publications, work on university committees and with professional organizations at the state, regional, and national level would be included as well.

The enumeration of the different types of goals does NOT mean that each individual is expected to set goals in every category for each performance evaluation period. If appropriate for clarification, the staff member may elect to specify the approximate percentage of time, or the actual number of hours, anticipated to reach specific goals. The staff member should point out where the successful attainment of a goal may depend on circumstances beyond the individual's control.

2. The staff member meets with the primary supervisor to review and agree upon the goals, keeping in mind the definitions given above.

3. The staff member, primary supervisor, and others providing input should confer as necessary to reach agreement on the content of the goals and objectives document.

4. If at any time during the evaluation period, circumstances that will affect realization of the staff member's proposed goals and objectives arise, the staff member and supervisor should revise the Goals and Objectives Document accordingly. Examples of such changes are: Loss of a staff member (requiring the hiring and training of another or leading to additional work while the position is vacant); prolonged absence due to illness or other reason; change or dislocation in the physical environment; changes in primary responsibilities; opportunity for extra or changed professional contributions.

V. ANNUAL ACTIVITY REPORT AND PERFORMANCE EVALUATION

The purpose of the annual performance evaluation is to review accomplishments and progress towards achievement of goals to identify areas for growth and development. The evaluation is based on the annual activity report, comments made during the annual review conference, and evaluative comments made by the primary supervisor and, in some cases, additional evaluative comments supplied by other persons.

1. Activity report

At the time of the annual evaluation, the staff member prepares an activity report for the primary supervisor to cover the evaluation period (1 April through 31 March) based on the goals and objectives agreed upon in previous year's planning conferences. (Because of the overlap of planning and evaluation cycles the report made, for example, March of 1992 will cover activities agreed to in July of 1990 but completed between April and July of 1991, as well as those agreed to in July of 1991 and complete or ongoing as of March 1992.) The report should also include activities unforeseen at the time of the planning conference. Normally the supervisor will have been notified as opportunities for such additional activities have arisen. The activity report formally documents these activities and their outcomes.

After consultation with the staff member the primary supervisor will, as appropriate, provide copies of the report for others involved in the evaluation.

2. The conference

The review conference involves the primary supervisor and the staff member. It will focus primarily on the activity report, but other matters may be introduced either by the staff member or by the supervisor.

In particular there may be times when a supervisor has received input into the evaluation process so close to the time of the evaluation conference that the supervisor has not been able to communicate it to the staff member. Such information should be communicated to the staff member during the evaluation conference. This is in no way meant to imply that information should be withheld until the annual performance appraisal conference. Discussions related to performance problems should always be dealt with promptly throughout the year.

To assist supervisors in conducting the conference and in preparing the written evaluation, a set of criteria has been developed. These criteria are intended as guides only. The list is not exhaustive nor is it intended that it apply in its entirety to all staff members.

3. Evaluative comment from other sources

If the primary supervisor, after consulting with the staff member, feels that performance related to specific goals and objectives requires comment from other individuals then the supervisor should request it. This information may be supplied in written or oral form, but if oral (by telephone or in person) then the primary supervisor will make a written summary.

4. Written evaluation

On the basis of the activity report, evaluation conference and oral or written comments from any other persons involved, the primary supervisor completes the written evaluation of the staff member's performance for the evaluation period. A copy of the completed document is sent to the staff member.

Supervisors should be careful to avoid personal bias when evaluating a staff member. Ratings should be based on the entire year under review. Isolated incidents or recent events should not be allowed to influence unduly a rating. The staff member's personal qualities should be considered by the evaluator only to the extent that they can be demonstrated to affect the performance of the staff member's professional duties.

In cases where performance has been unsatisfactory in some way, the evaluation documentation shall include the steps to be taken by staff member and supervisor to improve performance in the problem area(s).

5.   First review by staff member

The staff member reviews the performance evaluation documentation. The staff member may request an additional meeting with the primary supervisor to discuss disagreements or may return the summary with written comments. All documentation of the performance evaluation conference must be signed by the staff member signifying that all of the material upon which a rating is being based has been seen, and returned to the primary supervisor.

If, despite further discussion, the staff member continues to have reservations about the primary supervisor's final report, he or she may attach a signed statement of these concerns. Any supervisory response to this last document must be seen and signed by the staff member who may include a final comment.

6.   Submission of documentation to Director or UL

With all documentation attached, the primary supervisor forwards this summary to the appropriate Director (or UL), consults with the Director (or UL) regarding the performance evaluation, and communicates a recommended rating (based on the scale, p.486) of the staff member to the Director (or UL).

7.   Equity review

In order to accomplish systemwide equity review among all staff members for the purpose of determining a salary increase, the Executive Council will review and discuss all evaluations. Taking into consideration the primary supervisor's recommended rating, the Executive Council will determine the final rating for individual staff members based on comparison across divisions/departments. There will be no change in the relationship of recommended ratings of staff within a group evaluated by a primary supervisor without prior discussion with that supervisor.

The Directors/ULs may in some cases ask for clarification of the evaluation and the recommended rating or for additional information, if available, to support the recommended rating.

Once the final rating has been determined, each evaluation (with attached documentation) will be signed and returned to the primary supervisor who will then provide the staff member with an opportunity to review it.

8. Final review by staff member

The staff member reviews the documentation (now including a numerical rating) received from the primary supervisor, signs it, may attach written comments to it, and returns it to the primary supervisor. The completed evaluation package is then returned to the appropriate Director (or UL, as appropriate).

9. Appeals

Appeals of the outcome of an evaluation must be made **in writing** by the staff member to the University Librarian within 10 days of receiving the rating. If the outcome of this appeal does not satisfy the staff member, further appeal must be in strict accordance with University of Iowa grievance procedures for Professional and Scientific Staff.

VI. SALARY SETTING

The salary amounts associated with particular numerical ratings will not be determined until after the systemwide equity review has been completed, because those amounts will vary depending on: (1) the number of individuals who receive each rating; (2) the amount of money made available for salary increases, which typically becomes known to the Library Administration toward the end of the evaluation process.

The number of staff receiving each numerical rating will be made public at the conclusion of the salary-setting process.

CRITERIA FOR USE IN THE EVALUATION OF PROFESSIONAL AND SCIENTIFIC STAFF AT UNIVERSITY OF IOWA LIBRARIES

Supervisors should address the following elements in the annual performance review as they relate to the performance of the staff member's responsibilities. Criteria are not listed in order of importance.

- Organization or work and planning
- Managerial/supervisory/administrative skills
- Problem analysis/investigation/resolution
- Approachability/responsiveness/working relationships
- Initiative/attitude
- Quality of work/quantity of work
- Communication
- Expertise
- Professional commitment

RATING SCALE FOR ANNUAL PERFORMANCE REVIEW

5 **Distinguished performance**
[across-the-board pay increase plus merit pay increase]

4 **Noteworthy performance**
[across-the-board pay increase plus merit pay increase]

3 **Full performance**
[across-the-board pay increase plus merit pay increase]

2 **Diminished performance**
Strategy for improvement must be outlined by supervisor, though there is no threat to continued employment.
[across-the-board pay increase only; no merit pay increase]

1 **Unacceptable performance**
Strategy for improvement must be outlined by supervisor, continued performance at this level will lead to termination.
[no across-the-board pay increase, no merit pay increase]

UNIVERSITY OF IOWA LIBRARIES

P & S Performance Evaluation

Name _____ Rank _____

Position _____ Date of Employment in this Rank _____

Review Year _____ Date of Employment _____

   I. Professional's summary of activities (attached).

  II. Professional's performance goals and any other pertinent documents (attached).

 III. Supervisor's summary of performance conference.

       Signature of Supervisor _____ Date _____

       Signature of Professional _____ Date _____

       Name of Professional (typed) _____ Date _____
       (A signature by the professional indicates only that the individual has read this evaluation. It does not necessarily indicate agreement.)

 IV. Professional's response to evaluation (optional, attached).

  V. Performance rating (check one).

       1 _____ 2 _____ 3 _____ 4 _____ 5 _____

Signature of Director or University Librarian

_____ Date _____

Signature of Professional

_____ Date _____

Name of Professional (typed) _____ Date _____

 IV. Professional's response to rating (optional, attached).

Appendix E
Budget and Justification Forms

Miami - Dade County Public Library
1997–1998 PROPOSED OPERATING BUDGET
LIBRARY

PURPOSE

Operates the County libraries and provides library information and services.

MANAGEMENT DIRECTION

*Select library materials, service delivery methods, and programs that satisfy the diverse interests of the community

*Seek private funding for enhancement of collections, furnishings, and programming

*Continue to seek Community Development Block Grant (CDBG) funding for maintenance projects and maximize all available funds in order to properly maintain library facilities

*Start process for new Book Trust refunding initiative; the current Book Trust approved by voters in 1988, is expected to be depleted by the end of FY 1999–2000

*Continue planning the new regional library on Miami Beach

1996–97 SERVICE STATUS

*Completed installation and implementation of new library information system, "PELICAN"

*State Aid to Libraries funding is $279,000 less than anticipated

*Completed North Dade re-roofing and air conditioning upgrade ($324,000) from insurance proceeds; also completed Americans with Disabilities Act (ADA)-required facility upgrades ($100,000) with CDBG funds

	1995–96	1996–97	1997–98
WORKLOAD MEASURES	Actual	Projected	Estimated
Circulation Per Capita	6.35	6.41	6.93
Materials Per Capita*	2.37	2.37	2.37
Materials Budget Per Capita*	3.07	2.68	2.46
Registered Borrowers	687,000	687,000	687,000
Program Attendance	432,000	454,000	454,000

*Materials defined as books, periodicals, videos, tapes, and other audio/visual/computer media

RECOMMENDATIONS: The recommended FY 1997–98 Library District budget is $32.88 million, which is 0.6 percent less than the current year budget of $33.079 million due in part to a reduced transfer from the Book Trust ($5 million compared to $5.518 million in prior year); the proposed property tax revenue budget for FY 1997–98 is $22.587 million, based on a recommended millage rate of .327 mills, which is the estimated FY 1997–98 rolled-back rate for the Library District, the recommended Library District budget assumes receipt of $3.2 million in State Aid to Libraries funding, a decrease of $194,000 from the FY 1996–97 budgeted amount

- The same staffing levels are budgeted for FY 1997–98 as for the prior year and the current year attrition rate of 9.5 percent is maintained; at these levels, all current library hours of operation will be maintained

  All current County-funded special library services will be continued at existing levels

- The Library will pay $1.389 million for allocated building rent and management fees for County-owned facilities and a $757,000 administrative reimbursement to the general fund in FY 1997–98

- Library materials and automation will be maintained and enhanced with $5 million in Book Trust funds; as of September 30, 1997, the Book Trust, approved by voters in 1988, is estimated to have a balance of $13.616 million; at the historical rate of expenditures, the Book Trust is expected to be depleted by the end of FY 1999–2000

- The Library contingency reserve is budgeted at $300,000 while $470,000 is budgeted for major facility maintenance and repairs; this is in addition to $300,000 of current year and an anticipated $260,000 of FY 1997–98 recommended CDBG funding for ADA, roof, and other eligible renovation and repair activities, and $500,000 of available insurance proceeds that will also be used to offset the cost of repairs at older branches

- As in the current year, funding for priority facility repairs beyond dedicated funding amounts may also be made available from the contingency reserve

Used with permission of the Miami-Dade Public Library

Index